IFIP Advances in Information and Communication Technology 747

IFIP Advances in Information and Communication Technology

The IFIP AICT series publishes state-of-the-art results in the sciences and technologies of information and communication. The scope of the series includes: foundations of computer science; software theory and practice; education; computer applications in technology; communication systems; systems modeling and optimization; information systems; ICT and society; computer systems technology; security and protection in information processing systems; artificial intelligence; and human-computer interaction.

Edited volumes and proceedings of refereed international conferences in computer science and interdisciplinary fields are featured. These results often precede journal publication and represent the most current research.

The principal aim of the IFIP AICT series is to encourage education and the dissemination and exchange of information about all aspects of computing.

More information about this series at https://link.springer.com/bookseries/6102

Ganesh Bhutkar · Sheethal Tom · Debjani Roy ·
Jose Abdelnour-Nocera
Editors

Designing for Tomorrow: Innovation and Equity in Global Interaction Design

First IFIP WG 13.8 Interaction Design for International Development, IDID 2024
Mumbai, India, November 7–9, 2024
Proceedings

Springer

Editors
Ganesh Bhutkar
Vishwakarma Institute of Technology
Pune, Maharashtra, India

Debjani Roy
Srishti Manipal Institute of Art, Design
and Technology
Bengaluru, Karnataka, India

Sheethal Tom
IIE Varsity College
Cape Town, South Africa

Jose Abdelnour-Nocera
University of West London
London, UK

ISSN 1868-4238 ISSN 1868-422X (electronic)
IFIP Advances in Information and Communication Technology
ISBN 978-3-032-00776-6 ISBN 978-3-032-00777-3 (eBook)
https://doi.org/10.1007/978-3-032-00777-3

This Springer imprint is published by the registered company Springer Nature Switzerland AG
The registered company address is: Gewerbestrasse 11, 6330 Cham, Switzerland

Preface

This collection of chapters is an initiative from the IFIP working group 13.8 on Interaction Design and International Development (IDID) of Technical Committee (TC) 13. The chapters have been developed from contributions to the IDID Working Conference that took place at IIT Bombay, Mumbai, India in November 2024 in conjunction with the IndiaHCI 2024 conference. The aim of this working group is to pursue research and promote the discipline of Human-Computer Interaction (HCI) in an international context. It also provides a platform where both emerging and experienced researchers from academia and industry can converge to exchange their latest findings in the ever-evolving realm of HCI and International Development. This working group is committed to advancing HCI research, practices, and education on a worldwide scale, championing interaction design that caters to the needs of the developing world, and advocating for cross-cultural HCI practices, particularly within burgeoning economies. It also seeks to fortify the connections within the HCI community and related entities engaged in international and cross-cultural Information and Communication Technology (ICT) development. Seventeen research papers, including a keynote, were submitted to the conference. All the papers underwent a double-blind peer review process with an average of 2 and a maximum of 3 reviews. Finally, 14 papers were selected as full chapters for these IDID proceedings.

The book presents author/user experiences and research topics of Interaction Design and International Development. Chapter one discusses phishing attacks, their impact, and increased need for better anti-phishing measures, recommending a User Experience (UX) framework for anti-phishing cybersecurity training applications. Chapter two presents the need for theorization such as guidelines, models, and frameworks to enhance research influence, especially among Global South researchers. The opportunities for synthesizing and abstracting knowledge are yet to be optimized, which amounts to a loss of knowledge availability and value addition. Chapter three delves into the motivations of Indian millennials using Self-Determination Theory (SDT) from qualitative interviews with findings indicating adoption influenced by autonomy, competence, relatedness, and extrinsic variables. Chapter four addresses reviews of Nigerian users of current psychotherapy apps, highlighting weaknesses such as usability, subpar Artificial Intelligence (AI) chatbot capabilities, and lack of diversity in content supporting digital mental health interventions.

Chapter five looks at enhancing Android Pattern Locks (APL) with graphical overlays to enhance security and to assess their usability, memorability, and user acceptability using 36 emergent user studies. Outcomes indicate high usability and memorability levels with heightened APLs retaining high success rates. Chapter six examines technology use and personal well-being through the lens of minimalism within the context of an urban Indian setting. The study also provokes self-awareness with a view to facilitating more mindful, value-based technological decisions for future well-being. Chapter seven delves into the application of multiplayer serious games in cybersecurity awareness with the gameable 'Capture It' that can be repurposed. Results of user study indicate that a pre-game quiz has a positive effect on game performance, an indication that serious games are poised to make responsive and immersive learning experiences a possibility.

Chapter eight presents m-learning in rural regions of low- and middle-income countries from the perspective of HCI for Development (HCI4D). It explores gaps and prospects in lifelong learning for teachers, and their important themes, geographic reach, methods, and technological emphasis. Chapter nine discusses research applying Human-Centered Design (HCD) to insert user requirements into a status-tracking tool, prototyping and testing via input from domain experts. Results highlight the value of an easy-to-use tool that makes operational data accessible, places warnings in context, and improves situational awareness and team communication. Chapter ten proposes a smart dustbin prototype to maximize waste management through reduced manual inspection. The system monitors trash capacity in real time and alerts the authorities when the waste exceeds a threshold. Chapter eleven discusses the triggers and motivations for disordered gambling through models of behaviour such as Hook's Model, Fogg's Model, and the Habit Loop. This research takes a four-stage approach, resulting in Ryze, a narrative app promoting safe gambling, with prevention and awareness interventions against internet gambling addiction.

Chapter twelve compares Social Networking Site (SNS) design to the Haussmannization of Paris, exploring digital flânerie, algorithmic consumption, and the attention economy. Using digital ethnography, it examines memes, collective visibility, and online gentrification, while raising ethical concerns about consent, privacy, and user engagement. Chapter thirteen covers a twelve-day workshop conducted with six young adults, using gamified formats and insights taken from 30 Indian women to design a social communication toolkit for adolescent psychoeducation, promoting self-awareness, moral decision-making, and reproductive health knowledge. Chapter fourteen examines dark patterns in User Interface (UI) design, and five important factors such as frequency, trust, frustration, deception, and user experience impact that will enable users to identify manipulation. Based on analysis and user testing, it provides insights into their impact on usability across platforms.

We believe this book will be ideal for beginners as well as experts in HCI and International Development. It will receive an encouraging response from the communities of the global south.

Ganesh Bhutkar
Sheethal Tom
Debjani Roy
Jose Abdelnour-Nocera

IFIP TC13 – http://ifip-tc13.org/

Established in 1989, the International Federation for Information Processing Technical Committee on Human–Computer Interaction (IFIP TC 13) is an international committee of 35 member national societies and 10 Working Groups, representing specialists of the various disciplines contributing to the field of Human-Computer Interaction (HCI). This includes (among others) human factors, ergonomics, cognitive science, computer science and design. INTERACT is a flagship conference of IFIP TC 13, staged biennially in different countries in the world. The first INTERACT conference was held in 1984 running triennially and became a biennial event in 1993.

IFIP TC 13 aims to develop the science, technology and societal aspects of HCI by encouraging empirical research, promoting the use of knowledge and methods from the human sciences in design and evaluation of computer systems; promoting better understanding of the relation between formal design methods and system usability and acceptability; developing guidelines, models and methods by which designers may provide better human-oriented computer systems; and, cooperating with other groups, inside and outside IFIP, to promote user-orientation and humanization in system design. Thus, TC 13 seeks to improve interactions between people and computers, to encourage the growth of HCI research and its practice in industry and to disseminate these benefits worldwide.

The main orientation is to place the users at the center of the development process. Areas of study include the problems people face when interacting with computers; the impact of technology deployment on people in individual and organizational contexts; the determinants of utility, usability, acceptability and user experience; the appropriate allocation of tasks between computers and users especially in the case of automation; modelling the users, their tasks and the interactive system to aid better system design; and harmonizing the computer to user characteristics and needs.

While the scope is thus set wide, with a tendency towards general principles rather than particular systems, it is recognized that progress will only be achieved through both general studies to advance theoretical understanding and specific studies on practical issues (e.g., interface design standards, software system resilience, documentation, training material, appropriateness of alternative interaction technologies, guidelines, the problems of integrating multimedia systems to match system needs and organizational practices, etc.).

Organization

Conference Chair

Sheethal Tom	IIE Varsity College, South Africa

Program Chair

Torkil Clemmensen	Copenhagen Business School, Denmark

India HCI Liaison

Anirudha Joshi	IIT Bombay, India

Paper Chairs

Jose Abdelnour-Nocera	University of West London, UK/ITI/Larsys, Portugal
Debjani Roy	Srishti Manipal Institute of Art, Design and Technology, India

Poster and Demo Chairs

Daniel Cabezas López	Universitat Oberta de Catalunya, Spain
Antony William Joseph	Aalto University, Finland

Student Design Competition

Arthi Manohar	Brunel University London, UK
Christian Sturm	Technische Hochschule Ingolstadt, Germany

Proceedings Chair

Ganesh Bhutkar	Vishwakarma Institute of Technology, India

Webmaster

Daniel Cabezas López	Universitat Oberta de Catalunya, Spain

Student Volunteer Chairs

Atharva Mugalikar	Vishwakarma Institute of Technology, India
Swarup Vishwas	Vishwakarma Institute of Technology, India
Manas Avachat	Vishwakarma Institute of Technology, India

Programme Committee

Anant Bhaskar Garg	HRDEF, India
Avijit Sengupta	University of Queensland, Australia
Connie Bitso	University of Fort Hare, South Africa
David Lamas	Tallinn University, Estonia
Debarun Sarkar	Independent Researcher, India
Elisha Makori	University of Nairobi, Kenya
Ghazala Tabassum	University of Technology Sarawak, Malaysia
Jan Kroeze	University of South Africa, South Africa
Judy van Biljon	University of South Africa, South Africa
Mireia Ribera	Universitat de Barcelona, Spain
Paula Kotze	University of Pretoria, South Africa
Sandeep Athavale	TCS Research, India
Sayan Sarcar	Kochi University of Technology, Japan
Shaista Falak	University of Technology Sarawak, Malaysia
Sumita Sharma	University of Oulu, Finland
Sylvan Lobo	Tata Consultancy Services, India
Vishal Mehta	Independent UX Professional, USA
Chhaya Gosavi	MKSSS's CCOEW, India
Shrikant Salve	IIIT Pune, India
Yohannes Kurniawan	Bina Nusantara University, Indonesia

Contents

Designing a S-UX Framework to Combat Phishing and Foster Digital Responsibility

Noluntu Mpekoa [1(✉)], Sheethal Tom[2], Nobubele Shozi[3], and Noluxolo Gcaza[4]

[1] Academy of Computer Science and Software Engineering, University Johannesburg, Johannesburg, South Africa
noluntum@uj.ac.za

[2] School of Computer Science, IIE Varsity College, Cape Town, South Africa
stom@varsitycollege.co.za

[3] Council for Scientific and Industrial Research (CSIR), Pretoria, South Africa
nshozi@csir.co.za

[4] Nelson Mandela University, Port Elizabeth, South Africa
noluxolog@mandela.ac.za

Abstract. Cyberattacks have emerged as problems caused not only by technological issues but also by human factors that are often overlooked when designing interactive systems. Social engineering is an extremely effective type of cybercrime, where the attackers use human psychology to achieve their target which are in the form of data, account details, or IT devices for example. Phishing is one of the first methods that social engineers use to target victims and it accounts for the highest percentage of data breaches at 25% compared to the other types. Phishing is a deception technique that attackers use to steal sensitive information such as usernames, passwords, and online banking details from their victims. Despite phishing attacks being known for more than two decades, and the ongoing research for developing effective techniques against these attacks, the increasing trend of attacks confirms the lack of robust solutions and techniques against these attacks. There is a need for comprehensive research in the area of anti-phishing to improve the overall cybersecurity landscape. Hence this study aims to design and propose a User Experience (UX) Framework to safeguard against digital deception, that focuses on cybersecurity training applications. The study conducted an in-depth literature review on phishing and major phishing attacks. Next, the study explored interactive design by linking phishing with user experience design. Lastly, the improved S-UX framework is proposed for cybersecurity training applications in safeguarding users against digital deception. The proposed framework offers six high-level constructs which include security, experience, interactiveness, accessibility, robustness, and transparency. This study also provides recommendations on how to apply the proposed framework for cybersecurity training and real-world situations.

Keywords: Phishing · interactive design · UX framework · cybersecurity training

G. Bhutkar et al. (Eds.): IDID 2024, IFIP AICT 747, pp. 1–20, 2026.
https://doi.org/10.1007/978-3-032-00777-3_1

1 Introduction

The significant growth of internet usage and human negligence has paved the way for a fresh wave of cyber threats that manipulate human behaviour to compromise data protection [2]. In contrast to the traditional cyber-attacks that focus on targeting system vulnerabilities, these attacks such as phishing and social engineering target to exploit human vulnerabilities to obtain unauthorized access to sensitive data [16, 45]. This shift highlights a challenge in the field of cybersecurity: the human factor. The increasingly digitized and interconnected society is at serious risk from the complexity of hostile cyber-attacks [22, 46]. With the rise of cyber criminals, the role of interaction design in safeguarding digital interactions against deception has become predominant.

Phishing, a prevalent form of manipulation, showcases how human vulnerabilities can be exploited [5, 14, 46]. Phishers employ social engineering strategies to trick people into responding such as posing as legitimate companies, official government agencies or current events, all accompanied by statements that evoke fear, threat or excitement [7, 34]. The frequency and complexity of these attacks continue to rise despite the increasing awareness and extensive research done in this field. These challenges highlight the need for an approach to design and execute digital security measures. Traditional security measures, although important, are no longer adequate; instead, a resilient approach is required to counter deceit.

The importance of design and user experience has often been neglected in favour of focusing more on employing technology to combat cyber-attacks [4, 31]. However, the tactics used to counter these attacks should evolve as the nature of cyberattacks also evolves. Looking at cyber security challenges through the lens of interaction design provides a unique perspective. By focusing on improving the user's experience and behaviour, interface designers may create environments that not only give users guidance and information, but also reduce the likelihood of being deceived [28, 47]. The focus on this user-centered approach highlights the importance of creating systems that are secure and user-friendly; thereby decreasing the chances of falling victim to phishing attacks.

Cybersecurity dangers, like phishing and online fraud, are not just technological challenges; in addition they convey social and monetary hurdles to the vanguard that substantially affect underserved groups in our society [22, 35]. Certain populations at danger are those who participate in online transactions or community tech projects and undergo the brunt of these challenges more acutely than others do. Due to their lack of knowledge regarding how to protect themselves from these scams, these organizations are at a greater risk of exploitation in the digital realm [40]. The impact of fraud for those businesses goes beyond money. It hampers trust, which is a key factor in embracing digital tools intended to improve people's lives [35, 45]. It is thus crucial to create cybersecurity measures that protect those marginalized communities' hobbies and enable their participation in the economy without jeopardizing their security or confidence in it.

This paper is sectioned as follows: Sect. 2 discusses the literature on phishing and major phishing attacks, Sect. 3 presents the methods used to conduct the study, while Sect. 4 presents the proposed conceptual framework and Sect. 5 offers discussions and recommendations. Then Sect. 6 analyzes the proposed framework and lastly Sect. 7 concludes the paper.

2 Literature Review

Digital deception involves strategies and techniques designed to mislead users in digital environments to illicitly gain access, extract sensitive information, or inflict harm. It encompasses a wide spectrum of activities such as online fraud, identity theft, and misinformation, which exploit the interactive capabilities of digital media. [30] explore these facets, focusing on how the human element of security can be compromised through social engineering tactics, a core component of digital deception. These tactics manipulate psychological tendencies to trust and obey perceived authority, a vulnerability that phishing attacks frequently exploit [11, 30].

Phishing is a specific and highly effective type of digital deception where attackers masquerade as legitimate entities to lure individuals into providing confidential data. This form of deception uses electronic communications such as emails or text messages that appear to come from reputable sources—banks, popular social media platforms, or credible business institutions. [18] describes how phishing leverages the principles of social engineering to create a sense of urgency or fear, prompting users to reveal personal information, click on malicious links, or download compromised attachments.

Phishing attacks have significantly evolved, exploiting not just technological vulnerabilities but human psychology. These attacks manipulate human decision-making through tactics such as urgency, fear, and the semblance of authority. [48] emphasize that under cognitive load, individuals are more susceptible to such deceptions, suggesting a need for interfaces that reduce cognitive strain and heighten user alertness. This evolution underscores the necessity for adaptive cybersecurity strategies that are responsive to the dynamic tactics employed by cybercriminals [14, 48].

Several landmark phishing attacks have shaped the current understanding and response to digital threats. One of the most significant and sophisticated phishing attacks occurred in 2011 against RSA Security, a company known for its data security products [29, 36]. The attackers sent phishing emails to small groups of employees, one of which contained a malicious attachment that installed a backdoor upon opening. This breach demonstrated the effectiveness of spear-phishing and the importance of educating employees about the dangers of seemingly innocuous emails. It led to widespread changes in corporate policies regarding email attachments and heightened awareness about targeted phishing attacks.

A sophisticated phishing scam targeted millions of Google Docs users in 2017, where victims received emails that appeared to share a document for collaboration [9, 29]. Once the link was clicked, it led to a third-party app that asked for permission to access the user's email and contacts, replicating itself to spread further. This attack underscored the need for more stringent controls on third-party applications and better user education on the permissions granted to applications.

With the global pandemic came a surge in phishing attacks exploiting the widespread fear and uncertainty. Cybercriminals launched numerous campaigns disguised as communications from health organizations or government agencies providing information about COVID-19 [45]. These phishing emails often contained malicious links or attachments purportedly offering important updates but instead aimed to steal personal information or deliver malware [3, 6]. This wave of attacks prompted a renewed focus on adaptive cybersecurity solutions capable of responding to real-time global events and trends.

Phishing attacks also grew significantly in developing countries like South Africa (SA). According to [39, 51], SA was the third most affected country by phishing attacks during the period 2014–2016. The situation worsened during the COVID-19 time with a significant increase in attacks since then. Phishing has severely impacted industries like healthcare, banking, education and government departments. Many hospitals and other healthcare delivery organisations in SA became victims to cyberthreats during the pandemic time, exposing patient data and disrupting critical services [12]. The adoption of digital banking has also attracted cybercriminals who employ social engineering techniques like phishing to exploit sensitive user information [32]. Nyasvisvo and Chigada's study provides insights into the challenges faced by university students in SA who studied remotely and were exposed to phishing attacks [41]. A lack of awareness regarding cybersecurity and human vulnerability were identified as the main challenges faced by these students. Despite having the best internet facilities and infrastructure in Africa, factors like lack of digital literacy, inadequate security practices and economic inequalities make people in SA susceptible to such attacks [14, 39]. The phishing attack in 2021 on the South African Department of Justice which resulted in a loss of almost R33 million, further indicates the urgency of addressing these issues [31, 39].

These case studies highlight the evolving nature of phishing attacks and reinforce the argument that human factors such as awareness and vulnerability play an important role in enabling such attacks. They also underscore the necessity for continuous advancements in cybersecurity measures, user-centered design and accessible cybersecurity training programs. The following subsection explores the role of human factors in phishing attacks.

2.1 Human Factors on Phishing Attacks

Human factors are central to the success of phishing and social engineering attacks, exploiting the psychological and behavioral tendencies of individuals. Phishing attacks exploit fundamental psychological principles such as trust, authority, and urgency to deceive individuals. According to [18], phishing typically leverages these elements to create convincing scenarios that prompt users to voluntarily disclose sensitive information. This psychological manipulation is effective because it taps into automatic cognitive processing, where individuals react quickly to perceived authority figures or urgent situations without thorough analysis [18, 35].

Cognitive biases play a significant role in the success of phishing attacks. Kahneman and Tversky's work on decision-making under uncertainty provides insights into how biases like overconfidence, anchoring, and the familiarity heuristic can lead individuals to misjudge the authenticity of phishing attempts [24]. [44] specifically explore the impact of overconfidence in detecting phishing emails, demonstrating how this cognitive bias can lead to increased vulnerability. Their study reveals that individuals often overestimate their ability to identify phishing attempts, a misconception that can result in security breaches [44].

Individual differences, such as age, education, and cybersecurity knowledge, significantly influence susceptibility to phishing. Work by [40] shows that younger and older adults are particularly vulnerable to phishing due to different reasons; younger adults due to overconfidence in their tech-savviness, and older adults due to a lack of familiarity with digital norms and cues [32, 40]. This variation underlines the need for targeted cybersecurity education that addresses specific needs and vulnerabilities within diverse user demographics.

Understanding and addressing the human factors in phishing attacks is paramount for developing effective countermeasures. By considering psychological manipulation, cognitive biases, individual differences, and the efficacy of training programs, cybersecurity measures can be better tailored to the complexities of human behavior, ultimately enhancing the resilience of individuals and organizations against these deceptive attacks. The role of UX in combating phishing lies in translating the theoretical understanding of human factors into practical, user-centric solutions. The integration of rigorous psychological research into UX design is exemplified in the work by [14], who advocate for a holistic approach to cybersecurity that includes both technological defenses and human-centered design [14, 32].

2.2 Interactive Design and User Experience (UX) in Cybersecurity

Interaction design plays a pivotal role in enhancing the efficacy of cybersecurity by creating systems that are not only secure but also intuitive. [41] highlights how well-designed user interfaces can guide users through security practices and alert them to potential threats in real-time. Such enhancements in user experience promote better adherence to security protocols and reduce the likelihood of user errors, thereby strengthening the overall security posture of digital platforms.

The incorporation of AI and machine learning into interaction design is a promising development for cybersecurity. These technologies enable the creation of predictive and adaptive systems that can respond dynamically to user behaviors and environmental contexts. This allows security features and user interfaces to adjust in real-time, offering a personalized and proactive security approach.

Expanding on the educational aspect of cybersecurity, [25] demonstrate the effectiveness of game-based learning platforms. These platforms engage users in role-playing and co-design environments, significantly enhancing their understanding and detection of phishing schemes, thus making cybersecurity education both engaging and effective.

[17] provides valuable insights into the specific risks posed by Bluetooth Low Energy in smartwatches and offers practical solutions to mitigate these risks through improved interaction design. This contribution is significant as it enhances the understanding of wearable device security and underscores the importance of user-centered design in cybersecurity.

Furthermore, [43] explores the integration of biometric data, such as electroencephalography (EEG) and eye-tracking, into interaction designs to detect phishing attempts. This novel approach utilizes real-time feedback on user trust and suspicion levels, enhancing the security systems against phishing attacks.

In learning environments, [22] demonstrate how chatbots can be employed to educate users about phishing. By simulating phishing scenarios, these chatbots provide interactive learning experiences that improve users' ability to identify and respond to phishing emails, enhancing their resilience against cyber threats.

Lastly, [30] introduces an agent-based system that employs interactive communication agents, or chatbots, to detect phishing attempts in mobile-centric environments. This approach highlights the potential of interaction design to enhance end-user detection capabilities, making digital interactions more secure [30]. Similarly, [15] presents a visual analytics approach for identifying phishing activities in blockchain transactions. Their study underscores the importance of interactive and visual tools that assist users in understanding complex data patterns and recognizing phishing attempts, showcasing the effective application of interaction design in advanced digital platforms [15].

These studies collectively affirm the pivotal role of interaction design in enhancing phishing detection and prevention across diverse platforms. By making security measures intuitive and engaging, interaction design not only empowers users but also strengthens the overall security posture of digital systems, ensuring that users are better prepared to identify and counteract phishing threats.

3 Research Methodology

The main goal of this study was to develop a UX Framework to safeguard against digital deception. The framework was designed with an aim to enhance cybersecurity training applications while also exploring its potential to be applied in real-world community settings. The sub-objectives of this study are as follows:

- Describe phishing and conduct a review of major phishing attacks.
- Discuss interactive design.
- Design and propose a UX Framework that focuses on cybersecurity training applications and suggest real-world community settings.
- Offer recommendations on how to apply the proposed framework for cybersecurity training and real-world situations.

Therefore, a literature review was necessary to better understand and describe phishing and different phishing attacks that affect both individuals and communities. A literature review is a procedure for the collection and critical analyses of multiple research studies or papers [26, 27]. The main keywords used during the search were restricted to phishing, phishing attacks, social engineering and social engineering attacks. To capture as many relevant studies as possible, the electronic searches were performed using Google Scholar and other scientific journals and databases back to the year 2020. Articles and studies that were most related to the research theme were considered for this study. Titles, abstracts, and conclusions of conference papers and documents were reviewed.

Next, was the design of the UX Framework that focuses on cybersecurity training applications. [33] define the UX design framework as a structured approach that designers follow to create consistent and user-friendly digital products, websites, or applications. The most developed UX frameworks were considered, such as the BASIC UX Framework [20], User-Centered Design (UCD) Framework [39], Agile Framework [10], and the Secure-by-Design Framework [23]. The improved UX Framework is proposed for cybersecurity training applications as well as its adaptation for real-world community settings in safeguarding users against digital deception. This framework also serves as a tool to increase awareness and enhance security in community settings by combining security features with user experience design principles to create solutions that are secure and user-friendly for all users, regardless of their level of skills and resources.

4 Proposed Framework

This study aimed to develop a UX Framework to safeguard against digital deception. Therefore, this study merges two crucial components, which are User Experience (UX) and cybersecurity (security UX design). While user experience focuses on creating products that provide meaningful and relevant experiences to users [20, 33], security is all about integrating security measures into the user interface (UI) and the user experience (UX) of digital products and systems [23].

4.1 User Experience (UX) Design Frameworks

[33] define UX design framework as a structured approach that designers follow to create consistent and user-friendly digital products, websites, or applications. The

Table 1. Comparison of developed UX Frameworks.

BASIC UX Framework [20]	User-Centered Design (UCD) [39]	Agile framework [10]	Secure-by-Design framework [23]
Beauty	Empathy for Users	Customer experience (CX)	Create responsibility for cyber security risk
Accessibility	Focus on Usability	Harnessing technological and social change	Source secure technology products
Simplicity	Prototyping and Testing	Development timelines	Risk-driven approach
Intuitiveness	Continuous Improvement	Adaptive collaboration	Usable security controls
Consistency		Motivated individuals	Build in detect and respond security
		Effective communication	Flexible architectures
		High-quality UX as success benchmarks	Minimize the attack surface
		Sustainable development	Defend in depth
		Technical excellence is relative	Embed continuous assurance
			Make changes securely

most developed UX frameworks were considered, such as the BASIC UX Framework, User-Centered Design (UCD) framework, Agile framework, and the Secure-by-Design framework, which are depicted in Table 1.

As indicated previously, design and user experience has often been neglected in favour of focusing more on employing technology to combat cyber-attacks [4]. Hence, this study proposes and merges the strengths of the Secure-by-Design framework and Agile framework. The Secure-by-Design framework was selected for this study as it offers a proactive and holistic approach to cyber security, aiming at protecting privacy and data by instituting a security mindset from the outset, building in security throughout the design process and ensuring ongoing vulnerability management of digital products and services [23, 33].

Whereas the Agile framework incorporates elements of continuous planning, testing, integration, and other forms of continuous development with a customer-centered approach [10, 34]. The outcome of these two frameworks is a secure user experience that encourages users to interact with the product or services in a way that is not just user-friendly but also secure. By focusing on improving the user's experience and behaviour, interface designers may create environments that not only give users guidance and information, but also reduce the likelihood of being deceived [50]. The focus on this user-centered approach highlights the importance of creating systems that are secure and user-friendly; thereby decreasing the chances of falling victim to phishing attacks.

4.2 Proposed Conceptual Framework

The proposed conceptual framework is an amalgamation of the Secure-by-Design framework and Agile framework as presented in the previous section. The proposed conceptual framework is presented in Fig. 1.

The following section discusses the proposed S-UX framework and presents some recommendations.

5 Discussion and Recommendations

In relation to the construction of the conceptual framework, this study argues that the proposed S-UX framework differentiates between the key elements involved: the user-experience and security. Additionally, it considers the context of use (cybersecurity training applications). Within the Human-Computer Interaction (HCI) community, some researchers and practitioners tend to overlap concepts, which, although they are difficult to separate due to their dependent nature, it is important to recognize their individualities and strengths in their singularity. The proposed conceptual Secure User Experience (S-UX) Framework comprises six (6) constructs that form the basis for this framework, which are:

5.1 Security

One of the strengths of the S-UX framework lies in its clear distinction between user experience and security. Security as a construct focuses on establishing a secure foundation for the application. In the realm of cybersecurity, creating responsibility for cyber

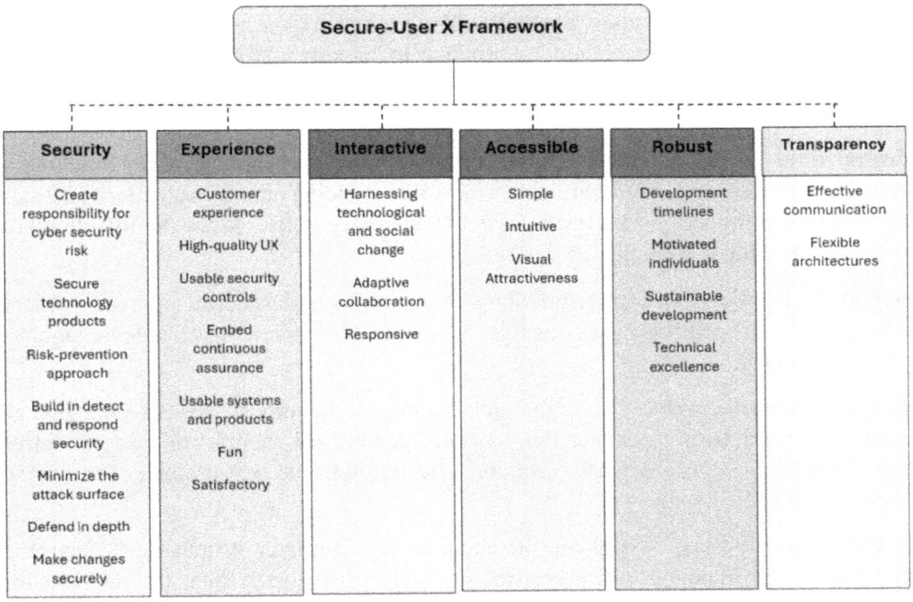

Fig. 1. Proposed Conceptual S-UX Framework.

security risk is paramount [34, 37]. By clearly defining roles and responsibilities, a culture of risk awareness and accountability is fostered. Furthermore, securing technology products entails implementing robust security measures throughout the design and development lifecycle. This includes adopting secure coding practices and proactive risk-prevention approaches to mitigate potential vulnerabilities. To effectively combat cyber threats, it's essential to build-in detect and respond security and minimize the attack surface by adopting a defense-in-depth strategy. The key concepts under the Security construct are discussed below:

Create Responsibility for Cyber Security Risk. Clearly defined roles and responsibilities for cyber security risks are imperative for ensuring that risks are adequately managed. The Govern component of the NIST Cybersecurity framework highlights the importance of shared responsibility of cyber security risk. Establishing and enforcing roles and responsibilities ensures that accountability and shared responsibility for cyber security risks exists through fostering a culture of risk awareness [37].

Secure Technology Products. This framework promotes the use of robust security measures in technology products to protect against deception techniques used by attackers. It is important that development follows secure coding practices that are embedded in the full development cycle [43].

Risk-Prevention Approach. This component highlights the importance of proactive measures to prevent security incidents rather than solely relying on reactive responses. Proactively identifying and mitigating potential vulnerabilities that could be exploited for deception is key to preventing security incidents [44].

Build in Detect and Respond Security. The framework acknowledges the need for built-in security features in technology products to help identify and effectively respond to potential security threats. Security features should be able to detect and respond to deceptive attempts proactively [49].

Minimize the Attack Surface. It is important to reduce the number of potential entry points for attackers by implementing measures like reducing unnecessary functionalities and software complexity. Minimizing the attack surface helps reduce the likelihood of successful deception attempts [38].

Defend in Depth. The framework emphasizes a layered security approach where multiple security controls work together to create a comprehensive defense against cyberattacks [43].

Make Changes Securely. This component highlights the importance of secure change management practices to ensure that system updates and modifications don't introduce vulnerabilities. Frameworks such as ITIL highlight the best practices for change management [42].

Cybersecurity plays a vital role in safeguarding computer systems and electronic information. As incidents of cybercrime continue to rise in Africa, the demand for cybersecurity professionals is becoming increasingly important to protect individuals, organizations, and their sensitive data. The significance of cybersecurity lies in its ability to shield various types of data from theft and damage, including sensitive information, personally identifiable information (PII), protected health information (PHI), personal data, intellectual property, and more [38].

To enhance the security of this data, individuals may adopt a variety of measures, such as employing strong passwords, utilizing multi-factor authentication, implementing screen locks, enabling hard-disk encryption, setting up local firewalls, and managing local administrator access with care [34]. Furthermore, embracing secure coding practices and proactive risk-prevention strategies can contribute an additional layer of security, helping to address potential vulnerabilities effectively.

5.2 Experience

Building on the secure foundation, this construct focuses on creating a positive user experience. A high-quality user experience is characterized by usable security controls and continuous assurance, which are crucial for fostering user engagement and satisfaction [1]. Applications can meet user expectations and security requirements by embedding continuous assurance processes and designing usable systems. Moreover, incorporating elements of fun and satisfaction enhances user engagement and contributes to a positive user experience. The key concepts of experience construct are as follows:

Customer Experience. Security considerations need to be within the broader context of giving the customer a positive user experience. [10] emphasize the importance of user involvement as a means to increase customer experience as they participate in the UX design and development process [38].

High-Quality UX. A high-quality user experience links to the customer experience. Usable and intuitive interfaces are crucial for users to interact with security features effectively [48].

Usable Security Controls. Designing usable security controls is crucial for balancing security requirements with user experience. According to [1], designing systems that are usable and secure at the same time is not an easy task and security is usually compromised for usability. However, this should not be the case as both functions are important and must be carefully considered for UX of cybersecurity training applications. A balance needs to be maintained between security and usability [42].

Embed Continuous Assurance. The framework emphasizes the importance of ongoing security assessments and user feedback to continuously improve the security posture and user experience. Continuous assurance ensures that all the latest cybersecurity threats are considered in the UX design [49].

Usable Systems and Products. Designing usable systems and products is essential for ensuring that users can effectively interact with technology. It is important to understand what a user wants from a system, how they want it and what they want to use it for [1].

Fun and Satisfactory. The concept of fun is an important element as user's need to enjoy the experience of using a cybersecurity application. This increases the user's engagement and satisfaction [34].

In underprivileged communities, digital platforms are becoming more and more popular these days. Designing systems that are usable and secure at the same time plays an important role in encouraging continuous engagement with the platforms [1]. For novice users, user experience assists in building confidence while using these platforms without falling victim to digital deception. The focus here should be on creating an intuitive, appealing, and easy-to-navigate interfaces or platforms.

5.3 Interactiveness

Interactiveness goes beyond user experience and emphasizes the importance of creating an engaging and interactive learning environment. Interactiveness pertains to the dynamic and responsive nature of digital systems that allow users to engage with technology across various platforms and devices. In the context of this research, interactiveness involves harnessing technological and social changes to ensure that cybersecurity applications remain adaptive and responsive to evolving user needs and behaviors [10].

Harnessing Technological and Social Change. This framework considers technological and social trend changes to ensure that UX for cybersecurity applications always meets users' expectations while providing security.

Adaptive Collaboration. The framework emphasizes the need for security measures to adapt to evolving technologies and user behaviors. Collaboration needs to exist between key stakeholders such as the user, developer and security personnel [10]. This ensures that applications developing using this framework always respond to changing requirements.

Responsive. Designing responsive technology products allows users to interact with them across various devices and platforms. Security features should be responsive to user needs and context to ensure that incidents of deception are minimized [48].

In a community-driven context, the interactivity of cybersecurity awareness platforms is essential for engaging users and increasing interest in cybersecurity. This interactivity takes into account technological and social changes, ensuring that the platforms are adaptable and responsive to user needs [10]. Cybersecurity awareness platforms play a vital role in helping citizens recognize and respond to threats, reducing the risk of incidents, ensuring compliance, and fostering a culture of security.

5.4 Accessibility

Accessibility refers to designing systems and interfaces that are inclusive and accessible to all users equally. In this research, this applies to creating secure and interactive systems that are simple to use, intuitive and visually attractive. This includes designing interfaces that are easy to navigate, provide clear user instructions and feedback and accommodate users with disabilities through accessibility. Simplicity, intuitiveness and visual attractiveness are discussed as key concepts below:

Simple. Designing secure interactive systems requires a delicate balance between robust security, intuitive usability, and full functionality [1]. This user-centered approach ensures a positive experience while safeguarding against cybersecurity threats. Designing simple and intuitive interfaces is essential for ensuring that technology products are accessible to all users, including those with disabilities.

Intuitive. Intuitiveness relates to how learnable a product and its features are [20]. Cybersecurity applications designed using the proposed framework help users understand how to interact with the applications without the need for extensive training or guidance.

Visual Attractiveness. The look and feel of a product contribute to its overall user experience [20, 36]. A product that is visually appealing is seen as being easier to use. Designing visually attractive interfaces enhances user engagement and satisfaction which contributes to user's using applications frequently.

Accessible and inclusive cybersecurity involves designing and implementing cybersecurity platforms that meet the needs of everyone [1]. In community-driven projects, particularly in rural areas, accessibility promotes active participation in digital platforms for all individuals, including those with disabilities and a lack of digital literacy skills. This increased participation supports the social and economic development of these communities. It is especially crucial to consider the most vulnerable members of our society, such as children, to protect them from threats like phishing, pornography, cyberbullying, identity theft, and violations of privacy.

5.5 Robustness

The concept of robustness relates to the resilience and reliability of applications to withstand threats while maintaining functionality and security. It is important to add a robust layer of security while designing the system or integrate security into other features and system usages [1]. This includes implementing rigorous testing and validation at every step of the development time, adopting industry best practices and continuously monitoring and updating security measures. Development timelines, sustainable development and technical excellence are discussed under the construct of robustness:

Development Timelines. This framework considers the importance of development timelines to ensure that applications are developed on time and within budget. To ensure robustness, it is important to implement rigorous testing and validation at each step of the development timeline [42].

Sustainable Development. Promoting sustainable development practices helps ensure that technology products are developed in a manner that is environmentally and socially responsible.

Technical Excellence. This framework maintains the importance of technical excellence. Striving for technical excellence in product development helps ensure that technology products are built to high standards of quality and reliability. This ensures that the cybersecurity applications are able to protect users from deception attempts.

For community-based projects involving the use of cybersecurity awareness platforms, robustness is important to ensure long-term viability of the platforms. Such platforms should be able to handle threats while ensuring security and usability. Therefore, it is important to add a robust layer of security while designing these platforms [1]. This entails putting in place stringent testing and validation at every step of the development time, applying industry best practices and continuously monitoring and updating security measures [42].

5.6 Transparency

According to [46], transparency of a system has an impact on a user's experience. For example, if users are aware how their information is being handled on a certain system, this significantly improves the trust they have in a system and in turn improves their trust and their willingness to use the system [46]. Transparency relates to maintaining clear and open communication channels, ensuring transparency in data handling and processing and promoting accountability for security measures and practices:

Effective Communication. This framework considers transparent communication channels with stakeholders important as it facilitates collaboration and ensures that everyone is informed and aligned.

Flexible Architectures. Flexible and adaptable architectures ensure that cybersecurity applications developed using this framework are able to evolve and adapt to the changing cybersecurity landscape. This ensures that these applications are able to adapt to new threats in the environment [46].

In South Africa, where many communities are underprivileged, there is a need for them to feel secure that their information is handled properly and is not at risk of fraud.

When users are provided with proper communication regarding how the data is handled and stored, they develop greater trust in the community-based platforms and this encourages continuous engagement with the system [46].

The recommendations from this study put forward the Secure User Experience (S-UX) Framework to safeguard against digital deception. The six constructs proposed are discussed in detail in this section, considering both the user experience and security whilst using cybersecurity awareness applications.

5.7 Linking Framework Constructs to Real Scenarios

To illustrate the practical implementation of the proposed S-UX framework, consider the CyberCulture Foundation, which operates within a rural community in Gqeberha, Eastern Cape. This foundation is dedicated to fostering cybersecurity awareness among children aged 6 to 12, with the goal of cultivating responsible digital citizens. They have developed an engaging application that provides comprehensive cybersecurity awareness training through interactive modules, quizzes, and challenges that address essential topics such as phishing, malware, and password management. The cybersecurity awareness platform aims to equip children with the knowledge and skills necessary to navigate online challenges, including phishing, inappropriate content, cyberbullying, identity theft, and issues related to privacy. Users are encouraged to track their progress, earn rewards, and participate in friendly competitions with others. The six constructs can be effectively utilized in this context as follows:

Security: The cybersecurity awareness platform places a strong emphasis on safeguarding the information of children. It implements essential security measures, including multi-factor authentication, continuous authentication, and data encryption, all of which play a vital role in ensuring comprehensive protection [47].

Experience: To ensure that children can effectively engage with the cybersecurity awareness platform, it is crucial to prioritize user experience. Presentations that are visually appealing and age-appropriate, combined with a user-friendly interface, will enhance the learning experience and make the exploration of new cyber concepts both enjoyable and engaging for young learners [42].

Interactiveness: A cybersecurity awareness platform should aim to provide personalized experiences for users. Incorporating game-like features can enhance student engagement and satisfaction. By integrating elements such as competition, challenges, and rewards, cybersecurity awareness platform can foster a motivational environment where students are inspired to actively participate in their learning journey [35].

Accessibility: It is essential for a cybersecurity awareness platform to consider incorporating voice-guided instructions in multiple languages while ensuring compatibility with budget-friendly devices. Additionally, offering users the option to cache information for later upload when they have access to a stable internet connection would enhance usability. These accessibility features contribute significantly to fostering inclusivity [42].

Robustness: A robust and dependable cybersecurity awareness platform is essential, particularly due to its data redundancy and backup capabilities, which ensure continued operation in the face of potential disruptions. The platform undergoes rigorous testing to confirm its ability to manage data effectively. Additionally, considerations for sustainable development strategies are integrated to promote the platform's efficient and lasting operation [47].

Transparency: The users of the cybersecurity awareness platform are informed in advance about the learning outcomes, assessments, competitions, and rewards, ensuring they are well-prepared for what to expect. Additionally, users are made aware of the types of data collected by the platform, including location and other personal information, fostering transparency and trust [36].

In this context, the S-UX framework demonstrates its potential in addressing various challenges by enhancing security, usability, and accessibility within a key community system. Additionally, it fosters increased cybersecurity awareness among users and encourages the development of responsible digital citizens. By implementing this framework in a practical setting, such as the CyberCulture Foundation's cybersecurity awareness platform, this study illustrates how a user-centered approach can positively influence both the technical and social dimensions of a community-driven initiative.

6 Analysis of the S-UX Framework

Despite phishing attacks being recognized for over two decades, the ongoing research aimed at developing effective techniques to combat these threats indicates a concerning increase in such attacks across Africa. This trend highlights a lack of robust solutions and strategies to address phishing. There is a pressing need for comprehensive research in the field of anti-phishing to enhance the overall cybersecurity landscape. The goal is to combat digital deception by fostering responsible digital citizenship. Responsible digital citizens contribute to a safer and more positive online environment, which can yield numerous social benefits [36, 42, 44], including:

- Building a safe online community
- Promoting respect and tolerance
- Encouraging civic participation
- Developing critical thinking skills
- Preparing for professional applications
- Promoting digital inclusion
- Empowering vulnerable communities

The S-UX framework proposes a new approach to safeguard against digital deception that is focused on cybersecurity training applications by integrating secure by design principles with the agile development methodology. This section analyzes this integration and explores the advantages and limitations of the S-UX framework. The traditional agile methods prioritize speed, flexibility and functionality over security and this leads to inadequate consideration for security and potential vulnerabilities that can be exploited. Security measures in the agile process tend to be reactive in nature [8]. The integration of secure by design with agile methodology enables the implementation of proactive security measures throughout the design process [44]. Security measures are incorporated into the design process from the beginning. This proactive step ensures that security is prioritized and the early identification and mitigation of security risks increases the security posture of the designed application and user experience. The proactive measures provided by the S-UX framework leads to early risk identification and mitigation which contributes to the overall protection against threats such as digital deception.

The agile methodology relies on short iterative cycles and continuous feedback amongst key stakeholders [8]. These short and iterative cycles are vital as they ensure that the applications being designed are accessible, interactive, robust and secure. These rapid development cycles can result in limited consideration for security. This gap raises concerns about the robustness and resilience of the developed applications against evolving cyber threats [19]. The integration of secure-by-design principles with agile methodology offers the advantage of flexibility and adaptability as discussed in sections above. Security can be incorporated without compromising on the agile process of designing. This also ensures that security related feedback can continuously be integrated at shorter feedback intervals to enhance the design of the digital deception applications.

The S-UX framework is made up of multiple constructs, each with its own set of principles and the complexity of its implementation has not been tested. The proposed framework offers six high-level constructs which includes security, experience, interactiveness, accessibility, robustness, and transparency. In underprivileged communities, digital platforms are becoming more and more popular. Designing systems that embodies the above constructs play an important role in encouraging continuous engagement with the platforms [47]. User experience is critical as it assists in building confidence while using these platforms without falling victim to digital deception. Users sometimes perceive additional security measures as being cumbersome [1]. It will therefore be important that the S-UX framework is evaluated to determine user acceptance. The cybersecurity threat landscape is also ever evolving with new cyber threats. Measuring the effectiveness of the S-UX framework against the evolving landscape and validating its impact requires further research to develop metrics for measuring the framework's performance.

7 Conclusion

User Experience (UX), an established field of research, presents some risks, such as providing users with experiences that they do not wish. Cybersecurity has recently become essential in order to protect businesses and individuals from spammers and cyber criminals. This study therefore merged two important aspects which are user experience and security in order to guide the development of secure cybersecurity awareness applications. This study seeks to improve the overall cybersecurity landscape and thereby contributes to the broader body of knowledge. Hence this study designed and proposed a Secure User Experience (S-UX) Framework to safeguard against digital deception, that focused on cybersecurity training applications, as well as its adaptation for real-world community settings. This framework also serves as a tool to increase awareness and enhance security in community settings by combining security features with user experience design principles to create solutions that are secure and user friendly for all users, regardless of their level of skills and resources.

The study merged the strengths of the Secure-by-Design framework and Agile framework. The result was a conceptual Secure User Experience (S-UX) Framework that comprises six (6) constructs which are security, experience, interactiveness, accessibility, robustness and transparency. These constructs cover issues around user experience and security that are needed for the development of cybersecurity training applications. Apart from its application in cybersecurity training, this framework has broader implications in societal and communal contexts where digital platforms are used. This framework may help increase trust among users in communities, which improves their use and engagement with such platforms. Additionally, this framework offers a systematic approach to protect users and safeguard them from deception involved in digital activities, thereby enabling communities to develop safely in the face of a digital fraud.

More work can still be done such as:

- Evaluation of the proposed framework.
- Implementation of the proposed framework in real-world community settings to ensure the framework's applicability.
- For each S-UX construct, a template and general guidelines are required.

References

1. Akinlade, E., Adeleye, E.: Designing a secure interactive system: balancing the conflict between security, usability, and functionality (2022)
2. Alghamdi, H.: Can phishing education enable users to recognize phishing attacks?. Dublin Institute of Technology ARROW at DIT (2017)
3. Al-Qahtani, A.F., Cresci, S.: The COVID-19 scamdemic: a survey of phishing attacks and their countermeasures during COVID-19. IET Inf. Secur. **16**(5), 324–345 (2022)
4. Amoroso, E.: Cyber attacks: protecting national infrastructure. Elsevier (2012)
5. Arachchilage, N.A.G., Hameed, M.A.: Integrating self-efficacy into a gamified approach to thwart phishing attacks. arXiv preprint arXiv:1706.07748 (2017)
6. Arachchilage, N.A., Hameed, M.A.: Teaching Johnny to thwart phishing attacks. Mach. Learn. Comput. Cyber Secur. Principle, Algorithms Pract., 337 (2019)
7. Atkins, B., Huang, W.: A study of social engineering in online frauds. Open J. Soc. Sci. **1**(03), 23 (2013)
8. Baca, D.: Developing secure software t in an agile process (Doctoral dissertation, Blekinge Institute of Technology) (2012)
9. BBC News.: Google Docs users hit by phishing scam. BBC News (2017). https://www.bbc.com/news/business-39798022
10. Chamberlain, S., Sharp, H., Maiden, N.P.: Towards a framework for integrating agile development and user-centred design. In: Abrahamsson, P., Marchesi, M., Succi, G. (eds) International Conference on Extreme Programming and Agile Processes in Software Engineering, pp. 143–153. Berlin, Heidelberg: Springer, Berlin, Heidelberg (2006). https://doi.org/10.1007/11774129_15
11. Chen, T.C., Dick, S., Miller, J.: Detecting visually similar web pages: application to phishing detection. ACM Trans. Internet Technol. (TOIT) **10**(2), 1–38 (2010)
12. Chuma, K.G., Mthethwa, S.N.: Cyberthreats, vulnerabilities and cyberattacks targeting hospitals in Pretoria, South Africa during the covid-19 pandemic. Acta Criminologica: Afr. J. Criminol. Victimol. **37**(1), 23–45 (2024)

13. Coetzee, A.: A Conceptual Model for Phishing Awareness: A South African Study. University of Johannesburg (South Africa) (2022)
14. Crossler, R.E., Johnston, A.C., Lowry, P.B., Hu, Q., Warkentin, M., Baskerville, R.: Future directions for behavioral information security research. Comput. Secur. **32**, 90–101 (2013). https://doi.org/10.1016/j.cose.2012.09.010
15. Desolda, G., Di Nocera, F., Ferro, L., Lanzilotti, R., Maggi, P., Marrella, A.: Alerting users about phishing attacks. In: HCI for Cybersecurity, Privacy and Trust: First International Conference, HCI-CPT 2019, Held as Part of the 21st HCI International Conference, HCII 2019, Orlando, FL, USA, July 26–31, Proceedings 21, pp. 134–148. Springer International Publishing, Cham (2019). https://doi.org/10.1007/978-3-030-22351-9_9
16. Dhamija, R., Tygar, J.D., Hearst, M.: Why phishing works. In: Proceedings of the SIGCHI Conference on Human Factors in Computing Systems, pp. 581–590 (2006)
17. Dong, J., Qin, Z., Fang, Z., Chen, X., Huang, Z., Guo, H., Chen, S.: Visual analytics for phishing scam identification in blockchain transactions with multiple model comparison. In: Proceedings of the 16th International Symposium on Visual Information Communication and Interaction, pp. 1–9 (2023)
18. Fatima, R., Yasin, A., Liu, L., Wang, J.: How persuasive is a phishing email? A phishing game for phishing awareness. J. Comput. Secur. **27**(6), 581–612 (2019)
19. Fawle, H., LeBlanc, D.: Smartwatch Vulnerability Analysis: Focusing on Bluetooth Low Energy (2024)
20. Hadnagy, C.: Social Engineering: The Art of Human Hacking. John Wiley & Sons (2010)
21. Hamari, J., Koivisto, J., Sarsa, H.: Does gamification work? A literature review of empirical studies on gamification. In: 2014 47th Hawaii International Conference on System Sciences, pp. 3025–3034. IEEE (2014)
22. Hartson, R., Pyla, P.S.: The UX book: agile UX design for a quality user experience. Morgan Kaufmann (2018)
23. Hassan, A.: Challenges to Implementing Financial Inclusion in Sub-Rural Areas in Bauchi State. Master's thesis. American University of Nigeria (2022)
24. Hobert, S., Følstad, A., Law, E.L.C.: Chatbots for active learning: a case of phishing email identification. Int. J. Hum. Comput. Stud. **179**, 103–108 (2023)
25. Ilina, A., Bekiarova, N., Ivaylo, I.: Cyber Globalization as an In/Stability Factor. In: Proceedings of INTCESS (2019)
26. Kadam, S.P., Joshi, S.: Secure by design approach to improve security of object oriented software. In: 2015 2nd International Conference on Computing for Sustainable Global Development (INDIACom), pp. 24–30, IEEE (2015)
27. Kahneman, D., Tversky, A.: Judgment under uncertainty: heuristics and biases. Science **185**(4157), 1124–1131 (1974)
28. Khan, M.A., Merabet, A., Alkaabi, S., Sayed, H.E.: Game-based learning platform to enhance cybersecurity education. Educ. Inf. Technol., 1–25 (2022)
29. Knopf, J.W.: Doing a literature review. PS: Polit. Sci. Polit **39**(1), 127–132 (2006)
30. Kralik, D., Visentin, K., Van Loon, A.: Transition: a literature review. J. Adv. Nurs. **55**(3), 320–329 (2006)
31. Kruger, M.: Towards a cybersecurity skills framework for South Africa (2023)
32. Mbelli, T.M., Dwolatzky, B.: Cyber security, a threat to cyber banking in South Africa: an approach to network and application security. In: 2016 IEEE 3rd International Conference on Cyber Security and Cloud Computing (CSCloud), pp. 1–6. IEEE (2016)
33. Miller, B., Miller, K., Zhang, X., Terwilliger, M.G.: Prevention of phishing attacks: a three-pillared approach. Issues Inf. Syst. **21**(2) (2020)
34. Mitnick, K.D., Simon, W.L.: The art of deception: controlling the human element of security. John Wiley & Sons (2003)

35. Mocanu, B.C., et al.: NextEDR-Next generation agent-based EDR systems for cybersecurity threats. In: 2024 32nd Euromicro International Conference on Parallel, Distributed and Network-Based Processing (PDP), pp. 183–190. IEEE (2024)
36. Moneva, A., Leukfeldt, E.R., Klijnsoon, W.: Alerting consciences to reduce cybercrime: a quasi-experimental design using warning banners. J. Exp. Criminol. **19**(3), 835–862 (2023)
37. Moore, R.J., Arar, R.: Conversational UX design: a practitioner's guide to the natural conversation framework. Morgan & Claypool (2019)
38. Mouratidis, H., Kang, M.: Secure by design: developing secure software. Dev. Eval. Secur.-Aware Softw Syst. 1 (2012)
39. Mpekoa, N.: An analysis of cybersecurity architectures. In: International Conference on Cyber Warfare and Security, vol. 19, No. 1, pp. 200–207 (2024)
40. Naidoo, R.: Analysing urgency and trust cues exploited in phishing scam designs. In: 10th International Conference on Cyber Warfare and Security, p. 216 (2015)
41. Nyasvisvo, B., Chigada, J.M.: Phishing attacks: a security challenge for university students studying remotely. Afr. J. Inf. Syst. **15**(2), 3 (2023)
42. Parmar, B.: Protecting against spear-phishing. Comput. Fraud Secur. **1**, 8–11 (2012)
43. Pascoe, C., Quinn, S., Scarfone, K.: The NIST Cybersecurity Framework (CSF) 2.0 (2024)
44. Razaq, L., Ahmad, T., Ibtasam, S., Ramzan, U., Mare, S.: "We even borrowed money from our neighbor" understanding mobile-based frauds through victims' experiences. In: Proceedings of the ACM on Human-Computer Interaction, vol. 5, pp. 1-30 (2021).
45. Salinas, E., Cueva, R., Paz, F.: A systematic review of user-centered design techniques. In: Marcus, A., Rosenzweig, E. (eds) Design, User Experience, and Usability. Interaction Design: 9th International Conference, DUXU 2020, Held as Part of the 22nd HCI International Conference, HCII 2020, Proceedings, Part I 22, pp. 253–267. Springer International Publishing, Cham (2020). https://doi.org/10.1007/978-3-030-49713-2_18
46. Sheng, S., Holbrook, M., Kumaraguru, P., Cranor, L.F., Downs, J.: Who falls for phish? A demographic analysis of phishing susceptibility and effectiveness of interventions. In: Proceedings of the SIGCHI Conference on Human Factors in Computing Systems, pp. 373–382 (2010)
47. Shete, S.: AI in cybersecurity and user interface design beyond chatbots. J. Artif. Intell. Cloud Comput. **164**(2), 2–4 (2023). SRC/JAICC-179.https://doi.org/10.47363/JAICC/2023
48. Soffer, H.: Old age and the potential for web fraud: an in-depth analysis. SSRN (2023).https://doi.org/10.2139/ssrn.46025384602538
49. Thomopoulos, G.A., Lyras, D.P., Fidas, C.A.: A systematic review and research challenges on phishing cyberattacks from an electroencephalography and gaze-based perspective. Personal and Ubiquitous Computing, pp. 1–22 (2024)
50. Valdés-Rodríguez, Y., Hochstetter-Diez, J., Diéguez-Rebolledo, M., Bustamante-Mora, A., Cadena-Martínez, R.: Analysis of strategies for the integration of security practices in agile software development: a sustainable SME Approach. IEEE Access (2024)
51. Veerasamy, N., Mashiane, T., Pillay, K.: Contextualising cybersecurity readiness in South Africa. In: 14th International Conference on Cyber Warfare and Security, pp. 467–475 (2019)
52. Venkatesha, S., Reddy, K.R., Chandavarkar, B.R.: Social engineering attacks during the COVID-19 pandemic. SN Comput. Sci. **2**, 1–9 (2021)
53. Vitale, J., et al.: Be more transparent and users will like you: a robot privacy and user experience design experiment. In: Proceedings of the 2018 ACM/IEEE International Conference on Human-Robot Interaction, pp. 379–387 (2018)
54. Wang, J., Li, Y., Rao, H.R.: Overconfidence in phishing email detection. J. Assoc. Inf. Syst. **17**(11), Article 1 (2016)
55. Wang, Z., Zhu, H., Sun, L.: Social engineering in cybersecurity: effect mechanisms, human vulnerabilities and attack methods. IEEE (2021)

56. Williams, E.J., Polage, D.: How persuasive is phishing email? The role of authentic design, influence and current events in email judgements. Behav. Inf. Technol. **38**(2), 184–197 (2019)
57. Willis, L.E.: Deception by design. Harv. JL Tech. **34**, 115 (2020)

Theorisation as Beneficiation in Interaction Design and International Development: A Global South Perspective

Judy van Biljon[✉]

University of South Africa, 28 Pioneer Ave, Roodepoort, South Africa
vbiljja@unisa.ac.za

Abstract. Widely varying contexts, rapidly accumulating changes to our environments and technological progress make Interaction Design for International Development (IDID) a challenging endeavour where it is essential to have a body of scientifically acceptable principles as disciplinary commons. Scientific principles can be formulated as theorisations, including rules, guidelines, models, methods, taxonomies, frameworks or theories which can guide research design, processes, development and improvement of interaction design practices and technologies. Many Global South countries have vast reserves of precious metals, which could be used to generate much needed funding for socio-economic development if the environmental impact and beneficiation are managed sustainably. Beneficiation in the mining industry is a process whereby impurities are removed to abstract a higher value product. Missing out on the beneficiation opportunities in the mining industry is a compelling problem for many Global South countries. Similarly, researchers and specifically Global South researchers miss out on the benefits of theorising as a beneficiation mechanism in research. Acknowledging the historic isolation and marginalisation of researchers from the Global South and the inhibition of alternatives to mainstream knowledge production. This paper focuses on a different aspect, the potential of theorisation to mobilise and amplify the voices of developing country researchers specifically by considering the potential of synthesising and abstracting findings beyond isolated insights. This question is investigated by a systematic literature review of papers published from 2020 to 2024 in the Computer-Human Interaction Conference. While the number of papers mentioning theory has increased since 2020, most findings report insights as the contribution; few papers abstracting theorisations like criteria, principles, guidelines or models, which would make the research knowledge more accessible and transferable. While acknowledging the challenges to theorisation this could imply an underused opportunity for value addition through theorisation.

Keywords: Theorisation · Human-Computer Interaction · Global South

Published by Springer Nature Switzerland AG 2026
G. Bhutkar et al. (Eds.): IDID 2024, IFIP AICT 747, pp. 21–32, 2026.
https://doi.org/10.1007/978-3-032-00777-3_2

1 Introduction

Besides rich reserves of gold and diamonds, South Africa has the largest share of the world's platinum and manganese and large shares of chrome and vanadium reserves but this comparative advantage from a national resource endowment perspective has not been fully leveraged to build a dynamic industrial economy [1]. Beneficiation, the processing of a mineral beyond the stage where it represents saleable raw material, is key to leveraging this resource endowment. The various factors impacting beneficiation include policies on domestic value-addition, energy requirements, transport and logistic costs and a decline in research and development over the past 20 years [1]. Here, a parallel is drawn between the challenge of beneficiation in the mining industry of the Global South (GS) and the challenge of theory development in Interaction design for international development (IDID). IDID and the related Human-Computer Interaction for Development (HCI4D) are challenging research domains due to widely varying contexts, rapidly accumulating changes to our environments, datafication and digitisation. When designing for a complex future with many uncertainties, it is important to develop theories and create a body of scientifically acceptable principles as disciplinary commons in interaction design [2]. Theories are necessary to guide research design, processes, development, and for the improvement of Human-Computer Interaction (HCI) practices and technologies [3]. Like beneficiation in the mining industry, theory development can be considered a process whereby impurities are removed to abstract a higher value product. Global South countries, like South Africa, do not reap the full benefit of the mining industry due to various factors that limit optimal beneficiation. Do Global South researchers miss out on the benefits of theorising as value addition, like Global South countries miss out on the value addition of beneficiation in the mining industry? If so, the problem may not be limited to Global South countries and lack of theorisation may not be the only reason. Therefore, a brief overview of challenges to research in the GS is presented. That is followed by an investigation into evidence of theorisation in HCI publications before focusing on the case of Global South countries. This paper investigates theorisation, specifically awareness of the importance of theorisation and adding value to research findings by synthesising and abstracting findings beyond isolated insights. This question is investigated by a systematic literature review of papers published from 2020 to 2024 at the Computer-Human Interaction (CHI) Conference. The findings indicate that the number of papers mentioning theory has increased since 2020. Most findings report the theoretical contribution as *insights* with few papers abstracting *criteria, principles, guidelines, models, etc.,* which would make the research knowledge more accessible and transferable. While acknowledging the challenges to theorisation this could imply a lack of awareness of the potential value addition by theorisation. Related literature is reviewed in Sect. 2, and the research design in Sect. 3. The findings from the literature review are presented in Sect. 4 and the paper concludes with the findings in Sect. 5.

2 Related Literature and Terminology

2.1 Theory

Drawing on the Information Systems discipline for a mature narrative on theorisation, this section provides a brief overview of what theory is, why it is important and where to focus for increasing impact. Theories provide a *representation* of someone's perceptions of how a subset of real-world phenomena should be described [4]. A complete theory contains four essential elements, namely the *what* and *how* elements that constitute the domain of the theory, the *why* (explanation) element and the temporal and contextual limitations that set the boundaries [5]. These elements are now described in more detail:

- What are the factors (constructs, concepts and variables) that should be considered as part of the explanation of the social or individual phenomenon of interest? In selecting the factors, the theorist needs to balance the competing virtues of comprehensiveness with parsimony.
- How are the factors related? Connecting the metaphorical 'boxes' that represent the factors adds order to the conceptualization by adding links that can be tested for causality.
- Why is this explanation plausible? In other words, what are the underlying psychological, economic or social dynamics that justify the selection of factors, and the causal relationships proposed?
- The temporal and contextual conditions: When, who and where, limit the propositions generated from a theoretical model and set the boundaries of generalisability.

Theories are important to facilitate the systematic treatment of a topic to explain, predict or make sense of some aspects of human behaviour [6]. Theorisation allows the researcher to abstract their knowledge on fundamental and universal ideas to provide a consistent and related set of concepts and principles that we can compare with reality. Weick [7] recommends moving beyond the dichotomy of what theory *is* and *is not* to view theory as a continuum of approximations. These 'emergent products' summarise progress, give direction, and serve as place markers that have vestiges of theory but are not themselves theories [7].

Hassan, Lowry and Thornhill [8] suggest the following as 12 useful products of theorisation in Information Systems: question, paradigm, law, framework, myth, analogy, metaphor, model, concept, construct, statement and hypothesis. Besides the brief overview provided in this section, a detailed discussion on theorising and the products of theorising are beyond the scope of this paper. Weber [4] and Hassan, Lowry and Thornhill [8] are recommended for their coverage of theorising and the products of theorising in Information Systems since these products are relevant to Interaction Design.

Theory usage across disciplines is dissimilar. The following are theory uses in HCI suggested by Hornbæk [9] and augmented theory uses from Design Science Research suggested by Gregor [10], as depicted in Table 1. The Design Science Research perspective (underlined in column 1) aligns with HCI as both domains involve the development and evaluation of artefacts in response to the research objective.

The next section introduces the context of interaction design and international development.

Table 1. Theory uses in Human-Computer interaction [9, 10]

Theory use	Contribution	Example
Background or explanation (<u>Link to existing literature)</u>	Overview of related theories, specifically the theories the paper builds on	'Previous studies concluded …' 'We depart from …'
Methodological tool for design and action (<u>Informs design)</u>	To inform data capturing instruments, often only some constructs of the theory is used	'We base our conceptual model on theories … We use the following constructs … in the questionnaire'
Analysis and description (<u>Guides evaluation</u>)	Provides an analytic lens for data analysis, often only taxonomic use	'The thematic analysis was informed by categories from …'
Discussion and explanation (<u>Explain user behaviour)</u>	Theories used to explain results, often disconnected from the other parts of the paper; rarely implications for theorisatoin	'Let us use … as a lens to explain our results"
Design explanation and prediction (<u>Enhances predictive power)</u>	To justify functionality theoretically	'The functionality … is included because of … (theory or theorisation product)

2.2 Interaction Design and International Development

Interaction Design and International Development (IDID) involves the domains of interaction design and international development. Human-Computer Interaction and International Development research focusing on human-centred design has gone under different names, one of those being Human-Computer Interaction for Development (HCI4D) [11]. Abdelnour-Nocera and Rangaswamy [12] argue that technologies for humans considering diverse cultural and contextual positions should be part of the default agenda for the HCI4D research domain. There is ambiguity and even controversy surrounding the meaning of the term "development", and a fundamental duality between those studies that focus on understanding technology "for development" (where there is a commitment to human and socio-economic development) and those studies that focus on understanding technology in developing countries [13]. For the purposes of this paper, no distinction will be made between the terms IDID and HCI4D.

2.3 Challenges to Global South Research

The visibility of African human-computer interaction research and practice, in Africa and internationally, is challenged by the practices of technology production, education, and research tend to reproduce meanings that associate the continent with absence [14]. Dependence on foreign scholarly direction can create a gap between research and reality in a way that affects the success of ICT programmes in African countries [15]. Furthermore, this problem is not limited to African research, Bai [16] suggests that the Global South has become a playground for Western scholars in information and communication technologies for development. Alatas [17] proposes the term *academic dependency* whereby social research in the Third World takes its cues from research in the First World (especially the UK, US and France) in terms of a research agenda, theoretical perspectives and methods while the designated role for researchers of the Third World is empirical data collection. This resonates with the findings of Bai [16] on the role of researchers in information and communication technologies for development where many of the Global South countries are considered less developed and are classified as Third World.

Collyer [18] contends that the publishing process, which is fundamental to academic knowledge production in its capacity to assist with the formation and maintenance of knowledge networks and disciplines, is implicated in the isolation or marginalisation of specific social groups and the inhibition of alternatives to mainstream knowledge production. These mechanisms allow knowledge produced in the Global South to be systematically marginalised, under-valued or made inaccessible to other researchers. A consequence is significant inequality in citation counts between the Global North and South, and despite the existence of knowledge production in the Global South, Southern scholarship is rarely cited by either Northern or Southern scholars [18]. A detailed discussion of the psychological, social and structural impediments to knowledge production and dissemination of researchers from the Global South is beyond the scope of this paper, but the consequences for the development and mobilisation of indigenous theories are evident. Recognising this problem is not novel, but most published research stops short of proposing solutions on how to amplify the voices of developing country researchers [15].

3 Research Design

3.1 Method

This study employs a systematic literature review (SLR) to investigate the research question. The systematic literature review (SLR) is a recognised method of supporting literature analysis in a research domain [19], especially when the aim is to construct evidence-based lessons from the accumulated research [20]. We followed the systematic literature review based on the Preferred Reporting Items for Systematic Reviews and Meta-Analyses (PRISMA) method [21] and which resulted in a corpus of literature to support the analysis. The processes of data collection, data condensation, data display, drawing conclusions, and verifying conclusions were applied, either allowing the publications to suggest themes (open coding) or using pre-existing themes to constrain and inform the analysis (directional coding) [22]. The directional coding themes were based on examples of previous literature review, for example, the themes of paper frequency and main authors' country. Open coding was used for areas specific to this study, for example, the theory types that emerged from the data.

3.2 Data Corpus

The Computer-Human Interaction Conference was selected since that is widely considered the flagship conference in the Computer-Human Interaction field and the papers and publication information are accessible through the ACM library. The review was conducted in the week of 2 September 2024, covering papers from the period 2020 to 2024. Conference papers in the English language were included but workshop papers were excluded. The number of papers per conference is as follows: 2020 (760), 2021 (238), 2022 (637), 2023 (879), 2024 (1057). When there was a section specifically for theory papers, e.g., the 'Models and Theories' section in 2022, those papers were all added. The procedure produced 3571 papers, for which the titles, abstracts and keywords were screened using the keyword "theory", thereby 103 papers were selected and the full papers downloaded. The full texts were read to validate relevance as papers explicitly stating a contribution to theory and 3 irrelevant papers were removed. The remaining 99 papers constituted the data corpus, as depicted in Fig. 1.

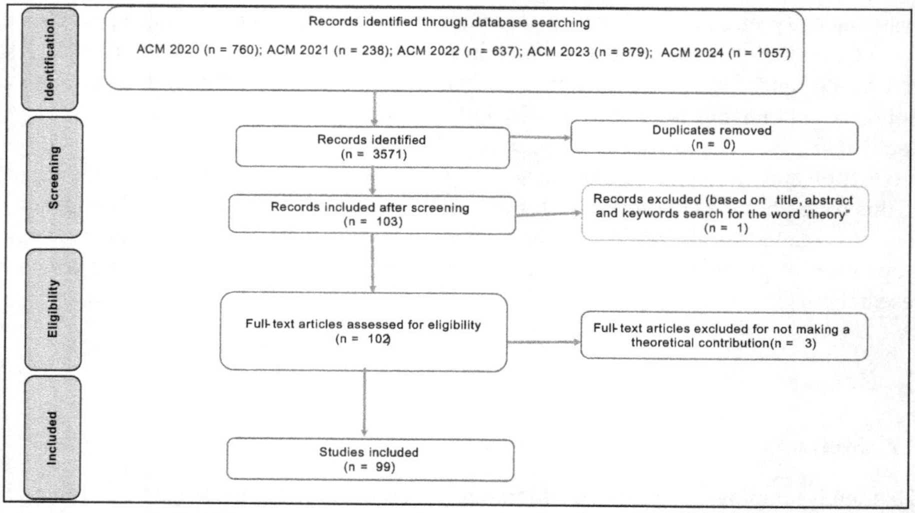

Fig 1. Paper selection process according to PRISMA method

The number of publications mentioning the word 'theory' as a percentage of the total publications in the proceedings is depicted in Table 2. The number of papers that mentioned the term theory increased annually except for 2022. In 2022, the CHI proceedings was published as sections rather than in one document, this complicated the search and could account for the smaller number of theory papers identified in 2022.

3.3 Limitations

As mentioned, the format of the CHI2022 proceedings complicated the search and may have introduced anomalies. Research in an interdisciplinary field like IDID is complicated by the disciplinary nuances associated with different terms, as mentioned in Sect. 2.

Table 2. CHI proceedings selected for analysis

Year	Number of publications	Selected	Percentage of publications
2020	760	5	0.7
2021	238	14	5.9
2022	637	5	0.8
2023	879	30	3.4
2024	1057	45	4.3

Furthermore, it can be argued that IDID is a subset of HCI4D like the interaction design research is a subset of the Human-Computer Interaction discipline. To be inclusive the terms HCI4D and IDID were both included and will be used interchangeably. Despite a rigorous approach enforced by the strict application of the SLR as method, any literature survey can be faulted for having made contestable decisions (both intentionally and unintentionally) about which works to include and which elements to emphasise in the works identified. We also acknowledge the ambiguity and limitations surrounding the use of the term "theory".

4 Results and Findings

4.1 Results

The 99 papers selected for mentioning the term *theory* were analysed to investigate where the paper originated from geographically (first author country), in which section of the paper the references to theory were found and what theories were mentioned. Figure 2 depicts the frequency per country. The best represented countries are the USA (45), UK (9), Germany (8), Canada (7), Australia and Sweden both 4, Switzerland 3, China and Singapore both two and the following one each: Belgium, Denmark, France, Ghana, Hong Kong, Ireland, Luxembourg, Poland and Saudi Arabia.

The only Global South country is Australia, which is a developed country, and the only African country is Ghana. The lack of papers from developing countries in the Global South mentioning theory confirms an earlier argument that the HCI4D domain lacks theoretical focus [23] since most developing economies are in the Global South.

Figure 3 depicts the references to theory expressed as a percentage per section of the paper. Unsurprisingly, the literature review section has the most references to theory. The relatively low number of references to theory in the conclusion and future research sections is interesting and seems to indicate that the connections to theory in terms of the contribution and future research contributions are lacking.

Figure 4 depicts a frequency-based word cloud of the related theories mentioned in the literature reviews. Those theories are from Psychology and Sociology and exclude HCI approaches like Participatory Design (PD), Contextual Design, Human Centred Design (HCD) or Value-Sensitive Design (VSD) due to the focus on the term theory.

Previous research on HCI4D theorisation identified underreporting in the sense that the methodological approaches were mostly identified on a high level as quantitative, qualitative or mixed methods without providing detail on the research design and methods [24]. The few theories identified included Actor-Network theory, Activity theory

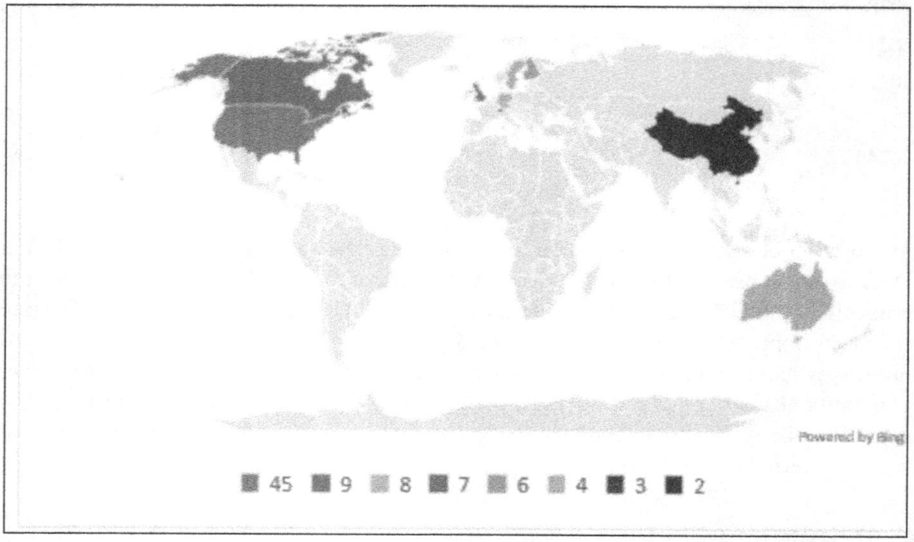

Fig 2: Geographic location of the publication's first authors

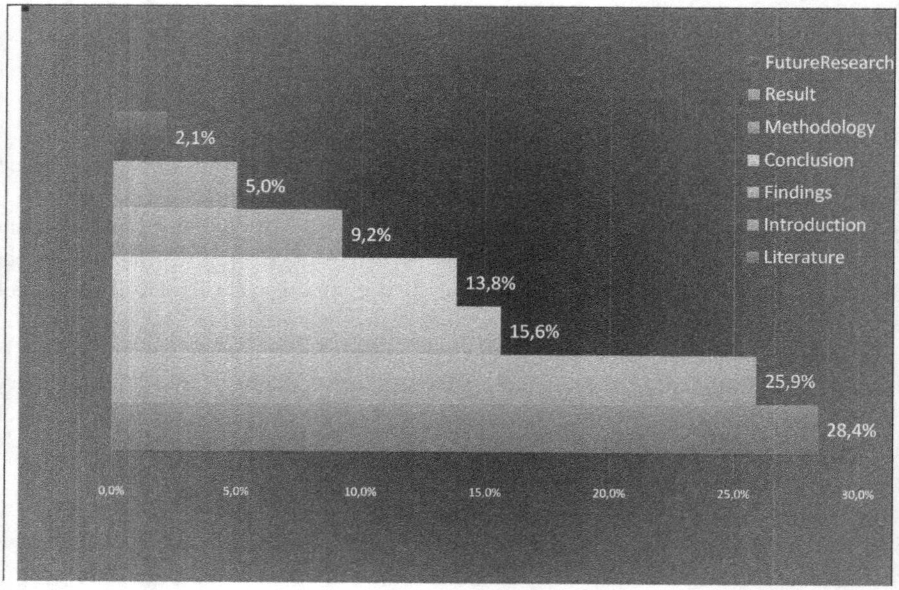

Fig 3. References to theory expressed as a percentage for each section

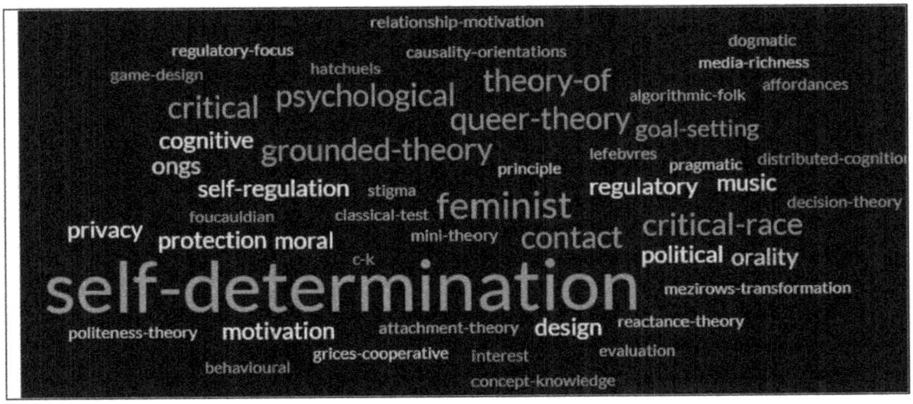

Fig 4. Word cloud based on frequencies of the theories mentioned

and Grounded theory, while the methods included literature reviews, case studies, action research, participatory design, Design science research and Ethnography [24].

Theorising is about making claims in the form of theories or products of theorisation. Labelling those with appropriate, recognisable labels makes these products of theorisation more manageable for the researcher and accessible for knowledge transfer to and by other researchers.

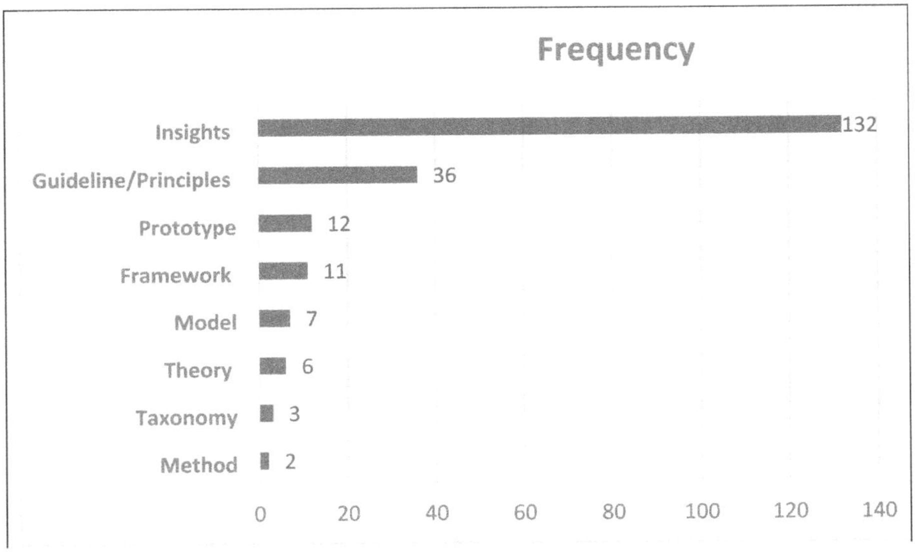

Fig 5. Frequencies of theorisation types produced

Figure 5 depicts the theorisation types produced as contributions, using the categories of insights, guidelines, models, methods and theories. Most papers (132) produced insights, followed by Guidelines (36) and Prototypes (12). Frameworks (11).

Models (7). Theories (6), Taxonomy (3) and Method (2). Some studies listed more than one contribution and hence the total is more than 99.

4.2 Findings

In summary, CHI papers mentioning the term 'theory' have increased annually over the past 5 years. Theory is mostly presented in the Literature review and Introduction sections, with a diminishing tendency towards the end of the paper. The theoretical contributions were presented mostly as *insights*. This may suggest a lack of awareness of the value of further processing and abstractions towards higher level theorisations such as guidelines or models. The theories mentioned in the literature review as a point of departure were mostly from disciplinary fields like Psychology or Sociology with few, if any, indigenous HCI4D theories.

5 Conclusion

This study investigated the potential of theorisation to mobilise and amplify the voices of researchers specifically by considering the synthesising and abstracting of findings beyond isolated insights. Considering the CHI proceedings from 2020 to 2024 and the 99 papers that mentioned theory, none were from developing countries in the Global South. This confirms earlier claims that IDID lacks theoretical focus. While acknowledging that isolated insights based on rigorous research may have great impact there could also be hidden potential in those insights. Potential, which will only emerge from a concerted effort towards theorising, i.e., efforts to further abstract and connect the factors (constructs, concepts and variables) while thinking about the explanation for the theorisation as well as the temporal and contextual conditions.

The findings indicate that most studies publish *insights* as a contribution. This implies that the products of theorisation may not be developed optimally by CHI researchers in general and those in the Global South specifically. In some cases, useful interim theorisations like questionnaires developed during the study are underreported. Future work is needed to validate these findings with a larger sample of conferences and journal publications. Furthermore, the barriers and enablers to research generation and mobilisation as experienced by researchers in the Global South need to be investigated towards proposing solutions on how to amplify the voices of IDID researchers in the Global South.

Acknowledgement. This article is based on the research supported by the South African Research Chairs Initiative of the Department of Science and Technology and the National Research Foundation of South Africa (Grant No. 98564). The author declares no financial or personal relationships that may have inappropriately influenced the writing of this article. The views expressed in this article are those of the author and not an official position of the institution or funder.

Disclosure of Interests. The authors declare that they have no financial or personal relationships that may have inappropriately influenced them in writing this article.

References

1. DTIC (Department of Trade, Industry and Competition) (2020) Mineral Beneficiation. http://www.thedtic.gov.za/wp-content/uploads/Beneficiation19-June2020.pdf. Accessed 13 Dec 2024
2. Nardi, B.: Designing for the future: but which one? Interactions **23**, 26–33 (2015)
3. Zakariashvili, M.: HCI – Human Computer Interaction Yesterday... Today... Tomorrow.... Transactions of Telavi State University, vol. 1, pp. 152–164 (2022). https://doi.org/10.52340/tuw.2022.20
4. Weber, R.: Evaluating and developing theories in the information systems discipline. J. Assoc. Inf. Syst. **13**, 1–30 (2012). https://doi.org/10.17705/1jais.00284
5. Whetten, D.A.: What constitutes a theoretical contribution? Acad. Manag. Rev. **14**, 490–495 (1989). https://doi.org/10.5465/amr.1989.4308371
6. Davison, R.M., Díaz Andrade, A.: Promoting indigenous theory. Inf. Syst. J. **28**, 759–764 (2018). https://doi.org/10.1111/isj.12203
7. Weick, K.E.: What theory is not, theorizing is. Adm. Sci. Q. **40**, 385–390 (1995). https://doi.org/10.2307/2393789
8. Hassan, N.R., Lowry, P.B., Mathiassen, L.: Useful products in information systems theorizing: a discursive formation perspective. J. Assoc. Inf. Syst. **23**(2), 418–446 (2022)
9. Hornbæk, K.: Implications for Theory. Aarhus, Denmark (2022)
10. Gregor, S.: The nature of theory in information systems. MIS Q. **30**, 611–642 (2006). https://doi.org/10.2307/25148742
11. Winters, N., Toyama, K.: Human-Computer Interaction for Development: Mapping the Terrain. Information Technologies and International Development 5: iii-viii (2009). https://itidjournal.org/index.php/itid/article/view/419/187
12. Abdelnour-Nocera, J., Rangaswamy, N.: Reflecting on the design-culture connection in HCI and HCI4D. Interactions **25**, 8–9 (2018). https://doi.org/10.1145/3264381
13. van Biljon, J., Renaud, K.: Reviewing a Decade of Human-Computer Interaction for Development (HCI4D) Research, as One of Best's "Grand Challenges". Afr. J. Inf. Commun. **27**, 1–15 (2021). https://doi.org/10.23962/10539/31368
14. Bidwell, N.J.: Decolonising HCI and interaction design discourse. XRDS: Crossroads. ACM Mag. Stud. **22**, 22–27 (2016). https://doi.org/10.1145/2930884
15. van Biljon, J.: Development informatics research and the challenges in representing the voice of developing country researchers: a South African view. Afr. J. Inf. Commun. (AJIC) **18**, 75–94 (2016). https://doi.org/10.23962/10539/21757
16. Bai, Y.: Has the Global South become a playground for Western scholars in information and communication technologies for development? Evidence from a three-journal analysis. Scientometrics **116**, 2139–2153 (2018). https://doi.org/10.1007/s11192-018-2839-y
17. Alatas, S.F.: Academic dependency and the global division of labour in the social sciences. Curr. Sociol. **51**, 599–613 (2003). https://doi.org/10.1177/00113921030516003
18. Collyer, F.M.: Global patterns in the publishing of academic knowledge: global North, global South. Curr. Sociol. **66**, 56–73 (2016). https://doi.org/10.1177/0011392116680020
19. Paré, G., Trudel, M.C., Jaana, M., Kitsiou, S.: Synthesizing information systems knowledge: a typology of literature reviews. Inf. Manage. **52**, 183–199 (2015). https://doi.org/10.1016/j.im.2014.08.008
20. Kitchenham, B., Pearl Brereton, O., Budgen, D., Turner, M., Bailey, J., Linkman, S.: Systematic literature reviews in software engineering - A systematic literature review. Inf. Softw. Technol. **51**, 7–15 (2009). https://doi.org/10.1016/j.infsof.2008.09.009
21. Moher, D., Liberati, A., Tetzlaff, J., Altman, D.G., Group, P.: Preferred reporting items for systematic reviews and meta-analyses: the PRISMA statement. Ann. Intern. Med. **151**, 264–269 (2009). https://doi.org/10.1371/journal.pmed.1000097

22. Miles, M.B., Huberman, M., Saldana, J.: Qualitative Data Analysis: A Methods Sourcebook, 4th ed. Thousand Oaks, California (2019)
23. Kumar, N., Dell, N.: Towards informed practice in HCI for development. Proc. ACM Hum.-Comput. Interact. **2**, 1–20 (2018). https://doi.org/10.1145/3274368
24. van Biljon, J.: Knowledge mobilization of human–computer interaction for development research: core issues and domain questions. Inf. Technol. Dev. **26**(3), 551–576 (2020). https://doi.org/10.1080/02681102.2020.1767022

Exploring Indian Millennials' Motivations for Using Wearable Activity Trackers (WATs) Through the Lens of Self-Determination Theory (SDT)

Indranil Saha[1(✉)], Deepak Ranjan Padhi[2], and Rahul Jain[2]

[1] National Institute of Fashion Technology, Kolkata, India
indranil.saha@nift.ac.in
[2] National Institute of Fashion Technology, Bhubaneswar, India
{deepak.padhi,rahul.jain}@nift.ac.in

Abstract. The emergence of wearable activity trackers (WATs) has transformed the way individuals monitor and manage their health and fitness. Over the past decade, these devices have gained immense popularity among young adults, particularly millennials, who are known for their embracement of technology and their pursuit of a healthier lifestyle. However, there is a lack of research examining the usage, interaction patterns, and overall motivation of millennials with activity trackers, especially in the Indian context. This study aims to explore the motivations of Indian millennials with WATs through the lens of Self-Determination Theory (SDT), a widely recognized theoretical framework that emphasizes the importance of intrinsic and extrinsic motivational factors in shaping human behavior. Employing a qualitative approach, we conducted in-depth semi-structured interviews with a diverse sample of Indian millennials (n = 10) experienced in using WATs. The findings suggest that the adoption and continued use of these devices are influenced by a complex range of factors, including the fulfillment of autonomy, competence, and relatedness needs, alongside extrinsic influences, as delineated in SDT. These insights can inform the design and development of more effective and engaging wearable technology solutions.

Keywords: User Experience Design · Human-Computer Interaction · Self-Determination Theory

1 Introduction

In recent times, wearable activity trackers (WATs) have been popular tools for tracking, monitoring, and enhancing an individual's physical activity levels, fitness progress, and overall health. According to Grand View Research (2022), fitness and activity trackers account for a significant share of the global wearable technology market which is expected to reach USD 186.14 billion by 2030 at a CAGR of 14.6% [1]. The growing

Published by Springer Nature Switzerland AG 2026
G. Bhutkar et al. (Eds.): IDID 2024, IFIP AICT 747, pp. 33–51, 2026.
https://doi.org/10.1007/978-3-032-00777-3_3

health and fitness consciousness of consumers, the rapid advancements in sensor technology, and the growing accessibility and popularity of fitness bands and smartwatches are the primary factors driving the substantial adoption of this category [2, 3]. Additionally, the COVID-19 pandemic in recent years has also amplified the adoption of WAT as consumers became dependent on these devices for real-time monitoring by measuring health and wellness parameters such as SPO2 level, heart rate, etc. amidst lockdown and social distancing guidelines [4].

With the growth of wearable technology, millennials, individuals born between the early 1980s and mid-1990s and known for their tech-enabled lifestyles and health-consciousness, represent a demographic that drives significant demand for WAT [3, 5, 6]. Studies have shown that millennials are more likely to adopt new technologies and integrate them into their daily lives compared to previous generations [5, 6]. Furthermore, millennials have been reported to prioritize health and wellness, often using digital tools and applications to manage their fitness and health goals [6]. Recent studies have reported that millennials primarily incorporate WAT in their daily routines to manage their fitness goals, with 30–33% claiming ownership of wearable devices to track their physical activity globally [7]. The extensive adoption of WAT and the lack of specific studies targeting Indian millennials in this category necessitate an investigation of the motivations, experiences, and behavioral implications associated with using these devices within this demographic group.

While data shows that India is already a substantial market for wearables [2], it is crucial to investigate how effectively Indian millennials are using these devices. This study aims to explore not just the adoption rates but also the depth and effectiveness of WAT usage among this demographic. Understanding these aspects is essential because purchasing does not necessarily equate to effective usage.

Applying SDT as a theoretical framework [8], this study examines how autonomy, competence, and relatedness needs influence millennials' interactions with WAT. The objective of this research is twofold. The first is to explore the motivations and experiences in using WAT for monitoring physical activities and the second is to examine the impact of WAT interaction on behavior change and self-regulation – both targeting Indian millennial users. This research enhances the existing comprehension of how SDT influences interactions and engagement with WAT among Indian millennials.

2 Review of Literature

2.1 User Interaction of WAT Among Indian Millennials

Wearable technologies refer to advanced devices that are seamlessly incorporated into garments, accessories, or even the body itself [9]. These devices cater to various needs and preferences and often offer customized functions to the users. A wearable activity tracker (WAT) is one such high-end device typically worn like traditional watches with associated connectivity and interactivity established through the user's mobile applications (apps) [10]. WATs primarily prioritize the users' health-related functions over features like calling and messaging, thus, distinguishing themselves from smartwatches [11]. WATs enable their users to manage their health effectively by its capability of tracking multiple health and activity parameters such as step count, calorie consumption, heart rate, oxygen levels, etc. [12]. Existing research studies on the adoption patterns of WATs explore the users' rationale and attitudes towards these devices [12]. The existing studies have revealed that users' motivation to engage in physical activities to maintain healthier lifestyles is the primary reason for their continuous usage of WATs; however, the goals and interactions associated with these devices keep evolving [12, 13]. Interestingly, studies focusing on younger demographics have argued that increased physical activity levels can be attributed to using WATs [11].

For millennials, the factor they identify the most is technology, owing to the transition from analog to digital environments. While technology doesn't entirely define millennials' identity, the role of technology adoption in facilitating their self-expression is immensely acknowledged [11, 14]. In line with this, WATs are increasingly popular tools for maintaining fitness and activity levels among millennials as being physically active holds significant social value for them [2, 3]. As heavy users of technology, millennials are inclined to integrate wearable devices into their daily lives for real-time health monitoring [6]. Moreover, they are willing to share lifestyle information with peers through digital platforms, which reflects their engagement with technology and social connectivity [15]. Their consumption habits and tech-savvy nature set them apart from earlier generations (e.g., baby boomers[1] and GenX[2]) and position them as a critical segment for WATs [6, 15]. Characterized by rapid adoption and agility with new technologies, this demographic represents a significant market for WATs, necessitating the need for further investigation into their motivations and behavioral patterns for using such devices [6, 15].

2.2 The Self-Determination Theory (SDT)

Comprehension of the motivations influencing millennials' interaction with WATs requires an in-depth exploration of the implicit psychological processes. In the context of the current study, Self-Determination Theory (SDT) proposes a human need-oriented theoretical framework [8] for investigating user motivation and behavioral patterns within the area of wearable devices. Ryan and Deci (2000) proposed SDT which suggests that individuals' motivation can be categorized into intrinsic and extrinsic motivations, each representing different levels of internalization and autonomy [8]. Intrinsic motivation refers to engaging in an activity as it brings inherent pleasure and satisfaction, whereas, extrinsic motivation involves engaging in an activity for the discrete external rewards it brings [8, 16]. Within the framework of SDT, meeting individuals' basic psychological needs for autonomy, competence, and relatedness is crucial in promoting internalization and nurturing extrinsic motivation [8]. *Autonomy* refers to the desire for self-direction and choice, *competence* reflects the need for command and effectiveness in one's actions, and *relatedness* incorporates the need for meaningful connections and belongingness within social contexts. It is argued that social contexts supporting users' autonomy, competence, and relatedness enhance the internalization process. This, in turn, promotes more autonomous forms of extrinsic motivation [16, 17].

[1] Individuals born between 1946 and 1964.

[2] Individuals born between 1965 and 1980.

Four different levels of internalization can be observed within the array of extrinsic motivations. *External regulation* represents the lowest level of internalization, where individuals engage in activities solely to obtain rewards or avoid penalties. *Introjected regulation* involves a partial internalization of external pressures or contingencies, where individuals perform the behavior to enhance self-esteem or avoid guilt or shame. *Identified regulation* signifies a higher level of internalization, where individuals engage in activities because they value the outcomes associated with the behavior. Finally, *integrated regulation* represents the highest level of internalization, where the behavior is fully assimilated into one's sense of self and identity, reflecting alignment with deeply held personal values and objectives [8].

Intrinsic motivation has received considerable attention in research; however, there is a gap in studies examining various types of extrinsic motivations, particularly within the context of WATs [8, 16, 17]. In the context of the current study on WAT interaction among Indian millennials, understanding how the fulfillment of these basic psychological needs influences user motivations, experiences, and behavioral patterns is essential for informing the design and implementation of effective interventions. By examining the relationship between extrinsic motivation, internalization processes, and supporting environments, this research aims to provide insights into how millennials engage and interact with WATs in ways that promote long-term adherence and positive behavioral outcomes.

3 Methods

This section will describe the research design, data collection methods, and data analysis procedures employed to investigate the motivations behind WAT usage among Indian millennials.

3.1 Research Design

This study employed a semi-structured qualitative interview approach to investigate WATs use among Indian millennials. This approach ensured an in-depth exploration of participants' perceptions regarding their WATs interactions. At the same time, this approach also allowed a degree of flexibility to explore further extensions of topics that emerged during the interviews. The study was guided by SDT, which is an established theory of motivation that focuses on the psychological needs that drive users' choices and behaviors [8]. As discussed in the literature review, the theory acknowledges intrinsic and extrinsic motivations for WAT usage among Indian millennials.

3.2 Participants

The target population for this study was Indian millennials (age group: 28 - 43 years as of May 2024). Purposive sampling was used to recruit participants who currently use WATs. Inclusion criteria ensured participants had adequate experience using WATs for at least 6 months to gain insights from qualified users. Participants were recruited through a combination of social media outreach and professional networks. The sample size was determined by reaching saturation – the point at which no significant new information emerged from further interviews [18, 19]. Data saturation was reached after conducting ten interviews. Table 1 summarizes the demographic information of the participants. A total of 7 males and 3 females participated in the data collection process. Most of the participants started using the WAT device after the year 2020. Table 3 lists the description of WATs used by the participants. It also enumerates the specific reasons for purchasing the WATs and the duration of usage.

Table 1. Participant demographics for Indian millennial WAT users

Participant pseudonyms	Age	Gender	Income	Occupation
Aakash	36	Male	12LPA	Graphic designer
Sujata	41	Female	12LPA	Architect
Prakash	30	Male	11LPA	Web developer
Raj	35	Male	13LPA	Educator
Ishaan	33	Male	13LPA	Business Consultant
Sunil	40	Male	15LPA	Banker
Ashima	34	Female	13LPA	Visual Artist
Uchit	35	Male	16LPA	Educator
Daanish	37	Male	12LPA	UX Designer
Manisha	29	Female	14LPA	HR Manager

3.3 Data Collection and Analysis

A pre-defined interview guide with fifteen questions that addressed the experiences and perceptions of using WAT was framed. The questions were framed based on how WATs fulfill or hinder the psychological needs for autonomy, competence, and relatedness and the intrinsic and extrinsic motivations for WAT usage. For example, questions related to customization and control of the WAT addressed the need for autonomy, questions about achievements and feedback targeted the sense of competence, and questions about sharing data and social interactions explored the need for relatedness. Semi-structured interviews were conducted in person with participants. They were audio-recorded with participant consent and transcribed verbatim for data analysis. The duration of the interviews ranged from 20 to 30 min (Table 2).

Thematic analysis was adopted to analyze the interview transcripts. This method involved identifying, coding, and interpreting recurring themes within the data, following a deductive approach. The themes were pre-determined based on SDT, specifically focusing on autonomy, competence, and relatedness for intrinsic motivations, and external regulation, introjected regulation, identified regulation, and integrated regulation for extrinsic motivations. The analysis was conducted in six key phases. Firstly, all interview transcripts were thoroughly read and re-read by the researchers to immerse themselves

Table 2. Sample questions connected to SDT asked during semi-structured interviews

Autonomy
How do you customize your WAT to fit your personal fitness goals? Can you describe a situation where you felt in control of your fitness tracking?
Competence
What achievements or milestones have you reached using your WAT? How does tracking your fitness progress with a WAT make you feel about your abilities?
Relatedness
In what ways do you share your WAT data or achievements with others? How does using a WAT affect your interactions with friends or family?

in the data. During this phase, initial notes were made on recurring ideas, phrases, or patterns that emerged across the interviews. For example, phrases like " I am happy that I can control...", or "I wanted to track...", or "I like that I can..." suggest a desire for self-direction and personalization in their use of WATs, aligning with the SDT concept of autonomy. Recurring ideas around tracking progress, achieving goals, and feeling a sense of accomplishment reflect the SDT concept of competence. Participants have used phrases like " achieving the goals motivates me," "I like that it challenges me," or "tracking motivates me." These phrases indicate a desire to feel effective and capable in managing their health and fitness. Participants have discussed that using their WATs they wanted to connect with friends or family, participate in fitness challenges, or share their achievements on social media. They have used phrases like "...getting acknowledged by people", or "It's fun to compare with friends..." etc. These phrases highlight the social aspect of using WATs and the desire for connection and belonging, aligning with the SDT concept of relatedness. After that, open coding was conducted on the entire dataset, where meaningful segments of data were identified and labeled with codes. This process involved coding the data manually, ensuring that all relevant content was captured. The coding was done independently by three researchers to ensure a comprehensive identification of potential themes. Thirdly, the initial codes were grouped into broader categories or themes based on their relevance to the research questions and the SDT framework. The themes were primarily guided by the pre-determined categories of autonomy, competence, and relatedness for intrinsic motivations, and external regulation, introjected regulation, identified regulation, and integrated regulation for extrinsic motivations. During this phase, the researchers engaged in several rounds of discussions to refine the themes, ensuring they were distinct, coherent, and accurately represented the data. Once the themes were identified, they were reviewed in the context of the entire dataset to ensure they captured the essence of the participants' experiences and motivations. The themes were also checked against the original coded extracts to confirm that they were grounded in the data. Intercoder reliability was assessed through a comparison of coding between the two researchers, with discrepancies being resolved through discussion and consensus, thus enhancing the reliability of the coding process. The final themes were clearly defined and named, with detailed descriptions provided for each.

This step involved summarizing the essence of each theme, how it related to the research questions, and how it connected to the broader SDT framework. Sub-themes were also identified where applicable to capture the complexity of the data. For example, the theme of "autonomy" included sub-themes such as "personal control" and "customization of WATs"; the theme of "competence" included sub-themes such as "goal setting and tracking" and "challenge and feedback"; the theme of relatedness included sub-themes such as "social comparison and competition" and "social acknowledgement," which were derived directly from the data but guided by the theoretical understanding within SDT. Finally, the thematic analysis was written in a structured manner, integrating the themes into the narrative of the findings section. Direct quotes from participants were used to illustrate each theme, ensuring that the participants' voices were central to the presentation of the results.

Table 3. Type of WATs used by Indian millennial participants (n = 10)

Parameter	Number
Reasons for purchase	
General health-tracking during covid	2
Fitness tracking	4
Attraction to multipurpose features	1
Influences of branding and trends	1
Unintended engagements (e.g. gifts)	2
Brand	
Boat	5
Apple	1
Xiaomi	4
Amazfit	1
Noise	1
Titan	1
Fossil	1
Number of WATs owned	
1	6
2	4
Length of use	
6 – 12 months	2
1–2 years	1
> 2 years	7

To ensure the validity and reliability of the qualitative data, several measures were implemented. Data saturation was achieved by conducting interviews until no new themes emerged, ensuring that the findings were comprehensive. The coding process involved three researchers to enhance reliability, with intercoder reliability assessed through comparisons and discussions to resolve discrepancies. To further validate the findings, the researchers used member checking, where participants were given the opportunity to review and confirm the accuracy of the transcriptions and interpretations. These steps were designed to minimize potential biases and enhance the credibility of the research, ensuring that the results are both reliable and valid.

3.4 Ethical Considerations

The study adhered to ethical research principles of informed consent obtained from all participants before commencing the interviews. Participants were assured of anonymity and confidentiality throughout the research process. To protect participant anonymity, this research uses pseudonyms instead of initials.

4 Results

This section discusses the insights of the semi-structured interview data gathered from the Indian millennial users of WATs. In line with the SDT, the analysis is categorized into two organizing themes – intrinsic and extrinsic motivations, which are further categorized into three (autonomy, competence, and relatedness) and four (external regulation, introjected regulation, identified regulation, and integrated regulation) subcategories, respectively. Each subcategory reports the intricacies of the quotes – ultimately addressing the research objectives of the current study.

4.1 Intrinsic Motivations in the Use of WAT by Indian Millennials

Autonomy. Several interviewees' desire for personal control and precision over their fitness tracking highlighted their intrinsic motivation for autonomy. For example, with his need for precision in the data provided by his wearable device, *Aakash*, a graphic designer commented, *"I just want to get rid of this [tracker] while I use this app. At this point, the watch is not that precise. That's why I only use it for a while."* His descriptions of the level of precision during straight and curved pathways while running further reflected his autonomy-driven quest for accurate self-monitoring. Such indications related to lack of precision weaken his sense of control and satisfaction associated with WAT. Moreover, some interviewees expressed that the ability to customize and regulate their health metrics was a major driver for their WAT usage. *Raj*, an educator, mentioned that he finds satisfaction in controlling different data points and features of the tracker: *"I am happy that I can control various parameters."* This autonomy in managing his health data aligns with the SDT framework, where self-regulation and personalization are crucial for intrinsic motivation. Similarly, *Sunil*, a banker, expressed his need to monitor specific health metrics like heart rate and calorie burn, commenting, *"I want to know about my heart condition, my heart rate, and how many calories I burn in this process."*

Additionally, many millennials' autonomous desire to improve their fitness suggested a proactive approach to health management. For example, *Ishaan*'s decision to overcome procrastination and purchase a WAT is explanatory: *"I thought I should stop procrastinating and buy this ASAP."* His proactive attitude is further supported by *Uchit*, who used the tracker to manage his running schedule: *"The initial motivation was just to track my running... I wanted to track the kilometers that I run. And also I wanted to track the time duration that I cover."* Furthermore, the interviewees also demonstrated a shift from traditional to modern tracking methods by highlighting autonomy through technological inclination. For instance, visual artist *Ashima*'s transition from analog to smartwatch was reflected by a deliberate choice aligned with her preferences. She asserted, *"I kind of was more keen on buying a smartwatch than an analog [watch]. And that's why I moved from analog to a smartwatch."* This decision signifies an autonomous preference to adopt modern technology that better serves her needs and lifestyle.

Competence. The interviewees described a sense of achievement through tracking their performance in WATs as an important motivating factor for usage. For example, *Aakash* explained how setting and achieving challenges through the Nike Run Club app motivated him: *"Initially, when I used the Nike Run Club, there were some achievements, like weekly 15 km, then monthly 100 km. So, I have to accept a challenge... okay, this month I am accepting the challenge of running 100 km."* His experience of running with a group of aspiring policemen and surpassing his previous limits – *"Before that, I never ran beyond 12 km"* demonstrates the role of competence in enhancing enthusiasm and achieving new milestones to push personal boundaries. The interviewees' sense of competence was further encouraged by positive reinforcement through rewards. For instance, *Prakash* appreciated the small competitions and rewards in his NoiseFit app, commenting, *"One good thing about this [WATs] is it has a nice app, which is available in the phone... they have these small, small competitions, where the app rewards you based on the goal that you have selected... So yes, it allows me to be motivated to follow a particular [activity]."* Similarly, *Ashima* found the animated gamified elements of Google Fit motivating: *"I think probably two or three times when I would have achieved that 15,000 steps a day. And then there will be like, this balloon of something like a celebration sort of a thing that happens in that app itself."*

Moreover, interviewees described that improvements in their physical fitness and the resultant enhancement in self-confidence significantly influenced them to continue using WAT. For instance, *Sujata*, an architect, shared, *"I lost a lot of weight and became more fit. Earlier I used to get tired easily. So somehow the tracking motivates you."* This portrayal of transformation indicates competence driven by measurable improvements in health and fitness. *Raj*, an educator, expressed a similar sentiment with his increased confidence since using his WAT in the gym: *"When I first started using it in the Gym last year. Since then, it has delivered perfectly on all fronts. I am pretty much confident."* Additionally, some interviewees also suggested that their personal fitness goals reflect their intrinsic motivation for competence. For example, *Sunil*, a banker, asserted how tracking helped him push his limits: *"When I see it today I burn almost more than 2000 cal...then the next day I try to burn more."*. By joyously recalling his cycling achievement, *Uchit* commented, *"I think one day, I had traveled almost 82 km cycling. So, 80 km. Yeah. That was actually very motivational that the app also had given a celebration that you targeted and achieved those things."* These instances represent how WATs help

Indian millennial users set, track, and achieve personal fitness goals through an intrinsic sense of competence.

Relatedness. Several interviewees' intrinsic motivation for relatedness was significantly driven by social validation and encouragement. For instance, indicating the motivating role of social recognition, *Aakash* stated, *"So I'm also getting acknowledged by people. For example, I was running and my friend from high school didn't know that I was running. I put it on Instagram, and the next day he joined me. Tomorrow I have a marathon, and both of us are going."* This validates the positive influence of social acknowledgment and companionship on Indian millennials' commitment to fitness goals. *Sujata* shared similar positive feedback from her social circle, *"People appreciate you, you know, if you are working on your fitness, I get appreciation that way."* Furthermore, community support and competitiveness were important aspects of the interviewees' sense of relatedness. *Aakash* described the influential role of his community towards his performance goals, commenting, *"This community also helped in a certain way, like achieving the goal. There's a guy who's running 10 km in 55 min. So I'm just trying to achieve that because he's not younger than me. He's running much faster than me."* This quote exemplifies how community interactions can push individuals to set and achieve higher standards. Likewise, *Ashima* also illustrated this point by referencing competition within her family: *"But yes, within the close circle if I see someone who has achieved something even I will also want to do the same thing with anyone from my family, friends, or close people whom I meet every day."* She further indicated that WATs help in connecting with her family members through shared health goals. She described how competing with her parents provided her additional motivation: *"I know my mom goes for a walk every day. I know my dad goes for a walk every day. So it will be good to, I mean, even compete with them. They are also getting a sense of competition from me."* These quotes highlight how family imparts a sense of relatedness and mutual encouragement. *Sunil*, although noting a smaller social circle, mentioned how his discussions about activity tracking influenced his friend to purchase a similar device: *"Actually, my friend circle is not very, very huge…I always talk to him [his friend] about this and I think he also needs to practice some activities. So, a few days before, he bought an Apple watch."*

Moreover, the interviewees were also influenced by their peers for WAT usage. While describing how his friend's activity tracking became a topic of discussion and motivation, *Daanish* mentioned, *"Yes, one of my friends used to post his app statistics of running. That becomes a point of conversation whenever we meet or talk."* The reflection of the motivating power of peer interactions and the role of social influence in maintaining fitness routines was evident in *Uchit*'s description also: *"When I shared the screenshots, I get to see a lot of people say or even I feel motivated, I do want to do workout those things, conversation happens with the peer group."*

Indian millennials' intrinsic motivation for using WATs is influenced by their desires for autonomy, competence, and relatedness. Autonomy is reflected by the pursuit of precise health data and proactive self-regulation, while goal achievement and self-improvement suggest competence. Consistently, relatedness is evident through social acknowledgment and community support. These motivations integrate and signify technology's role in facilitating personal growth and social connections for enhancing fitness and lifestyle choices.

4.2 Extrinsic Motivations in the Use of WAT by Indian Millennials

External Regulation. Several interviewees reflected on their extrinsic motivations by expressing perspectives on device functionality and performance. The effectiveness of WATs significantly influenced Indian millennial users' motivation through external regulation. For example, *Aakash* expressed his frustration with the accuracy of his device: *"I never use both for running and cycling because it could not measure my distance and time properly. So I use my mobile on my arm and put it there while starting my app."* This dependence on the device's adequate functioning for motivation reflects how external factors like device accuracy regulate user engagement. Similarly, *Ashima* also specified the inconvenience caused by battery drainage: *"But it was draining out my battery of the watch quite a lot...So it was a very big problem"*. These pieces of evidence establish the necessity to manage device limitations and the extent to which external factors influence usage. Interviewees also indicated that tracking habits and routines are crucial forms of external regulation. For instance, *Sujata* mentioned that step tracking became regular in her daily routine: *"So now it has become a habit to track the steps every day."* This suggests that external prompts and the tracker's feedback influence habitual tracking. Similarly, *Ishaan* described that achieving set targets has become part of his routine, commenting, *"Basically, a target is set in my app, I need to achieve it every day."* The establishment of these habits and routines represents the external regulation through consistent and repetitive tracking behaviors.

Moreover, the interviewees' descriptions suggested that external regulation was also manifested through social accountability. For example, *Uchit* mentioned, *"Many [health] insurance agencies also asked for the tracking reports, you know... records to see how active we are."* This suggests that Indian millennial users' motivation to use WAT is also shaped by external regulations such as reducing the health insurance premium amount to present a healthier lifestyle to the agency, further reflecting external social accountability as a motivator. Additionally, WATs utilize motivational prompts through interactive elements to drive user engagement and regulate user behavior. For example, *Ishaan* commented, *"It also sends notifications on my tracker that I overachieved my goals by 200% or 400% today."*

Introjected Regulation. Introjected regulation among Indian millennials using WATs often demonstrated feelings of obligation and guilt. This was evident in *Uchit*'s experience, where he attempted to balance work and family responsibilities with his fitness routine, commenting, *"It changed because of work culture? Probably also, you know, commitment at home. So this is why, okay, family responsibilities, and at the same time work responsibilities due to that, where I'm not able to do it regularly, but still I managed to do four days in a week."* This sense of obligation reflects an internalized sense of duty and associated guilt upon failing to meet self-imposed or social expectations. Moreover, interviewees often felt frustrated with their devices. This showed an internal conflict. They wanted to maintain their fitness goals but their devices had limitations that hindered their progress. For instance, *Sunil* was annoyed when his device failed during workouts, commenting, *"When I continue with my jumping rope mode...it stopped suddenly...it is very annoying for me because I never want to stop my jumping around."* Similarly, *Ishaan*'s WAT required to be removed and switched off to save battery life, despite he wanted to keep it on consecutively for days. He asserted, *"I have to remove it after I come back from work and then switch it off so I can save the battery and I don't need to charge it often."* This suggests the tension between user aspirations and practical constraints.

Interviewees also reported inconsistent usage due to external factors that ultimately led to feelings of inadequacy and self-criticism. *Aakash*, for instance, described a significant decrease in his WAT usage due to work and injuries: *"In the months of April and May, my frequency dropped down because of work and injuries. This year, every year, pretty much I hardly used it. I think I used it three times or four times only, and this year it has decreased."* The decrease in activity and following internal reflection on not meeting personal fitness goals highlight how external pressures can lead to internalized feelings of failure. Furthermore, Indian millennial WAT users often adjusted their goals to manage internal pressures. This shows a compromise between their aspirations and their practical realities. For example, *Ashima* discussed how she modifies her goals to remain motivated without feeling overwhelmed with the WAT targets. She commented, *"So there are options to set your goals. Like for example, if you're not wanting to work 15,000 steps a day, which is what they're recommending, then I can, you know, correct it to 7,000 to 10,000 a day. And if I'm not fulfilling that, also, they will. I mean, there are certain features of the app, which will tell you that you can push yourself a little bit more, these kinds of notifications come."* This adjustment process indicates an internal negotiation to maintain motivation while managing self-imposed pressures of meeting the daily targets.

Identified Regulation. Identified regulation among Indian millennials using WATs shows a strong alignment between the aesthetic and practical elements of their devices. This alignment strengthens their motivation to use these devices. *Raj*'s evolving usage of his smartwatch underscores this sentiment: *"Initially for aesthetic appeal, but later I hooked to it because of its utility."* This transition shows how identified regulation influences long-term engagement by aligning with users' health goals. Moreover, WATs became integral to users' remembrance of their tracker usage on special occasions. For example, *Ishaan*'s use of his tracker during his PhD convocation validated this integration: *"I remember on the day of my PhD convocation, I roamed around the whole huge campus so much that I achieved 400% of my walking limit on that day. I felt great."* Additionally, *Uchit*'s reliance on his tracker to remind him of his workout time aligns with his well-planned days and overall lifestyle that consciously values his personal goals: *"So sometimes I get notification that it's my running time. So that motivates me and reminds me that I have not done my workout."* Additionally, factors such as social influence and competitive spirits, supported by interviewees' quotes and reported in the intrinsic motivation section, also overlap with the extrinsic motivations driven by identified regulation.

Integrated Regulation. Interviewees' descriptions indicated integrated regulation as their fitness goals and the use of wearable activity trackers become a seamless part of daily life. For example, *Aakash*'s comment – *"The Nike Run Club has given me* *achievements like weekly 15 km, monthly 100 km club. So I have to accept a challenge, okay, this month I am accepting the challenge of running 100 km. So per day, 3.75 km, that's the motivation for me."* – this suggests his adherence to the challenges set in his app. The perception of WAT was also established as a valuable and supportive tool for social recognition and validation. *Ashima*'s appreciation of comparative data and virtual congratulations reflects this: *"So, they will just say that congratulations and you are on this much of point and Yeah, somebody will feel good. I mean, though, it is very much you know, not in person, but yeah, to see something that you have achieved and to show comparative data is also that okay, this much people would have walked like you."* This suggests how social elements, even digital acknowledgments, contribute to integrating the use of WATs into the user's identity and social practices. On the other hand, *Uchit*'s engagement with fitness tracking despite concerns about accuracy reveals an underlying belief in the value of the activity and the device: *"Even I don't know whether, whatever six kilometers, I am thinking that I'm running, whether it is accurate or not, I'm not sure. But still, it's just a belief."* This indicates that despite doubts about precision, the overall validation of effort provided by the WAT is enough to maintain motivation and integration into his fitness routine. Additionally, *Uchit*'s participation in tracking activities requested by health insurance agencies (quote mentioned previously) further demonstrates how the utility of the WAT goes beyond personal use and becomes integrated into broader fitness and health validation systems.

The use of WATs among Indian millennials is shaped by various forms of extrinsic regulation—external, introjected, identified, and integrated. These motivations range from device functionality and social influence to personal goal achievement. Both external factors and internal motivations influence long-term engagement and behavior change with WATs among Indian millennials.

5 Discussion

We conducted semi-structured interviews with 10 Indian millennials to gain insights into their motivations and behaviors towards digital technology adoption; WATs in our case. The primary objective was to investigate the incentives and encounters associated with the use of WATs for monitoring physical activities. Secondly, we assess the influence of WATs interaction on changing behaviors and self-regulation. By applying the SDT framework, we categorized our interview findings into intrinsic (autonomy, competence, and relatedness) and extrinsic (external regulation, introjected regulation, identified regulation, and integrated regulation) categories, providing in-depth insights into how these motivations influence user engagement and behavior change.

The existing data shows that India is already a significant market for wearables; however, the effectiveness of their usage among Indian millennials remains underexplored. This study addresses this gap by investigating whether Indian millennials are fully utilizing WATs to meet their health and fitness goals. The findings reveal that motivations driven by SDT – autonomy, competence, and relatedness – play a critical role in how these devices are used. For instance, autonomy emerged as a significant intrinsic motivator, with participants expressing a strong desire for personal control and precision in tracking their fitness activities. This suggests that while the adoption rates are high, the depth of engagement and effective usage may vary. Such complexity necessitates a deeper understanding of the motivational factors at play. By using SDT as a framework, this study moves beyond simply identifying motivations and explores the types of motivations (intrinsic vs. extrinsic) and their interplay. For example, while "autonomy" (wanting control over tracking) might seem individualistic, it's actually an intrinsic motivator linked to a deeper sense of ownership and personal growth, which can fuel sustained engagement.

However, we acknowledge that the study's sample size (n = 10) is relatively small and may limit the generalizability of the findings. This limitation is further compounded by the variability in the types and brands of WATs used by participants, which may affect their experiences and perceptions differently. While the qualitative approach provides rich, detailed insights into user motivations and behaviors, these findings should be interpreted mindfully. They represent initial observations that highlight important themes and patterns rather than definitive conclusions applicable to all Indian millennials.

The findings reveal that motivations driven by SDT—autonomy, competence, and relatedness—play a critical role in how Indian millennials use WATs. Autonomy emerged as a significant intrinsic motivator, with participants expressing a strong desire for personal control and precision in tracking their fitness activities. This highlights the importance of providing users with the ability to customize their WAT settings and functionalities, suggesting that autonomy-supportive features are essential for user engagement. Competence, reflected in the sense of achievement and mastery from meeting fitness goals, indicates that gamified elements and positive feedback can enhance user motivation. The role of relatedness, facilitated by social sharing and community support, underscores the need for WATs to include features that enable social connectivity and validation.

However, in the Indian context, the motivations of millennials appear to have unique nuances. For instance, while autonomy and competence are recognized motivators across cultures for wearable activity tracker adoption, the study's findings suggest a particularly pronounced emphasis on "relatedness" among Indian millennials. This aligns with established cultural frameworks [20] positioning India as a highly collectivistic society, where social harmony and group belonging are deeply valued. This cultural context emphasizes strong family and community ties, influencing social interactions and technology adoption. Prior research on technology use in India supports this notion, highlighting the importance of social connectivity and validation in shaping user behavior [21, 22]. Therefore, the desire to use WATs for social comparison, encouragement, and sharing achievements among Indian millennials likely stems from deeply ingrained cultural norms that prioritize community and social engagement.

Extrinsic motivations, such as external regulation, introjected regulation, identified regulation, and integrated regulation, also play a significant role. For instance, users were motivated by the functional aspects of the devices, such as accuracy and battery life, which directly influenced their satisfaction and continued use. Social accountability, such as health insurance requirements and competitive elements within fitness apps, also drove engagement, reflecting the interplay between personal and social factors in shaping behavior.

These findings align with existing literature on the importance of personalization, gamification, and social features in digital health tools, particularly through the lens of Self-Determination Theory (SDT). Previous studies have highlighted the significance of user autonomy in technology adoption and the effectiveness of gamified elements in maintaining user engagement [3, 8]. This study extends these insights to the specific context of Indian millennials, demonstrating that these motivational factors are equally relevant in this demographic. The emphasis on social connectivity resonates with broader HCI trends that focus on the social dimensions of technology use and the potential for digital platforms to enhance social well-being.

This study focuses on understanding the motivational factors for Wearable Activity Trackers (WATs) through the "why" behind their use rather than the "how" of user interaction with the devices. The findings highlight both similarities and differences when compared with similar studies in other cultural contexts. For example, studies in Western contexts often emphasize individualistic motivations such as personal fitness goals and self-improvement as primary drivers for WAT usage [3]. In contrast, the social aspects of WAT use, such as sharing achievements with friends and family and participating in community challenges, seem more significant in the Indian context. This difference suggests that while the core motivations align with SDT, the manifestation of these motivations may vary across cultures.

Furthermore, the study aligns with ongoing trends in HCI that emphasize the potential of digital platforms to enhance social well-being. The strong desire for personal control and customization from the "autonomy" theme suggests that WAT interfaces should prioritize flexibility and personalization, allowing users to customize goals, tracking metrics, and feedback mechanisms. This will make WATs adaptable to different user needs and preferences. Devices may also provide better user control by incorporating notification management and feature selection. The emphasis on goal setting, progress tracking, and feedback from the competence theme implies that WAT interfaces should focus on effective visualization, presenting data in a clear, meaningful, and motivating way, while offering personalized feedback based on individual progress and goals. Incorporating elements that promote engagement and a sense of achievement, such as challenges and gamification, could enhance user experience further.

Finally, the importance of social comparison and support related to the relatedness theme suggests that WAT interfaces could provide seamless social features, enabling easy connection with friends, family, or online communities. By facilitating group activities, competitions, and encouragement, WAT devices can better support community challenges and social connectivity, which are more significant in the Indian context. These insights not only contribute to the understanding of user motivations but also open new avenues for HCI researchers to develop and test applications that leverage these findings, significantly enhancing the usability and impact of wearable technologies in promoting health and well-being.

Additionally, it is important to note that the intrinsic and extrinsic parameters in users' findings are not mutually exclusive. Rather, they complement each other in shaping the users' interaction patterns with wearable activity trackers among Indian millennials. The results highlight the importance of understanding the motivational dynamics that drive the usage of these devices, which can inform the design and development of more effective and engaging wearable technology solutions. Further research focusing on user interaction, interface preferences, and usability could reveal more explicit HCI characteristics.

6 Research Contribution

6.1 Contribution to Research

This study addresses a gap in the literature by focusing on a specific demographic in the Indian context. It also adds valuable data to the limited body of research in this area. The research demonstrates the applicability of SDT in understanding technology adoption and usage behaviors among millennials. It offers a robust framework for future studies to explore motivational factors in other cultural or demographic contexts. Additionally, the qualitative approach enriches the understanding of user experiences and behaviors that quantitative data might not capture. These insights can inform subsequent larger-scale quantitative studies and enhance the theoretical discourse on technology adoption and motivation.

6.2 Contributions to Practice

The findings of this study offer practical design recommendations for WAT developers to enhance user engagement. Improving the accuracy and customization of tracking features to meet autonomy needs, incorporating gamified elements to foster competence, and enhancing social sharing features to satisfy relatedness needs are some key suggestions. For example, integrating features that facilitate social challenges, such as weekly step goals among friends or virtual group runs, can significantly enhance user engagement and satisfaction. Marketers can tailor their strategies based on the motivational factors identified, emphasizing control and personalization, showcasing achievements, and fostering a sense of community to appeal to the target demographic. Understanding the specific needs and motivations of Indian millennials can help WAT companies design products that align with user expectations, leading to higher satisfaction and sustained usage. Furthermore, addressing technical issues such as battery life and device accuracy can improve overall user experience. For health policymakers and fitness program designers, these insights can aid in developing initiatives that leverage WATs to promote physical activity and health monitoring among tech-savvy young adults.

7 Conclusion

The use of WATs among Indian millennials is shaped by an array of intrinsic and extrinsic motivations. Autonomy, competence, and relatedness are essential intrinsic motivators that can be improved by incorporating socially integrated, accurate, and customizable features. Extrinsic motivations, driven by device functionality, social influence, and personal goal alignment, highlight the need for reliable, supportive, and adaptable WAT designs. By addressing both intrinsic and extrinsic factors, designers can create WATs that not only attract initial interest but also foster long-term engagement and positive behavior change among users. This holistic approach ensures that WATs remain valuable tools for personal health management, catering to the evolving needs and preferences of Indian millennial users. This study's findings provide a foundation for engaging HCI researchers in future studies and offer practical insights for designing more effective and engaging WATs. By grounding the research in SDT and linking it to broader HCI trends, the study opens new avenues for developing digital health tools that are tailored to the specific needs and motivations of Indian millennials.

This study's findings, while intuitive in some respects, provide a crucial foundation for engaging HCI researchers in future studies. By examining the intrinsic and extrinsic motivations of Indian millennials for using WATs through the lens of SDT, this research offers valuable insights that align with broader HCI trends, such as personalized user experiences, gamification, and social connectivity in digital health tools. HCI researchers can build upon these findings to explore how personalization and customization in WATs can enhance user autonomy, leading to more engaging and effective health monitoring solutions. Additionally, the role of gamified elements in fostering a sense of competence suggests a basis for developing innovative motivational features in wearable technologies.

While the qualitative approach provides in-depth insights, the study solely relied on self-reported data from interviews. It does not include objective data on actual WATs usage patterns, such as activity logs or device usage statistics. Future research could benefit from a mixed-methods approach that combines qualitative interviews with quantitative surveys to validate and extend the results. The study does not account for the variability in the types and brands of WATs used by participants. Different devices may have distinct features, user interfaces, and accuracy levels, which can affect user experiences and perceptions. The study focuses on Indian millennials, which may limit the applicability of the findings to other cultural or geographical contexts. More diverse data, collected from different age groups or demographics, might reveal greater insights into WAT usage and interaction patterns. The findings of this study also suggest that future research should explore how cultural context influences the relative importance of different motivational factors in WAT usage. Studies comparing different cultural groups could provide further insights into how design features can be tailored to meet the specific needs of users in various regions. For practitioners, these insights underscore the importance of incorporating social features into WATs that resonate with the cultural values of the target market, particularly in regions where community and social connections are integral to daily life. Addressing these limitations in future research could provide deeper insights into the factors influencing WAT usage and engagement among different user groups.

References

1. GrandViewResearch: Wearable Technology Market Size, Share & Trends Analysis Report By Product (Head & Eyewear, Wristwear), By Application (Consumer Electronics, Healthcare), By Region (Asia Pacific, Europe), And Segment Forecasts, 2023–2030. https://www.grandviewresearch.com/industry-analysis/wearable-technology-market. Accessed 03 Jun 2024
2. Nayak, B., Bhattacharyya, S.S., Kumar, S., Jumnani, R.K.: Exploring the factors influencing adoption of health-care wearables among generation Z consumers in India. J. Inf. Commun. Ethics Soc. **20**, 150–174 (2022)
3. Gowin, M., et al.: Wearable activity tracker use in young adults through the lens of social cognitive theory. Am. J. Health Educ. **50**, 40–51 (2019)
4. Maille, B., et al.: Smartwatch electrocardiogram and artificial intelligence for assessing cardiac-rhythm safety of drug therapy in the COVID-19 pandemic. The QT-logs study. Int. J. Cardiol. **331**, 333–339 (2021)
5. Kasriel-Alexander, D.: Top 10 global consumer trends for 2015. Euromonitor International (2016)
6. Blazquez, M., Alexander, B., Fung, K.: Exploring Millennial's perceptions towards luxury fashion wearable technology. J. Fashion Market. Manage. Int. J. **24**, 343–359 (2020)
7. PYMNTS: Wearable Healthcare Tech Trend Driven by Millennials. https://www.pymnts.com/technology/2022/wearable-medtech-revolution-driven-generation-z-millennials/. Accessed 03 Jun 2024
8. Deci, E.L., Ryan, R.M.: Self-determination theory. Handbook of Theories of Social Psychology, vol. 1, pp. 416–436 (2012)
9. Choi, J., Kim, S.: Is the smartwatch an IT product or a fashion product? A study on factors affecting the intention to use smartwatches. Comput. Hum. Behav. **63**, 777–786 (2016)
10. Chuah, S.H.-W., Rauschnabel, P.A., Krey, N., Nguyen, B., Ramayah, T., Lade, S.: Wearable technologies: the role of usefulness and visibility in smartwatch adoption. Comput. Hum. Behav. **65**, 276–284 (2016)
11. Kamble, A., Desai, S., Abhang, N.: Wearable activity trackers: a structural investigation into acceptance and goal achievements of generation Z. Am. J. Health Educ. **52**, 307–320 (2021)
12. Shin, G., et al.: Wearable activity trackers, accuracy, adoption, acceptance and health impact: a systematic literature review. J. Biomed. Inform. **93**, 103153 (2019)
13. Kinney, D.A., Nabors, L.A., Merianos, A.L., Vidourek, R.A.: College students' use and perceptions of wearable fitness trackers. Am. J. Health Educ. **50**, 298–307 (2019)
14. Gascón, J.F.F., Alcalde, M.C., del Olmo Arriaga, J.L.: Impacto de las tecnologías de la información y la comunicación en la elección de universidad: el caso de internet y las redes sociales. Edutec. Revista electrónica de tecnología educative, a195–a195 (2012)
15. Fondevila-Gascón, J.F., Bernal, P.M., SanMiguel, P., Sádaba, T., Pérez-Bou, S.: Millennials and fashion: branding and positioning through digital interactions. In: Sádaba, T., Kalbaska, N., Cominelli, F., Cantoni, L., Torregrosa Puig, M. (eds) International Conference on Fashion Communication: Between Tradition and Future Digital Developments, pp. 117–128. Springer, Cham (2021). https://doi.org/10.1007/978-3-030-81321-5_10
16. Vansteenkiste, M., Niemiec, C.P., Soenens, B.: The development of the five mini-theories of self-determination theory: an historical overview, emerging trends, and future directions. The decade ahead: theoretical perspectives on motivation and achievement, 105–165 (2010)
17. Zhang, T., Wang, W.Y.C., Lin, Y.C., Tai, L.-H.: Understanding user motivation for evaluating online content: a self-determination theory perspective. Behav. Inf. Technol. **34**, 479–491 (2015)
18. Roxo, M.T., Brito, P.Q.: Augmented reality: what motivates late millennials towards fashion mobile apps? In: Enlightened Marketing in Challenging Times: Proceedings of the 2019 AMS

World Marketing Congress (WMC) 22, pp. 315–327. Springer, Cham (2020). https://doi.org/10.1007/978-3-030-42545-6_102
19. Glaser, B.: Strategies for qualitative research. In: The Discovery of Grounded Theory, pp. 2–6 (1967)
20. Hofstede, G.: Culture's consequences: comparing values, behaviors, institutions, and organizations across nations. Thousand Oaks (2001)
21. Pandey, P., Zheng, Y: Social positioning matters: a socialized affordance perspective of mHealth in India. Inf. Syst. J. **33**(4), 703–732 (2023)
22. Ganguly, N., Kumaraguru, P.: The positive and negative effects of social media in India. Commun. ACM, **62**(11), 98–99 (2019)

Overview of Challenges Faced by Nigerians in Using Psychotherapy Apps Integrated with Artificial Intelligence Conversational Chatbots: Analysing User Reviews for Technological Advancement in Nigeria

Chizoba Agwaonye[1], José Abdelnour-Nocera[1](✉), Neda Azarmehr[1], and Anicia Peters[2]

[1] University of West London, London, England
{agwachi,Jose.abdelnour-Nocera,Neda.Azarmehr}@uwl.ac.uk
[2] National Commission on Research Science and Technology, Windhoek, Namibia
apeters@ncrst.na

Abstract. Nigeria faces significant socioeconomic challenges, contributing to heightened anxiety and depression among its population. Despite the growing need for mental health support, psychotherapy apps specifically designed for Nigerians remain scarce. User feedback on existing apps reveals critical shortcomings, emphasizing the need for innovations tailored to local therapeutic requirements. This research focuses on integrating the unique needs of Nigerian users into the design of psychotherapy apps, particularly those featuring AI conversational chatbots, which have shown promise in providing therapeutic support. However, there is limited research on the specific design requirements for AI-integrated psychotherapy apps targeting Nigerians. To address this gap, the study analysed user reviews of 10 psychotherapy apps available on Apple's App Store and Google Play. A thematic analysis of 200 reviews identified key user priorities, including a well-designed user interface, user-friendliness, and functional AI chatbots. Conversely, poor usability and suboptimal AI performance were common reasons for users abandoning these apps. Additional concerns included a lack of content variety, repetitive chatbot responses, and security and privacy issues. The findings underscore the urgent need for improved app design to enhance user engagement and effectiveness. By addressing identified deficiencies—such as usability, AI functionality, and content diversity future psychotherapy apps can better meet the needs of Nigerian users. This research provides actionable insights for developing innovative, culturally relevant digital mental health solutions to support therapy for anxiety and depression in Nigeria.

Keywords: Psychotherapy Apps · AI chatbots · Users Experience · Human Computer Interaction

Published by Springer Nature Switzerland AG 2026
G. Bhutkar et al. (Eds.): IDID 2024, IFIP AICT 747, pp. 52–66, 2026.
https://doi.org/10.1007/978-3-032-00777-3_4

1 Introduction

Nigeria is currently experiencing a critical shortage of mental health infrastructure and services, exacerbated by minimal government expenditure on mental healthcare [1]. The deficit of mental health care professionals, particularly psychologists needed for counselling individuals during periods of emotional dysregulation, exacerbates the situation, leaving many Nigerians without adequate support [2]. Additionally, a substantial proportion of Nigerians do not seek therapy for anxiety and depression due to a lack of awareness about available therapy sessions and their benefits [3]. Research suggests that psychotherapy apps integrated with artificial intelligence (AI) can effectively manage depression and anxiety [4]. These digital tools provide scalable and accessible mental health support, which is crucial in mitigating the gaps left by the shortage of mental health professionals. To optimize these AI-integrated psychotherapy apps for Nigerian users, it is essential to conduct a comprehensive analysis of user reviews. User feedback provides critical insights into the app's usability, accessibility, and overall user experience. By systematically examining these reviews, developers can identify common issues, user preferences, and areas needing improvement, thereby enhancing the app to better meet the needs of Nigerian users [5]. Anxiety and depression have become significant public health concerns in Nigeria, severely impacting individuals' mood, cognition, and their ability to perform daily tasks such as work and study [4] In severe cases, anxiety can lead to suicidal tendencies. Individuals suffering from anxiety and depression often require various forms of psychological support to manage their conditions [6]. However, many Nigerians cannot afford the fees for psychological support provided by human psychologists. Consequently, many individuals turn to psychotherapy apps as a source of support for depression. Studies have shown that AI conversation agents can deliver therapeutic treatment via psychotherapy apps, enabling users to share their emotional moments with the AI and receive support [7]. During periods of emotional dysregulation, AI-based conversational agents can handle complex tasks such as providing social support and making therapeutic decisions in a human-like manner [8]. Currently, there are a few psychotherapy apps available on the Apple Store and Google Play for users to download. Given the proliferation of these applications, it is unlikely that all have undergone thorough assessments for effectiveness, usability, and safety. While some studies indicate that psychotherapy apps can effectively reduce issues such as depression and anxiety, they also highlight high dropout rates and reliability concerns as significant barriers to widespread adoption and sustained use [9]. For example, studies by Adaora et al. [10] reported high attrition rates in digital therapeutics for managing anxiety. The reasons behind these high attrition rates remain underexplored, particularly from the user perspective. Therefore, it is crucial to examine app efficiency, user experience, and satisfaction from the user's viewpoint to identify factors contributing to high attrition and dropout rates and propose innovative measures to sustain user engagement in Nigeria.

2 Background Study

Nigeria has faced numerous challenges across various sectors of national life, contributing to a significant rise in mental health issues among its citizens [11]. Persistent insecurity in multiple regions, combined with inflation and unemployment, has exacerbated the rates of depression and anxiety. The poverty rate has also surged, with over 55% of the population living below the poverty line and struggling to afford basic necessities such as food, housing, and healthcare [12]. Consequently, depression and anxiety have emerged as pressing concerns. Adewuya et al. [13] report that approximately 20% of Nigerians experience depression annually. Psychological treatment is essential to address these issues, but it remains unaffordable for many Nigerians Psychotherapy apps offer a promising solution by making psychological treatment more accessible. These apps, particularly those integrated with AI conversational chatbots, can engage users in therapeutic conversations and provide support for anxiety management, which could significantly benefit Nigerians. While chatbots cannot fully replicate traditional therapy, they can administer psychotherapeutic interventions that require minimal therapeutic expertise [14]. For example, some chatbots use natural language processing (NLP) to mimic a therapeutic conversational style and teach users various therapeutic techniques [15]. Emotionally intelligent psychotherapy apps often incorporate multiple therapeutic methods, such as dialectical behavior therapy and motivational interviewing [9, 16]. Despite their potential, these AI-integrated psychotherapy apps face significant challenges, notably high dropout or attrition rates. Studies have developed two versions of such apps for individuals with depression: one delivers therapeutic support through instant messaging using NLP to simulate human interactions, while the other incorporates various therapeutic approaches, including acceptance and commitment therapy and mindfulness [17, 18]. Both versions exhibited high attrition rates, despite demonstrating positive impacts on reducing depressive symptoms. Understanding the reasons for these high attrition rates and proposing innovative measures tailored to Nigerian users is crucial. Research by Inal et al. [19] indicates that poor usability significantly reduces user engagement. For instance, Lewis and Sauro [20] found that users with depressive disorders often struggled with the time-consuming process of entering and retrieving mood data. Additionally, privacy concerns can deter users from engaging with psychotherapy apps. Lustgarten et al. [21] discovered that many psychotherapy apps have privacy policies that do not align with user safety expectations. Understanding users' experiences is essential for designing effective psychotherapy apps. This research investigates the drawbacks of publicly available psychotherapy apps and offers innovative measures to enhance their performance, particularly for Nigerian users. Through a qualitative analysis of user reviews, this study identifies key design factors influencing user adherence to AI conversational chatbots and provides valuable insights for developing more usable, engaging, and effective psychotherapy app.

2.1 Literature Review

The limited availability of human psychologists and high psychology consultation fees have led to a greater reliance on electronic mental health services [22]. The digital mental health approach, utilizes virtual reality, artificial intelligence, and m-health apps, has shown significant effectiveness [23]. Nowadays, this has underscored its importance as a flexible and accessible resource, especially for underserved populations like those in Nigeria, is becoming increasingly clear. While the future of digital mental health services appears promising, challenges remain regarding equitable access, ongoing training needs, and technological advancements [24]. In a real-world observational study by Shih et al. [25], the effectiveness of various care modalities (limited, text-based coaching, clinical, and hybrid care) in treating depression and anxiety was assessed. Approximately 40% of participants responded fully to treatment across these modalities, with no significant differences in effectiveness noted among text-based coaching, clinical care, and hybrid approaches [25]. Although higher usage typically resulted in better outcomes across most modalities, the hybrid care group maintained consistent results regardless of usage levels. These findings underscore the promising potential of digital behavioral health interventions, particularly AI chatbot coaching. Another study by Feusener et al. [26]. Found substantial improvements in obsessive-compulsive disorder (OCD) symptoms among patients receiving digital Exposure and Response Prevention (ERP) teletherapy, with around 62.9% classified as full responders and a 43.4% reduction in OCD symptoms alongside enhanced quality of life. Comorbid symptoms of depression, anxiety, and stress also improved significantly, all achieved within a few weeks and with an average of less than 11 total therapist hours, indicating both cost and time efficiency [26]. This treatment model was found to be as effective as traditional face-to-face therapy while also reaching patients in remote areas. However, limitations include the lack of follow-up data for many patients and variability in treatment flexibility [26]. AI chatbot-driven digital mental health services have emerged as a viable method for delivering a variety of healthcare services, including psychotherapy. Their advantages extend beyond geographical barriers to provide specialized support across different therapy sessions. Nonetheless, the global rollout of mental health apps necessitates standardized laws and assurances regarding data privacy. Professionals must receive adequate training in digital mental health interventions, as outdated or absent legislation poses challenges. Ethical considerations, patient confidentiality, and informed consent processes are critical aspects of this discourse [27]. Psychotherapy apps hold great promise for expanding access to mental health services, particularly in remote or underserved regions. As technology progresses, innovative delivery methods, such as immersive virtual reality experiences, could further enhance treatment efficacy. However, realizing this potential will depend on addressing challenges such as establishing strong data privacy protections, standardizing regulations, and ensuring equitable access. Continuous professional development and training in AI chatbot therapy techniques will also be essential, with future success relying on a balance between technological innovation and ethical healthcare practices.

3 Methodology

3.1 Review Analysis

To investigate psychotherapy apps currently available for smartphones and their users' experiences, the researcher conducted a review of these apps and analyzed a set of user reviews. Apple App Store for iOS and Google Play for Android provide platforms where users can download apps and assess them by giving ratings and writing comments. These publicly available user reviews offer a comprehensive evaluation of the apps from the users' perspectives. Reviews typically contain both positive and negative feedback, highlighting specific features or aspects that users dislike. Therefore, user reviews are considered a rich source of information and valuable insights [28]. Analyzing user reviews to gather insights has become a common approach among researchers. For instance, Rogers et al. [29] found that user reviews contain valuable comments, user experiences, bug reports, and feature requests, which can help address unmet user needs.

To identify a set of currently popular psychotherapy apps, a systematic search was conducted in both the Android Play Store and the Apple App Store in June 2024. The search utilized the following keywords: (anxiety or depression) AND (artificial intelligence chatbot) AND (psychotherapy treatment or therapeutic support).

Inclusion Criteria: Apps were considered eligible if they met all the following criteria: 1) The app should have an AI conversational chatbot; 2) it should be for therapeutic support. 3) The app is available in English; 4) It was last updated no earlier than 2017; and 5) It has at least 4.3 out of 5 ratings and above (this was because apps with 4 out of 5 ratings and above were considered to be effective).

Exclusion Criteria: The reviews were considered ineligible for the following reasons: 1) If they weren't written in the English language 2) when the written words are shorter than 15 characters. 3) If it is a positive review.

Ratings were chosen as the measure of popularity because this metric is consistently provided by both Android and iOS app stores. Criteria regarding popularity and recent updates were employed to exclude low-quality apps that are not maintained or widely used currently. The initial screening of each app was independently conducted by the researcher. This process involved reading the app's name and description in the app stores to determine eligibility for a detailed feature and review analysis.

3.2 Data Collections and Review Analysis

This study examined users reviews of the psychotherapy app. The dataset used comprises 118838 reviews, which were extracted from the app stores (Apple and Google Play). The collected datasets were all the reviews written between 2020 and 2024. Each review was screened using the exclusion criteria. After the screening, 650 reviews (comments written with words that are more than 15 characters and are negative reviews from Nigerians) remained. After accessing the reviews for eligibility, 200 reviews (sentences that are correct and complete) were selected and grouped into different themes for the thematic analysis. Thematic analysis was chosen because it allows the analysis of an enormous data set, thereby helping with the interpretation of textual patterns while accounting for the context [30]. The study employed a qualitative thematic analysis and was conducted using the six- phase framework proposed, which consists of the following steps: (1) familiarizing oneself with the data; (2) generating preliminary codes; (3) searching for themes; (4) identifying themes; (5) reviewing themes; and (6) writing up the results.

A single thematic analysis was conducted for the app reviews because it helps promotes comparative insight which will ensure robustness of the analysis. The researcher reviewed each app review and identified relevant themes. Axial coding was then employed to refine and extract the central themes present in the data.

3.3 Apps Selection

After screening following the exclusion and inclusion criteria, 10 apps were selected, including Android apps and iOS apps (Table 1). All of the selected apps are designed for therapeutic support and have an artificial intelligence chatbot for communication with the users. Since the researcher is interested in apps designed specifically for therapeutic support with AI, all the psychotherapy apps without AI conversational agents were excluded. Thus, all of the apps included in our review are designed for a general population. The researcher included both Android and iOS versions for vast data collections.

During the collection of user reviews, it was observed that some users can provide both ratings and reviews for an app, while others only provide either rating or review (i.e., assign it a score between 1 and 5 stars) without leaving a written review. These metrics make the number of star ratings vary with the total number of user reviews of the apps.

Table 1. List of Apps Reviewed

Names of Apps	Play Store	Star Rating Value	No of Ratings	No of Reviews
Wysa	Apple/google	4.8 out of 5	6600	886
MindDoc	Apple/google	4.3 out of 5	38000	4750
Mind Spa	Apple/google	4.4 out of 5	2200	1137
Hector	Apple/	4.5 out of 5	106	11
Elomia	Apple	4.3 out of 5	174	19
Dr. Lisa	Apple	5 out of 5	3	1
Youper	Apple/google	4.8 out of 5	2100	502
Vos	Apple/Google	4.7 out of 5	473	32
Headspace	Apple/google	4.8 out of 5	346000	100000
Rootd	Google	4.6 out of 5	33000	11500

4 Results

For this study, the researcher focused only on the most critical reviews of the psychotherapy apps as identified by users. This is because the sole purpose of this research is to understand the reasons for users' disengagement with the AI conversational chatbot of a psychotherapy app and the weaknesses of the app. User reviews were denoted by [UR].

4.1 Drawbacks Identified by User in the Reviews Are

Data Loss: Data collected using a tracking application is extremely important to users, particularly those who spend a significant amount of time storing their data for future reference. If the app develops an issue that causes users to lose this data, they may never use the app again. For example: " I used to love this app and I mainly used it as a way to vent as I have no one to talk to. And I could compare how I was feeling back then to now and see how things have changed. But tonight, I went to re-read stuff from 2019 and it's all just gone". I'm probably not going to use this app anymore because I feel like I have lost my dairy and what is the point if everything will just disappear". [UR = 15].

Lack of User Control: Users liked to be able to control the app features and functionalities and be able to use them without too many constraints. For example," I'm overall very happy to have access to this tool but I would like to make a suggestion for improvement with regards to the track my mood section. I believe it would be helpful to be able to fully customize the icon/options on the screen (e.g. work, school, partner, family, outdoor etc.) so that it can be relevant to each individual as possible. I cannot relate to certain 'by default' Icons and therefore I don't find it necessary for them to be present as options, however I cannot delete them or rename them so that they represent more closely a relevant element in my life. The ability to fully control the Icon option would be a five-star rating for me. [UR = 20].

Repetition of Responses: Users appreciate AI conversational chatbots that ask different questions during therapy sessions rather than repeating the same questions, which tends to bore users, especially during long conversations. For example, "It was helpful at the beginning but the more you use it you will realize that it just asks the same questions constantly and the conversation doesn't really go anywhere".[UR = 35].

Lack of Security: Psychotherapy apps are designed to gather users' data, and there is a need for this data to be protected. Users appreciated mobile apps that enabled them to gather their data without storing it. For Example," Their app logs and store your IMEI number which is a privacy concern, there is no legitimate reason to log imei number, I've seen the source code and can confirm that my imei number is stored in their app/server". [UR = 10].

Not Ease to Use: For a psychotherapy app to be efficient for its users, they will be able to use it effortlessly. If the app becomes complicated to use, the users tend to get discouraged. For example, " quite disappointed with the update. I did it without thinking. The old version was very simple but had a very clear and easy to track mood. Now I feel everything is behind a paywall and I don't know how to use most of the new features. Really disappointed because it really was a great tool before. I wish I never updated the app to be honest". [UR = 12].

Lack of App Features Variety: The users would like to access different features that will enable them to utilise the app to its fullest. Users complained about some missing features. For example," I'm unable to add weblinks and video. It only export text from the app". [UR = 7].

AI sounds Robotic: It is expected of users to converse intimately with the AI chatbot as though they are having a conversation with a human; this will make the therapy sessions with the conversational agent real. For example, ''I think everything in the app is well designed, the help they offer is good and they have the right idea. However, there is lot of things they should improve on. I had a lot of trouble connecting with the app, it didn't feel like an actual friendship (which is to be expected with this type of Ai). I think the developer should try to improve the app as a character, to make them more relatable and easier to bond with. I would definitely recommend this app if you have trouble looking on the bright side". [UR = 18].

Low Memory Storage: Users have experienced that AI tends to forget previous conversations after some days, thereby making them incoherent in their responses. For example, ''it helps in some sense but gosh it's hard work. I find myself having to repeat my situation over and over so there is not much memory of what you have covered. These are the reasons I don't want 'X' in my life. I'm scared of X. please remind me when I'm weak so I don't reach out. The App accepts this. Me: I'm feeling week and need you to remind me. App: I think you should reach out. Me: I have written X a letter it's not very nice content. App: I'm sure X would appreciate the letter. Me: 100% X would appreciate it:). No friend would give you that advise. I think if it had a bit more memory and could talk to you directly about situations it would be better for me but it does help and can see how it could potentially be a life saver for someone". [UR = 29].

Lack of In-Depth Responses: It is always appreciated when the AI chatbot provides a detailed response. During a conversation with the chatbot, the user expects to have a lengthy discussion with the chatbot as if they are conversing with a human. For example," I downloaded this app after I'd been through a difficult time and promptly deleted it after a week. It's quite cute, with a calming colour scheme and aesthetic but the actual Ai wasn't great; you had to be very clear with it (once, after my pet passed away, I said ''I'm feeling awful because my dog had to be put down today, but I'm glad she didn't have to suffer any longer) it replied; it's good to hear you are feeling glad! What else are you happy about? It's okay, with access to real therapist and breathing exercises but it's definitely not the best therapy app I've tried. it also spouts the usual take deep breaths' mantra that I'm sick of at this point". [15].

Unaffordability: Some users complained about the payment cost of the app. For example," I really love how the Ai talks to me but I don't have the money to afford to keep talking to it. I think the Ai chat should be free, you can talk to it whenever you want for free. I don't have money to keep talking to your Ai but it really does help me and I need it the most right now so please make it free. It will help a lot of people not just me [37] (Fig. 1).

4.2 The Innovative Measures that Can Be Used to Enhance Users (Nigerians) Performance Following the Drawbacks on the Psychotherapy App.

Data Loss

Implementing robust data management systems that provide users with control over their personal data, including options to back up and restore information. By enhancing data management, users can feel secure knowing their important information is safe, addressing concerns over data loss [31].

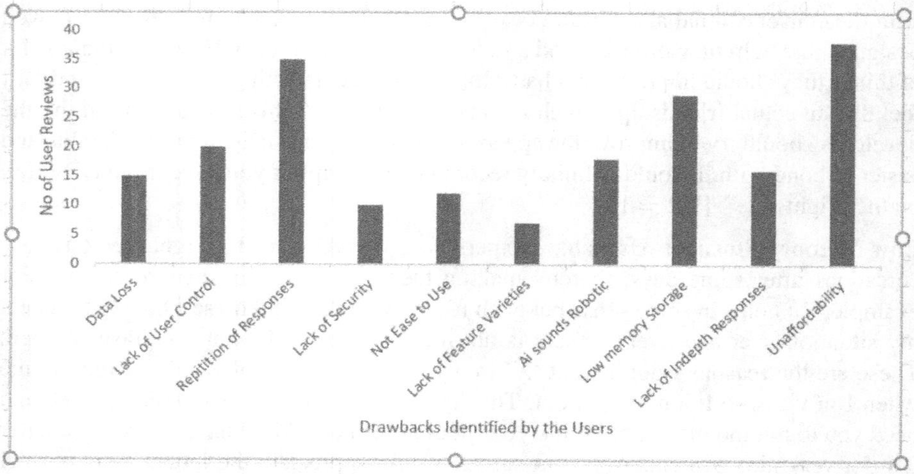

Fig. 1. A Graph of Identified drawbacks vs User Reviews

Lack of User Control
Introducing customizable user interfaces that allow users to select and modify icons and options based on their personal experiences. Incorporating feedback mechanisms where users can suggest features, enables the app to adapt to their needs continuously [32].

Repetition of Responses
By leveraging NLP advancements to improve AI conversational capabilities. This will reduce repetition through better language processing, thereby boosting the AI to provide more varied and engaging interactions to address user boredom during therapy sessions [33].

Lack of Security
Employing end-to-end encryption for user data will ensure privacy and security. Additionally, clearly communicating data handling practices, including the option for users to manage what data is collected and how it's used will foster user's trust in the using apps for mental health therapy [34].

Not Easy to Use
By designing a user-friendly onboarding process with interactive tutorials to guide new users. Also, implementing a simplified user interface with easy navigation and a help section that offers quick solutions to common issues is of great advantage to user [35].

Lack of App Features Variety
Introducing culturally relevant content and support for various media types (e.g., video, links). More so, expanding features to include multimedia and culturally relevant scenarios enhances the app's utility and relevance for diverse users [36].

AI Sounds Robotic
Training AI to recognize local dialects and slang will improve communication effectiveness among users. Additionally, making the AI more relatable and culturally aware will likely make users to feel a stronger connection thereby enhancing the therapeutic experience [37].

Low Memory Storage
Developing a memory-enhanced feature that allows the psychotherapy app to recall previous conversations and user preferences over time. This could include summarizing past interactions for users to elevate continuity in conversations [38].

Lack of In-Depth Responses
Incorporating culturally relevant examples and scenarios, using NLP to provide nuanced answers. This will enrich the depth of responses that ensures users feel understood and supported thereby, improving overall satisfaction with the app [39].

Unaffordability
Offering tiered pricing models, including a freemium version with essential features, and subsidized options for low-income users. Also Partnering with NGOs and government programs to provide free access to the app for those in need, particularly focusing on vulnerable populations in Nigeria [5].

4.3 Lists of Ethical Issues in Using AI for Therapy Sessions and How They Can Be Addressed

Quality of Care
AI may lack the effective understanding and empathy that human therapists provide, potentially leading to unsatisfied responses during therapy. This can be avoided by conducting extensive clinical trials to evaluate the efficiency of the AI mental health interventions compared to traditional therapy.

Informed Consent
Users must understand how AI operates, what data is collected, and how it will be used. If users are unaware of AI's limitations, it can lead to misplaced trust. Considering this, there should be a developed educational resource that will users understand the differences between AI and therapy of using human psychologist.

Confidentiality and Privacy
The collection and storage of sensitive mental health data pose risks. The Breaches of users' data privacy could lead to significant harm, including stigma or discrimination. Users should be made aware of how their data is used and whether it's shared with third parties, requiring clear privacy policies. To secure users' data, implementation of robust encryption and security protocols are necessary. Additionally, there should be clear outline of data collection, usage and sharing practice in user agreement thereby allowing users to opt out of specific data uses.

Accountability
With psychotherapy app, it can be challenging in determining whether is the developers, AI or organization is responsible for errors or misinformation during the therapy session. Therefore, it is necessary to establish structured overview for accountability in case of errors, including responsibilities of developers, users and organization.

Bias and Inequality
AI can perpetuate or amplify existing biases in mental health care if trained on non-representative datasets, potentially leading to discriminatory practices. To overcome this, the use of diverse and representative datasets is encouraged for training AI models. Also, this will mitigate bias and ensure that the system works equitably across different populations.

Dependence on Technology
As AI tools become more prevalent, there may be a decrease in human therapists' roles, which could impact the overall quality of mental health care. This can be curbed by implanting mechanism for users to provide feedback about their relevance on AI thereby helping the mental health medical professional to understand and address dependency issues.

Cultural Sensitivity
AI systems may not be able to adequately understand or address cultural differences and nuances, leading to ineffective or harmful interactions. For this reason, it is necessary to incorporate cultural sensitivity training into AI development processes to ensure that the AI can recognize and respond appropriately to diverse cultural context.

5 Discussion and Adaptation of Psychotherapy Digital Advancement for Nigeria

Nigeria has the potential to establish nationwide therapy sessions through the implementation of psychotherapy apps, thereby providing remote therapeutic support to its citizens. With 67% of Nigerians owning mobile phones, such technological solutions could significantly bridge the existing gaps in psychotherapy treatment within the country [40]. Furthermore, designing these apps to incorporate local Nigerian languages and cultural sensitivities could greatly enhance the self-management of anxiety and depression among users. Psychotherapy apps present a valuable opportunity to aid users in managing their anxiety more effectively. By analyzing user reviews, this study has identified several key drawbacks, thereby offering a comprehensive understanding of users' overall experiences with these apps. Common issues uncovered include data loss, lack of user control, repetitive responses, privacy concerns, limited features, the nature of AI responses, low memory storage, and high costs. The predominant focus of user comments on usability underscores the critical importance of this factor in the development of effective psychotherapy apps. Many psychotherapy apps available on the App Store and Google Play fail to adequately assess AI functionality and usability. This oversight leads to design and interface problems that, if addressed, could enhance user engagement and reduce dropout rates. Reviews suggest that these apps should cater to a broad audience by allowing customization to meet individual needs and preferences, thereby improving user satisfaction and experience. Specific complaints from users included the repetitive and often incomprehensible responses from AI, which led to dissatisfaction with their interactions. Additionally, subscription costs were highlighted as a significant barrier to app usage. While free apps with valuable content encourage engagement, the limited content in free versions often results in low user engagement. Analyzing user reviews, as conducted in this study, is essential for identifying the drawbacks of psychotherapy apps and provides insights for technological advancements in their design. For instance, the key themes in this user reviews have highlighted usability issues such as navigation difficulties and accessibility challenges. Systematic analysis of these issues will lead to targeted improvements, ensuring that psychotherapy apps are optimized for ease of use and user engagement in Nigeria. Furthermore, comparing user reviews across similar applications can highlight competitive advantages and market trends, aiding in understanding user preferences and informing strategic product development decisions. Overall, user reviews offer a wealth of information that significantly contributes to the HCI research community. By systematically analyzing this qualitative data, researchers and designers can gain valuable insights into user experiences, usability issues, feature prioritization, emotional responses, and more. As the landscape of digital applications continues to evolve, harnessing the power of user feedback will be essential for creating more effective, inclusive, and user-centered technologies.

6 Conclusion

This study outlined the user reviews of psychotherapy apps and the innovative measures that can be used to enhance the users experience of AI integrated psychotherapy apps by Nigerians. Understanding user opinions is crucial for designing effective applications that will be adopted and utilized by the target audience. To this end, a qualitative study was conducted on 10 psychotherapy apps from Apple's App Store and Google Play. Thematic analysis was used in evaluating 200 user reviews to identify key themes. From the identified drawbacks backs, themes were created and recommendation that will improve users in Nigeria was provided for each theme. This research revealed significant insights into the weaknesses of existing psychotherapy applications by identifying the features and qualities that users found unsatisfactory and also suggesting potential improvements. The findings highlight several critical aspects of app design that should consider when integrating AI conversational chatbots to enhance the user experience, usability, adherence, and overall effectiveness for Nigerians. The innovative measures include implementing robust cloud backup solutions, introducing customizable user interfaces that allows users to modify icons, utilizing machine learning algorithms to analyses users' interaction and employing end to end encryption for user data. Ultimately, this analysis of user's reviews helps to highlights the diversity of varying needs thereby underscoring the importance of inclusive design practices. The study provides design recommendations aimed at improving the design of psychotherapy apps for better tomorrow of Nigerians.

6.1 Limitations

The study analysed 200 user reviews from a dataset of 118,838 reviews, which might not fully capture the diversity of user experiences or represent the broader population's views on these apps. Additionally, reviews were selected based on specific criteria (e.g., only negative reviews written in English by Nigerian users), which could introduce bias and limit the generalizability of the findings. The study's focus on apps updated until 2024 limits its applicability in accounting for future technological advancements in AI chatbots, which could address some of the identified issues (e.g., repetitive responses, lack of memory storage) over time.

References

1. Wada, Y.H., et al.: Mental health in Nigeria: a neglected issue in public health. Public Health Pract. **2**, 100166 (2021). https://doi.org/10.1016/j.puhip.2021.100166
2. Armiya'u, A.Y., Yildirim, M., Muhammad, A., Tanhan, A., Young, J.S.: Mental health facilitators and barriers during Covid-19 in Nigeria. J. Asian Afr. Stud. **59**(2), 354–376 (2024). https://doi.org/10.1177/00219096221111354
3. Aderounmu, B., Azuh, D., Onanuga, O., Oluwatomisin, O., Ebenezer, B., Azuh, A.: Poverty drivers and Nigeria's development: Implications for policy intervention. Cogent Arts Hum. **8**(1), 1927495 (2021). https://doi.org/10.1080/23311983.2021.1927495
4. Gual-Montolio, P., Jaén, I., Martínez-Borba, V., Castilla, D., Suso-Ribera, C.: Using artificial intelligence to enhance ongoing psychological interventions for emotional problems in real- or close to real-time: a systematic review. IJERPH **19**(13), 7737 (2022). https://doi.org/10.3390/ijerph19137737
5. Borghouts, J., et al.: Barriers to and facilitators of user engagement with digital mental health interventions: systematic review. J. Med. Internet Res. **23**(3), e24387 (2021). https://doi.org/10.2196/24387
6. Carpenter, J.S., et al.: Circadian depression: a mood disorder phenotype. Neurosci. Biobehav. Rev. **126**, 79–101 (2021). https://doi.org/10.1016/j.neubiorev.2021.02.045
7. Filatova, E.V., Shadrina, M.I., Slominsky, P.A.: 'Major Depression: One Brain. One Disease, One Set of Intertwined Processes', Cells **10**(6), 1283 (2021). https://doi.org/10.3390/cells10061283
8. Adam, M., Wessel, M., Benlian, A.: AI-based chatbots in customer service and their effects on user compliance. Electron Markets **31**(2), 427–445 (2021). https://doi.org/10.1007/s12525-020-00414-7
9. Ahmad, R., Siemon, D., Gnewuch, U., Robra-Bissantz, S.: Designing personality-adaptive conversational agents for mental health care. Inf. Syst. Front. **24**(3), 923–943 (2022). https://doi.org/10.1007/s10796-022-10254-9
10. Lim, S.M., Shiau, C.W.C., Cheng, L.J., Lau, Y.: Chatbot-delivered psychotherapy for adults with depressive and anxiety symptoms: a systematic review and meta-regression. Behav. Ther. **53**(2), 334–347 (2022). https://doi.org/10.1016/j.beth.2021.09.007
11. Nwosu, A., Boardman, S., Husain, M.M., Doraiswamy, P.M.: Digital therapeutics for mental health: Is attrition the Achilles heel? Front. Psychiatry **13**, 900615 (2022). https://doi.org/10.3389/fpsyt.2022.900615
12. Labinjo, T., Serrant, L., Ashmore, R., Turner, J.: Perceptions, attitudes and cultural understandings of mental health in Nigeria: a scoping review of published literature. Ment. Health Relig. Cult. **23**(7), 606–624 (2020). https://doi.org/10.1080/13674676.2020.1726883

13. Olasode, T., Eke, C., Olaleye, O.O.: Has economic growth reduced poverty in Nigeria? A critical analysis of the last two decades. JED **4**(2), 232–256 (2022). https://doi.org/10.20414/jed.v4i2.5506
14. Adewuya, A.O., et al.: Epidemiology of depression in primary care: findings from the mental health in primary care (MeHPriC) project, Lagos, Nigeria. Int. J. Psychiatry Med. **57**(1), 6–20 (2022). https://doi.org/10.1177/0091217421996089
15. Haque, M.D.R., Rubya, S.: An overview of chatbot-based mobile mental health apps: insights from app description and user reviews. JMIR Mhealth Uhealth **11**, e44838 (2023). https://doi.org/10.2196/44838
16. Svikhnushina, E., Pu, P.: PEACE: a model of key social and emotional qualities of conversational chatbots. ACM Trans. Interact. Intell. Syst. **12**(4), 1–29 (2022). https://doi.org/10.1145/3531064
17. Jiang, Y., Yang, X., Zheng, T.: Make chatbots more adaptive: Dual pathways linking human-like cues and tailored response to trust in interactions with chatbots. Comput. Hum. Behav. **138**, 107485 (2023). https://doi.org/10.1016/j.chb.2022.107485
18. Goldberg, S.B., et al.: Machine learning and natural language processing in psychotherapy research: Alliance as example use case. J. Counseling Psychol. **67**(4), 438–448 (2020). https://doi.org/10.1037/cou0000382
19. Reyes, A.T.: The process of learning mindfulness and acceptance through the use of a mobile app based on acceptance and commitment therapy: a grounded theory analysis. Issues Ment. Health Nurs. **43**(1), 3–12 (2022). https://doi.org/10.1080/01612840.2021.1953652
20. Inal, Y., Wake, J.D., Guribye, F., Nordgreen, T.: Usability evaluations of mobile mental health technologies: systematic review. J. Med. Internet Res. **22**(1), e15337 (2020). https://doi.org/10.2196/15337
21. Lewis, J.R., Sauro, J.: Usability and user experience: design and evaluation. In: Salvendy, G., Karwowski, W., (Eds.) Handbook of Human Factors and Ergonomics, 1st ed., Wiley, pp. 972–1015 (2021). https://doi.org/10.1002/9781119636113.ch38
22. Lustgarten, S.D., Garrison, Y.L., Sinnard, M.T., Flynn, A.W.: Digital privacy in mental healthcare: current issues and recommendations for technology use. Curr. Opin. Psychol. **36**, 25–31 (2020). https://doi.org/10.1016/j.copsyc.2020.03.012
23. Lattie, E.G., Stiles-Shields, C., Graham, A.K.: An overview of and recommendations for more accessible digital mental health services. Nat. Rev. Psychol. **1**(2), 87–100 (2022). https://doi.org/10.1038/s44159-021-00003-1
24. Gan, D.Z.Q., McGillivray, L., Han, J., Christensen, H., Torok, M.: Effect of engagement with digital interventions on mental health outcomes: a systematic review and meta-analysis. Front. Digit. Health **3**, 764079 (2021). https://doi.org/10.3389/fdgth.2021.764079
25. Ramos, G., Chavira, D.A.: Use of technology to provide mental health care for racial and ethnic minorities: evidence, promise, and challenges. Cogn. Behav. Pract. **29**(1), 15–40 (2022). https://doi.org/10.1016/j.cbpra.2019.10.004
26. Bulkes, N.Z., Davis, K., Kay, B., Riemann, B.C.: Comparing efficacy of telehealth to in-person mental health care in intensive-treatment-seeking adults. J. Psychiatr. Res. **145**, 347–352 (2022). https://doi.org/10.1016/j.jpsychires.2021.11.003
27. Chaharshughi, B.T., Izadi, R., Naghavi, A.: Tele-psychotherapy for individuals with obsessive-compulsive disorder during the COVID-19 outbreak: a qualitative study. J. Educ. Health Promot. **13**(1) (2024). https://doi.org/10.4103/jehp.jehp_372_23
28. Chan, A.H.Y., Honey, M.L.L.: User perceptions of mobile digital apps for mental health: acceptability and usability - An integrative review. Psychiatr. Ment. Health Nurs. **29**(1), 147–168 (2022). https://doi.org/10.1111/jpm.12744
29. Wu, H., Deng, W., Niu, X., Nie, C.: Identifying key features from app user reviews. In: 2021 IEEE/ACM 43rd International Conference on Software Engineering (ICSE), Madrid, ES, pp. 922–932. IEEE (2021). https://doi.org/10.1109/ICSE43902.2021.00088

30. Rogers, D., Preece, A., Innes, M., Spasic, I.: Real-time text classification of user-generated content on social media: systematic review. IEEE Trans. Comput. Soc. Syst. **9**(4), 1154–1166 (2022). https://doi.org/10.1109/TCSS.2021.3120138
31. Braun, V., Clarke, V.: Conceptual and design thinking for thematic analysis. Qual. Psychol. **9**(1), 3–26 (2022). https://doi.org/10.1037/qup0000196
32. Ahmad, K., Maabreh, M., Ghaly, M., Khan, K., Qadir, J., Al-Fuqaha, A.: Developing future human-centered smart cities: critical analysis of smart city security, data management, and ethical challenges. Comput. Sci. Rev. **43**, 100452 (2022). https://doi.org/10.1016/j.cosrev.2021.100452
33. Bitrián, P., Buil, I., Catalán, S.: Enhancing user engagement: the role of gamification in mobile apps. J. Bus. Res. **132**, 170–185 (2021). https://doi.org/10.1016/j.jbusres.2021.04.028
34. Zidaru, T., Morrow, E.M., Stockley, R.: Ensuring patient and public involvement in the transition to AI-assisted mental health care: a systematic scoping review and agenda for design justice. Health Expect. **24**(4), 1072–1124 (2021). https://doi.org/10.1111/hex.13299
35. Eisenstadt, M., Liverpool, S., Infanti, E., Ciuvat, R.M., Carlsson, C.: Mobile apps that promote emotion regulation, positive mental health, and well-being in the general population: systematic review and meta-analysis. JMIR Ment. Health **8**(11), e31170 (2021). https://doi.org/10.2196/31170
36. Zaina, L.A.M., Fortes, R.P.M., Casadei, V., Nozaki, L.S., Paiva, D.M.B.: Preventing accessibility barriers: guidelines for using user interface design patterns in mobile applications. J. Syst. Softw. **186**, 111213 (2022). https://doi.org/10.1016/j.jss.2021.111213
37. Pisoni, G., Díaz-Rodríguez, N., Gijlers, H., Tonolli, L.: Human-centered artificial intelligence for designing accessible cultural heritage. Appl. Sci. **11**(2), 870 (2021). https://doi.org/10.3390/app11020870
38. Chaudhry, B.M., Debi, H.R.: User perceptions and experiences of an AI-driven conversational agent for mental health support. mHealth **10**, 22 (2024). https://doi.org/10.21037/mhealth-23-55
39. Chen, S., Nakamura, M.: Generating personalized dialogues based on conversation log summarization and sentiment analysis. In: The 23rd International Conference on Information Integration and Web Intelligence, Linz Austria: ACM, pp. 217–222 (2021). https://doi.org/10.1145/3487664.3487695
40. Santos-Vijande, M.L., Gómez-Rico, M., Molina-Collado, A., Davison, R.M.: Building user engagement to mhealth apps from a learning perspective: Relationships among functional, emotional and social drivers of user value. J. Retail. Consum. Serv. **66**, 102956 (2022). https://doi.org/10.1016/j.jretconser.2022.102956
41. Ibeneme, S., Ukor, N., Ongom, M., Dasa, T., Muneene, D., Okeibunor, J.: Strengthening capacities among digital health leaders for the development and implementation of national digital health programs in Nigeria. BMC Proc. **14**(S10), 9 (2020). https://doi.org/10.1186/s12919-020-00193-1

More is Still Easy: Adding Dimensions to Android Pattern Locks to Enhance Security for Emergent Users Without Compromising Usability and Memorability

Ishita Sharma(✉) and Anirudha Joshi

Indian Institute of Technology, Bombay, Mumbai 400076, Maharashtra, India

Abstract. Android Pattern Locks (APLs) are a prevalent yet vulnerable password mechanism. Despite their potential for heightened security compared to 4-digit PINs, users often resort to simple and common APLs, particularly emergent users. We enhance the APLs with additional dimensions of single-select graphical layers to increase the password space and report a systematic, within-subjects, counterbalanced study involving 36 emergent users comparing two enhanced versions of APLs against the original, to evaluate aspects of usability, memorability, graphical layer popularity, and user preferences. Our results indicated a 100% success rate in first-time usability in all 3 password mechanisms, and no significant differences in 4-day memorability with 94.44% success rates in the original APL and 2-Layer + APL, and 100% success rate in the 5-Layer + APL. We present an analysis of the security and memorability of these enhanced APLs and discuss the implications of our results.

Keywords: HCI · Multidimensional Passwords · Graphical Passwords · Mobile Security · Enhanced Pattern Lock Mechanisms · Interaction Design · Emergent Users

1 Introduction

Following global shifts in mobile and internet technologies, there has been a notable trend towards cost reduction of devices, rendering them increasingly accessible. This phenomenon is due to the evolving dynamics of needs, desires, and aspirations within glocal mindsets [20]. The increased availability of affordable internet-enabled smartphones among low-income groups has sparked interest in academia and industry to cater to not only traditional users but also "emergent" users [8]. Devanuj and Joshi [13] define emergent users as: "new users, who may have less education, who may be poor, who are often located away from commercial and political centers and are culturally different from not only the traditional (that is, urban and educated) users but from each other as well."

Published by Springer Nature Switzerland AG 2026
G. Bhutkar et al. (Eds.): IDID 2024, IFIP AICT 747, pp. 67–89, 2026.
https://doi.org/10.1007/978-3-032-00777-3_5

With the increasing use of technology among emergent users, the importance of secure and usable user authentication mechanisms also increases. There are three types of user authentication mechanisms, namely knowledge-based (what-you-know), possession-based (what-you-have), and biometric-based (who-you-are) [29]. While all types are in use, what-you-know mechanisms continue to be dominant. Within these, three knowledge-based authentication methods are most commonly employed on smartphones, namely personal identification numbers (PINs), Android pattern locks (APLs), and alphanumeric passwords.

Alphanumeric passwords are considered to be the most secure due to their extensive password space (7×10^{14} for a typical 8-character password). However, the complexity of alphanumeric passwords can make them hard to remember, often leading to users creating predictable passwords [1], [33] or writing them down [22], compromising security. Alphanumeric passwords are even less suitable for emergent users due to potential literacy issues, language barriers, and text input difficulties [3]. PINs are widely used, yet they offer a smaller password space (10^4 for a 4-digit PIN), making them moderately difficult to remember and also prone to users selecting easily guessable combinations [21].

APLs (Fig. 1a) are a popular gesture-based graphical password mechanism, and have a somewhat larger password space than 4-digit PINs (389,112 for a 3×3 grid) [25]. However, as we discuss below, users tend to select from a significantly smaller subset of APLs, often with just four nodes, reducing the combinations to only 1,624 [25], [5]. In contrast, users choose PINs in relatively less predictable ways [26]. Despite their limitations, APLs could be a mechanism of choice among

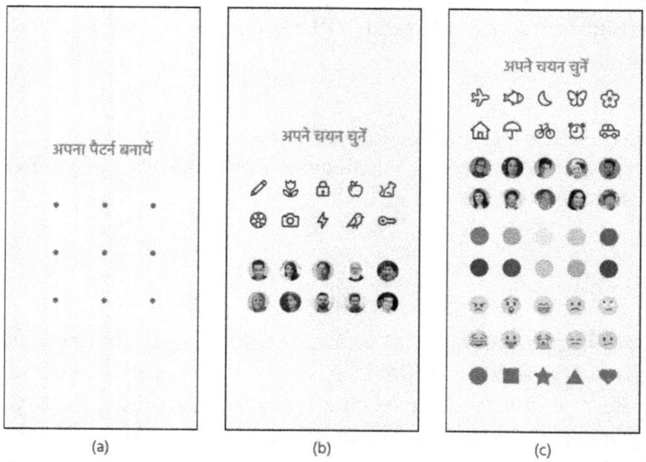

Fig. 1. We designed three password mechanisms: (a) The standard APL, referred to in our study as the 'Only APL' condition (b) The first enhanced version with 2 single-select graphical layers that appear prior to the APL, referred to as '2-Layers + APL' condition, (c) The second enhanced version with 5 single-select graphical layers that appears prior to the APL, defined as '5-Layers + APL' condition.

emergent users as they require no textual literacy and are language-free. Hence, it is worth exploring how the security of APLs could be increased for these users.

In this paper, we investigate an alternative approach. We supplement APLs with additional dimensions consisting of "single-select graphical layers". We define a graphical layer as a set of visual tokens. For example, Fig. 1b has two layers where layer 1 consists of a set of icons and layer 2 consists of a set of faces. The user is asked to select one icon and one face as a part of their password (hence, "single-select" per layer). This simple act increases the password space of the APL by 10^2. A 5-layer version (Fig. 1c) increases the password space by 5×10^4.

It has been known for a long time that though the human mind has a limited capacity of 7 ± 2 units for absolute judgment in a particular dimension (e.g. size of a square), having stimuli with multiple dimensions helps to increase this limit (e.g. adding colour) [28]. Human faces, for example, have several dimensions, and hence we are able to differentiate between thousands of faces. We hypothesise that our single-select graphical layers will not decrease the usability and memorability of the overall password (because these are dimensions unrelated to the APL) while increasing the password space. We present a within-subjects counterbalanced study that compares the performance of emergent users (N=36) with "Only APL" (the original APL without any enhancements), "2-Layer + APL" (2 graphical layers added prior to the APL), and "5-Layer + APL" (5 graphical layers added prior to the APL). We make the following contributions:

1. We propose the concept of multidimensional passwords to enhance the security of a password mechanism without compromising usability and memorability.
2. We report successes of first-time usability and 4-day memorability of the three password mechanisms and demonstrate that adding dimensions of up to 5 single-select graphical layers does not cause any loss to usability or memorability of the overall password mechanism.
3. We present an analysis of the number of attempts, time taken, and the percentage of success and failures at each attempt.
4. We demonstrate that it is possible to design password mechanisms that can be used by emergent users and recalled after 4 days with above 80% success rates.
5. We analyse the popularity of tokens in the chosen graphical layers and biases that may exist in them.
6. Through qualitative analyses, we also report user preferences and behavior related to graphical passwords.

2 Background

Graphical Passwords. Graphical passwords, where users interact with graphical elements to authenticate themselves, were pioneered by Blonder [9]. These include Draw-a-Secret [19], Deja Vu [14], Passdoodle [37], Story [11], Pass-go [18], and Passfaces [11]. These methods have been extensively researched, with recall-based schemes requiring users to reproduce pre-defined APLs or sequences of graphical elements. Passfaces, utilizing human face visualizations, leverage the human ability to recognize faces for authentication. A recent study found that Celebrity passfaces [3] are significantly effective among emergent users due to their visual nature, but their widespread adoption remains limited.

Android Pattern Lock. APLs, a simplified variant of Pass-Go [18], were introduced by Google in 2008 and have become a popular user authentication method on Android smartphones for traditional as well as emergent users. To unlock the device, users are prompted to draw a personalized sequence of connected nodes on a 3×3 grid, forming an APL that follows certain rules. A valid APL must connect at least four nodes where each node may only be connected once, following a sequential progression from the first unconnected node. It cannot reuse nodes already connected unless it links to additional unconnected nodes along its path [32]. Considering these constraints, the total number of possible APLs on a 3×3 grid amounts to 389,112 [36] (Table 1).

Table 1. Number of APL Combinations [25]

Nodes	Valid Combinations
4	1624
5	7152
6	26,016
7	72,912
8	140,704
9	140,704
Total	389,112

However, research indicates that users tend to select from a significantly smaller subset of APLs [5]. A study showed that 44% APLs were initiated from the top left-most node of the screen, and 77% APLs began in one of the four corners [25]. A significant percentage of APLs comprised just four nodes, reducing the available combinations to 1,624 (Table 1). APLs tended to move from left to right and top to bottom, contributing to the ease of guessing and reducing the password space further. APLs are susceptible to various forms of attack, owing to their limited complexity. These attacks include shoulder-surfing [6] and video-based reconstruction [38], as well as smudge-based side channel attacks [4].

Proposals for enhancing APL security have been numerous. Early studies range from modifications to mitigate shoulder-surfing [12], [39] and smudge attacks [30], [24] while retaining the primary design of APLs, to more radical suggestions such as rearranging the APL points into a ring [34] or increasing the size of the grids itself [5]. Similarly, a study in 2020 proposed Double patterns [15], or the creation of two superimposing APLs on the same 3 × 3 grid, effectively enhanced password complexity. However, this approach is unsuitable for emergent users due to its increased complexity, potentially increasing usability challenges already faced by this demographic. Password meters, proposed to enhance APL selection diversity [2], [32], may not always correlate with security and may alter user behavior through their presence [17]. Another study in 2021 [40] proposed four new unlock pattern structures - Trapezium, House 1, Circle, and House 2, comparing them to the original Android pattern. While all had similar recall rates, House 1, Circle, and House 2 patterns showed higher entropy, offering stronger security than the original. In a study conducted in 2023 [35], motion event data was collected using the Android API, which tracked the user's touch behavior while drawing a pattern, which was then analyzed to differentiate between users based on their unique touch dynamics. Similarly, another study in 2024 [41] proposed the FingerPattern method to enhance the Android pattern lock by analyzing the unique fingerprint-dependent friction sound during input.

Dimensionality. Graphical elements have multiple dimensions. For example, a simple rectangle can have a length, breadth, colour, outline colour, outline thickness, and more. It has been known that dimensions make visuals more distinct to perceive and remember. The classical paper by Miller [28] discusses the absolute judgment of humans with uni-dimensional and multi-dimensional data and their ability to retain bits of information. Miller proposed that individuals typically possess the cognitive capacity to retain, manipulate, and process approximately 7 ± 2 uni-dimensional pieces of information within their working memory.

However, some studies challenge Miller's work. For example, [10] and [27] propose dynamic frameworks influenced by chunking strategies and individual differences, suggesting that working memory capacity may fluctuate around 3 ± 2 chunks of information. The multi-component model of working memory [7] suggests separate subsystems for verbal and visuospatial information processing, indicating that working memory capacity may exceed Miller's magical number 7 through rehearsal strategies and chunked information manipulation. Another study [16] suggests that the capacity of working memory may vary depending on the sensory modality of the stimuli, emphasizing the importance of considering stimulus characteristics in understanding working memory limitations.

Despite these challenges, the incorporation of additional dimensions in stimuli generally enhances perceptual discrimination and memory performance. A study [23] demonstrated that dimensions in visual stimuli are responsible for a majority of variance in memorability through regression analysis. The study also discovered that semantic dimensions more strongly influence what is remembered than visual properties. Multiple dimensions can reduce the cognitive load associated with remembering uni-dimensional items and different semantic associations can be leveraged by individuals to remember this information, for example, through emotional or personal experiences. This finding highlights the notion that the richness of sensory information contained in multidimensional stimuli may afford greater discriminability and facilitate more robust memory representations. Therefore, incorporating additional dimensions may improve the accuracy of absolute judgment. However, to the best of our knowledge, no one has systematically explored the notion of adding dimensions to passwords to enhance their security without compromising usability and memorability.

3 Design

3.1 Enhanced versions of the Android Pattern Locks

As mentioned above, we created two enhanced versions of the APLs, one with two single-select graphical layers (Fig. 1b) and one with five (Fig. 1c). The three password mechanisms were named "Only APL", "2-Layer + APL", and "5-Layer + APL". The 2-layer version had 10 tokens for each layer, increasing the password space by 10^2. Initially, we had planned a 5-layer version with 10 tokens for each layer (increasing the password space by 10^5) but found that this made the tokens too small and intimidated emergent users in a pilot test. Hence, we switched to 4 layers with 10 tokens and 1 layer with 5 tokens, which increased the password space by 5×10^4.

The 2-layer version used icons for layer 1 and celebrity faces (we utilized faces of prominent individuals recognisable by our target users, like famous actors, politicians, and cricketers, available in the public domain) for layer 2. The 5-layer version used icons for layer 1, celebrity faces for layer 2, colours for layer 3, emojis for layer 4, and shapes for layer 5. Similar to the work of Asif et al. [3], each token was unique. None of the tokens repeated across layers or versions. This eliminated the need to remember the order of the tokens during input. A pilot test among emergent users confirmed the recognisability of each token. Tokens within each layer were shuffled randomly to counter shoulder-surfing and smudge attacks. Iterative refinement, guided by pilot study feedback from emergent users, improved token identifiability and reduced visual density. In the 5-layer version, we found that sometimes emergent users tend to get intimidated by the number of choices presented. To simplify this experience, we introduced layers sequentially, enabling participants to focus on one layer at a time.

We posit that using multiple dimensions like icons, faces, colors, shapes, and emojis offers diversity within each layer, allowing participants to encode information in various forms. This diversity may reduce the cognitive load associated with remembering a single-dimensional item, as individuals may utilize different semantic associations for processing each token. Visually distinct elements may add mnemonic dimensions, making tokens inherently memorable and aiding encoding and retrieval processes. For example, an individual may associate a specific token with a concept, an object, a memory, a feeling, or a personal experience. Furthermore, breaking down the information into smaller, manageable chunks or categories distributed across layers enhances memorability. Rather than overwhelming participants with a large amount of information presented simultaneously, the layering approach enables gradual processing and encoding of each token [28]. We developed prototypes for each version to record choices, task duration, attempts, and errors at password creation and recall. A Samsung Galaxy M11 was used as hardware to host the test prototypes.

3.2 Study Design

The objective of our study was to compare the performance of emergent users with the three versions of the APL mechanism. Through this study, we attempt to answer the following research question, "How do emergent users perform in terms of first-time usability, 4-day memorability, and time taken to set and recall the variations of the APL?" Our primary hypothesis was that adding dimensions to the APL does not affect its usability or memorability for emergent users.

In line with the research conducted by Shammee et al. [31] and Asif et al. [3], we asked participants to do two types of recall: Immediate recall and Delayed recall (interval of 4 days). Recall 1 represents the mechanism's first-time usability and immediate memorability. Emergent users may encounter challenges when learning to use a password mechanism, potentially leading to failure in recalling the password after a brief distraction task. Therefore, the success rate in the first recall serves as an indicator of the mechanism's initial usability for first-time users. Success in the second recall serves as the primary endpoint of our study, reflecting the mechanism's memorability over time or "delayed memorability". We assessed participants' success in recalling the passwords, documented any failures, identified whether the errors were in graphical layers or APLs, recorded the number of attempts made, and measured the time taken to set and recall the password. This is further outlined in the Method section below.

3.3 Method

We recruited 36 emergent users (18 female) with education less than 10 years of schooling. The age range of the participants ranged from 19 to 56 years. Among them, 30 participants had smartphones and 6 had feature phones. Out of the 6 users who had feature phones, 4 were somewhat familiar with smartphones and had interacted with them a couple of times. Refer to Table 2 for a detailed summary of the participant demographics. Each participant participated in four sessions (Each session separated by at least 4 and at the most 5 days, depending on the availability of the participant) and used the three password mechanisms (Only APL, 2-Layer + APL, and 5-Layer + APL) in a counterbalanced order. The total duration of the study per participant was 12 - 13 days.

In the first session, the participant was briefed about the study and their informed consent was taken. The participant was then trained on the first password mechanism that they were assigned to use. Participants were told to follow the standard APL rules mentioned earlier. If the participant was unfamiliar with APLs, they were given some time to understand and interact with it and then the concept of graphical layers was introduced. They were also demonstrated to use backspace. The training task was not recorded.

After the training, the participant set a password using the assigned password mechanism and confirmed it. After confirmation, they completed a distraction

Table 2. Summary of Participant Demographics (N = 36).

Demographic	Description	Number
Age	18-24 years	5
	25-34 years	8
	35-44 years	12
	45-56 years	11
Gender	Male	18
	Female	18
Education	No formal education	1
	Primary (up to Class 5)	6
	Middle (Class 6-8)	7
	Secondary (Class 9-10)	22
Experience with Smartphones	No Familiarity	2
	Basic Familiarity (0-2 years)	17
	Moderate Familiarity (2-5 years)	6
	Good Familiarity (5-10 years)	7
	Advanced Familiarity (10+ years)	5
Mobile Lock	None	7
	APL	13
	Fingerprint + APL	5
	PIN	11

task, where the participant was asked to play a simple visual memory game for 5 minutes. They then performed Recall 1.1 (the immediate recall of the first mechanism). If they couldn't recall the password, they were allowed multiple attempts until the participant gave up. For the purpose of our analysis, the attempts were capped at 10. This concluded the first session. In a subsequent session four days later, participants completed Recall 1.2, set and confirmed a password for the assigned second password mechanism, completed another distraction task, and performed Recall 2.1. Sessions three and four followed a similar pattern. After the fourth session, a post-test was administered, which assessed user behavior, difficulty ratings, and password selection strategies. Refer to Fig 2.

Participants were compensated for their time attending each session (INR 100 per session attended). Additionally, two types of incentives were provided. Firstly, since this was a multi-session study, we provided a "session bonus" to encourage them to participate in each session (INR 10 for the first session, INR 20 for the second session, INR 30 for the third session, and INR 40 for the fourth session). Secondly, to encourage participants to recall their passwords correctly, we provided them with a "successful recall bonus". If a participant was successful in recalling the Only APL condition in Recall 1 and Recall 2, they were given an INR 50 bonus. If a participant was successful in recalling both the graphical layers and the APL in 2-Layer + APL condition in Recall 1 and Recall 2, they were given an INR 100 bonus. Failing to recall a graphical layer would decrease

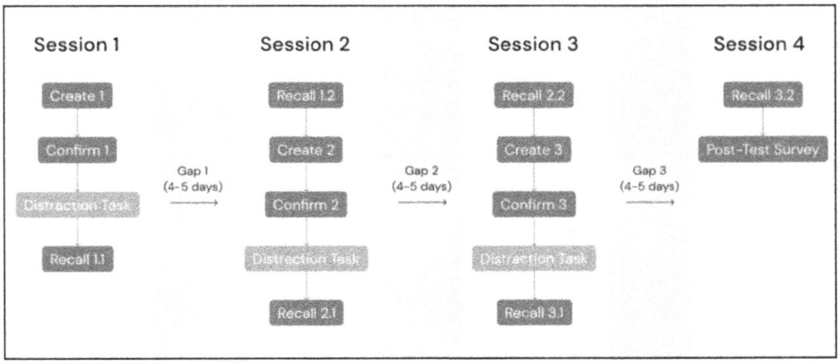

Fig. 2. Overview of Study Methodology

the bonus by INR 25 per layer as long as the APL was input correctly. In any case, if the APL was forgotten, no bonus would be given for that condition. Similarly, in 5-Layer + APL, a maximum of INR 150 was allotted to each participant. Failure per graphical layer would decrease the bonus by INR 25 and a recall failure due to APL would result in no bonus for this condition. The stakes involved mirrored real-life scenarios in which a password has a value attached to it. Hence, those who attended all four scheduled sessions were compensated a minimum of INR 500 and a maximum of INR 800. Participants were informed about the incentives before taking their informed consent.

Thus, we conducted a systematic, within-subjects, counterbalanced four-day recall study with emergent users, which had one independent variable (Type of Password Mechanism) with 3 levels (Only APL, 2 Layers + APL, and 5-layers + APL), and 6 dependent variables, namely Recall 1 success (Usability), Recall 2 success (Memorability), Time taken to create the passwords, Time taken for Recall 1, Time taken for Recall 2, and the Number of attempts taken. No repetition of tokens and shuffling of tokens were treated as control variables for this study.

4 Results

4.1 Success Rates

As previously mentioned, the success rate in Recall 1 reflects the usability of the password mechanism, while the success rate in Recall 2 (after 4 days) reflects memorability. The results are summarised in Table 2. As seen in Recall 1, all participants were successful in all 3 password mechanisms. In Recall 2, two participants failed in the Only APL (95% C.I. = [80.91%, 99.41%]) condition and two participants failed in the 2-Layer + APL (95% C.I. = [80.91%, 99.41%]) condition, while all were successful in the 5-Layer + APL (95% C.I. = [88.53%, 100%]). As hypothesised, the difference between conditions was not significant (X^2 = 2.076, p = 0.1496). This was our primary endpoint. To our surprise, no failures were recorded in the most complex condition (5-Layer + APL).

Table 3. Success rates of the 3 password mechanisms in Recall 1, Recall 2 (All participants), and Recall 2 (only those participants who were successful in Recall 2). The last row also presents the results of the Chi-Square test.

	Recall 1 (First Time Usability)			Recall 2 (4-Day Memorability)		
	Only APL	**2-Layers + APL**	**5-Layers + APL**	**Only APL**	**2-Layers + APL**	**5-Layers + APL**
Success	36	36	36	34	34	36
Failure	0	0	0	2	2	0
Total	36	36	36	36	36	36
Proportion(%)	100.00%	100.00%	100.00%	94.44%	94.44%	100.00%
95% C.I. from	88.53%	88.53%	88.53%	80.91%	80.91%	88.53%
95% C.I. to	100%*	100%*	100%*	99.41%	99.41%	100%*
	$\chi^2 < 0.0005, p = 1.000$			$\chi^2 = 2.076, p = 0.1496$		

4.2 Time Taken

The time taken to input password mechanisms indirectly informs the choice emergent users make while setting up their passwords. Most often users want a password that can be entered quickly. Although the time taken to set up and recall the password was not our primary endpoint, we report the data here to inform the design of future graphical password mechanisms for emergent users. Table 3 and Fig. 3 summarise the time taken to set up, the time taken for Recall 1, and the time taken for Recall 2 for each password mechanism. In both Recall 1 and Recall 2, the time taken includes aggregated attempt time until successful entry or until the 10th attempt.

Table 4. Time taken (in seconds) for Recall 1 and Recall 2 in all 3 password mechanisms.

	Setup Time			Recall 1 Time			Recall 2 Time		
	Only APL	**2-Layers + APL**	**5-Layers + APL**	**Only APL**	**2-Layers + APL**	**5-Layers + APL**	**Only APL**	**2-Layers + APL**	**5-Layers + APL**
N	36	36	36	36	36	36	36	36	36
Mean	17.92	34.97	55.36	3.06	8.56	20.03	14.56	23.44	45.42
95% C.I. from	14.126	26.465	47.631	2.44	7.34	15.56	2.20	10.92	29.50
95% C.I. to	21.707	43.48	63.091	3.67	9.77	24.50	26.91	35.97	61.33
	F = 46.426, p < 0.0005			F = 47.038, p < 0.0005			F = 7.773, p = 0.002		

A repeated measures ANOVA revealed that there was a statistically significant effect of the password mechanism on the time taken to set up the passwords ($F(1, 34) = 46.426$, $p < 0.0005$, observed power = 1.000). Post hoc comparisons using Bonferroni correction found that the mean value of time taken for setup was statistically significant between all 3 password mechanisms: Only APL and 2-Layers + APL ($p = 0.001$, 95% C.I. = [-27.0791, -6.320]); 2-Layers + APL and 5-Layer + APL ($p < 0.0005$, 95% C.I. = [-30.451, -10.327]); and, Only APL

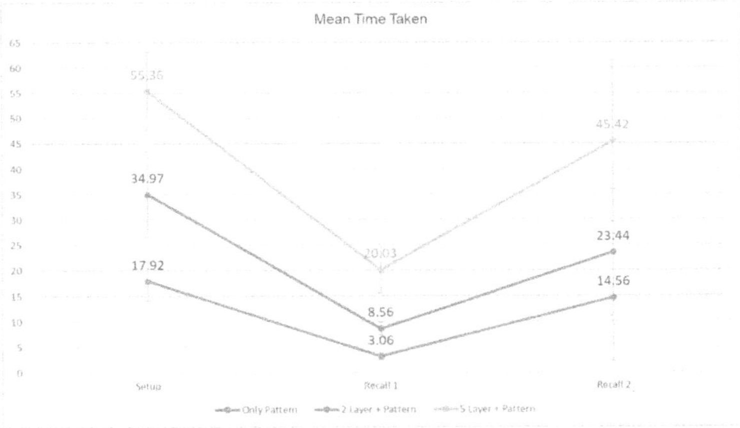

Fig. 3. Mean Time Taken in Recall 1 and 2 in all 3 password mechanisms.

and 5-Layer + APL ($p < 0.0005$, 95% C.I. = [-47.161, -27.728]). The setup time for each password mechanism understandably increases with the addition of multiple graphical layers (2 and 5) to the APL.

Similarly, a repeated measures ANOVA revealed there was a significant effect of the password mechanism on the time taken for Recall 1 ($F(2,33) = 55.817$, $p < 0.0005$, observed power = 1.000) with a grand mean of 10.546 (95% C.I. = [8.963, 12.129]) seconds, where the average time taken for Recall 1 of 5-Layers + APL was approximately double of 2-Layers + APL. Post hoc comparisons using Bonferroni correction found that the mean value of time taken for Recall 1 was statistically significant between all 3 password mechanisms: Only APL and 2-Layers + APL ($p < 0.0005$, 95% C.I. = [-7.013, -3.987]); 2-Layers + APL and 5-Layer + APL ($p < 0.0005$, 95% C.I. = [-16.768, -6.177]); and, Only APL and 5-Layer + APL ($p < 0.0005$, 95% C.I. = [-22.459, -11.486]).

Lastly, a repeated measures ANOVA revealed there was a significant effect of the password mechanism on the time taken for Recall 2 ($F(2,33) = 7.988$, $p = 0.001$, observed power = 0.937) with a grand mean of 27.806 seconds (95% C.I. = [17.047, 38.566]), which is quite larger than Recall 1. This can be partially attributed to the 4-day gap between the two recalls. Post hoc comparisons using Bonferroni correction found that the mean value of time taken for Recall 2 was statistically significant between Only APL and 5-Layers + APL ($p = 0.001$, 95% C.I. = -50.394, -11.328]) and 2-Layers + APL and 5-Layer + APL ($p = 0.016$, 95% C.I. = [-40.571, -3.373]). The difference between Only APL and 2-Layers + APL was not significant ($p = 0.618$).

A linear regression analysis depicted a small but significant effect of the number of graphical layers and setup time ($F(1, 106) = 59.875$, $p < 0.0005$), with an R^2 value of 0.361, indicating that 36.1% of the variance in setup time may be explained by the number of graphical layers. Similarly, the linear regression analysis depicted an even smaller but significant effect of the number of graphical layers and Recall 2 time (F(1, 106) = 10.83, p = 0.001), with an R^2 value of 0.09, indicating that only 9% of the variance in setup time may be explained by the number of graphical layers. Each graphical layer adds about 8.3 seconds to the setup time and about 6.9 seconds to the Recall 2 time. The predicted setup time (t_{setup}) and recall time ($t_{recall2}$) taken for a password mechanism with l number of graphical layers can be stated as:

$$t_{setup} = (18.069 \pm 3.055) + (8.314 \pm 1.074) \times l \tag{1}$$

$$t_{recall2} = (12.75 \pm 6.00) + (6.94 \pm 2.11) \times l \tag{2}$$

We noticed that women take longer to set up passwords compared to men. We found that the mean difference of 15.019 seconds (p = 0.002, 95% C.I. = [6.044, 23.993]). However, gender does not significantly impact the setup time of the three password mechanisms (p = 0.303). Tests of Between-Subject Effects also revealed that the interaction of gender and password mechanism on recall 1 time is statistically significant (F = 4.732, p = 0.037, observed power = 0.561). There is almost no difference in Only APL between men and women, however, the difference in time taken for immediate recall between the genders seems to increase as the number of layers in the password mechanisms increases. In Recall 2 the interaction between gender and password mechanism is not significant (p = 0.227), unlike Recall 1. The mean time taken for Recall 2 between females (Mean = 28.148 s, 95% C.I. = [12.930, 43.366]) and Males (Mean = 27.463 s, 95% C.I. = [12.245, 42.681]) are almost equivalent. However, it can be observed that the mean time for Recall 2 in 2-Layers + APL (Mean = 19.000 s, 95% C.I. = [1.139, 36.861]) and 3 (Mean = 52.944 s, 95% C.I. = [30.389, 75.499]) among females has quite a difference. Due to sociological differences, women may tend to have less exposure to technology which may have contributed to these findings. Since this was not something that we had hypothesised, we did not investigate this issue systematically. It could be a part of future work.

4.3 Number of Attempts

We did not restrict the number of attempts taken by participants, however, none of the participants who took more than 7 attempts were successful (See Table 4). Hence, for the purpose of this analysis, the number of attempts were capped at 10. Only one participant (who had taken 27 attempts before giving up) was thus capped at 10 attempts, the second highest number of attempts being 8 (gave up). Participants who used APLs on their own devices were used to entering the APL rapidly, which was occasionally not recognized by the prototype used in this study, leading to multiple attempts before a successful entry. However, as the study was counter-balanced, these errors did not affect the overall study.

We employed Friedmann's test (as the number of attempts was taken as an ordinal variable) and found no significant differences between all 3 password mechanisms in the number of attempts taken by emergent users in Recall 1 (asymptotic $\chi^2 = 2.000, P = 0.368$) or Recall 2 (asymptotic $\chi^2 = 1.105, P =$

0.575). As seen in Table 4, the mean number of attempts taken by participants in Recall 1 (Immediate Recall) is considerably less than the mean number of attempts taken in Recall 2 (Only successful participants). Thus, the graphical layers don't seem to add to the number of attempts required by participants during recalls.

Table 5. Number of Attempts for Recall 1, Recall 2 (All Participants) and Recall 2 (Successful Only).

	Recall 1 Attempts			Recall 2 Attempts (All Participants)			Recall 2 Attempts (Only Successful Participants)		
	Only APL	**2-Layers + APL**	**5-Layers + APL**	**Only APL**	**2-Layers + APL**	**5-Layers + APL**	**Only APL**	**2-Layers + APL**	**5-Layers + APL**
N	36	36	36	36	36	36	33	33	33
Mean	1.06	1.03	1.11	1.64	1.50	1.75	1.21	1.21	1.55
Minimum	1	1	1	1	1	1	1	1	1
Maximum	2	2	2	8	10	7	2	4	7
Mean Rank	1.99	1.94	2.05	2.04	1.93	2.03	1.98	1.94	2.08
	$\chi^2 = 2.000$, $p* = 0.368$			$\chi^2 = 0.776$, $p* = 0.679$			$\chi^2 = 1.105$, $p* = 0.575$		

*Asymptotic significance

4.4 Attempt and Failure Analysis

In recalls where participants needed multiple attempts, we analyzed the errors that participants made in each attempt. Tables 5 and 6 record the part of the password mechanism where errors occurred in 2-Layer + APL and 5-Layer + APL password mechanisms respectively. Most participants were able to recall the graphical layers easily but had difficulty recalling the APLs. One probable reason could be that participants were instructed to create 3 different APLs throughout the duration of the study - a new APL for each password mechanism tested. This may have caused confusion in recalling the correct APL. This could also have been a technical limitation of our prototype, which was a web app (i.e. not a native Android app). Many participants rapidly entered their APL which was sometimes too fast for the testing prototype. These errors have been marked with a * in Tables 5 and 6.

All participants successfully recalled the shape layer (perhaps due to fewer items in the shape layer). Difficulty with the emoji layer was primarily due to confusion between specific emojis (for example, emoji 6 and 8 in Fig. 1c). Errors in the Color Layer mostly stemmed from confusion between light and dark versions of the same hue (for example, light blue and dark blue). APL-related errors included forgetting the APL, rapid entry, confusion with earlier APLs, or misclicks. Recall success rates were 97.22% in Recall 1 and 83.33% in

Table 6. Analysis of errors and attempts for 2-Layer + APL. Areas where participants did not make an error are marked with a tick mark, whereas areas where the error occurred are marked with a cross.

Participant	Recall	Icon	Passface	APL	Total Attempts
P02	1	✓	✓	×*	2
P05	2	✓	×	✓	2
P10	2	✓	✓	×	3
P12	2	✓	✓	×*	2
P27	2	✓	✓	×	10
P31	2	×	✓	×	4
P34	2	✓	✓	×	3
Total = 7		1	1	6	

Table 7. Analysis of errors and attempts for 5-Layer + APL. Areas where participants did not make an error are marked with a tick mark, whereas areas where the error occurred are marked with a cross.

Participant	Recall	Icon	Passface	colour	Emoji	Shape	APL	Total Attempts
P03	2	✓	✓	✓	✓	✓	×	2
P05	1	×	✓	✓	✓	✓	✓	2
P05	2	×	×	✓	×	✓	×	6
P06	2	✓	✓	✓	×	✓	✓	2
P09	1	✓	✓	✓	✓	✓	×	2
P11	1	✓	✓	✓	×	✓	×	2
P24	1	✓	✓	✓	✓	✓	×	2
P25	2	×	✓	✓	✓	✓	✓	2
P26	2	✓	×	×	×	✓	✓	7
P27	2	✓	✓	×	✓	✓	×	4
P31	2	✓	✓	✓	✓	✓	×	3
P33	2	✓	✓	✓	✓	✓	×*	3
P34	2	✓	✓	✓	✓	✓	×	3
Total = 13		3	2	2	4	0	9	

Recall 2 for 2-Layers + APL, and 88.88% in Recall 1 and 75% in Recall 2 for 5-Layers + APL.

We also analyzed the failures in all 3 password mechanisms. See two examples in Fig. 4. Recall 1 had no recorded failures while Recall 2 had 4 recorded failures: 2 in Only APL and 2 in 2-Layers + APL. Out of the 4 failures, 2 were by the same participant. 5-Layers + APL recorded no failures. Commonalities were observed among the four instances of failure, all of which were attributed solely to difficulties in recalling APLs. Notably, participants did not encounter issues with forgetting any of the graphical layers, suggesting a distinct challenge specifically with APL memorization. In cases of failures, we showed the participants the APL they had set and asked them to describe it. These participants struggled to describe their APLs as they did not resemble recognizable shapes or letters. Additionally, three out of the four failures occurred as the second or third APL in sequence, indicating a propensity for confusion with previously set passwords. Further APL analyses were conducted regarding the security of the

APLs created by emergent users, their visual complexity, and similarities, however, APL analysis is out of the scope of this paper. Future work may provide in-depth analyses of the same.

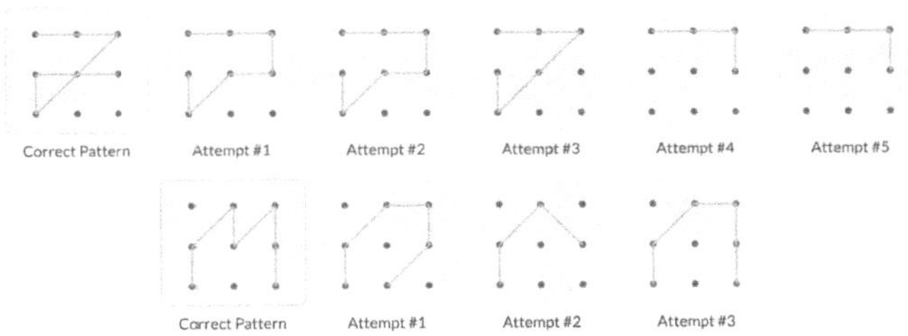

Fig. 4. 2 Cases of attempts taken and APLs created before recorded failures.

4.5 Popularity of Graphical Layers

We analyzed the choices in graphical layers to understand biases that may exist in them. By performing binomial two-tailed goodness-of-fit tests, we were able to determine the p values of items and their probability of selection. Please refer to Fig. 1b and 1c and Table 7. It was interesting to note that Sindhutai Sapkal (who was chosen 3 times) was only chosen by female participants. In 5-Layer + APL, The Icon Layer showed balanced selections in the 5-Layers + APL. Anil Kapoor and MS Dhoni were primarily chosen by males while Indira Gandhi was primarily chosen by females. In the Colour Layer, warmer colors like Red, Yellow, and Pink had the most selections (72.22%) with Red itself having 33.33%. Gender differences were noted in the emoji layer, with men preferring Angry and Teasing and women preferring Smiling. In qualitative analyses, men expressed that they were angry often ("*Mujhe gussa bohot aata hai*") and so they chose this emoji. Women more often expressed that staying happy and laughing is important ("*Humesha haste rehna chahiye*") and so they chose the same. The Annoying emoji was the most ambiguous among participants with diverse interpretations like "normal", "sleeping", "angry" and "eyes closed". The difficulty in nomenclature or assigning meaning to arbitrary items may lead to a lack of selections by participants. In the Shapes Layer, the Heart and Star were chosen most (83.33%), with women preferring the heart shape and men preferring the star shape. Square and circle shapes were chosen only once. Out of all the layers, Icons and celebrity faces seem to be the least biased layers overall. Eliminating tokens like the Apple icon, Narendra Modi, and Amitabh Bachchan, that create bias in the layers would produce balanced and arguably more secure graphical layers (Table 8).

Table 8. Analysis of popularity of tokens in graphical layers. Positions of the tokens with respect to Fig. 1 are mentioned in brackets in the token column.

Enhanced version	Graphical Layer	Token (position)	Frequency (Out of 36)	Percentage	p-value
2-Layer + APL	Icon	Apple (4)	8	22.22%	0.024
2-Layer + APL	Icon	Lightning (8)	0	0.00%	0.046
2-Layer + APL	Celebrity Faces	Narendra Modi (4)	14	38.89%	< 0.0005
2-Layer + APL	Celebrity Faces	Aishwarya Rai (2)	0	0.00%	0.046
2-Layer + APL	Celebrity Faces	Mamta Banerjee (3)	0	0.00%	0.046
2-Layer + APL	Celebrity Faces	Sai Tamhankar (7)	0	0.00%	0.046
5-Layer + APL	Celebrity Faces	Amitabh Bachchan (1)	12	33.33%	0.0001
5-Layer + APL	Celebrity Faces	Dada Kondke (10)	0	0.00%	0.046
5-Layer + APL	Celebrity Faces	Hema Malini (2)	0	0.00%	0.046
5-Layer + APL	Celebrity Faces	Pratibha Patil (8)	0	0.00%	0.046
5-Layer + APL	Colour	Red (1)	12	33.33%	0.0001
5-Layer + APL	Colour	Brown (6)	0	0.00%	0.046
5-Layer + APL	Colour	Light Green (8)	0	0.00%	0.046
5-Layer + APL	Emoji	Teasing (7)	11	30.56%	0.0006
5-Layer + APL	Emoji	Laughing (6)	8	22.22%	0.0235
5-Layer + APL	Emoji	Annoyed (9)	0	0.00%	0.046
5-Layer + APL	Emoji	Frowning (10)	0	0.00%	0.046
5-Layer + APL	Shape	Heart (5)	19	52.78%	< 0.0005
5-Layer + APL	Shape	Star (3)	11	30.56%	0.1411

4.6 Qualitative Responses

At the end of the study, the participants responded to a post-test questionnaire (see responses in Fig. 5) and were asked to openly comment on the three password mechanisms. As expected, ratings showed 'Only APL' as easiest but less secure and engaging, '5-Layers + APL' as most secure but less easy to use/recall, and '2-Layers + APL' as balanced in ease of use/recall and perceived security/engagement.

Participants were also asked to select one of 3 password mechanisms as their preferred mechanism and give their reasons for the same. Participants did not indicate any particular trend in their preferences (13 participants chose 'Only APL', 13 chose '2-Layers + APL', and 10 chose '5-Layer + APL'). Participants preferring the 'Only APL' mechanism found it easy, fast, and less error-prone, which may be attributed to the original APL being easy to enter as it gets registered in one's muscle memory over time. In case they made an error in other mechanisms, they would have to enter the entire password all over again, leading to frustration. Participants preferring the '2-Layer + APL' mechanism appreciated its memorability and enjoyed selecting favorite icons/celebrity faces, despite slightly longer input times. They considered it safer than 'Only APL'. Engaging passwords may be more memorable, even if slightly time-consuming. Participants preferring the '5-Layers + APL' mechanism valued its security with multiple layers and shuffled tokens, despite concerns about misclicks and mental

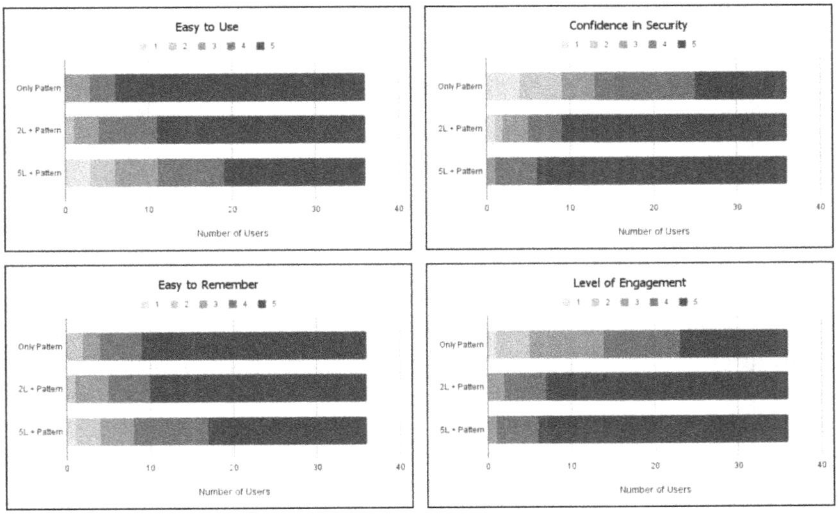

Fig. 5. Participant Ratings gathered on a 5-point Likert Scale for the 3 password mechanisms regarding easy to use (1=very hard to use, 5 = very easy to use), confidence in security (1= very unconfident, 5= very confident), easy to remember (1=very hard to remember, 5 = very easy to remember), and level of engagement (1=very unengaging, 5 = very engaging).

workload. Yet no misclicks were observed in the study in the graphical layers for any of the participants, with a few observed during APL input. Many participants stated that '5-Layers + APL' seemed difficult to use, but with practice, they were confident that they could recall it. Although recalling the 5-layer password demanded attention, participants rarely forgot it.

We also performed an affinity analysis utilizing the data gathered from the post-test sessions, encompassing insights into user experiences, encountered challenges, notable observations, and rationales behind their selections. Many participants opted for graphical items due to their memorability, personal preferences, popularity, or relevance to their daily lives or identities (for example, participants who worked as security guards often chose a star in the shape layer because they associated the star with their uniform). Frequently, participants indicated that if their preferred selection appeared in a specific password mechanism, they labeled it as their favorite, regardless of the number of layers involved. The icon and celebrity face layers were clear and straightforward for participants to distinguish between. Many participants found faces enjoyable to interact with, particularly because they could select their favorite celebrities. Colors and shapes were deemed the easiest to recall, while emojis presented a challenge for some participants, particularly those with limited prior exposure to them.

Emojis are culturally rooted. The emoji layer presented ambiguity for our participants because they could not assign meaning to them. This underscores the necessity for meaningful items and layers that are easily 'nameable' or identifiable. Particularly, emojis such as "Annoyed" (9) and "Frowning" (10) proved challenging for participants to interpret, often leading to misidentifications such as "sleeping," "normal," or "angry" (Translated). Emojis like "happy" (3) and "teasing" (7) caused confusion because of their emotional resemblance. Additionally, the "crying" (8) and "laughing" (6) emojis were often associated with the tears depicted, leading participants to mistake the laughing emoji for crying.

Our study included some participants who were new to smartphones and had never interacted with them before. Many of these participants expressed difficulty with lock mechanisms and often relied on default settings for passwords, indicating that setting up passwords seemed complicated to them. Interestingly, participants who were not accustomed to smartphones found APLs challenging, while graphical layers were easier for them to grasp. New smartphone users tended to prefer graphical layers over APLs. Some participants noted that recalling difficult APLs was more challenging than recalling five graphical layers. This suggests that graphical passwords are not only easier to use but also preferred by new smartphone users from our demographic.

5 Discussion and Conclusion

We developed two enhanced versions of the APL to increase their security by adding dimensions comprising single-select graphical layers. By design, we made sure the password space of these enhanced versions was greater than the original APL. The shuffling of tokens enhanced the security further. We compared the three password mechanisms in a systematic, within-subjects, counterbalanced four-day recall study with 36 emergent users. There were no significant differences in the success rates between the original APL and the enhanced versions in all recalls. We demonstrated that it is possible to increase the security of a password mechanism without compromising its usability and memorability. Leveraging recognition-over-recall in the design of graphical passwords could provide more accessible authentication methods that benefit many emergent users. Further research could explore the long-term usability and memorability of the enhanced APLs. To the best of our knowledge, our study is the first that establishes that adding dimensions to a password can enhance the security of password mechanisms without reducing their memorability and usability even among emergent users.

We found that the first-time usability of all 3 mechanisms was equivalent, with a success rate of 100% (95% C.I. = [88.53%, 100%]), indicating good usability. However, the study had only 36 participants and could be slightly underpowered (Power = 0.771). The 4-day memorability of all 3 mechanisms had no significant differences with similar success rates of 94.44% (95% C.I. = [80.91%, 99.41%]) for Only APL and 2-Layer + APL, and 100% (95% C.I. = [88.53%, 100%]) for 5-Layer + APL, concluding that the enhanced versions of the APL were as memorable as the original.

An interesting finding was that the most complex condition, i.e. 5-Layer + APL had a 100% success rate (95% C.I. = [88.53%, 100%]) among emergent users. Several participants noted that initially, the screen with five layers seemed slightly intimidating, leading them to carefully consider their selections assuming they might struggle to remember. However, during the recall phase, they found the task surprisingly easy as they only had to locate their selection within the group of options rather than recall an exact value. This heightened attention during input could have contributed to a higher success rate. Nonetheless, given the relatively small sample size of 36 participants, the study may have been underpowered. Follow-up studies with a larger participant pool may provide a more accurate analysis.

Although the enhanced versions understandably took longer to set up (8.3 seconds per layer), the set-up process would occur only once during the creation of the password. Recall time also increased (by 6.9 seconds per layer). The extended input time presents a notable drawback, particularly for daily usage scenarios. However, enhanced security mechanisms may be better suited for relatively less frequent tasks, and hence the extra time required may not be of concern. Future research could investigate the application of enhanced APLs in scenarios where passwords are used infrequently, such as net banking. Qualitative analyses revealed that participants perceived the creation and recall of the enhanced APLs as akin to a memory game rather than a conventional password mechanism for data security. This experience was characterized by heightened engagement and positive reception among participants. Participants demonstrated a willingness to invest additional time in locating their tokens due to the engaging nature of the process.

We also observed considerable bias in user preferences towards certain tokens in some graphical layers. For example, 52.78% participants picked the heart in the shape layer ($p < 0.0005$), out of which 63.1% were women. Most participants (72.22%) chose warmer colours like Red, Yellow, and Pink. This difference may be attributed to the specific hex colours chosen in this study. Future studies could consider exploring the appropriateness and balance of colors within our cultural context. Overall, however, adding graphical layers prior to the APL will not increase the practical password space unless there is enough variance in the tokens chosen. Layers like icons and celebrity faces are relatively unbiased and may provide sufficient variance and security even if users create simple APLs.

Participants found icons, celebrity faces, colours, and shapes easier to distinguish between than emojis. In hindsight, the choice of our emojis (the layer where some users faced some difficulties) could have been better. All emojis chosen in our study were yellow, similar in size and shape and some had expressions varying only in degree (for example, laughing (6) and smiling (3)). Not only should choices of tokens be nameable, but they should also be nameable by emergent users. The nameability of tokens would allow stronger association and better recall. Interpretation of tokens may be culturally dependent. Interpretations of tokens by researchers may not match the interpretations by emergent users (for example, researchers interpreted emoji 9 as "annoyed", however, some participants interpreted it as "sleeping," "normal," or "angry". Tokens need to be systematically evaluated with target users before use. Tokens also need to be distinct from each other.

All failures recorded were due to participants forgetting their APLs and none were due to the graphical layers. This could be because the study protocol instructed each participant to create three different APLs. These participants created complex APLs that were difficult to recall after 4 days. Remembering multiple single-select graphical layers was a much easier task than recalling newly set complex APLs, as per many emergent users. Future research could determine the threshold at which the number of graphical layers becomes too excessive. Additionally, most attempts revealed that most errors in attempts occurred in APLs, suggesting that single-select graphical layers may exhibit lower error rates compared to APLs. Future research could further investigate the scalability and optimal configuration of graphical layers to improve authentication experiences for emergent users.

We argue that the graphical layers are inherently scalable. The scalability opportunities include increasing the number of graphical layers, increasing the number of tokens per layer, expanding the number of selections per layer (moving away from single-select), introducing multiple screens of graphical layers preceding the APL lock, and utilizing tokens with concepts more familiar and clear to emergent users, such as food, fruits or other culturally significant tokens. Personalisation of the graphical layers is another avenue that may be explored. While there could be a limit to the number of graphical layers that can be used in a particular password by a user, we do not see any limit to the number of unique graphical layers that can be created. This could (potentially) help emergent users change passwords (by completely changing some or all graphical layers), without causing confusion. This approach may open doors for adoption in various domains, such as financial institutions, that remain an intimidating experience for most emergent users due to multiple authentication rounds. By harnessing the high memorability and usability of graphical layers, institutions can enhance security without burdening emergent users with the need to learn the Latin script.

Several limitations should be acknowledged in this study. Firstly, the number of participants recruited for this study was only 36, which limited the number of errors observed in our dataset and indicated a potentially underpowered analysis. Future investigations could benefit from recruiting a larger and more diverse participant pool to better explore the implications of the findings across various demographic groups. Secondly, due to time constraints, the number of recalls and the duration between Recall 1 and Recall 2 were limited. Including an additional recall could provide insights into the long-term memorability of the enhanced APLs. Thirdly, the emergent user corpus in this study predominantly comprises lower-income residents of Mumbai and migrant workers who have relocated to Mumbai. Incorporating participants from a broader geographic spectrum (including rural areas) would offer a more nuanced insight into how the regional localization of the corpus impacts both password selection and memorability. Furthermore, notable trends emerged where specific tokens were favored by a substantial portion of participants, potentially skewing the overall distribution of password choices. A subsequent study that excludes these highly prevalent tokens could yield a more reliable and impartial distribution of password selections. These limitations underscore the necessity for future research endeavors to mitigate these constraints by increasing the sample size, integrating additional recall sessions, diversifying participant demographics, and investigating the ramifications of excluding commonly chosen tokens.

References

1. Adams, A., Sasse, A.: Users are not the enemy. Commun. ACM **42**, 40–46 (1999). https://doi.org/10.1145/322796.322806
2. Andriotis, P., Tryfonas, T., Oikonomou, G.: Complexity metrics and user strength perceptions of the pattern-lock graphical authentication method. In: Tryfonas, T., Askoxylakis, I. (eds.) Human Aspects of Information Security, Privacy, and Trust, pp. 115–126. Springer, Cham (2014). https://doi.org/10.1007/978-3-319-07620-1_11
3. Asif, Z., et al.: Graphical passwords for emergent users: a four-day recall comparative study on PIN, passfaces and celebrities. In: Indian Conference on Human-Computer Interaction, Dehradun (2023)
4. Aviv, A., et al.: Smudge attacks on smartphone touch screens. In: Proceedings of the 4th USENIX Conference on Offensive Technologies, WOOT'10 (2010)
5. Aviv, A.J., Budzitowski, D., Kuber, R.: Is bigger better? Comparing user-generated passwords on 3x3 vs. 4x4 grid sizes for android's pattern unlock. In: Proceedings of the 31st Annual Computer Security Applications Conference. ACSAC '15. New York, NY, USA: Association for Computing Machinery, pp. 301–310 (2015). https://doi.org/10.1145/2818000.2818014
6. Aviv, A.J., et al.: Towards baselines for shoulder surfing on mobile authentication. In: Proceedings of the 33rd Annual Computer Security Applications Conference, pp. 486–498 (2017). https://doi.org/10.1145/3134600.3134609
7. Baddeley, A.D., Hitch, G.: Working memory. In: Bower. G.H. (ed.) Psychology of Learning and Motivation, vol. 8, pp. 47–89. Academic Press (1974). https://doi.org/10.1016/S0079-7421(08)60452-1
8. Balkrishan, D., et al.: Making and breaking the user-usage model: WhatsApp adoption amongst emergent users in India. In: Proceedings of the 8th Indian Conference on Human-Computer Interaction. IndiaHCI '16. Association for Computing Machinery, New York, NY, USA, pp. 52–63 (2016). https://doi.org/10.1145/3014362.3014367
9. Blonder, G.E.: Graphical password (1996). https://www.freepatentsonline.com/5559961.html
10. Cowan, N.: The magical number 4 in short-term memory: a reconsideration of mental storage capacity. Behav. Brain Sci. **24**(1), 87–114 (2001). https://doi.org/10.1017/S0140525X01003922
11. Davis, D., Monrose, F., Reiter, M.: On user choice in graphical password schemes (2004). https://www.semanticscholar.org/paper/On-User-Choice-in-Graphical-Password-Schemes-Davis-Monrose/25f4ac8e021b7304227e0d3f4ce01741b0ce9f92

12. De Luca, A., et al.: Now you see me, now you don't: protecting smartphone authentication from shoulder surfers. In: Proceedings of the SIGCHI Conference on Human Factors in Computing Systems. CHI '14. Association for Computing Machinery, New York, NY, USA, pp. 2937–2946 (2014). https://doi.org/10.1145/2556288.2557097
13. Joshi, D.A.: Technology adoption by emergent' users: the user-usage model. In: Proceedings of the 11th Asia Pacific Conference on Computer Human Interaction. APCHI '13. Association for Computing Machinery, New York, NY, USA, pp. 28–38 (2013). https://doi.org/10.1145/2525194.2525209
14. Dhamija, R., Perrig. A.: Deja Vu: a user study using images for authentication (2000)
15. Forman, T., Aviv, A.: Double patterns: a usable solution to increase the security of android unlock patterns. In: Proceedings of the 36th Annual Computer Security Applications Conference. ACSAC '20. Association for Computing Machinery, New York, NY, USA, pp. 219–233 (2020). https://doi.org/10.1145/3427228.3427252
16. Fougnie, D., Marois, R.: What limits working memory capacity? Evidence for modality-specific sources to the simultaneous storage of visual and auditory arrays. J. Exp. Psychol. Learn. Memory Cogn. **37**(6), 1329–1341 (2011). https://doi.org/10.1037/a0024834
17. Golla, M., et al.: Work in progress: on the in-accuracy and influence of android pattern strength meters. In: Proceedings 2019 Workshop on Usable Security. Internet Society, San Diego, CA (2019). https://doi.org/10.14722/usec.2019.23025
18. Hai, T., Carlisle, A.: Pass-go: a proposal to improve the usability of graphical passwords. Int. J. Netw. Secur. **7** (2008)
19. Jermyn, I., et al.: The design and analysis of graphical passwords. In: Proceedings of the 8th conference on USENIX Security Symposium, vol. 8, p. 1. SSYM'99. USENIX Association. USA (1999)
20. Kant, V., Joshi, A.: Challenges in supporting the emergent user. In: Proceedings of the 9th Indian Conference on Human Computer Interaction, pp. 67–70. ACM, Bangalore India (2018). https://doi.org/10.1145/3297121.3297131
21. Keating, P.: How predictable is your PIN number? (2012). https://ascentor.co.uk/cyber-security-resources/how-predictable-isyour-pin-number/
22. Kotadia, M.: Microsoft: write down your passwords (2005). https://www.zdnet.com/article/microsoft-write-down-your-passwords/
23. Kramer, M.A., et al.: The features underlying the memorability of objects. Sci. Adv. **9**(17), eadd2981 (2023). https://doi.org/10.1126/sciadv.add2981
24. Kwon, T., Na, S.: TinyLock: affordable defense against smudge attacks on smartphone pattern lock systems. Comput. Secur. **42** (2013). https://doi.org/10.1016/j.cose.2013.12.001
25. Løge, M.D.: Tell me who you are and I will tell you your unlock pattern, MA thesis, NTNU (2015). https://ntnuopen.ntnu.no/ntnuxmlui/handle/11250/2380967
26. Markert, P., et al.: This PIN can be easily guessed: analyzing the security of smartphone unlock PINs. In: 2020 IEEE Symposium on Security and Privacy (SP), pp. 286–303 (2020). https://doi.org/10.1109/SP40000.2020.00100
27. Mathy, F., Feldman, J.: What's magic about magic numbers? Chunking and data compression in short-term memory. Cognition **122**(3), 346–362 (2012). https://doi.org/10.1016/j.cognition.2011.11.003
28. Miller, G.A.: The magical number seven, plus or minus two: some limits on our capacity for processing information. Psychol. Rev. **63**(2), 81–97 (1956). https://doi.org/10.1037/h0043158

29. Newhouse, W.: Multifactor authentication for e-commerce, Technical report, NIST SP 1800-17. National Institute of Standards and Technology, Gaithersburg, MD, NIST SP 1800–17 (2019). https://doi.org/10.6028/NIST.SP.1800-17
30. Schneegass, S., et al.: SmudgeSafe: geometric image transformations for smudge-resistant user authentication. In: Proceedings of the 2014 ACM International Joint Conference on Pervasive and Ubiquitous Computing, pp. 775–786. UbiComp '14. Association for Computing Machinery, New York, NY, USA (2014). https://doi.org/10.1145/2632048.2636090
31. Shammee, I.T., et al.: A systematic literature review of graphical password schemes. J. Comput. Sci. Eng. **14**(4), 163–185 (2020). https://doi.org/10.5626/JCSE.2020.14.4.163
32. Shammee, I.T., et al.: A systematic literature review of graphical password schemes. J. Comput. Sci. Eng. **14**(4), 163–185 (2020). https://doi.org/10.1016/j.jisa.2014.10.009
33. Suo, X., Zhu, Y., Owen, G.: Graphical passwords: a survey, p. 472 (2005). https://doi.org/10.1109/CSAC.2005.27
34. Tupsamudre, H., et al.: Pass-roll and pass-scroll: new graphical user interfaces for improving text passwords. In: Proceedings 2nd European Workshop on Usable Security. Internet Society, Paris, France (2017). https://doi.org/10.14722/eurousec.2017.23004
35. Tusko, G., Meng, W., Lampe, B.: Look closer to touch behavior-enabled android pattern locks: a study in the wild. In: 2023 IEEE 22nd International Conference on Trust, Security and Privacy in Computing and Communications (TrustCom), pp. 1196–1205 (2023). https://doi.org/10.1109/TrustCom60117.2023.00163
36. Uellenbeck, S., et al.: Quantifying the security of graphical passwords: the case of android unlock patterns. In: Proceedings of the 2013 ACM SIGSAC Conference on Computer and Communications Security, pp. 161–172. CCS '13. Association for Computing Machinery, New York, NY, USA (2013). https://doi.org/10.1145/2508859.2516700
37. Varenhorst, C., Van Kleek, M., Rudolph, L.: Passdoodles; a lightweight authentication method (2004)
38. Ye, G., et al.: A Video-based Attack for Android Pattern Lock. ACM Trans. Priv. Secur. **21**, 1–31 (2018). https://doi.org/10.1145/3230740
39. von Zezschwitz, E, et al.: Easy to draw, but hard to trace? On the observability of grid-based (un)lock patterns. In: Proceedings of the 33rd Annual ACM Conference on Human Factors in Computing Systems, pp. 2339–2342. CHI '15. Association for Computing Machinery, New York, NY, USA (2015). https://doi.org/10.1145/2702123.2702202
40. Zhang, L., et al.: Does the layout of the Android unlock pattern affect the security and usability of the password? J. Inf. Secur. Appl. **62**, 103011 (2021). https://doi.org/10.1016/j.jisa.2021.103011
41. Zhou, M., et al.: FingerPattern: securing pattern lock via fingerprint dependent friction sound. IEEE Trans. Mobile Comput. **23**(6), 7210–7224 (2024). https://doi.org/10.1109/TMC.2023.3338148

Provoking Through Probing: Investigating Technology Consumption Through the Lens of Minimalism

Nikita Dadbhawala[1](✉), Debjani Roy[1], and Rushabh Dadbhawala[2]

[1] Srishti Manipal Institute of Art, Design and Technology, Manipal Academy of Higher Education, Bengaluru, India
nikita.rushabh@gmail.com, debjani.roy@manipal.edu
[2] Bengaluru, India
rushabh.nikita@gmail.com

Abstract. This study examines if ubiquitous technology that creates complexity and incompatibility along with ease and efficiency is truly beneficial. It investigates the possibility of achieving balance between technology and wellbeing through lens of minimalism. The study done in urban Indian setup uses gamified physical probes prompting participants to reflect on their choices and gain insights into their behaviour. By posing progressively difficult questions that delve into hidden facets of wellbeing, environment, and media consumption, the study leads participants to assess the influence of their choices on their quality of life, leading them to self-awareness and self-realization. The study aims to enable participants to be conscious towards technology use, to consider not just immediate utility but also long-term effects on health and environment. By highlighting invisible costs, the study aims to empower individuals to make informed decisions that align with their wellbeing and values.

Keywords: Technology · Devices · Minimalism · Design Probes · Consciousness · Self-Reflection · Wellbeing · Awareness · Behaviour

1 Introduction

In our ever-evolving world, technology has become an invisible companion that has seamlessly encroached all aspect of our lives. Working, cooking, shopping, traveling, or managing finances, technology accompanies us at every turn. Over the past 15 years, this omnipresent force has transformed how we perform each task, offering convenience, productivity, and ability to multitask. However, amidst the benefits of penetration of technology, it becomes critical to question how mindful the technology consumption in everyone's life is. This study seeks to understand whether technology enhances experiences or overwhelms with choices. It explores whether technology fosters mindful engagement or contributes to digital fatigue. It investigates the dichotomy of technology and minimalism, understanding its implications on sustainable wellbeing.

R. Dadbhawala—Independent Researcher

Published by Springer Nature Switzerland AG 2026
G. Bhutkar et al. (Eds.): IDID 2024, IFIP AICT 747, pp. 90–103, 2026.
https://doi.org/10.1007/978-3-032-00777-3_6

In exploring perspectives around technology, it is observed that technology brings efficiency and convenience, but at the cost of simplicity in utilization [1]. To counter this complexity, Julia Swann proposes that products ought to be designed with minimalist technology, enabling individuals to do more with less [2]. The other side of the spectrum is the over consumption of technology. The philosophies of technology use may range from completely avoiding it, to using it in every part of the life [3]. Between the two extremes lies the question of health and wellbeing, not just of the physical body but also of the mind.

As technology simplifies certain tasks, individuals may no longer be mindful of the invisible aspects of these solutions. For instance, smartphone camera and online backup are an effective combination that it is difficult to realise the amount of digital data that is generated [4].

Technology is not just bound to the realm of smartphones, laptops, and tablets. It is also present in physical devices such as refrigerators, robot vacuum cleaners, appliances, etc. As technology churns itself faster than people can adopt, devices must either undergo frequent upgrades or be left with incompatible devices that won't work together. Presence of advanced products in the market causes users to discard them even though they are still functional [5]. While devices reach their end-of-life very soon, individuals are unaware how to properly discard technology from their lives.

An activity that is common and routine, is no longer mindful. It happens subconsciously with minimum awareness about its impact in the broader scheme of sustainable wellbeing. While we acutely focus on convenience and achievement of goals, we lose focus on the costs that we pay in the form of health, environment impact, and sustainable wellbeing.

The study aims to assess individuals' technology usage and their awareness of the reasons behind their technology choices. It explores the outcomes they experience from consuming technology for various purposes and whether it brings the benefits that were expected. It compels the participants to question technology's impact on their lives, be it privacy, environment, lifestyle ailments, mindless consumption, or addiction. It even tries to understand whether individuals can strike a harmonious balance between technology engagement and personal wellbeing. It does so by looking at technology through the lens of minimalism. It weighs the effects of technology through the aspects of minimalism, enabling individuals to look beyond the surface.

This study, through the use of design probes, is an experiment to nudge participants to self-reflect on their choices with respect to consumption of technology. The paper discusses the initial results of the study conducted with specific demography, to identify evidence that would facilitate a larger study with diverse demography.

1.1 Method

The study was conducted in an urban Indian context, with 24 participants. It included systematic literature review, in depth in-context inquiry and experiment through probes. The current study presents the initial results with limited sample size. The study was divided into three phases.

Phase 1: involved the systematic review of existing literature and categorization of the aspects of minimalism and technology. The understanding of these aspects became the foundation for building the structure of the research study.

Phase 2: was the pilot study through in-context interviews and observations with 6 individuals from 3 families. Its purpose was to observe and gather initial information about the usage of technology in the daily life of people and their perspectives around these consumptions. The insights drawn from Phase1 and Phase2 were integrated to design probes to investigate minimalism and technology.

Phase 3: covered testing of the probe with 18 individuals from 9 families and analysis of the data.

2 The Study

2.1 Phase 1: Theorising Technology and Minimalism

Hannay and McGinn have stated, "The basic function of technology is the expansion of the realm of practical human possibilities." [6]. The study builds on this statement and proposes that "Technology is the minimizing of human efforts and the maximizing of human possibilities." Its impact is evident in the ease, efficiency, and effectiveness it brings to daily lives.

Kang and others define Minimalism as a sustainable living approach where people deliberately choose a lifestyle practice of "less" without compulsions especially financial [7]. Hence, in the context of the study, "Minimalism is a practice of conscious consumption by choice without any constraints".

Based on these definitions and related readings, the study enumerated the fundamental aspects of Minimalism and Technology which served as the foundation for this research. The terms that emerged from the review were further clustered in three categories: Devices, Behaviour and Realisation, as shown in Table 1. Each stage of the study was planned and structured around these aspects. They were further validated by collecting users' perspectives facilitated by the design probes. The categories that emerged from the interviews were further mapped with the categories emerged in the systematic literature review. The diverse thoughts and perspectives collected from the participants converged into these aspects, serving as the metric, based on which the probes were created.

2.2 Phase 2: Initial Investigation

To identify key patterns of technology consumption in daily life, an initial study was done with three families (comprising six participants) from diverse socio-demographic backgrounds (age, lifestyle, and family structure), in the Indian urban context. The interview agenda was defined to ensure a smooth flow and coverage of several perspectives around device and technology consumption.

The in-context interviews were conducted in an informal conversational manner along with observational study. Each interview lasted for over an hour, considering the participants' interest and engagement. Probing questions were asked to help participants recall the devices and technologies they used. Systematic transitions across various stages of the interview, from icebreaking to in-depth conversations, without losing the flow and interest of the participants, was a key requirement for further study. However, the use of verbal conversation restricted the envisioning of technology and devices usage in their current surrounding.

The extended duration of the qualitative study posed challenges for participants in recalling details and the reliance on verbal exchange led to a loss of information. These challenges facilitated to identify the cues to build the probes for the further detailed study.

Table 1. Categorized Aspects of Minimalism and Technology

Aspects	Devices	Behaviour	Realisation
Minimalism			
Consumption [8]	✔	✔	
Consumerism [8]	✔	✔	
Behavioural Patterns		✔	
Environmental Impact [9, 10]			✔
Awareness [7]			✔
Consciousness [7]			✔
Wellbeing [11]			✔
Technology			
Standardisation [12]	✔		
Trends [12]	✔	✔	
Innovations [12]	✔	✔	
Advancements [12]	✔	✔	
Complexity [12]		✔	
Consumer Sovereignty [12]		✔	
Health Benefit [12]		✔	✔
Health Hazard [12]			✔
Environmental Impact [12]			✔

2.3 Phase 3: Probe Design, Experimentation

Probe Design. To create a more engaging experience, to allow participants to reflect on their choices, and to discover deeper insights, probes were designed [13, 14]. Drawing on the learnings from the initial investigation, eight probes were designed that they covered all aspects of technology and minimalism that were identified in the literature review. The eight probes were grouped into three categories: Devices, Behaviour, and Realisation.

Set 1: Mapping Devices. The initial two probes, as shown in Fig. 1, were designed with the objective of gathering baseline data on the family's device ecosystem. The first probe utilized an apartment floor plan as a representation of the house and capture information on shared devices. Conversely, the second probe used participant avatars to collect data pertaining to personal devices. Tokens bearing icons for avatars, devices and behaviours were placed on the probes to record the data shared by the participants. This, in turn, aided the participants to recall their devices and behaviours in later stages of the conversation.

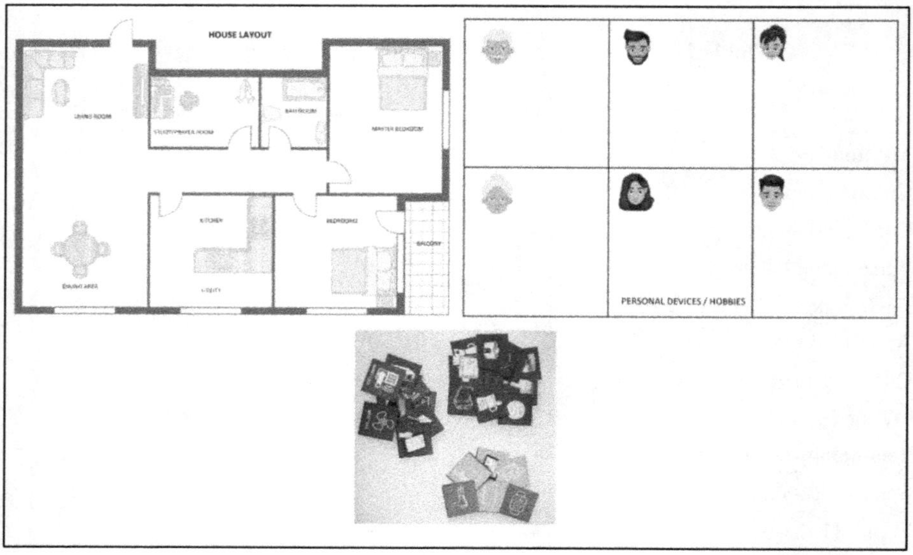

Fig. 1. Mapping Devices through Probes and Tokens

Set 2: Probing into Behaviour. The second set, as shown in Fig. 2, concentrated on specific activities and occasions, including physical exercise, hobbies, family bonding, experiences from the COVID-19 pandemic, work- from-home, and multitasking. This set aimed to elucidate participants' behavioural patterns associated with these activities, both with and without the use of technology. As the probes graduate from collecting basic information to exploring behaviour, the conversation with participants became increasingly profound, thereby uncovering nuances of their decision-making processes.

Set 3: Probing into Realisation. The final set of probes, as shown in Fig. 3, delved into participants' level of consciousness and self-awareness regarding their technological practices, extending beyond mere device usage. It explored themes such as end-of-life management and disposal of devices, their environmental impacts, digital and virtual practices, and activity timelines reconstructed across three points in time (Present day, 5 years prior, and 15 years prior) to gauge the evolution of technology integration within their lives. Additionally, this set investigated the health advantages and potential

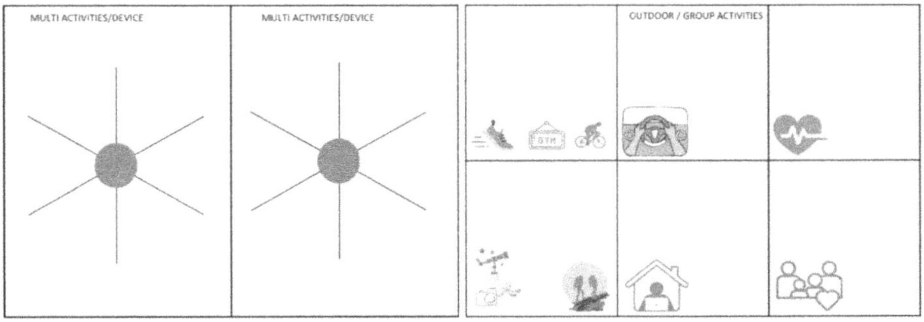

Fig. 2. Behaviour Probes

risks associated with technology use, while appraising the factors building or disrupting overall wellbeing.

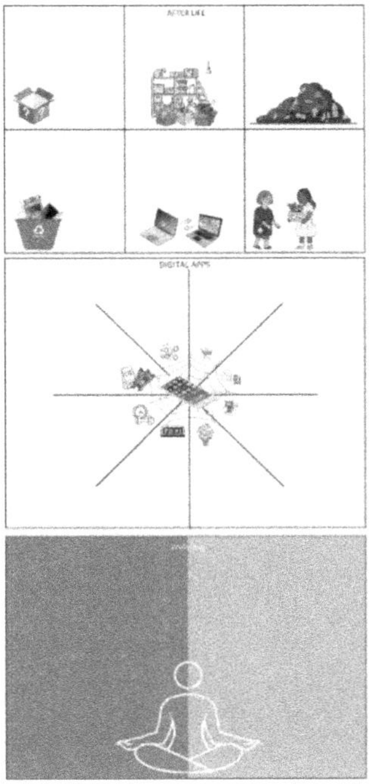

Activities	Today	5 Years Ago	15 Years Ago	Wish
Groceries				
Movie				
Shopping				
Investments				
Banking				
Exercise				
Train Ticket				
Air Ticket				
Music				
News				
Local Travel				
Talking				
Socialising				

Fig. 3. Realisation Probes

All three sets were intentionally designed to visually depict an individual's journey with technology consumption, spanning from acquisition to disposal. This approach aimed to study participants' realisations regarding the multifaceted impacts, both positive and negative, of technology on their lives.

Provoking through Probing. The probes were tested on nine families (comprising 18 participants) representing various family structures: nuclear families, joint families, bachelors living alone, and senior citizens living alone. This diversity in socio-demographics along with the lifestyles brought out insights into the varied behavioural patterns and technology requirements of the participants. Figure 4 highlights the demographic diversity of all participants (including Pilot phase).

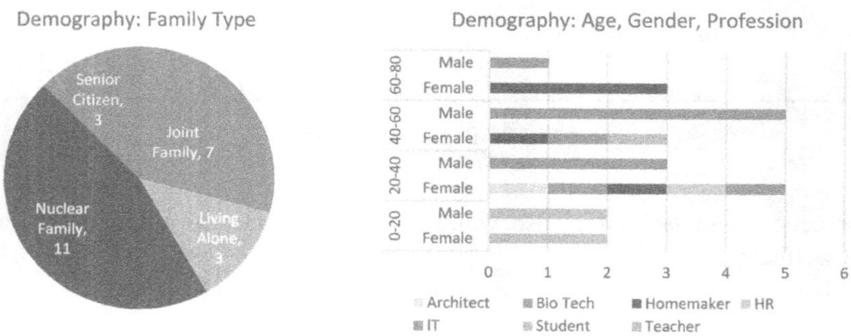

Fig. 4. Participant Demographic Details

The interview experience was designed like playing a board game with each probe like a game level, as shown in Fig. 5. The participants interacted with the probe using a set of tokens which represent their avatars, devices, and behaviours. As one progressed, the probes asked increasingly "difficult" questions. This game like interaction where participants placed tokens on the board created an engaging, immersive experience. Due to their simplicity and graphical representation, the probes overcame barriers such as language and age.

Fig. 5. Probes during an Interview

Thematic Analysis. The interviews were recorded and transcribed. The transcriptions were coded to derive quantitative data. Thematic analysis was done by coding the data, further categorizing them based on devices, behaviour, and realisations. The analysis led to the emergence of patterns based on varied aligned and contrasting perspectives, discussed in the insights section.

3 Insights

The exercise of Probing Interviews helped participants visually reflect on their real-life technology usage. It enabled participants to recognize the complete spectrum of technology and devices present in their lives. By revealing hidden or unnoticed behaviours, these probes raised awareness about the impact of devices on overall wellbeing.

Participants became aware that technology is incredibly transparent and omnipresent. Prior to this exercise, they hadn't fully realized the extent of devices woven into their daily lives.

3.1 Relation Between Technology Acquisition and Age

Analysis revealed a clear pattern regarding the number of personal and shared devices owned by the participants, as shown in Fig. 6. Across age groups, younger participants tend to acquire more devices for specific activities, whereas senior citizens often prefer to stick to traditional methods and avoid purchasing additional devices. E.g. coffee maker v/s filter coffee apparatus.

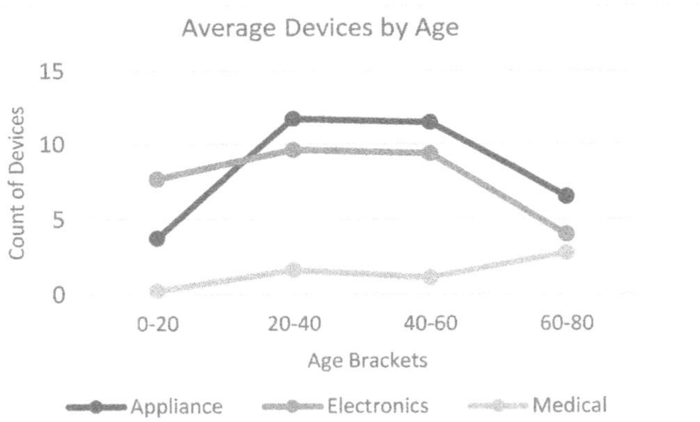

Fig. 6. Relationship between devices and age.

3.2 Technology and Family Bonding

Individuals living away from their families perceived social media as beneficial for their wellbeing and strengthening of family bonds as it facilitated connections with loved ones. In contrast, those residing with their families believed that technology, particularly social media, negatively impacted their well-being and weakened the family ties. TV and OTT were popular mediums for quality family time across the age groups. Refer to Fig. 7 for an overview of all such activities and devices.

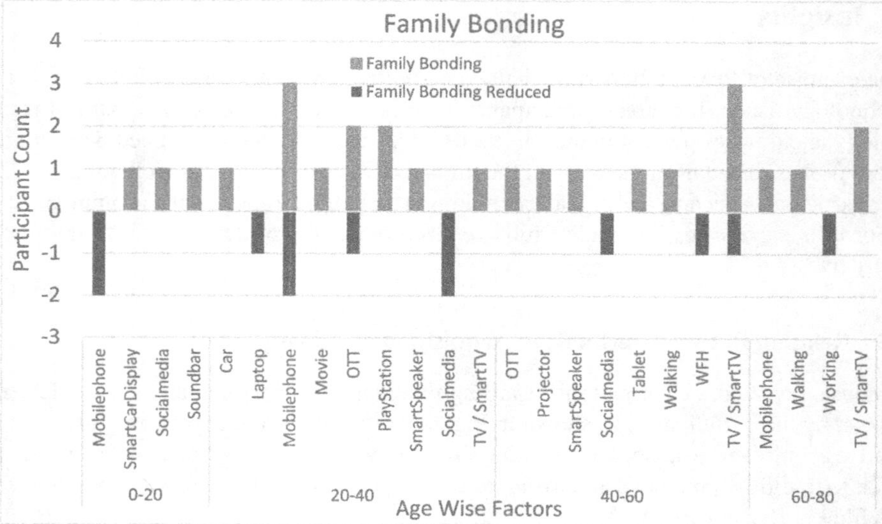

Fig. 7. Activities and Devices influencing Family Bonding

3.3 Discarding Technology and Its Environmental Impact

Participants found recycling and disposal of devices challenging. Most of the unused gadgets accumulated in boxes within the homes, as shown in Fig. 8. Many of these devices were retained due to time constraints and lack of awareness about their disposal.

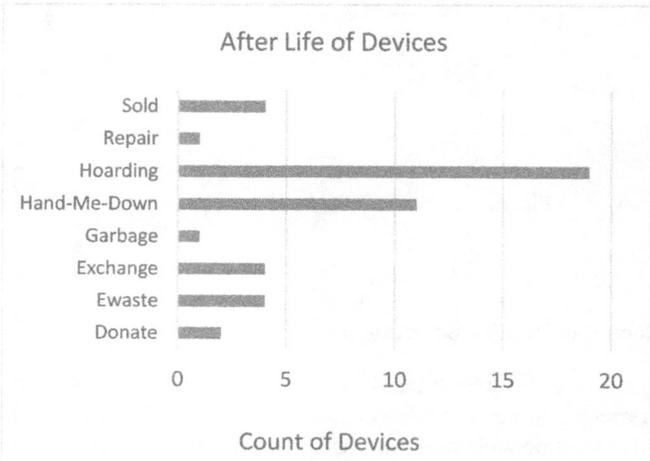

Fig. 8. After Life and Disposal of Devices

3.4 Digital Technology and Behavioural Patterns

The probe on digital behaviours made the participants realise that they hoard unused apps on their devices. Multiple apps were installed on the phone as a backup for specific needs (e.g. Cab services). Most of the participants were unaware how to enforce data privacy settings on their phones.

People seek automation for mundane activities like banking, ticketing, and local travel to enhance ease and convenience, as shown in Fig. 9. However, for more personal activities—those with an emotional quotient—such as talking, socializing, and shopping, individuals desire both online and offline experiences, as shown in Fig. 10.

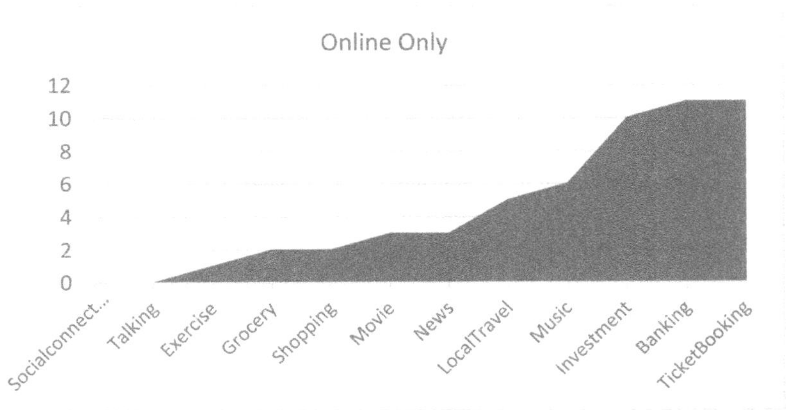

Fig. 9. How do participants want to perform the mundane activities?

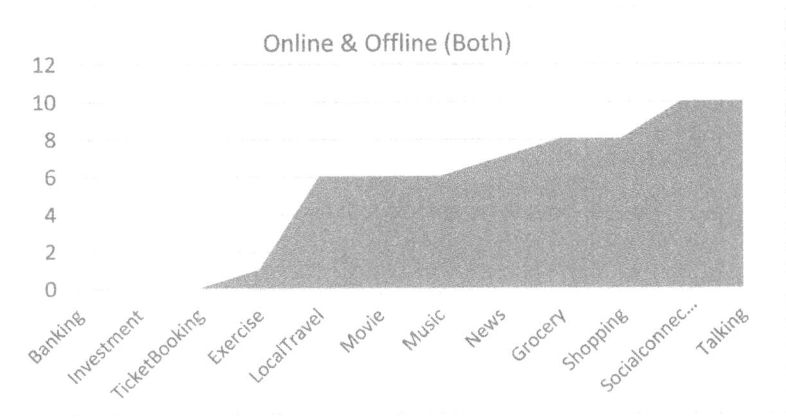

Fig. 10. Preferences for Mundane v/s Experiential Activities

3.5 Technology and Wellbeing

While the participants expressed a variety of ways in which they gain their wellbeing, the number of ways in which one loses wellbeing are fewer, similar, and common. Another noteworthy insight here is that the sources of gaining wellbeing are filled with hobbies, activities, and bonding with loved ones. But the causes of losing wellbeing are primarily related to work and mindless consumption via technology, as shown in Fig. 11.

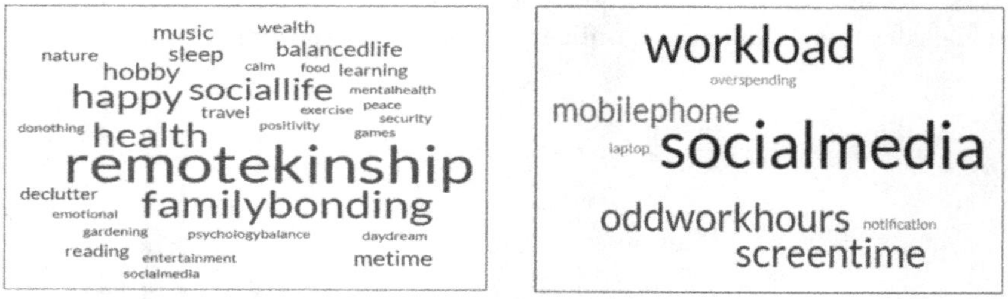

Fig. 11. Word Cloud of Factors Building (blue) and Disrupting (red) Wellbeing. (Color figure online)

3.6 Participants' Realisations

Fig. 12. Participants engrossed in the Probing Interviews

Several participants expressed a sense of seeing their lives reflected in miniature. The visual and physical representation quantified the technology and devices they actively used, those lying around, and even those left unused. Many participants reported experiencing self-reflection during the interview itself (Fig. 12).

Individuals generally perceive laptops, smartphones, tablets, wearables, and such devices as technology. But the participants were pleasantly surprised that there were more appliances in the kitchen than devices in the rest of the house. These devices also entail a huge technology quotient, but they are generally not categorized as "high-tech" devices.

One participant expressed the realisation that despite the presence of so much technology and devices around us, why does one still feel the lack of time? Is technology really helping us do more, or is technology making things difficult?

A young mother with small children appreciated the convenience of multitasking using available technology but also expressed occasional feelings of missing out on physical activities that created contentment, pleasure, or happiness, such as reading and shopping.

A participant noticed how much clutter is accumulated in the name of convenience. Impulse buying and consumerism has led to items ending up in landfills or contributing to e-waste. The participant postponed some decisions with the realisation that such device/technology is not critical. Sometimes, not making a purchase is the wisest choice.

Some participants realised that technology usage can be reduced in situations where it is optional, thereby conserving resources and time. One participant recognized the virtues of planned grocery shopping over instant online delivery.

A participant expressed that awareness of technology consumption often lingers in the background, but when confronted with concrete data through this research interview, the impact became more pronounced. It highlighted areas with wastage or ineffective technology utilisation.

Reflecting on the past 15 years, participants came to recognize the increased dependence on technology—a shift that wasn't as pronounced back then.

A participant felt that the interview was like seeing a miniature version of their existence, revealing both important and superfluous aspects. Reflecting on the interview experience made them realise that they can exercise more control on technology consumption rather than technology consuming them.

A participant appreciated the opportunity to revisit their habits. Over the years, though the family has been mindful of device usage both personally and within their home, this exercise served as a helpful check-in, reminding of the surplus electronics that can be decluttered. The participant's conscious consumption journey has been going on for a long time, and it had become a habit that most of their devices and apps serve specific purposes with clear reasons behind their use. Overall, it was a valuable exercise to reassess and refine the choices.

A participant acknowledged that life doesn't come to a halt without an aspirational device and allowed himself to postpone their purchases.

After self-realisation through this exercise each participant expressed the need for continuous self-assessment tool / system of utilisation of the technology.

4 Summary and Future Scope

The overall experiment made it evident to the participants that technology is ubiquitous and present all around them. The gamified probes played an important role in helping participants arrive at their own realisations with respect to their technology consumption.

The participants were able to look at their relationship with devices and technologies from all spheres of their life in a single glance, be it shared appliances, personal electronics, hobbies, health, or work. This enabled the participants to have a very high recall regarding their behaviours with technology. They were able to see which devices were valuable to them and, more importantly, which devices were not. Progressing further in the interviews, they were able to justify as well as question their technology decisions as they became aware of their interactions with devices.

From utility to behaviours to wellbeing, the participants led themselves into deeper introspections at every step of the way by confronting increasingly "difficult" questions. They were able to look at technology through the lens of minimalism to become aware of the invisible aspects of technology (such as hoarding, environmental impact and media consumption) which hitherto went unnoticed. Through the course of the experiment, the participants arrived at the crossroads of self-realisation where they could appraise whether their technologies and behaviours led them to create wellbeing or reduce it.

Moving forward, this study can be refined by including a larger sample from diverse location and demography. The insights from this research study can be leveraged to create gamified self-assessment platform for conscious technology consumption.

Acknowledgements. We would like to thank all the participants whose willing involvement in the research activities was indispensable to this study. We would like to thank Srishti Manipal Institute of Art, Design and Technology for giving the opportunity to conduct the study.

References

1. Sugandha, G.: Minimalism in design: a trend of simplicity in complexity. ShodhKosh J. Vis. Perform. Arts **4** (2023). https://doi.org/10.29121/shodhkosh.v4.i2.2023.539
2. Minimalist Technology: Leveraging tech for happier living. https://www.goneminimal.com/minimalist-technology/. Accessed 25 April 2024
3. Newport, C.: Digital Minimalism: Choosing a Focused Life in a Noisy World. Penguin Random House, United States of America (2019)
4. Vitale, F., Janzen, I., McGrenere, J. . Hoarding and minimalism: tendencies in digital data preservation. In: Proceedings of the 2018 CHI Conference on Human Factors in Computing Systems (CHI '18). Association for Computing Machinery, New York, NY, USA, Paper 587, pp. 1–12 (2018). https://doi.org/10.1145/3173574.3174161
5. Yamamoto, H., Murakami, S.: Product obsolescence and its relationship with product lifetime: an empirical case study of consumer appliances in Japan. Resour. Conserv. Recycling **174**, 105798 (2021). https://doi.org/10.1016/j.resconrec.2021.105798
6. Bruce, H.N., McGinn, R.E.: The anatomy of modern technology: prolegomenon to an improved public policy for the social management of technology. Daedalus **109**(1), 25–53 (1980). http://www.jstor.org/stable/20024647
7. Kang, J., Martinez, C.M.J., Johnson, C.: Minimalism as a sustainable lifestyle: Its behavioral representations and contributions to emotional wellbeing. Sustain. Prod. Consumption **27**, 802–813 (2021). https://doi.org/10.1016/j.spc.2021.02.001
8. Dopierała, R.: Minimalism – a new mode of consumption? Przegląd Socjologiczny **66**, 67–83 (2017)
9. Blackburn, R., Leviston, Z., Walker, I., Schram, A.: Could a minimalist lifestyle reduce carbon emissions and improve wellbeing? A review of minimalism and other low consumption lifestyles. WIREs Clim. Change **15**(2), e865 (2024). https://doi.org/10.1002/wcc.865
10. Oliveira de Mendonça, G., Coelho Rocha, A.R., Bogéa da Costa Tayt-son, D.: The minimalist process: an interpretivist study. J. Consum. Behav. **20**, 1040–1050 (2021). https://doi.org/10.1002/cb.1912

11. Lloyd, K., Pennington, W.: Towards a theory of minimalism and wellbeing. Int. J. Appl. Posit Psychol. **5**, 121–136 (2020). https://doi.org/10.1007/s41042-020-00030-y
12. Brooks, H.: Technology, evolution, and purpose. Daedalus **109**(1), 65–81 (1980). http://www.jstor.org/stable/20024649
13. Wallace, J., McCarthy, J., Wright, P.C., Olivier, P.: Making design probes work. In: Proceedings of the SIGCHI Conference on Human Factors in Computing Systems (CHI'13), pp. 3441–3450. Association for Computing Machinery, New York, NY, USA (2013). https://doi.org/10.1145/2470654.2466473
14. Sanders, E.B.-N., Stappers, P.J.: Probes, toolkits and prototypes: three approaches to making in codesigning. CoDesign **10**(1), 5–14 (2014). https://doi.org/10.1080/15710882.2014.888183

Capture It: Exploring Cybersecurity Assessment Using a Multiplayer Repurposable Game

Gokul Jayakrishnan(✉), Vijayanand Banahatti, and Sachin Lodha

TCS Research, Tata Consultancy Services Ltd., Pune, India
{gokul.cj,vijayanand.banahatti,sachin.lodha}@tcs.com

Abstract. Multiplayer games are generally popular due to their more social and competitive gameplay experience. Serious games are a category of games used to educate and engage users. If made to be repurposable, serious games can also cater to various learning contexts with minimal modifications. Considering the above findings, we performed an exploratory study with a repurposable, anchor-driven multiplayer serious game 'Capture It'. In this study with 358 participants, the team-based game was used to assess the cybersecurity awareness levels of enterprise participants using a competitive ask-and-answer method. Every correct answer lets the team capture parts of a virtual territory. Here, we also tested the influence of a pre-game quiz on the in-game performance of the teams. Our findings indicate a positive impact of the pre-game quiz on participants' in-game performance. We share our results and a broader scope of the game to guide future research in this domain.

Keywords: Anchor-driven · Repurposable · Multiplayer serious game · Cybersecurity awareness · Assessment

1 Introduction

Digital games have been identified as a means of enhancing collaborative learning [27, 31]. Multiplayer gaming is also one of the best approaches for game-based learning [11]. Research shows that motivation and teamwork among learners can be enhanced through collaborative learning [22]. A study on how computers in low-income countries support learning activities [2, 45] showed that a single computer (in home) was used to strengthen social relations and promote learning and creativity among several members. Building upon this insight, we explored a means to promote learning using a prototype single-device multiplayer game. Here, a human anchor or a moderator can moderate the digital game from their own device. The participants can interact with the game through the anchor, without the need of individual personal devices. Our aim was to develop a repurposable game framework, which can easily be modified to suit various learning contexts. A game can be repurposed [18] if its learning resources or objects created for one learning context can be modified for a new learning context [50]. As an initial step, our current study aims to use the game for assessing cybersecurity awareness among an enterprise audience.

Published by Springer Nature Switzerland AG 2026
G. Bhutkar et al. (Eds.): IDID 2024, IFIP AICT 747, pp. 104–124, 2026.
https://doi.org/10.1007/978-3-032-00777-3_7

In the enterprise sector, cybersecurity training typically occurs as part of security compliance rather than as an engaging experience. Therefore, if employees perceive the training as 'extra work', it could result in negative effects on the training [70]. An engaging experience such as an interactive game could cater to multiple users and could help them to break out of the compliance check criteria and interact with the training proactively. Serious games are computer games created for the primary purpose of education rather than entertainment [58]. Studies on serious games for cybersecurity education have generally shown positive results, demonstrating that active engagement and learning are achievable through these games. Several serious games have been used to train and assess user awareness, as reported in the literature [19, 35, 55, 59, 64], with positive results. While most cybersecurity serious games are single-player, a recent multiplayer serious game, Housie [34], has demonstrated relatively high participation and good performance. Housie could be considered as an assessment in the form of a game where participants were engaged in quickly answering a set of cybersecurity-related questions and the leaderboard was based on how quickly they could answer the questions [34]. This game inspired us to approach the Corporate Security Office (CSO) of the organization (under study) for planning a team-based game for the employees. The CSO team was keen on assessing the security awareness of the employees with a new team-based assessment approach. To make this assessment more engaging and to ensure that the employees do not find the assessment as 'an extra work' [58], we used a game-related assessment approach (GRA) [51].

Literature shows that presentation of assessment as a game plays a part in increasing the user's motivation [66] and also in eliciting better reactions from them [25]. Considering the acceptability of Housie [34], the general outlook of gamified assessments [25, 66], the positive results from serious games for cybersecurity education [19, 35, 55, 59, 64], and building inspiration from the study on usage of a single computer to spread learning and creativity [2, 45], we developed the prototype 'Capture It'. It is a multiplayer, serious game-based assessment framework, which can be played even using a single computer. The game was deployed within an enterprise under study with the assistance of their CSO team. It was then used to assess the security awareness of the employees. The game was anchored by a human moderator to augment communication between the participants, as studies show that games should offer several processes of collaboration, including voice and text [28, 56].

We also introduced a cybersecurity quiz as a pre-test before the game-based study. This was intended to measure the participants' existing knowledge levels. Prior studies by Little, et al. [40] and Murphy et al. [43] also suggest the benefits of a pre-test (or prequestions) on subsequent learning of related content, and we sought to investigate this for a cybersecurity context within an enterprise. Thus, in this exploratory study using an anchor-driven multiplayer game, our research question focused on identifying **'if a pre-game quiz has any impact in a multiplayer serious game setting within an enterprise context'**. As per certain previous cybersecurity serious games [33, 34], participants' demographics also seem to affect their performance, which was also suggested by Zahid et al. [71]. In our study, we also attempted at finding any such effects. This paper details the design and development, study, and results of our 'Capture It' game based assessment.

2 Background and Related Work

2.1 Cybersecurity Awareness

Despite the increase in security measures, the rise in cyberattacks is alarming. A recent Gartner report suggests that by 2025, lack of training, negligence, and/or human error will cause over 50% of cyber incidents [5]. The Anti-Phishing Working Group (APWG) and even the FBI reports that the increase in cyber-attacks is at an alarming rate [1, 3]. In an organization, the employees are the first line of defense against cyberthreats [6]. A security breach or a cyber-attack can cause large financial and reputational losses to an organization [6]. The need for cybersecurity awareness among the enterprise employees is at an all-time high, especially due to the increased implementation of artificial intelligence (AI) and related advanced technologies. In addition to traditional cybersecurity awareness training methods, such as documents, slideshows, and instructor-led sessions, gamification has also been found to be popular and more engaging [7].

2.2 Game-Based Learning and Gamification

Learning using a game is a useful pedagogical idea that existed throughout history [41]. In today's context, game-based learning (GBL) denotes the use of video games and interactive mechanisms for the purpose of education [23]. On the other hand, gamification deals with the use of game mechanics, aesthetics, and thinking to attract users to solve problems [21, 41]. It is basically the use of game elements in non-gaming situations [53]. Different forms of games can be used for teaching various concepts to users ranging from children to adults. One of the most efficient means to do this takes the form of a multiple-choice test, where the use has shown to benefit learning among primary school students [41, 48, 52, 57]. It is also found to be effective for university students and adults [57]. It has been found to increase motivation and improve the quality of learning among users [41]. A gamification literature study done by Caponetto et al. [14] reviews around 120 gamification-related papers and reports that gamification techniques are popular in a wide range of educational setting. A more recent study by Saleem et al. [53] suggests that the key learning elements used in gamification include points, badges, leaderboard, levels, rewards, feedback, and challenges. The study reports that gamification can be a valuable tool for gaining knowledge, and can help in decision-making, cooperation, communication, and to improve specific skills. The study also recommends that the game or gamified setting should be easy to understand, should be familiar to learners, duration should be short, and the game should have simplicity and clarity [53]. As per reports by eLearning tools platform Kiwi LMS [8], 90% of employees evaluated for a restaurant gamification-based study were found to be more productive when they use gamification. Over 72% people surveyed also believe that gamification inspires them to work harder [8]. Besides GBL and gamification, serious games are a category of games created specifically for the purpose of education.

2.3 Serious Games for Cybersecurity Awareness

Serious games are often termed as mental contests played with specific rules and a computer. It uses entertainment to further training [72]. As per Ben Sawyer, the co-founder of 'Serious Games Initiative', serious games are games designed for a purpose other than just entertainment [54]. The use of serious games in cybersecurity education is increasing, and this could likely be due to its inherent ability to sustain the interest of the learners [36]. Several serious games for cybersecurity education have been tried and tested with successful results. Games such as Anti-phishing phil [55], What.Hack [63], Phishy [19], and PickMail [33] were created to train users on phishing emails and links, each having pre-test and post-test methods to analyze the participants' knowledge improvement after playing the game. The process involves quantitative analysis by comparison of the pre-test scores to the post-test scores. Apart from single player games, a study by Awojana et al. [11] suggests that multiplayer mode is one of the best approaches for game-based learning.

Considering multiplayer games for cybersecurity awareness, Security Requirements Educational Game (SREG) [68] is a card game that uses attackers and vulnerabilities. This game was found to be effective in teaching security vulnerabilities and attacks to the participants. SecurityCom [60] is a multiplayer game, involving team interaction, for teaching team concepts in information security within an organizational context. Hivemind Network [37] is a multiplayer game consisting of challenges and puzzles. It helped users get familiar with network topologies and services. Cyberpoly [64] is a multiplayer serious game based on Monopoly board game, where multiple players can play simultaneously and answer various questions and initiate cyber-attacks on other players. The participant data shows that the game was engaging and motivational to learn cybersecurity concepts. Cyberspace Odyssey [26] is a multiplayer, 3D game that allows students to learn and practice basics of computer network. The associated study showed that the game can be used as an effective teaching tool. Housie [34] is a BINGO-themed [20] multiplayer serious game used to assess enterprise users' knowledge on various areas of cybersecurity. Housie was played by over 56,000 participants, and the game evaluated participants' performance in various security topics. The game was found to be a success among enterprise audience.

2.4 Game-Based Assessment

Engagement is a determining factor for attitude and motivation that could increase participation in an assessment [30]. A study has shown that motivated individuals can achieve higher academic performance [32]. Game-based assessment incorporates game elements in assessing performance of the subjects. They have shown to elicit enjoyment, motivation, flow, and learning [39]. Such assessments have found to be effective in several areas, including employee selection and performance [24, 44], stimulate learning and group collaboration [42], and in academic quiz platforms [17] to name a few. A learning assessment of students using 'Kahoot!' game also fostered interaction with friends with a fun, competitive, and engaging experience [62]. In such assessments, feedback plays a major role as it is shown to impact the learning and achievement [29]. Studies show that gamified assessment, with feedback, can support learning [67].

Due to the following organizational requirements, we devised a new serious game for assessing the security awareness of enterprise employees. The requirements included limited time of play (maximum of 20 min), multiplayer element of gameplay, the need to increase participant engagement, requirement of a human host or mediator to carry out the game (who is a part of organization's security team), the requirement to make the game available in any device and operating system, and the need to make the entire game modular and 'repurposable' [18, 50]. We adopted an established model of game-based assessment design, which follows theoretical foundations [39, 65] (mentioned in Sect. 3.1) and includes gamification elements, to design and develop our gamified assessment using the serious game 'Capture It'.

3 Design of Capture It

3.1 Design Model

We designed Capture It by following the gamification model from Werbach and Hunter [47, 65], which showcases a thoughtful design and player-centric approach. As per this proposal of gaming elements, the dynamics, mechanics, and components form a pyramid (in the above order), organized in a decreasing order of abstraction [47].

'Dynamics' is the most abstract level and deals with implicit elements that do not directly participate in the game. It consists of elements such as emotions, narrative, progression, relationship, and restrictions. 'Mechanics' refers to the processes that drive player actions and foster engagement. It is related to dynamics. The elements of mechanics constitute resources (in-game), uncertainty/chance, competition, cooperation, challenges, feedback, rewards, and victory. 'Components' are the specific elements in a game, they relate to each other to generate mechanics. It includes avatars, levels, virtual goods, badges, unlockable content, mission, points, gifts, teams, ranking etc. The integration between the three elements is found to increase the probability of generating memorable experiences in a game [47, 65].

While designing Capture It, we considered the dynamics and identified the mechanics that suited the dynamics and the components that aided the mechanics (Table 1). The details on how the game mechanics is related to the established gamification model [47, 65] is given in Sect. 3.6. This method was similar to that done by Kocadere et al. [39] while designing a gamified assessment. In terms of immersion, Gordon Calleja [13], in 'In-Game: From Immersion to In-corporation' integrates both the player's cognitive and affective responses to gameplay and proposes 'Incorporation' framework over 'Immersion'. He mentions that players are not just passive participants but actively make decisions based on game's rules and mechanics. He also mentions that players experience a wide range of emotions, which play a significant role in engagement and suggests that multiplayer games enhance player experiences by social interactions. Our game mechanics were such that the players feel active during the game and also become involved in the game due to the anchor-player communication. We added rewards and feedback, and 'audience questions' to increase the engagement factor.

3.2 Repurposability

The prototype game 'Capture It' was designed to be a human anchor-driven, semi-automated multiplayer (team-based) game that uses a competitive quiztheme to engage the teams to capture more cells of a virtual territory. One of our main design decisions

Table 1. 'Dynamics – Mechanics – Components' used in Capture It.

Dynamics	Mechanics	Components
Emotions	Challenge Reward Chance Competition Cooperation	Answering specific questions, limited time Capturing territory, Gaining flags/badges Uncertainty in answers, categories Teams, cells captured, time for correct answers Communication
Narrative	Chance	Uncertainty in answers Uncertainty in experience of opponents Time of responses
Progression	Reward Feedback Victory	Cells capture, flags/badges Instructional content, badges Territory captured
Relationships	Communication	Team-mates and between anchor and team, audience
Restrictions	Challenges	Limited 'virtual goods' (categories, cells)

was to make the game framework 'repurposable', in other words, to be able to cater to different learning contexts [18, 50]. Capture It game is modular, and every component can be easily replaced or substituted by another component. The learning content and the assets, such as the static images and backgrounds, can be easily replaced, allowing developers to modify the game entirely in a short period. The game, playable between two teams, was also designed in a way that the human anchor can choose the number of members for the teams, from four to 10. Repurposing makes the transition between learning contexts smooth and easy. Capture It can easily be repurposed to meet a wider range of learning needs, thus appealing to a broader audience. In the context of this study, Capture It was used for assessing cybersecurity awareness. The team size was fixed at 10 members per team to maximize participation.

3.3 Capture It Game Design and Mechanics

The design of the game went through a collaborative and iterative process where both security and design teams worked parallelly to streamline the game elements and interactions such that the players feel both, a sense of urgency and achievement while playing the game. This was intended to augment the 'microinvolvement' of gameplay, as suggested by Calleja [13], which deals with the moment-to-moment engagement with the gameplay.

We explored several mechanics for the game such as a soccer premiere leaguethemed game, a card game-like game mechanics, and so on. However, since our target demographic consisted of users from ages 21 and above, belonging to varied gender and backgrounds, we finalized the 'capture the territory' theme as this is a more universal (like that of chess or war) and well-known theme unlike specific sports-related themes.

The game still provided an appropriate introduction and 'how to play' steps to the players. The game makes use of the learning science principle of reflection by providing appropriate feedback to the players [12]. A basic game flow is shown in Fig. 1. Game mechanics refer to the rules, systems, and ways in which players interact with a game [10]. In Capture It, a human anchor or moderator, commonly known as host or quizmaster [61], plays a main role in the gameplay as it is their responsibility to ensure both the teams take part and the team members are given equal opportunity. The anchor also engages in conversations with the team members and team captains.

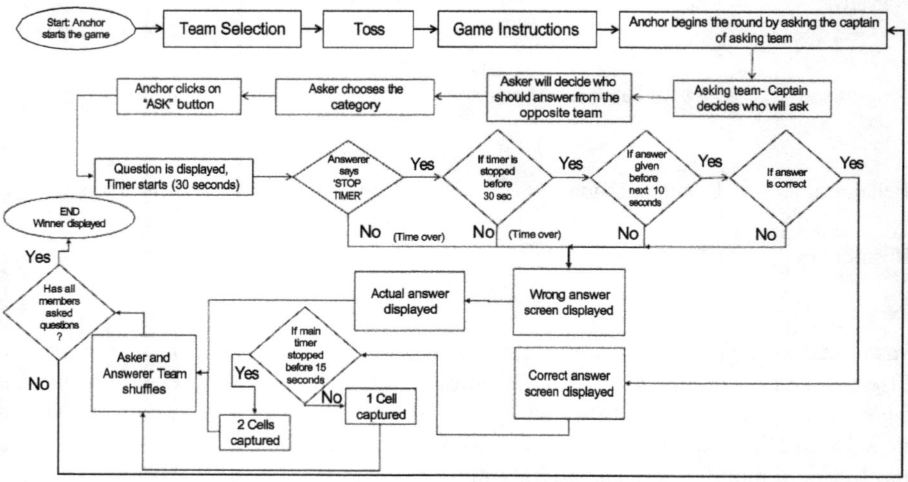

Fig. 1. Game flow of Capture It.

The game can be played in both online (through the Microsoft Teams ^{TM} application or any other group chat application) or offline modes (in a room where the participants and the anchor can sit together and play. Here, the game can be projected onto a screen from the anchor's computer device). In the context of this study, Capture It was used to assess the cybersecurity knowledge of the participants on certain categories of cybersecurity and general security.

3.4 Security-Related Learning Content in the Game

Capture It game focused on a set of five categories of security, taking inspiration from the multiplayer game 'Housie' [34]. The categories are:

1. **Application Security**: It includes the security measures at an application level to prevent unauthorized access, code leakage, data corruption, and keep unwanted perpetrators from gaining access to applications [69]. Example: What does OWASP stand for?
2. **Network Security**: It is a broader version of computer security, as it deals with securing networks containing multiple computers that share resources, ensuring that

all data (both in storage and in transit) and resources are protected [38]. Example: What is a socket?
3. **Operational Security**: It is a security and risk management process to prevent unauthorized access of sensitive information. It includes identifying several actions that could result in a potential data leakage [4]. Example: Questions on business continuity management
4. **End-user education**: This category involves questions on general security awareness area. It focuses on the tools and skills required to protect users themselves and their organizations from potential cyberattacks or loss of data [9]. Example: Conditions for a strong password, and
5. **Information Security**: It involves a state in which both information and data are secure [38]. Information security generally encompasses the study of mathematical concepts, cryptography, communication protocols, and best practices for managing data and information [38]. Example: What are the dangers of cross-site scripting?

Every question had a set of answer choices.

3.5 How the Game Works?

The game's user interface screen (UI) has the territory (randomly generated for every game) marked in green (see Fig. 2 a). The anchor begins the game by interacting with the captain of the team who decides to ask first, selected by a virtual coin toss. The captain decides who gets to ask the question from their team. Based on the captain's response, the anchor clicks the appropriate button with the player's name, on the UI (see Fig. 2 a, b). Once the 'asker' is selected, the anchor asks them to choose the preferred 'answerer' from the opposite team. The terms 'asker' and 'answerer' are respectively the 'questioner' and 'respondent' in a quiz [46, 61], and so these terms will be used further in this paper, for better clarity. Once the questioner chooses the respondent, the former must also choose an appropriate category (from the five available categories) of questions to ask (see Fig. 2 b). Once these steps are done, the anchor presses the "Ask Question" button which will display a question corresponding to the category selected (see Fig. 2 c). We gave the choice for the questioner to choose the respondent as this also brings in a strategic element to the game, where the former could choose a person from the opposite team who they think is not familiar in a specific cybersecurity topic and ask them a question from that specific category to increase the chances of scoring (cells in the territory). This works best if the team members know each other beforehand, which also increases the fun element and competitiveness of the gameplay.

3.6 Mechanics and Design Model

The design of Capture It mechanics (in the context of security awareness) as per the established gamification model from Werbach and Hunter [47, 65] (see Table 1) is as follows:

1. **Challenge**: The main challenge for the players in the game is to answer the specific category-related question within the allotted time. This element of mechanics was added to raise the dynamics of emotion.

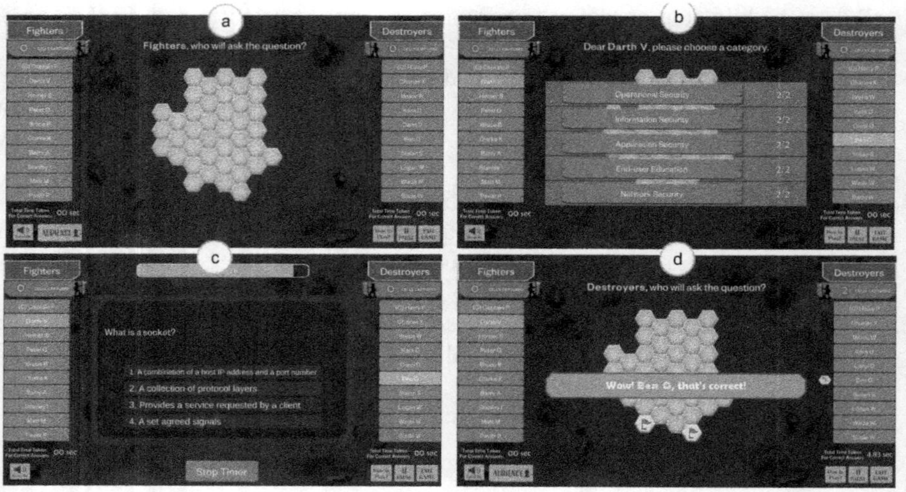

Fig. 2. Game Screens: a) the randomly generated territory with team members on either side of the screen, b) The categories of questions that the 'asking' team member can choose from, c) The question and options getting displayed based on the category of question asked, and d) Once the answer is provided, appropriate scores are updated (as cells captured), and territory captured will be displayed using flags. The respondent will also see flags against their name indicating that they have given the correct answer. The anchor can click on the 'Audience' button at any moment in the game and the next question will be redirected to the audience, who can then answer it by speaking or typing in the chat box (if the game is conducted online, especially through Microsoft Teams ^{TM}).

2. **Chance**: The uncertainty in the categories of questions asked was attributed to chance. A participant who is familiar with category such as 'Application Security' might obtain a question related to 'Information Security', and this is entirely based on chance and the mindset of the opponent. All the questions in the game had equal weights.
3. **Rewards**: For every correct answer, the player receives a badge based on how fast they have responded. If the answer was given before 15 s, the player earns a 'two-flagged' badge (Fig. 2 d) and if it is after 15 s (and before 30 s), there is a 'one-flagged' badge. The number of cells captured by the player also depends on the time of answer, with two cells for 0–15 s and one cell for 15–30 s.
4. **Feedback**: The game even though is an assessment to gauge the participants' security awareness, also implements a feedback mechanism that displays the correct answer for every question. This was implemented to augment learning during the process.
5. **Competition**: Serving the dynamics of emotion, the team members competed against each other to score the greater number of cells within the territory. The badges, cells, and time taken for correct answers increased the competition element. In case of a tie among the teams (in terms of cells collected), the winner was decided based on the 'least time for correct answers'.
6. **Cooperation**: The mechanics of cooperation among teammates were also present, as they could communicate with each other and with the anchor during the game, which

was intended to boost player morale. This mechanic served the dynamics of emotions and relationships. The audience were also an active part of the game, and participants who have expired their turns to answer were also involved in the audience. Whenever the anchor decides to ask an 'audience question', they could answer through the chat boxes of the messaging application (for example, MS Teams ^{TM}).

For Capture It, we decided to keep the game controls simple to ensure that even participants (or anchors) with little or no gaming experience can easily play.

3.7 Game Technology

Capture It game was developed using the Unity Game engine. The assets and UI items were created using Adobe Photoshop CC, Adobe Animate CC and Adobe Illustrator CC. The game runs as an executable '.exe' file (for Windows) and a '.app file' (for Mac machines) depending on the operating system of the anchor's computer. The.exe/.app files were passcode-locked for ensuring security and only the anchor could open it from their machines by entering the appropriate passcode. The data that was collected throughout the game such as participants' responses, team scores (cells captured), and time information, was automatically stored within the anchor's computer device as a data file, which the anchor then shared with the research team for analysis.

4 Exploratory Study

The study with Capture It game was exploratory in nature, and we intended to gauge the awareness levels of the enterprise employees based on five categories of security (Sect. 3.4). The game was preceded by a pre-game quiz on the same security topics that the game focused on. We focused on finding out if a pre-game quiz and any other factors (such as demographics) can influence the performance of the participants in the game.

4.1 Study Hypotheses

With this exploratory study, we investigated if a serious game-based assessment can give any insights about participants' performance in various cybersecurity areas. We also used this study to test two hypotheses:

- Hypothesis 1: A pre-game quiz will have an effect on the performance of the teams within the game. We hypothesize that a test before the game can motivate the participants into being more focused and motivated for the serious game. The positive effect of 'prequestions' on a learning context was previously reported by certain studies [15, 40, 43], and we investigated this for a cybersecurity, serious game context.
- Hypothesis 2: There will be significant differences in performances between the various demographic groups. This hypothesis is based on certain previous serious games studied for enterprise audiences, which show that certain age groups ([34] suggests that the age-group 41–50 performed the best in Housie, multiplayer game) and genders ([33], suggests that males performed better in Pickmail, single-player game) show varying performance in serious games.

4.2 Methodology

The initial game was launched in an enterprise setting for a small set of participants. The game was developed in collaboration with the security group and business group of an organization under study. The security group had chosen a team of information security managers (ISMs) as anchors to interact with various employees of the organization and conduct the games among various teams. The ISMs sent emails to the employees of their respective business units asking them to participate. Based on availability (known either by replies to the aforementioned emails or through direct communication), the ISMs then selected participants from different project teams belonging to different business units. Then, the playing teams were registered by the ISMs based on the data provided by the employees. The ISMs collected the demographic information from the participants (voluntarily, and the participants were free to not disclose any information) and registered the teams. This demographic information included gender, age group (21 and above), and cybersecurity knowledge (what the participants think of their awareness levels to be, having five categories: Novice, Beginner, Intermediate, Advance, and Expert). After the participants were selected, the pre-game quiz was sent to them as an online link. Later, the teams (with 10 participants each) were created just before the game began, with the same set of participants that were earlier selected. The team-creation was independent of the participation in the pre-test.

4.3 Participants

Overall, 358 participants were part of the initial study as players and among them, 241 participants responded to the questions on demographic details (Male: 67.7%, Female: 31.9%, Prefer not to say: 0.4%). Based on age groups, the participants belonged to 21–30 (46.5%), 31–40 (43.2%), 41–50(7.9%), and Above 50 (2.0%), with 0.4% responding as 'Prefer not to say'. The winners (based on teams) from the business units were also rewarded using the organization's virtual currency, with which they could make purchases from within the organization's portal. The responses to the questions and performance in the game were captured for team-wise analysis.

4.4 Pre-Game Quiz

The pre-game quiz contained 10 questions, with two questions from each of the category focused in the game. A previous study [40] reports that multiple-choice pre-testing has been found to be better for learning related information and suggests instructors to conduct such pre-tests before providing learning content. This inspired us to proceed with a multiple-choice-based pre-game quiz to the participants. Five sample questions from the quiz are given below:

1. Taking backup of data on regular basis ensures __________ of data during crisis (Answer: Availability, Category: Information security)
2. It is a form of an attack on a website. Its acronym is XSS. (Answer: Cross-site scripting, Category: Network Security)
3. What is a person doing if they are following you into an access restricted area without using their own access card? (Answer: Tailgating, Category: Operational Security)

4. A software designed to detect and destroy malware. (Answer: Anti-virus, Category: Application Security)
5. Default password must be changed immediately at ________ log-on. (Answer: First, Category: End-user Education)

The participants did not get the results of the quiz nor the answers before the game. This was to ensure that the quiz, in itself, did not impart any learning or affect the awareness of the participants. The game was conducted on the same day as the pre-test (with no repeating questions), so the participants most likely did not get any extra time to brush up their skills before the game as well.

4.5 Study Results

After completing the 'Capture It' games, we analyzed the results based on team performance, participants' performance, and the security categories to validate our hypotheses 1 and 2, respectively.

Team-Wise Analysis. We identified 18 unique games where teams played with unique participants, forming 36 teams. For the analysis, we removed the duplicated responses from the participants. For example, if a participant 'A' had participated in game 'G1' first, as a part of team 'T1', and then later on, participated in game 'G2' as a part of team 'T2', we only considered the participant for the game 'G1' as the latter was a duplicated entry of the participant. The answers in the game were marked as '0' (incorrect) or '1' (correct), and hence, in this context, the mean score also depicts the mean correctness. Overall, we found a mean score (correctness) of 0.49 (std: 0.18, var = 0.03) within the games. The mean correctness of the participants for the pre-game quiz came to be 0.66 (std: 0.09, var = 0.008).

While performing the analysis for teams, we found that the teams (with at least 2 participants or more) whose members gave responses to the pre-game quiz showed better performance in the game. For teams in which at least 5 participants answered the pre-game quiz (Group A) showed a significantly better response in the game (mean correctness = 0.52, var = 0.03) as compared to those teams where two to five participants attempted it (Group B, mean correctness = 0.39, var = 0.01). We only considered those teams where at least two participants did the pre-game quiz as anything below that could not be considered as a team. Statistical significance was also found using independent samples t-test ($t(14) = 2.05$, $p < 0.05$). Also, Cohen's d indicated a large effect size (0.71), suggesting a meaningful difference between the two groups. The mean of the Group A was found to be higher than Group B as we hypothesized.

Participant-wise Analysis. Table 2 shows the participants' category-wise performance within the game. Based on the category of the questions, our analysis shows that 'end-user education' has the highest in-game mean correctness percentage, followed by 'application security'. 'Information security' shows the least mean correctness, with only 0.39 (or 39%). At the same time, when we consider the demographics of the participants (the 241 participants who provided their demographic details), we found that the males (M = 0.57, var = 0.25) showed a higher correctness as compared to females (M = 0.44, var = 0.25). For the different age groups, we found that 21–30 group showed the highest

Table 2. Category-wise correctness in the game.

Category of question asked in the game	Mean correctness in the game	Variance
Application Security	0.60	0.24
End-user Education	0.63	0.23
Information Security	0.39	0.24
Network Security	0.41	0.24
Operational Security	0.42	0.25

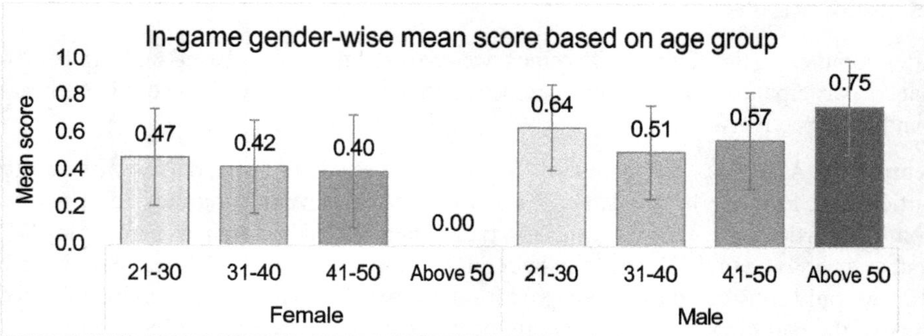

Fig. 3. Mean scores (also depict correctness) in the game based on gender and age group of the 241 participants. Error bar depicts variance of scores.

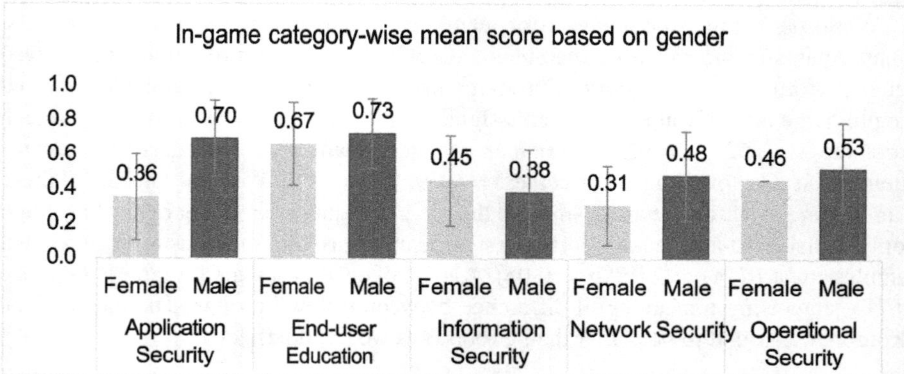

Fig. 4. Mean scores (also depict correctness) in the game based on category and gender (241 participants). Error bar depicts variance of scores.

mean correctness in the game (M = 0.57, var = 0.25), followed by the 41–50 group (M = 0.52, var = 0.26). Group 31–40 has a mean correctness of 0.48 (var = 0.25). The above 50 category has a mean correctness of 0.6, however it has very small number of participants to make it count.

Considering the gender and age group of the participants, we found that females showed relatively lesser mean correctness in all age groups as compared to males (see Fig. 3). This trend was similar in the category-wise mean correctness as well (see Fig. 4), with 'network security' and 'information security' showing the least correctness overall. Even though the means showed a higher value, we could not find any statistical significance between the performance of males and females using a chi-squared test, as the $p - value > 0.05$.

Effects of Design Elements. We had added the design mechanics of 'Challenges' and 'Rewards' (Sect. 3.6) by providing a time-based limitation for answering, to raise the element of 'emotion'. Faster correct responses (under 15 s) would earn '2 cells' on the territory. We analyzed the participants' correctness to the in-game questions based on the time they took to answer. We expected a higher correctness in answers that were given in less than 15 s.

Of the total 358 participants, over 90% responded before 15 s half-time.

Their mean correctness of answers comes to 0.51. Whereas the mean correctness of answers given at or after 15 s comes to 0.26. We found a significant difference in the means using a chi-squared test ($\chi^2 = 6.858, p < 0.05$). This shows that participants tried to give the correct answers before the half-time, thereby ensuring that they capture '2 cells'. The game provided immediate feedback of answers. Qualitative feedback of the game provided by the participants suggest the game was accepted by them positively. In Capture It, there was live interaction between the participants, moderated by the anchor. Majority of the teams were also consisting of friends and colleagues from the same projects. This gave rise to more engagement between the players. The audience questions were added to keep the participants stay alert and focused in the game. The qualitative feedback from the audience such as "amazing game", "best game of the season", "it was really fun playing this" and so on suggest that the participants had a fun experience playing the game.

5 Discussion

5.1 Effect of Pre-Game Quiz

For team-wise analysis, we found that those teams in which at least 50% of the participants participated in the pre-game quiz, the performance within the game was higher overall. This finding sheds light on how the pre-game quiz might have motivated the participants. The reasons could be closely related to the effect of priming, which suggests that a prior stimulus could influence a person's response to a subsequent stimulus. The study by Chen, et al. [16] reports that priming individuals with learning and performance goals can enhance their motivation and effort, thereby leading to increased performance in tasks. While we cannot directly compare 'priming' with the motivation here, we found an increased performance for those who took the pre-test. The performance could also be due to increased engagement in the game because of the pre-game quiz. The participants must have felt that the familiarity in the topics could help them in the game.

A previous study also suggests that multiple-choice pre-test questions could induce deeper processing of information contained in the question [40]. One could argue that there is also a small probability of selection bias in this result, however we believe the chances of it are minimal because the participants were selected by the ISMs and there was no voluntary participation. The only reason for non-participation was unavailability due to work-related engagements. We believe our Hypothesis 1 was found to be true with a statistical significance. This also augments the findings by previous studies that report the positive effects of pre-tests [40, 43].

5.2 On Gameplay, Categories and Demographics

From analyzing the results of the participants' gameplay, we found that individually, there is a high performance in the categories 'application security' and 'end-user education', whereas 'information security' showed the least performance. While the game participants form just a very small portion of the organization's employee base, this still raises concerns regarding the awareness levels. This points to the need for a more frequent and comprehensive training and awareness plan that needs to be followed.

The demographic-wise differences in the performance also show the same trend among categories. While the females show a relatively lesser performance (see Fig. 3), we could not find any statistical significance in this performance difference. Thus, we could not prove our Hypothesis 2 for the current serious game. This contradicts some earlier findings from different studies [33, 34]. This needs to be further researched in a follow-up study. The '21–30' age group showed the highest mean correctness. This could be attributed to the security training and assessments that the employees are exposed to during the initial period of their tenure. This also points to the need for periodic and continuous training, rather than once in a year or once in a quarter training and the need for knowledge retention methods. The '41–50' group comes in second, which could also be attributed to the security training experience they had received over the years. While these findings do not conclusively give a reason as to why certain age groups show reduced performance, it is important to note that continuous training can be helpful in keeping the knowledge retained across participants. Also, as we can see differences in mean correctness among demographics (see Figs. 3 and 4), we believe further studies with a higher participation can provide better insights regarding the performance of various demographic groups.

5.3 Recommendations for the Community

For the future work in the area of serious games for security awareness, we recommend that the method should include various categories of security, and this will help to identify the weak areas for the particular organization.

Studies should include demographic-wise analysis as there have been instances where there were clear differences between the performance.

We found mean differences, however, were not able to validate it statistically. Further studies might help in bringing a consensus of demographic differences vs. security awareness levels of users. A recent study by Zahid et al. [71] found that demographics indeed has an influence on cybersecurity awareness, particularly the gender. The study also suggests that identifying the demographic factors that affect cybersecurity awareness can help in improving the strategies and risk mitigation techniques [71].

The incorporation of time-based challenges in a game could trigger the quick response of participants, which is highly required in real-world scenarios. In our case, the correctness of participants who responded quickly was higher than those responded slower.

While designing team-based serious games, we recommend the use of pregame tests for the users to get familiar with the topics and this could also help them get motivated for the same. This motivation could also be carried forward to real-world situations, which needs to be studied further.

5.4 Considerations for a Broader Scope

Capture It can be easily repurposed to various learning contexts and audience. Below are several areas where the game can be utilized.

Due to the minimal device requirements (as the game resides in the anchor's device, and is playable in offline mode), the game can be beneficial to individuals from economically disadvantaged communities and developing countries who lack access to computers or mobile phones.

As per a journal on digital literacy, a smart blend of online and offline teaching methods can help in improving digital literacy [49], which can then promote education and learning. Capture It offers a solution to incorporate such a hybrid learning method to a wider audience.

The game can be adapted to assess student awareness in various subjects, including physics, history, mathematics, and more.

The game could be used during class lectures for a quick and engaging trivia session. The multiplayer nature of the game could be effectively moderated by the anchor to foster cooperation and communication among students.

5.5 Limitations

This is an exploratory study, and it focuses on enterprise employees and the results are to be considered specific to the participants studied. The study focuses on a very small demographic of the respective organization, and further studies need to be done in order to verify the results and to generalize the findings. Also, the findings may turn out to be different if this study is to be done for a general audience, who are not enterprise employees; this needs to be validated. While we believe that there are effects of the pregame quiz on the participants (as per our findings), we acknowledge that the results could also have been influenced by certain other factors which would need further studies to verify. We believe there is a difference in performance among the various demographics, however, we failed to obtain significant results in this. We believe that with a higher participation, this could be identified. Since this is an exploratory study on the use of a serious game for assessing security awareness, we did not include a control condition or a knowledge retention study. The current study mainly focused on online participation and the offline participation is yet to be explored.

5.6 Future Scope

As an immediate follow-up to this study, we plan to modify our game experiment by creating two categories of participants. One category will include those who completed the pre-test, and the second category will include those participants who did not complete the pre-test. Comparison between the effects of the game for online and offline participants will also be a major topic of study. We also aim to conduct a long-term retention study to find the effects of the game on participants' knowledge retention. The future study will also include measures to judge how the communication between the participants and the anchor can affect the performance outcome (if any).

6 Conclusion

We designed and developed the repurposable game 'Capture It' and used it to assess the security awareness of enterprise employees in five categories of security. This exploratory study was to identify if a serious game can be used for assessment and if any meaningful findings can be obtained from it. We found that the general awareness in areas such as 'Application security' and 'End-user education' was high with 'Information security' showing the least performance overall. By answering our research question, we found that the teams where participants completed a pre-game quiz showed better correctness within the game. We could not find any significant demographic-based differences in the correctness. Our initial findings suggest that adding a time-based challenge can affect the correctness of answers and participants will attempt to 'beat the clock', which could prove useful in real-life where they would have to act swiftly, for example in judging a phishing email and to avoid clicking on it. Capture It can be effectively repurposed to focus on a wider range of learning contexts to a larger audience. As our future work, we plan to include measures to judge how communication between participants can affect the outcome in performance. We also plan to include control condition and the use of a post-game assessment to see how the awareness assessment can affect participants' long-term knowledge retention.

References

1. APWG trends report. https://apwg.org/trendsreports/. Accessed 16 April 2024
2. The conversation, Madagascar report. https://theconversation.com/how-kidsin-a-low-income-country-use-laptops-lessons-from-madagascar-93305. Accessed 24 Sep 2024
3. FBI crime report. https://www.ic3.gov/Media/PDF/AnnualReport/2023IC3Report.pdf. Accessed 24 Sep 2024
4. Fortinet. https://www.fortinet.com/resources/cyberglossary/operational-security. Accessed 24 Sep 2024
5. Gartner reports press release. https://www.gartner.com/en/newsroom/press-releases/2023-02-22-gartner-predicts-nearly-half-of-cybersecurity-leaders-willchange-jobs-by-2025. Accessed 24 Sep 2024
6. The hidden cost of poor security awareness training on your organization. https://www.linkedin.com/pulse/hidden-cost-poor-security-awareness-training-your-robertsiedt/. Accessed 24 Sep 2024

7. Reasons you need gamification. https://www.terranovasecurity.com/blog/reasons-you-need-gamification-insecurity-awareness/. Accessed 24 Sep 2024
8. Kiwi LMS, homepage. https://startkiwi.com/blog/gamification-in-the-workplacetactics-for-restaurant-gamification. Accessed 24 Sep 2024
9. TAV Technologies. https://tavtechnologies.aero/en-EN/services/servicescybersecurity/pages/end-user-education. Accessed 24 Sep 2024
10. Adams, E., Dormans, J.: Game Mechanics: Advanced Game Design. New Riders (2012)
11. Awojana, T., Chou, T.S.: Overview of learning cybersecurity through game based systems. In: 2019 CIEC (2019)
12. Bellotti, F., et al.: Designing serious games for education: from pedagogical principles to game mechanisms. In: Proceedings of the 5th European Conference on Games Based Learning, pp. 26–34. University of Athens Greece (2011)
13. Calleja, G.: In-Game: From Immersion to Incorporation. MIT Press (2011)
14. Caponetto, I., Earp, J., Ott, M.: Gamification and education: a literature review. In: European Conference on Games Based Learning, vol. 1, p. 50. Academic Conferences International Limited (2014)
15. Carpenter, S.K., Rahman, S., Perkins, K.: The effects of prequestions on classroom learning. J. Exp. Psychol. Appl. **24**(1), 34 (2018)
16. Chen, X., Latham, G.P.: The effect of priming learning vs. performance goals on a complex task. Org. Behav. Hum. Decis. Process. **125**(2), 88–97 (2014)
17. Cheong, C., Cheong, F., Filippou, J.: Quick quiz: a gamified approach for enhancing learning (2013)
18. Chettoor Jayakrishnan, G., Banahatti, V., Lodha, S.: GOVID: repurposing serious game for enterprise COVID-19 awareness. In: Proceedings of the 12th Indian Conference on Human-Computer Interaction, pp. 11–18 (2021)
19. CJ, G., Pandit, S., Vaddepalli, S., Tupsamudre, H., Banahatti, V., Lodha, S.: Phishy-a serious game to train enterprise users on phishing awareness. In: Proceedings of the 2018 Annual Symposium on Computer-Human Interaction in Play Companion Extended Abstracts, pp. 169–181 (2018)
20. Coco, A., Woodward, I., Shaw, K., Cody, A., Lupton, G., Peake, A.: Bingo for beginners: a game strategy for facilitating active learning. Teach. Sociol. **29**(4), 492–503 (2001)
21. Cózar-Gutiérrez, R., Sáez-López, J.M.: Game-based learning and gamification in initial teacher training in the social sciences: an experiment with MinecraftEdu. Int. J. Educ. Technol. High. Educ. **13**, 1–11 (2016)
22. Felder, R.M., Brent, R.: Designing and teaching courses to satisfy the abet engineering criteria. J. Eng. Educ. **92**(1), 7–25 (2003)
23. Ge, X., Ifenthaler, D.: Designing engaging educational games and assessing engagement in game-based learning. In: Gamification in Education: Breakthroughs in Research and Practice, pp. 1–19. IGI Global (2018)
24. Georgiou, K., Gouras, A., Nikolaou, I.: Gamification in employee selection: The development of a gamified assessment. Int. J. Sel. Assess. **27**(2), 91–103 (2019)
25. Gkorezis, P., Georgiou, K., Nikolaou, I., Kyriazati, A.: Gamified or traditional situational judgement test? A moderated mediation model of recommendation intentions via organizational attractiveness. Euro. J. Work Org. Psychol. **30**(2), 240–250 (2021)
26. Graham, K., et al.: Cyberspace odyssey: a competitive team-oriented serious game in computer networking. IEEE Trans. Learn. Technol. **13**(3), 502–515 (2020)
27. Hämäläinen, R.: Using a game environment to foster collaborative learning: a design-based study. Technol. Pedagog. Educ. **20**(1), 61–78 (2011)
28. Hämäläinen, R., Manninen, T., Häkkinen, P., Järvelä, S.: Learning to collaborate: designing collaboration in a 3D game environment. Internet High. Educ. **9**(1), 47–61 (2006)

29. Hattie, J., Timperley, H.: The power of feedback. Tijdschrift voor Medisch Onderwijs **27**(1), 50–51 (2008). https://doi.org/10.1007/BF03078234
30. Hawari, N., Zain, N.H.M., Baharum, A.: The need of gamified assessment for engaging learning experience. Bull. Electr. Eng. Inf. **9**(2), 722–728 (2020)
31. Huo, Y.: A pedagogy-based framework for optimizing learning efficiency across multiple disciplines in educational games. Int. J. Inf. Educ. Technol. **9**(10), 704–709 (2019)
32. Ibanez, M.B., Di-Serio, A., Delgado-Kloos, C.: Gamification for engaging computer science students in learning activities: a case study. IEEE Trans. Learn. Technol. **7**(3), 291–301 (2014)
33. Jayakrishnan, G., Banahatti, V., Lodha, S.: PickMail: a serious game for email phishing awareness training. In: Usable Security and Privacy (USEC) Symposium, vol. 2022 (2022)
34. Jayakrishnan, G.C., Banahatti, V., Lodha, S., Sirigireddy, G., Nivas, S.: Housie: a multiplayer game for cybersecurity training and evaluation. In: Extended Abstracts of the 2022 Annual Symposium on Computer-Human Interaction in Play, pp. 17–23 (2022)
35. Jayakrishnan, G.C., Sirigireddy, G.R., Vaddepalli, S., Banahatti, V., Lodha, S.P., Pandit, S.S.: PassWorld: a serious game to promote password awareness and diversity in an enterprise. In: Sixteenth Symposium on Usable Privacy and Security (SOUPS 2020), pp. 1–18 (2020)
36. Kam, H.J., Ormond, D.K., Menard, P., Crossler, R.E.: That's interesting: an examination of interest theory and self-determination in organisational cybersecurity training. Inf. Syst. J. **32**(4), 888–926 (2022)
37. Karagiannis, S., Magkos, E.: Engaging students in basic cybersecurity concepts using digital game-based learning: computer games as virtual learning environments. Advances in Core Computer Science-Based Technologies: Papers in Honor of Professor Nikolaos Alexandris, pp. 55–81 (2021)
38. Kizza, J.: Computer Network Security (2005). https://doi.org/10.1007/b106962
39. Kocadere, S.A., Çağlar, Ş: The design and implementation of a gamified assessment. J. e-Learn. Knowl. Soc. **11**(3) (2015)
40. Little, J.L., Bjork, E.L.: Multiple-choice pretesting potentiates learning of related information. Mem. Cognit. **44**, 1085–1101 (2016)
41. Liu, Z.Y., Shaikh, Z.A., Gazizova, F.: Using the concept of game-based learning in education. Int. J. Emerg. Technol. Learn. (2020)
42. Moccozet, L., Tardy, C., Opprecht, W., Léonard, M.: Gamification-based assessment of group work. In: 2013 International Conference on Interactive Collaborative Learning (ICL), pp. 171–179. IEEE (2013)
43. Murphy, D.H., Little, J.L., Bjork, E.L.: The value of using tests in education as tools for learning—not just for assessment. Educ. Psychol. Rev. **35**(3), 89 (2023)
44. Nikolaou, I., Georgiou, K., Kotsasarlidou, V.: Exploring the relationship of a gamified assessment with performance. Span. J. Psychol. **22**, E6 (2019)
45. Nogry, S., Varly, P.: Everyday laptop use by children in a southern country: a mixed-method approach. J. Res. Technol. Educ. **50**(1), 18–33 (2018)
46. Nugraha, E., Salsabila, S., Ramadhiani, T.: Implementing online quiz application in EFL classroom. Educ. Linguist. Comput. Sci., 308–314 (2021)
47. Paixa˜o, W.B.D., Cordeiro, I.J.D.: Gamification practices in tourism: An analysis based on the model by werbach & hunter (2012). Revista Brasileira de Pesquisa em Turismo **15**, e–2067 (2021)
48. Park, J., Kim, S., Kim, A., Mun, Y.Y.: Learning to be better at the game: Performance vs. completion contingent reward for game-based learning. Comput. Educ. **139**, 1–15 (2019)
49. Pawar, M.A.: Role of digital literacy among teachers and students in 21st century india. Educ. Resurgence J. **3**(6), 93–101 (2021)
50. Protopsaltis, A., et al.: Scenario-based serious games repurposing. In: Proceedings of the 29th ACM International Conference on Design of Communication, pp. 37–44 (2011)

51. Ramos-Villagrasa, P.J., Fernández-del-Río, E., Castro, Á.: Game-related assessments for personnel selection: a systematic review. Front. Psychol. **13**, 952002 (2022)
52. Romero, M., Proulx, J.N.: Conceptions and instructional strategies of pre-service teachers towards digital game based learning integration in the primary education curriculum. IJDLDC **7**(2), 11–22 (2016)
53. Saleem, A.N., Noori, N.M., Ozdamli, F.: Gamification applications in e-learning: a literature review. Technol. Knowl. Learn. **27**(1), 139–159 (2022)
54. Sawyer, B.: Serious games: improving public policy through game. Foresight and Governance Project (2001)
55. Sheng, S., et al.: Anti-phishing phil: the design and evaluation of a game that teaches people not to fall for phish. In: Proceedings of the 3rd Symposium on Usable Privacy and Security, pp. 88–99 (2007)
56. Spyridonis, F., Daylamani-Zad, D., O'Brien, M.P.: Efficient in-game communication in collaborative online multiplayer games. In: 2018 10th International Conference on Virtual Worlds and Games for Serious Applications (VS-Games), pp. 1–4. IEEE (2018)
57. Sung, H.Y., Hwang, G.J., Lin, C.J., Hong, T.W.: Experiencing the analects of confucius: an experiential game-based learning approach to promoting students' motivation and conception of learning. Comput. Educ. **110**, 143–153 (2017)
58. Susi, T., Johannesson, M., Backlund, P.: Serious Games: An Overview (2007)
59. Tupsamudre, H., et al.: Gap: a game for improving awareness about passwords. In: Serious Games: 4th Joint International Conference, JCSG 2018, Darmstadt, Germany, November 7–8, 2018, Proceedings 4, pp. 66–78. Springer (2018)
60. Twitchell, D.P.: Securitycom: a multi-player game for researching and teaching information security teams. J. Digital Forensics Secur. Law **2**(4), 1 (2007)
61. WaiShiang, C., Khairuddin, M.A.B., et al.: How to model an engaging online quiz? The emotion modeling approach. J. Telecommun. Inf. Technol. (2022)
62. Wang, A.I., Tahir, R.: The effect of using kahoot! For learning–a literature review. Comput. Educ. **149**, 103818 (2020)
63. Wang, J., Hodgson, R., Cristea, A.I.: Memorable: a multi-player customisable serious game framework for cyber-security learning. In: International Conference on Intelligent Tutoring Systems, pp. 313–322. Springer (2022)
64. Wen, Z.A., Lin, Z., Chen, R., Andersen, E.: What. hack: engaging anti-phishing training through a role-playing phishing simulation game. In: Proceedings of the 2019 CHI Conference on Human Factors in Computing Systems, pp. 1–12 (2019)
65. Werbach, K., Hunter, D.: For the Win, vol. 51. Wharton Digital Press, Philadelphia (2012)
66. Wiernik, B.M., Raghavan, M., Caretta, T.R., Coovert, M.D.: Developing and validating a serious game-based assessment for cyber occupations in the us air force. Int. J. Sel. Assess. **30**(1), 27–47 (2022)
67. Wood, L., Teras, H., Reiners, T., Gregory, S.: The role of gamification and game-based learning in authentic assessment within virtual environments. In: Research and Development in Higher Education: The Place of Learning and Teaching, pp. 514–523 (2013)
68. Yasin, A., Liu, L., Li, T., Wang, J., Zowghi, D.: Design and preliminary evaluation of a cyber security requirements education game (SREG). Inf. Softw. Technol. **95**, 179–200 (2018)
69. Yoder, J., Barcalow, J.: Architectural patterns for enabling application security. In: Proceedings of the 4th Conference on Patterns Language of Programming (PLoP'97). vol. 2, p. 30. Citeseer (1997)
70. Yoo, C.W., Sanders, G.L., Cerveny, R.P.: Exploring the influence of flow and psychological ownership on security education, training and awareness effectiveness and security compliance. Decis. Support. Syst. **108**, 107–118 (2018)

71. Zahid, I.A., Hussein, S.A., Mahdi, S.M.: Measuring individuals cybersecurity awareness based on demographic features (2023)
72. Zyda, M.: From visual simulation to virtual reality to games. Computer **38**(9), 25–32 (2005)

Designing Digital Learning Interventions for Primary School Teachers in Rural and Remote, Low- and Middle-Income Areas: A Systematic Review

Daniel Cabezas López[1](✉), Enric Mor Pera[1](✉), Jose Abdelnour Nocera[2](✉), and Nurha Yingta[2](✉)

[1] Faculty of Computer Science, Multimedia and Telecommunications, Universitat Oberta de Catalunya, Barcelona, Spain
{dcabezasl,emor}@uoc.edu

[2] School of Computing and Engineering, University of West London, London, UK
jose.abdelnour-nocera@uwl.ac.uk, 21363511@student.uwl.ac.uk

Abstract. M-learning has established itself as a popular and effective educational method, leveraging the universality of mobile devices. This approach is particularly valuable for continuous training of teachers in rural areas of low- and middle-income countries. This paper presents a systematic review of the literature on m-learning from the perspective of Human-Computer Interaction for Development (HCI4D), focusing on these regions. Databases including Science Direct, ACM, and Google Scholar were searched, ultimately selecting 52 articles published between 2014 and 2024 through specific inclusion and exclusion criteria. The PRISMA framework guided the analysis, uncovering various gaps in m-learning for longlife learning in rural areas. The review identified important gaps and opportunities at the intersection of HCI4D and m-learning in relation to themes of interest, geographical coverage, preferred methodologies and technological focus.

Additional Keywords and Phrases: HCI4D · Design Models · Digital Learning · m-learning · Global South · Rural Areas · Lifelong Learning · Primary School Teachers

1 Introduction

In October 2019, the World Bank and UNESCO introduced a new indicator called Learning Poverty to address low levels of education and track progress towards the goal of all children acquiring basic skills [56]. Prior to the COVID-19 pandemic, 53% of children in low and middle-income countries could not read comprehensively by the age of 10, and this percentage was projected to only decrease to 44% by 2030, far from the universal lite[1]racy goal of the Sustainable Development Goals. According to the

Published by Springer Nature Switzerland AG 2026
G. Bhutkar et al. (Eds.): IDID 2024, IFIP AICT 747, pp. 125–143, 2026.
https://doi.org/10.1007/978-3-032-00777-3_8

2022 Global Learning Poverty Report [57], developed by various organizations, school closures due to the pandemic exacerbated this crisis, with estimated learning poverty at 70%, further widening educational disparities. This underscores the urgent need to take steps to mitigate this learning poverty and avoid a catastrophic educational deficit.

For the last two decades, the field of research, Human Computer Interaction for Development (HCI4D [1, 6, 47]), has adapted and created traditional HCI methods to design and deploy solutions in developing countries, with an emphasis on local experiences and the adaptation of methodological frameworks from different disciplines.

In HCI4D research, education has been one of the most studied fields over the past decade [6]. One of the main pillars, fundamental to combating educational poverty, is the professional development of teachers [58]. Despite this, promoting the professional development of teachers in rural areas of low- and middle-income countries (LMICs) faces significant challenges, such as limited access to technology, lack of resources, and the scattered distribution of the population [59].

Rural areas are often characterized by what they lack: large and dense populations, robust infrastructure (e.g., internet access), economic resources, and proximity to specialized knowledge. According to Jean Hardy, Susan Wyche, and Tiffany Veinot [16], rural HCI research conducted in developing regions largely focuses on areas with limited or no infrastructure (or records the introduction of infrastructure), and communities that have not been normatively associated with the use of digital technology (e.g., oral cultures, people with limited formal education).

Another element that underpins this review was introduced by UNESCO in 2013 with the document "Policy guidelines for mobile learning," mobile learning. This new form of learning involves using mobile technology, either alone or with other ICTs, to facilitate learning anytime and anywhere. Mobile technologies, such as mobile phones and tablets, are diverse and constantly evolving, with more than 3.2 billion mobile phone subscribers worldwide. Mobile learning, a branch of ICT in education, becomes a highly useful element in low-resource contexts due to its affordability and ease of acquisition. Unlike wired computers, mobile learning assumes that students have uninterrupted access to technology. A Dell and Kumar [10], presented an empirical analysis of HCI4D literature (2009–2016) highlighting a trend where the rapid increase in the use of mobile devices worldwide, especially in LMICs, had led to mobile devices becoming a significant focal point within the field of Human-Computer Interaction for Development (HCI4D). On the other hand, van Biljon and Renaud [6], in the results of their empirical analysis of HCI4D literature, suggested that the research was community-focused and designed with mobile phones as the most important technology in HCI4D research.

The last element underpinning this research is based on understanding the methodological approach of this discipline. Toyama [47] argues that research in HCI4D has adopted a set of recognized methodologies, grouped into three main categories: qualitative methods and user studies, iterative design and prototyping, and evaluation. Additionally, HCI4D also contemplates a fourth activity: reflection, which considers the broader social implications of research. Van Biljon and Renaud [6] position HCI4D as an interdisciplinary field that adapts traditional HCI methods to design solutions in developing countries, highlighting the importance of the human element in technology design and focusing on geographic differences in performance. HCI4D focuses on local experiences, adapting conceptual and methodological frameworks from HCI to make them locally relevant. According to Abdelnour-Nocera and Densmore [1], integrating HCI concepts and tools into locally relevant technology design requires a deep consideration of the perspectives and practices of indigenous communities. This process involves taking into account the beliefs, values, and forms of knowledge characteristic of these communities to gain new insights into what is considered useful, usable, and a good user experience.

This paper presents a systematic review of the existing body of research in HCI4D and m-learning as part of a wider project to help reduce learning poverty through the continuous professional development of teachers in rural areas of LMICs.

Furthermore, the article is organized into sections, including research questions and objectives, review methodology, results, synthesis of research and discussion with future directions.

1.1 Research Question and Aims

The present systematic review aims to answer the following research question:

What is known about HCI4D research in designing m-learning interventions for primary school teachers, specifically in rural/remote areas of low- and middle-income countries (LMICs)?

The aim of this research is to understand the state of the art of HCI in relation to the design of m-learning interventions for primary school teachers, specifically in rural/remote areas of LMICs. This will be achieved through a systematic review of the current literature. The systematic review was chosen because it allows for exhaustive data collection and analysis, providing greater confidence in the results obtained and offering a rigorous approach to identifying patterns, gaps, and trends that are essential for mapping the state of the art. The systematic review was selected due to its ability to provide a comprehensive and rigorous overview of the existing landscape, enabling the identification of gaps and trends in the field. Unlike other approaches, the systematic review uses a more structured and transparent method, ensuring that all relevant studies are considered comprehensively. This approach best fits the objective of mapping the state of the art, as it provides a detailed analysis and allows for solid conclusions regarding the opportunities and limitations of current research.

Following the PRISMA framework [60] the objectives of this review are:

- To summarize and map the available literature on HCI design of digital learning for primary school teachers in rural areas of LMICs from 2014 to 2024.
- To identify research gaps in the following fields: research themes, geographic coverage, methodological approach, technological focus.
- To make recommendations for future studies of HCI for m-learning designed for primary school teachers in rural areas of LMICs.

These issues will be key to establishing a doctoral research line at the Universitat Oberta de Barcelona. This project will focus on the ongoing training of teachers in the Sahrawi camps in Tindouf, Algeria, implemented through the RASDALE working group at the University of Seville (US).

2 Research Methodology

This systematic review was conducted with the purpose of covering a wide range of articles while keeping the search manageable. The search chain was designed based on the research question of the study, ensuring that all relevant articles that included topics on the knowledge area addressed, the place of intervention, the population group, and the areas of intervention were captured. Three tools were used for this study, two database: Science Direct (Elsevier), the Association for Computing Machinery (ACM); and one search engine: Google Scholar.

As part of this systematic review, a meta-analysis was conducted using statistical methods to objectively assess the outcomes [19], allowing us to arrive at a synthesis of evidence [55]. This aided in the interpretation of individual studies in the context of global knowledge about the HCI theme, offering a solid and transparent knowledge base that would allow converting the research into decision-making for future studies. The methodology identified four knowledge groups that will help evaluate the robustness of the evidence and analyze the studies to answer the question posed. These groups were: Research Themes, Geographic Coverage, Methodological, Technology Focus.

2.1 Selection Terms

The keywords used in the search for the systematic review were developed in two phases. In the first phase, 20 keywords were selected through the UNESCO Thesaurus [61] and ACM Computing Classification System [62] (see Table 1). Subsequently, in the second phase, each keyword was analyzed for its frequency of use in each search engine during the period between 2014 and 2024, in order to select the 8 main keywords that would be used in the search.

Table 1. Keywords.

Keywords	Elements
Human Computer Interaction, "HCI", Human Computer Interaction for Development, "HCI4D"	Knowledge area
Rural Areas, Remote areas, Developing countries	Intervention area
Primary school teachers, Teachers	Population
Teacher training, Lifelong learning, Lifelong education, Permanent Learning, Adult learning, Continuous learning	Intervention Objective
M-learning, Mobile learning, Mobile education, e-learning, Mobile e-learning	Technology

In Group 1 (see Table 2), the keywords 'Human-Computer Interaction,' 'HCI,' 'Human-Computer Interaction for Development,' and 'HCI4D' were reviewed, which define the area of knowledge addressed in the research. The data revealed that the most recurrent keyword during this decade was 'Human-Computer Interaction,' with more than 2.8 million mentions.

Table 2. Group 1.

Keyword	ScienceDirect	Google Scholar	ACM	Total
HCI	10814	459620	53,937	524371
Human Computer Interaction	14653	2779040	35156	2828849
HCI4D	6	5870	463	6339
Human Computer Interaction for Development	9	2004	463	2476

In group 2 (see Table 3), the terms "Rural Areas," "Remote Areas," and "Developing Countries," which specify the particular scope of intervention, were analyzed. The data indicated that the most common keyword within the scope of our research was "Developing Countries," with more than 1.1 million mentions, followed by "Rural Areas," with more than 472 thousand mentions.

Table 3. Group 2.

Keyword	ScienceDirect	Google Scholar	ACM	Total
Rural areas	271379	4456800	427	4728606
Remote areas	275558	1320870	409	1596837
Developing countries	967615	10062500	2,625	11032740

In group 3 (see Table 4), the terms "Primary School Teacher" and "Teacher" and "Developing Countries" were examined to define the target group of the intervention. The data showed that the most used keyword during this decade in the scope of our research was "Teacher," with more than 977 thousand mentions.

Table 4. Group 3.

Keyword	ScienceDirect	Google Scholar	ACM	Total
Primary School Teacher	55976	186798	94	242868
Teacher	129386	9618900	27,351	9775637

In group 4 (see Table 5), the keywords "Teacher Training," "Lifelong Learning," "Permanent Education," "Continuing Education," and "Adult Learning" were explored to delimit the area of intervention of the research. The data indicated that the most used keyword during this decade in the scope of our research was "Teacher Training," with more than 1.6 million mentions, followed by "Lifelong Learning," with more than 472 thousand mentions.

Table 5. Group 4.

Keyword	ScienceDirect	Goggle Scholar	ACM	Total
Teacher training	67125	1585350	1,497	1653972
Lifelong learning	26318	1348000	1,696	1376014
Lifelong education	31462	227526	115	259103
Permanent Learning	182	58156	22	58360
Adult learning	3385	416320	128	419833
Continuous learning	5623	342920	1,012	349555

Lastly, in group 5 (see Table 6), the terms "Mobile Learning," "Learning on Mobile Devices," "e-learning," "Mobile Education," and "Electronic Learning" were investigated to define a second area of intervention in the research. The data showed that the most used term was "Mobile Learning," with more than 686 thousand mentions, followed by "Learning on Mobile Devices" with more than 453 thousand mentions.

Table 6. Group 5.

Keyword	ScienceDirect	Goggle Scholar	ACM	Total
M-learning	821	452870	303	453994
Mobile learning	1616	684420	953	686989
Mobile education	119	40355	56	40530
Mobile e-learning	22	10734	8	10764

Following the analysis conducted, the main components of the search chain were as follows: "Human Computer Interaction" AND ("Developing Countries" OR "Rural areas" OR "Remote areas") AND "Teacher" AND ("Teacher training" OR "Lifelong learning") AND ("Mobile learning" OR "M-learning").

2.2 Search Process

Table 7 presents the inclusion and exclusion criteria used to ensure that the analysis does not contain superfluous information. By using separate lists for the exclusion criteria, the researchers aimed to maintain a precise and well-focused selection of studies, aligned with the research objectives. This method allows for the elimination of studies that do not meet the established criteria, ensuring that only the most pertinent and applicable ones are considered for further analysis.

2.3 Search Process

The search period covered the years from 2014 to 2024, with the aim of gaining a comprehensive overview of the state of the art in HCI4D over the past decade. After completing the search, the data was collected using Zotero software. This tool facilitated the entire process of selecting relevant articles, including removing duplicate entries, applying automatic filters, and organizing the articles into categorized folders. These folders were subsequently shared online, enabling all team members to easily access the files.

As reflected in Fig. 1 of the Identification of studies through databases and records [60], the search was conducted on March 11, 2014, and a total of 2671 results were obtained among the three databases. The first step was to eliminate duplicate articles. After conducting all the searches, we encountered many duplicate results. To solve this, we used the "remove duplicates" function of Zotero to keep only the unique entries. A

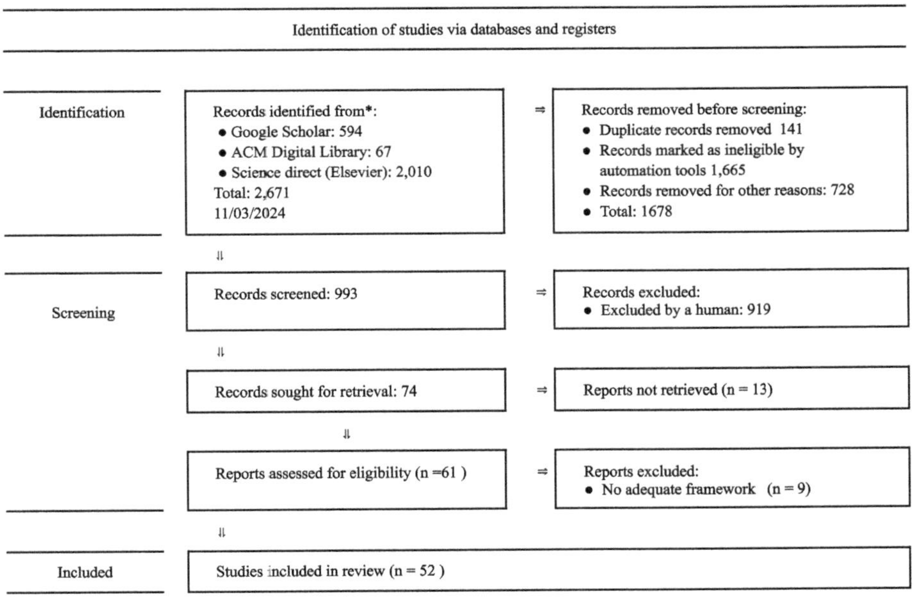

Fig. 1. PRISMA Flow Diagram.

Table 7. Keywords.

Exclusion Criteria	Exclusion Criteria
IC-1: The paper should be focused on HCI, HCI4D and ICT4D;	EC1: The paper is written in a language other than English.
IC-2: The article provides information about digital learning focused in the m-learning;	EC2: Publications that are not within the field of HCI or HCI4D
IC-3: The paper is thoroughly researched, scientifically robust, and has been published as a peer-reviewed journal article between 2014 and 2024.	

total of 141 duplicate records were excluded. In the next step, a total of 1678 articles that did not correspond to the knowledge area of HCI were automatically excluded. In the third step, a total of 885 articles were eliminated, excluded through the selection of titles/abstracts. In the fourth step, panels, workshops, editorials, extended abstracts, forums, and books were eliminated, leaving 74 documents for in-depth analysis, of which 13 were eliminated for not having access to the full text. Then, a thematic analysis was conducted to analyze the abstracts of the articles and draw conclusions based on common themes or patterns identified in each phase to answer the research question, and 9 were eliminated for not having an adequate research framework, leaving 52 studies included for the systematic review.

3 Results

As discussed in the methodology, the results of this systematic review were analyzed through a meta-analysis using statistical methods to objectively assess the outcomes [19], allowing us to arrive at a synthesis of evidence [55]. The methodology identified four knowledge groups to answer the question posed (Research Themes, Geographic Coverage, Methodological, Technology Focus). Thus, the results were as follows:

3.1 Themes of Interest

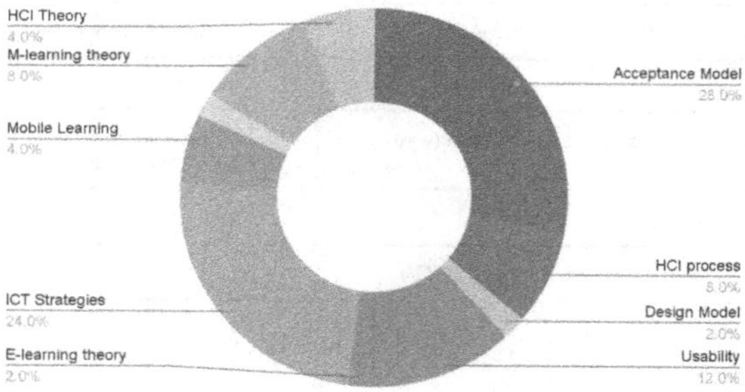

Fig. 2. Research Themes and Topics.

The dominant themes in the analyzed literature (see Fig. 2) evidence two predominant lines of research over the last decade: works that center their research on the technological acceptance of mobile devices for m-learning by teachers and students [3, 3, 7, 15, 24, 25, 31, 35, 36, 41, 43, 45, 46, 53], representing 28% of the analyzed documents, among these, the "Technology Acceptance Model" (TAM) stands out as predominant among the different models of technological acceptance; and works whose research base is found in the strategies of Information and Communication Technologies (ICT)[12, 13, 18, 20–22, 26, 37, 42, 49–51], comprising 24% of the analyzed documents. This category contains a great diversity of research on new technologies and learning strategies based on mobile technology. A 14% of the studies conducted focused on the field of Usability [9, 14, 28,

32, 38, 40, 54], encompassing from Heuristics, evaluation of m-learning platforms to universal accessibility, among others. The categories m-learning Theory [5, 27, 29, 34] and HCI models [8, 17, 39, 48] reached a quota of 8% respectively in the last decade. The rest of the studies were below 4%, and the themes found included HCI Theory (4%), Mobile Learning (4%), Design Model (2%).

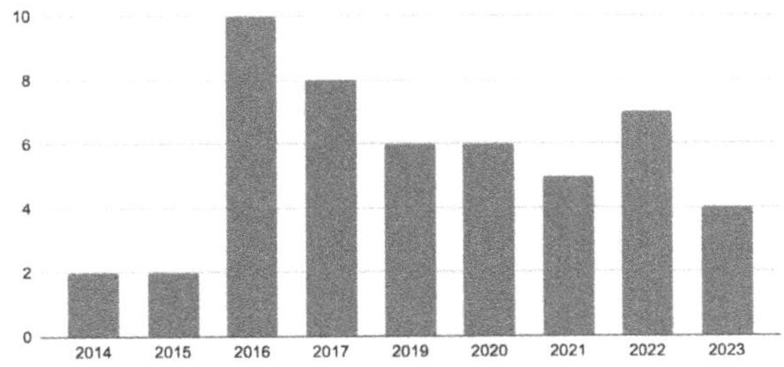

Fig. 3. Research between 2014 -2024.

Over the decade in which the study was based, no noteworthy trends were detected in the research, and the topics studied have remained stable over these years (see Fig. 3), except in the years 2014 and 2015 where there is low production of articles and in 2018 which is non-existent. The themes mentioned above have been recurrent over time.

3.2 Geographic Coverage

Fig. 4. Geographic coverage by countries.

This section provides an overview of the countries and regions towards which the studies in the field of HCI4D have been directed, as well as the educational levels that have been the object of research. Based on the geographic information statistics [63] (see Figs. 4 and 5), the results show that the most recurrent regions for research are Sub-Saharan Africa (South Africa, Tanzania, Kenya, Nigeria, and Uganda), where the studies focused on 32.4% [11, 12, 14, 20, 22, 24, 25, 29, 33, 36, 37, 53]; East Asia and the Pacific (Indonesia, Thailand, and Malaysia), with 21.6% of the publications [4, 8, 21, 32, 45, 48, 51, 52]; South Asia (India, Nepal, Pakistan, and Bangladesh), with 18.9% of the publications [17, 38, 38, 41, 44, 49]; Middle East and North Africa (Egypt, Iran, and Lebanon), with 8.1% [15, 42, 46]; Europe and Central Asia, with 2.7% [35]; and studies that focus their research on more than one region, with 13.5% [7, 23, 26, 30, 54].

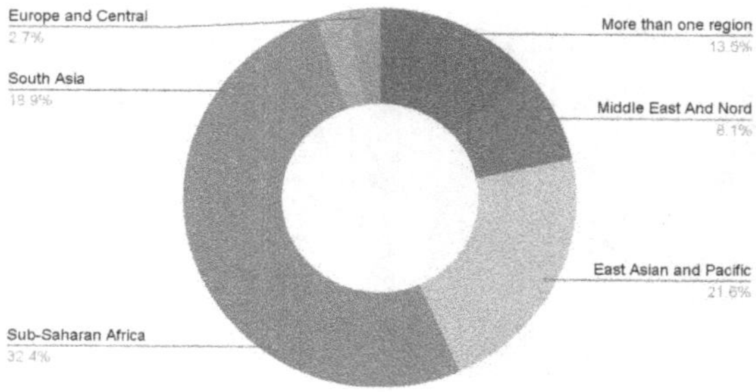

Fig. 5. Geography Coverage by regions.

The reviewed articles were classified according to the educational level that provided the focus of the research. It was revealed that more than half of the research (57.7%) [4, 7, 12, 13, 15, 20, 24, 30, 32, 33, 36, 37, 40, 46, 53] was conducted in higher education, followed by 26.9% [8, 9, 14, 22, 26, 48, 51] of the research in primary education. Relatively few studies were conducted in vocational education (3.8%) [43], secondary education (7.7%) [25, 35], and general education (3.8%) [11], as shown in Fig. 6.

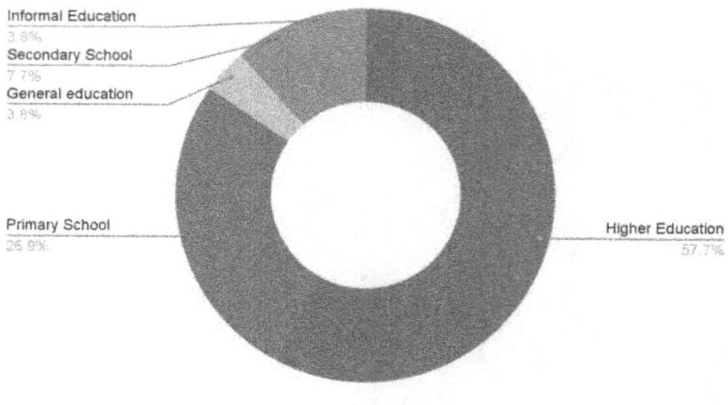

Fig. 6. Educational Level.

3.3 Methodological Approach

In HCI4D research, as in other domains, quantitative, qualitative, or mixed approaches are often adopted, depending on the aim of the study. According to the 52 articles reviewed, approximately half (49%) [4, 8–12, 15, 18, 20, 25, 31, 32, 35, 38, 41–43, 45,

46, 51, 52] used quantitative methods. Mixed methods were employed in 32% of the studies [3, 7, 13, 14, 22, 24, 26, 28, 29, 33, 34, 36, 37, 44, 48, 54], while the remaining 20% [5, 16, 21, 23, 27, 30, 39, 50] opted for qualitative approaches (see Fig. 7).

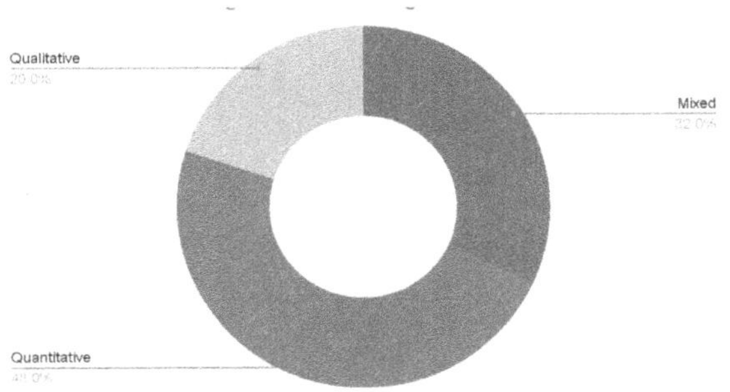

Fig. 7. Methodologies.

In relation to the percentage distribution of population groups in the sample of the analyzed studies, the most represented group was that of teachers, with 37.5% [9, 22, 25, 26, 29, 43, 44, 49, 51, 52], followed by students, with 34.4%[4, 7, 14, 15, 20, 21, 32, 35–37, 46]. The studies that included both teachers and students represent 28.1% [11, 12, 18, 24, 31, 33, 40, 41, 53]. Figure 8 illustrates the distribution of these population groups in the reviewed articles.

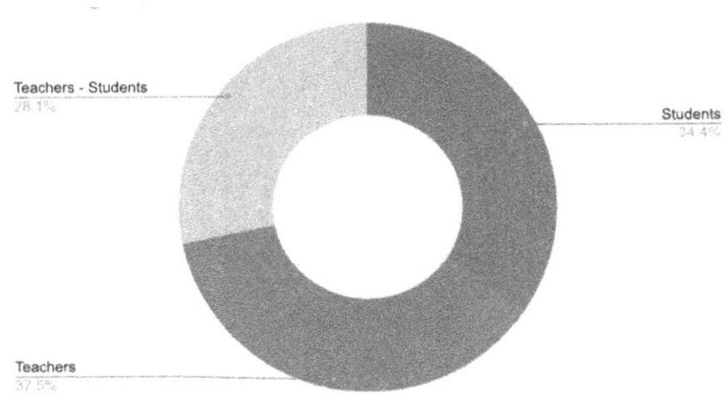

Fig. 8. Focus group.

In a study on the data collection tools most used by researchers (see Fig. 9), it was found that surveys are the most popular, used by 42% [4, 8–12, 15, 18, 20, 25, 31, 32, 35, 38, 41–43, 45, 46, 51, 52] of the researchers. Mixed methods of surveys and interviews follow, used by 20%[7, 22, 24, 29, 36, 37, 48]. Theoretical analyses and systematic reviews were employed by 14% [2, 3, 13, 17, 28, 34, 54] of the researchers each. Finally, experiments and case studies were used by 4% [21, 26, 26, 40, 53], and interviews only by 2% [49].

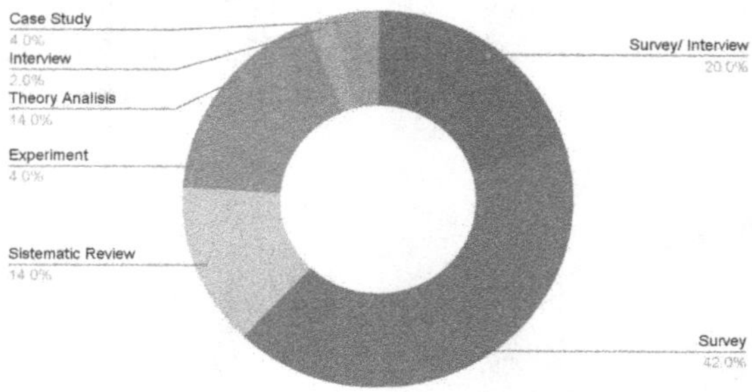

Fig. 9. Methodological approach/ Tools.

3.4 Technological Focus

In the present research, the technologies used for m-learning, which appeared in 88.5% of the analyzed research (see Fig. 10), were employed especially in LMICs. It was discovered that almost half of the studies (46%) [2, 4, 5, 7, 8, 13, 15, 18, 22, 25, 29, 30, 30, 31, 36, 37, 39, 40, 45, 48, 49] explored various aspects of Learning Management Systems (LMS). Likewise, 34% [10, 17, 20, 21, 23, 24, 26–28, 32, 38, 46, 50, 52, 54] of the reviewed works did not detail specific technologies, but focused on researching m-learning in general. Only 6% [3, 43] of the studies focused on design models and open-source platforms respectively (see Fig. 11).

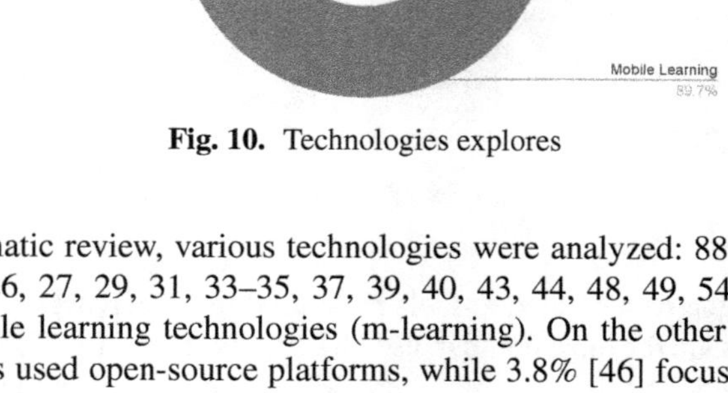

Fig. 10. Technologies explores

In the systematic review, various technologies were analyzed: 88% [3–5, 7–9, 11, 14, 15, 18, 21, 26, 27, 29, 31, 33–35, 37, 39, 40, 43, 44, 48, 49, 54] of the research focused on mobile learning technologies (m-learning). On the other hand, 7.7% [25, 41] of the studies used open-source platforms, while 3.8% [46] focused on web-based learning (see Fig. 10).

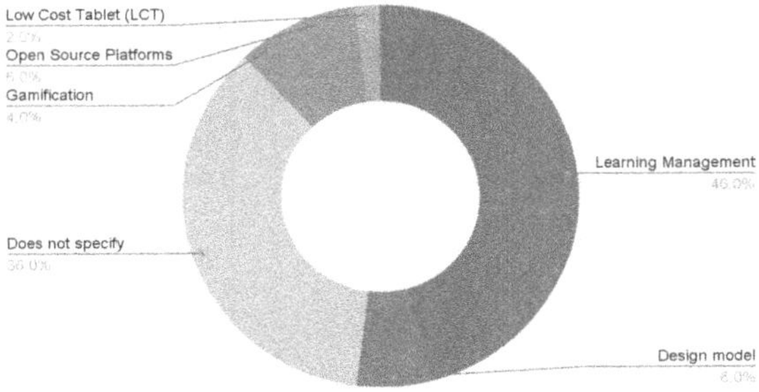

Fig. 11. Technology for m-learning

4 Synthesis of Research and Discussion

The present systematic review has synthesized the available knowledge on m-learning interventions designed for primary school teachers in rural and remote areas of low- and middle-income countries (LMICs) from an HCI4D perspective. The most prominent conclusions of the research are presented below:

4.1 Summary of Findings

The review identified multiple gaps and opportunities in the field of HCI4D and m-learning, specifically in the context of rural areas in LMICs. The main findings include:

- Research Topics: No emerging trends were observed in research topics during the period analyzed (2014–2024). The reviewed studies focused on recurring topics over time, with limited exploration of emerging areas such as Artificial Intelligence and gamification in teacher training.
- Geographic Coverage: The findings support those previously obtained by Van Biljon & Renaud (2021) [4] and, before them, by Dell and Kumar (2016) [10] who identified that research is concentrated in the same regions of the global South. There is significant geographic concentration in the research, with most studies conducted in Sub-Saharan Africa, East Asia and the Pacific, and South Asia, while regions such as Latin America, the Caribbean, the Middle East, and North Africa are underrepresented.
- Methodological Approach: According to the study conducted by Noorulhasan, Choudhary, Ahmad, Alqahtani, and Ibrahim (2023) [34], their research shows that primary education is primarily studied through surveys, followed by qualitative interviews and the analysis of secondary data. This result supports our findings, which indicate a significant predominance of quantitative and qualitative studies in the field, representing 68% of the total, in contrast to mixed studies (32%), which are more characteristic of the field of HCI4D [1, 6, 47]. Likewise, opportunities are identified to integrate mixed methods methodologies or develop innovative approaches in research design in HCI, especially in mobile learning projects aimed at primary school teachers in rural or remote areas of LMICs.

- Technological Focus: This study revealed that the predominant technologies in m-learning interventions are Learning Management Systems and other technological areas. However, there are significant opportunities to explore emerging technologies in m-learning applied to the training of primary school teachers. Areas such as design models, Artificial Intelligence, and gamification, although promising, are still poorly represented in the existing literature.

4.2 Implications for Research

The implications of this study highlight the need to diversify both the research topics and the geographic regions addressed. It is crucial to expand coverage to less-explored areas of the Global South, such as Latin America and the Caribbean, and to improve the integration of emerging technologies and innovative methodological approaches to enhance the effectiveness of educational interventions.

There are also opportunities to strengthen research around learning outcomes derived from m-learning and to develop standardized protocols that can guide future educational interventions in rural LMICs.

4.3 Study Limitations

This study has several limitations. First, the review was limited to studies published in English, which may have excluded relevant research in other languages. Additionally, the review focused on articles accessible in selected databases, which may also have limited the scope of the studies included.

4.4 Recommendations for Future Studies

To advance the field of HCI4D and m-learning, the following are necessary:

A. **Expand Geographic Coverage**: Conduct studies in underrepresented regions, such as Latin America and the Caribbean, as well as the Middle East and North Africa, to achieve a more equitable and complete view of the global educational landscape.
B. **Integrate Emerging Technologies**: Encourage the use of technologies such as Artificial Intelligence, gamification, and open-source platforms to enrich m-learning interventions.
C. **Adopt Mixed Methodological Approaches**: Incorporate mixed methodologies that combine qualitative and quantitative approaches, providing a more comprehensive and detailed analysis of the impact of educational interventions.
D. **Develop Standardized Design Protocols**: Create and standardize design protocols that guide the implementation of educational interventions in low-resource settings, ensuring the effectiveness and replicability of these efforts.

4.5 General Conclusion

The findings from this review indicate that m-learning has captured the attention of researchers in areas such as education, computer science, and engineering. Mobile learning technologies have been implemented across various educational levels to assess their effectiveness in a variety of contexts. However, there is a noticeable lack of studies that comprehensively address the research topic or fully align with the proposed keywords.

Significant research gaps have been identified, particularly in geographic regions such as the Middle East and North Africa, as well as Latin America and the Caribbean. There is also an urgent need to develop mixed methodological approaches and technologies adapted to remote areas that facilitate access to ongoing teacher training.

Future research should focus on closing the identified gaps, maximizing the use of mobile technologies and other ICTs to effectively support educators in underserved regions. It is essential to develop and standardize practices and design protocols that optimize educational interventions in low-resource settings, thus contributing to the reduction of educational poverty and advancing towards the Sustainable Development Goals (SDGs).

References

1. Abdelnour-Nocera, J., Densmore, M.: A review of perspectives and challenges for international development in information and communication technologies. Ann. Int. Commun. Assoc. **41**(3–4), 250–257 (2017). https://doi.org/10.1080/23808985.2017.1392252
2. Abdullah, F., Ward, R.: Developing a General Extended Technology Acceptance Model for E-Learning (GETAMEL) by analysing commonly used external factors. Comput. Hum. Behav. (2016). https://www.sciencedirect.com/science/article/pii/S074756321530251X
3. Alabdali, S.A., Pileggi, S.F., Cetindamar, D.: Influential factors, enablers, and barriers to adopting smart technology in rural regions: a literature review. Sustainability (2023). https://www.mdpi.com/2071-1050/15/10/7908
4. Almaiah, M.A., Abdul Jalil, M.M., Man, M.: Empirical investigation to explore factors that achieve high quality of mobile learning system based on students' perspectives. Eng. Sci. Technol. Int. J. **19**, 3, 1314–1320 (2016). https://doi.org/10.1016/j.jestch.2016.03.004
5. Baytiyeh, H.: Mobile learning technologies as a means of maintaining education delivery in crisis situations. J. Inf. Commun. Technol. (2019). https://www.igi-global.com/article/mobile-learning-technologies-as-a-means-of-maintaining-education-delivery-in-crisis-situations/229014
6. Van Biljon, J., Renaud, K.: Reviewing a Decade of Human-Computer Interaction for Development (HCI4D) Research, as One of Best's "Grand Challenges." Afr. J. Inf. Commun. AJIC 27 (May 2021) (2021). https://doi.org/10.23962/10539/31368
7. Campos, A.A.M.: Adopting smartphone applications for Second Language Acquisition: investigating readiness and acceptance of mobile learning in two Higher Education Institutions. search.proquest.com (2017). https://search.proquest.com/openview/c093cde2b228b7618d118df4dc9780ea/1?pq-origsite=gscholar\&cbl=2026366
8. N. A. Dahri, M. S. Vighio, O. A. Alismaiel, and2022. Assessing the Impact of Mobile-Based Training on Teachers' Achievement and Usage Attitude. International Journal of .... https://www.researchgate.net/profile/Nisar-Dahri/publication/360514521_Assessing_the_Impact_of_Mobile-Based_Training_on_Teachers_Achievement_and_Usage_Attitude/links/62c90402cab7ba7426ddd821/Assessing-the-Impact-of-Mobile-Based-Training-on-Teachers-Achievement-and-Usage-Attitude.pdf

9. Dahri, N.A., Vighio, M.S., Al-Rahmi, W.M.: Usability Evaluation of Mobile App for the Sustainable Professional Development of Teachers. International Journal of Retrieved from https://www.researchgate.net/profile/Nisar-Dahri/publication/363156144_Usability_Evaluation_of_Mobile_App_for_the_Sustainable_Professional_Development_of_Teachers/links/631046ccacd814437ff28d28/Usability-Evaluation-of-Mobile-App-for-the-Sustainable-Professional-Development-of-Teachers.pdf
10. Dell, N., Kumar, N.: The ins and outs of HCI for development. In: Proceedings of the 2016 CHI Conference on Human Factors in Computing Systems (CHI '16), 2016. Association for Computing Machinery, New York, NY, USA, 2220–2232 (2016). https://doi.org/10.1145/2858036.2858081
11. Erasmus, R.: A framework for designing South African mobile learning experiences through a participatory design process. scholar.sun.ac.za (2022). https://scholar.sun.ac.za/handle/10019.1/124819
12. Essel, H.B., Vlachopoulos, D., Adom, D.: Transforming higher education in Ghana in times of disruption: flexible learning in rural communities with high latency internet connectivity. J. Enterprising (2021). https://doi.org/10.1108/JEC-08-2020-0151
13. González-Zamar, M.D., Abad-Segura, E.: Managing ICT for sustainable education: research analysis in the context of higher education. Sustainability (2020). https://www.mdpi.com/2071-1050/12/19/8254
14. Hager, L., Almström, S.: Essential Factors for Usability and Acceptance of Mobile Learning in Ugandan Primary Schools: Minor Field Studies. diva-portal.org (2019). https://www.diva-portal.org/smash/record.jsf?pid=diva2:1354670
15. Hamidi, H., Chavoshi, A.: Analysis of the essential factors for the adoption of mobile learning in higher education: a case study of students of the University of Technology (2017). https://www.sciencedirect.com/science/article/abs/pii/S0736585317302277#:~:text=The%20factors%20related%20to%20adoption,of%20using%20a%20research%20model
16. Hardy, J., Wyche, S., Veinot, T.: Rural HCI research: definitions, distinctions, methods, and opportunities. Proc. ACM Hum. Comput. Interact. 3, CSCW (2019). https://doi.org/10.1145/3359298
17. Hossain, B., Fatima, M.J., Muzykant, V.L., Hoesin, C.F.I.S.: An overview of digital media literacy in digital Bangladesh. Jurnal Cita. https://www.academia.edu/download/107737331/34755_108081_1_PB.pdf
18. Iqbal, M.Z.: Versatile classroom management solution for teachers in developing countries. Hum. Comput. Interact 2017 (2017). https://doi.org/10.1007/978-3-319-68059-0_55
19. Aimee Sgourakis Jenkins. Guides: A Guide to Systematic Reviews and Evidence Synthesis Service @ ULS: What is Evidence Synthesis? Retrieved April 23, 2024 from https://pitt.libguides.com/SystematicReviews/EvidenceSynthesis
20. Kafuko, M.M., Namisango, F.: Perceived benefits of technology enhanced learning by learners in Uganda: Three band benefits. Int. (2016). https://researchportal.murdoch.edu.au/esploro/outputs/journalArticle/Perceived-benefits-of-technology-enhanced-learning/991005541242507891
21. Kim, J.: Voices of youth in reconceptualising and repositioning the role of mobile learning for sustainable development. Inf. Technol. Dev. (2020). https://doi.org/10.1080/02681102.2020.1749537
22. Kimaiyo, L.: Of teacher trainee's perceptions on ICT integration in primary schools: a study in public teacher training colleges in selected ....erepository.uoeld.ac.ke (2016). http://erepository.uoeld.ac.ke/handle/123456789/1066
23. Kolog, E.A., Devine, S.N.O., Egala, S.B.: Rethinking the implementation of artificial intelligence for a sustainable education in Africa: Challenges and solutions. Technol. (2022). https://doi.org/10.1108/S1877-636120220000029003

24. Kuliya, M., Usman, S.: Perceptions of e-learning among undergraduates and academic staff of higher educational institutions in north-eastern Nigeria. Educ. Inf. Technol. (2021). https://doi.org/10.1007/s10639-020-10325-x
25. Laugasson, E., Quaicoe, J.S., Jeladze, E.: Bridging digital divide in schools in developing countries: perceptions of teachers of free software opportunities. In: 2016 Held Part HCI (2016). https://doi.org/10.1007/978-3-319-39483-1_63
26. Lorenz, B., Banister, S.I., Kikkas, K.: Impacting the digital divide on a global scale-six case studies from three continents. In: Part HCI International 2015 Los (2015). https://doi.org/10.1007/978-3-319-20609-7_64
27. Mashudi, N.A., Mohd Izhar, M.A., Mohd Aris, S.A.: Human-computer interaction in mobile learning: a review. Int. J. Adv. Comput. Sci. Appl. **13**, 3 (2022). https://thesai.org/Publications/ViewPaper?Volume=13&Issue=3&Code=IJACSA&SerialNo=67
28. Miraz, M.H., Ali, M., Excell, P.S.: Adaptive user interfaces and universal usability through plasticity of user interface design. Comput. Sci. Rev. **40**(2021), 100363 (2021). https://doi.org/10.1016/j.cosrev.2021.100363
29. Moodley, K.: Mobile learning: a professional teacher technical identity development framework (2017). https://search.proquest.com/openview/a5bb30f3eb13663ce65feea64f3b96ea/1?pq-origsite=gscholar\&cbl=2026366\&diss=y
30. Muhammad, G.: Challenges in development of eLearning systems in higher education of the developing countries. London J. Res. Human. (2017). https://journalspress.com/LJRHSS_Volume17/142_Challenges-in-Development-of-eLearning-Systems-in-Higher-Education-of-the-Developing-Countries.pdf
31. Mutambara, D., Bayaga, A.: Learners' and teachers' acceptance of mobile learning: an exploratory study in a developing country. Int. J. Learn. (2021). https://doi.org/10.1504/IJLT.2021.117763
32. Muthuraman, A.A., Abdullah, S.: Perceived satisfaction towards emergency remote teaching amidst Covid-19 crisis: a case among undergraduate students in Penang, Malaysia. J. Institutional Res. South (2022). https://irep.ntu.ac.uk/id/eprint/49961/
33. Mwandosya, G.I., Suero Montero, C., Mbise, E.R.: Co-designing of a mobile educational tool for innovative teaching and learning at the college of business education, Tanzania. Turk. Online J. (2019). https://eric.ed.gov/?id=EJ1223769
34. Naveed, Q.N., Choudhary, H., Ahmad, N., Alqahtani, J.: Mobile learning in higher education: a systematic literature review. Sustainability (2023). https://www.mdpi.com/2071-1050/15/18/13566
35. Nikou, S.A., Economides, A.A.: Mobile-based assessment: integrating acceptance and motivational factors into a combined model of self-determination theory and technology acceptance. Comput. Hum. Behav. **68**(2017), 83–95 (2017). https://doi.org/10.1016/j.chb.2016.11.020
36. Ooko, M.: the adoption of technology to support teaching and learning in a distance learning programme at Africa Nazarene University (2016). https://core.ac.uk/download/pdf/43178319.pdf
37. Oyelere, S.S.: Design and development of a mobile learning system for computer science education in Nigerian higher education context (2018). https://erepo.uef.fi/bitstream/handle/123456789/18930/urn_isbn_978-952-61-2705-7.pdf?sequence=1
38. Pal, D., Vanijja, V.: Perceived usability evaluation of Microsoft Teams as an online learning platform during COVID-19 using system usability scale and technology acceptance model in Child. Youth Serv. Rev. (2020). https://www.sciencedirect.com/science/article/pii/S0190740920313992
39. Paulins, N., Balina, S., Arhipova, I.: Learning content development methodology for mobile devices. Procedia Comput. Sci. **43**(2015), 147–153 (2015). https://doi.org/10.1016/j.procs.2014.12.020

40. Pensabe-Rodriguez, A., Lopez-Dominguez, E., Hernandez-Velazquez, Y., Dominguez-Isidro, S., De-la-Calleja, J.: Context-aware mobile learning system: usability assessment based on a field study. Telemat. Inform. **48**(2020), 101346 (2020). https://doi.org/10.1016/j.tele.2020.101346
41. Raman, R., Vachhrajani, H., Shivdas, A.: Low cost tablets as disruptive educational innovation: modeling its diffusion within Indian K12 system. IEEE Innov. (2014). https://ieeexplore.ieee.org/abstract/document/7137053/
42. Said, G.R.E.: The use of ICT in personalizing self-learning in time of crisis: a human computer interaction perspective in a developing country. In: Proceedings of Seventh International Congress (2022). https://doi.org/10.1007/978-981-19-1607-6_10
43. Sánchez-Prieto, J.C., Olmos-Migueláñez, S., García-Peñalvo, F.J.: Informal tools in formal contexts: development of a model to assess the acceptance of mobile technologies among teachers. Comput. Hum. Behav. **55**(2016), 519–528 (2016). https://doi.org/10.1016/j.chb.2015.07.002
44. Shrestha, S.: Exploring mobile learning opportunities and challenges in Nepal: the potential of open-source platforms. repository.uwl.ac.uk (2016). http://repository.uwl.ac.uk/id/eprint/2962/
45. Sulisworo, D., Hidayati, D., Bala, R., Nasir, R.: The Anomali on Technology Readiness Profile of Elementary School Teachers in Online Learning Amid Covid-19. Ilkogretim (2021). https://www.academia.edu/download/91552171/218-1612429568.pdf
46. Tarhini, A.: The effects of cultural dimensions and demographic characteristics on e-learning acceptance. ArXiv Prepr. ArXiv160701492 (2016). https://arxiv.org/abs/1607.01492
47. Toyama, K.: Human–Computer Interaction and Global Development. Found. Trends Hum. Comput. Interact. 4, (January 2010), 1–79 (2010). https://doi.org/10.1561/1100000021
48. Trongtortam, S.: A decision support model for mobile technology enhanced teaching (2019). https://search.proquest.com/openview/2bc82da58e8cdd5ae2b13fcb41186a1a/1?pq-origsite=gscholar\&cbl=2026366\&diss=y
49. Varanasi, R.A., Vashistha, A., Parikh, T., Dell, N.: Challenges and issues integrating smartphones into teacher support programs in India. Proc. 2020 (2020). https://doi.org/10.1145/3392561.3394638
50. Wagner, D.A.: Technology for education in low-income countries: supporting the UN sustainable development goals. ICT-Support. Innov. Small Ctries. (2018). https://doi.org/10.1007/978-3-319-67657-9_3
51. Wang, J., Tigelaar, D.E.H., Admiraal, W.: Connecting rural schools to quality education: rural teachers' use of digital educational resources. Comput. Hum. Behav. **101**(2019), 68–76 (2019). https://doi.org/10.1016/j.chb.2019.07.009
52. Wang, X., Young, G.W., Iqbal, M.Z., Guckin, C.M.: The potential of extended reality in Rural Education's future–perspectives from rural educators. Educ. Inform. (2023). https://doi.org/10.1007/s10639-023-12169-7
53. Whale, A.M., Scholtz, B.M., Calitz, A.P.: Components of e-learning for enterprise systems' education in developing countries. In: Proceedings of the 9th IDIA Conference (2015). https://citeseerx.ist.psu.edu/document?repid=rep1\&type=pdf\&doi=f90cf502bbec835313437cde33425da05bf78dd7
54. De Wit, M., Plastow, N.A.: Recommendations to improve the usability of mobile learning for preschool teachers in Africa: a systematic scoping review. Int. J. Learn. Teach. (2021). http://ijlter.myres.net/index.php/ijlter/article/view/741
55. 2015. What is Evidence Synthesis? Retrieved April 23, 2024 from https://evidencesynthesis.org/what-is-evidence-synthesis/
56. New Target: Cut "Learning Poverty" by At Least Half by 2030. World Bank. 10/17/new-target-cut-learning-poverty-by-at-least-half-by-2030

57. The State of Global Learning Poverty: 2022 Update. World Bank. Retrieved April 10, 2024 from https://www.worldbank.org/en/topic/education/publication/state-of-global-learning-poverty
58. How to tackle Learning Poverty? Delivering education's promise to children across the world. World Bank Blogs. Retrieved April 10, 2024 from https://blogs.worldbank.org/en/education/how-tackle-learning-poverty-delivering-educations-promise-children-across-world
59. Insufficient investment in geographically remote schools | UNICEF. Retrieved April 10, 2024 from https://www.unicef.org/serbia/en/stories/insufficient-investment-geographically-remote-schools
60. PRISMA 2020. PRISMA statement. Retrieved April 22, 2024 from https://www.prisma-statement.org/prisma-2020
61. UNESCO Thesaurus. Retrieved April 24, 2024 from https://vocabularies.unesco.org/browser/thesaurus/en/
62. Computing Classification System. ACM Digital Library. Retrieved April 24, 2024 from https://dl.acm.org/ccs
63. Data | The World Bank. Retrieved April 24, 2024 from https://datatopics.worldbank.org/sdgatlas/archive/2017/the-world-by-region.html

Human-Centred Design Approach to Find User Requirements for a Status Monitoring System in a Remote and Autonomous Multivessel Operation

Antony William Joseph(✉) and Iiro Törmä

School of Arts, Design Architecture, Department of Design, Aalto University, Espoo, Finland
antony.joseph@aalto.fi

Abstract. The maritime industry is advancing towards the implementation of autonomous cargo shipping operations on a commercial scale, significantly transforming the nature of work for maritime officers. Vessels controlled from land-based operation centers and the capability to simultaneously operate multiple ships demands new control tools for effective monitoring. Our study seeks to understand the context and user requirements of future operators through HCD process. User requirements for a status monitoring tool were refined through expert participation and a first-phase prototype was designed and evaluated. Key findings reveal that an accessible tool providing a simplified view of operational assets, with alerts contextualized within the mission, enhances situational awareness and communication within heterogeneous teams. Our study contributes to the conference theme by addressing the future requirements of remote maritime operators concerning system status monitoring through HCD process.

Keywords: Human-Centred Design · Alert Management · MASS · Remote Maritime Operation · Situational Awareness · Shared Situational Awareness · Status Monitoring

1 Introduction

The maritime industry is actively in the development of advancements necessary to facilitate the implementation of autonomous cargo shipping operations on a commercial scale. Several trial projects in the field of maritime autonomous surface ships (MASS) have been conducted since the 2010s, such as Yara Birk cargo ship by Kongsberg and Yara, and the MUNIN project coordinated by Fraunhofer with funding from the European Commission [10].

The developers of MASS technologies anticipate numerous benefits from autonomous shipping, including enhanced safety at sea due to reduced human navigational errors and the absence of crew on board. Additionally, lower emissions and fuel costs are expected through route optimization, the potential for reduced cruising speeds,

Published by Springer Nature Switzerland AG 2026
G. Bhutkar et al. (Eds.): IDID 2024, IFIP AICT 747, pp. 144–156, 2026.
https://doi.org/10.1007/978-3-032-00777-3_9

and more efficient ship designs. Fully autonomous vessels eliminate the need for crew accommodations, crew safety equipment, sanitary systems, air conditioning, and bridge facilities, thus reducing investment costs [17, 19].

The concept of remote and autonomous maritime operations presents several challenges. Certification body Det Norske Veritas (DNV), which has developed preliminary guidelines for autonomous ships, emphasizes that the introduction of new technologies should not compromise safety for people or the environment, nor have a negative impact on other societal aspects. DNV asserts that new remote and autonomous operational concepts must offer equivalent or superior safety compared to conventional vessel operations [5]. Automation studies have extensively explored the challenges faced by operators of highly reliable systems. Bailey and Scerbo [1] showed that when operators have a high level of trust in the system they are monitoring, their performance in monitoring tasks tends to decline. Lutzhöft [14] explains that mariners prefer to take over the work actively from automation rather than functioning solely as passive observes.

Highly automated systems have the ability to generate a large amount of data and system alarms. Effective alarm management plays a crucial role in the usability of such systems. Inadequate design of alarm systems and alarm management can result in issues such as alarm fatigue, automation misuse, disuse, or abuse and potentially lead to catastrophic consequences [13, 20].

Autonomy involving Artificial Intelligence (AI) is gradually transforming the marine industry. For mariners, the advent of autonomous systems indicate significant changes in their work, particularly skill and competency requirements. Veitch et al. [26] observed that navigators operating ferries equipped with autonomous navigation and docking capabilities experienced a shift toward a backup role, a "button presser", which could possibility lead to issues such as boredom, skill degradation and stretched resources.

In this case study, general scenario features a team comprising one technical officer and two navigation officers who work in a single ROC supervising three autonomous vessels. The vessels are expected to be operating on short point-to-point routes in coastal waters. Operating multiple vessels simultaneously increases the necessity for a system that provides the operator with a comprehensive overview of the status of all systems that are important for a safe operation. In contrast to traditional maritime operations, the number of systems requiring supervision by a remote operator multiples with the increase in vessels. Therefore, an optimal solution must be developed to support remote operators in terms of usability.

The present case study takes the perspective of a future remote maritime engineering officer in a multivessel MASS operation. The study focuses on examining alarm management, situational awareness, teamwork and communication within the context of remote operations centers (ROCs) in the future. The introduction of remote and autonomous, multivessel shipping operations presents mariners with a new set of challenges. These operations demand a high level situational awareness and increased complexity compared to conventional shipping. This necessities a need for new tools to enable the team to promptly respond to unexpected situations.

The main research question of our study is What types of new requirements the change in the working context bring? To address this question, we employed human-centred design method [9], focusing on the early phases of the design process. To understand context and user requirements of future maritime operators, we involved diverse field experts in the study. By employing this methodology, the study seeks to create a tool that aligns with the needs and preferences of the users. The user requirements identified in this study may contribute to create a better working environment for future remote operators and could also provide insights for designing similar monitoring systems in other fields. Our case study contributes to the field of Human-Computer Interaction by identifying the requirements of the future remote officers' needs concerning expert system status monitoring and team communication.

2 Related Research

The evolution of maritime technology has been closely linked to the four industrial revolutions. The fourth industrial revolution, characterized by smart technologies utilizing digitalization and AI-driven capabilities, is now shaping the maritime sector [4, 12]. Due to safety critical and highly regulated nature of maritime operations, the adoption of cutting-edge smart technologies has been slower in the maritime Industry. However, with the emergence of autonomous shipping, the maritime began to embrace smart technologies.

The study of remote operators' situational awareness (SA) in Maritime Autonomous Surface Ships (MASS) operations, particularly in relation to teamwork, has not been extensively studied. In a systematic review conducted by Veitch and Alsos [25], which included 42 studies on human supervision and control of autonomous ships. Among these, situation awareness was referred in 9 studies, with it most prevalent paradigm in the field of Human-Computer Interaction (HCI).

Kari and Steinert [11] highlight that situational awareness in the context of MASS is often discussed in terms of human-machine interactions, but it is equally important to consider interactions within the operation team. The authors conclude that to achieve adequate levels of overall situational awareness, both perspectives should be considered. In an early study by Porathe et al. [22] on the emerging field of remote operation centers (ROCs), the authors emphasize how operators in future ROCs will lack important physical cues that traditional mariners rely on, for instance sensing the ship's movement caused by rough weather – something that is termed "ship sense" [22, 23].

Furthermore, Man et al. [16] explored a similar study in a simulated ROC environment and discovered several challenges faced by the operators in developing adequate situational awareness. They emphasize the need for "proactive", forward-looking alert systems in ROCs, considering that the remote operating team may require more time to react in a problem scenarios compared to traditional ships. Effective team communication and utilizing the expertise of different team members were identified as crucial factors. Additionally, the authors highlight the importance of adhering to appropriate working procedures and maritime regulations.

The previous research studies show that the interfaces and displays between human operators and automated systems can pose challenges [7, 21]. Endsley [7] perceives that automation by collecting and presenting essential information (Level 1 SA) and integrating it to support comprehension and projection requirements (Level 2 and 3 SA), has the potential to reduce workload and improve both situational awareness and performance.

The Ecological Interface Design framework, developed by Vicente and Rasmussen [27] is based on Rasmussen's studies on how expert workers engage in complex system reasoning during problem-solving [18]. The framework is guided by two principles: minimizing interference and facilitating error recovery [24]. Further, the author emphasizes the importance of presenting system data in a manner that integrates with higher-level objects, states, and events, aligning with the operator's conceptual language and level of abstraction used in their causal reasoning.

In summary, the literatures reviewed in the maritime sector do not address the user requirements of the future maritime operators adequately through human-centred design process. The shipping industry is going through a significant transformation towards more autonomous operations where vessels are controlled from land-based operations. Technologically advanced work environment will impact the nature of future work and job roles with new competencies and capabilities. Our study focuses on the early phases of the HCD process.

3 Methodology

The research question of our study focused on identifying the new requirements that arise from the changing working context using a human-centred design method (HCD) [9]. HCD is a widely applied method in the development of interactive systems. Primarily, it integrates the users' perspectives into the design process, ensuring that the resulting systems are usable [15]. Accordingly to ISO standard 9241–210 on Ergonomics of human-system interaction [9], this approach facilitates the creation of designs that are not only more satisfactory, effective, and efficient but also accessible, sustainable and supportive of users' overall well-being. The HCD method has four phases: 1) Understanding and specifying the context of use, 2) Specifying the user requirements, 3) Producing design solutions, and 4) Evaluating the design.

Table 1. Participants and activities included in the human-centred design process of the study.

Phase	Activity	Participants
Understanding the context of use	Semi-structed interviews	7
	Workshop	5
Specifying user requirements	Brainstorming	4
	Group interview	3
Producing designs and prototypes	Designer workshop	3
Carrying out user-based assessments	Participatory evaluation	3

To understand context and user requirements of future maritime operators, we involved diverse field experts in the case study from the client company who are experts in short sea shipping. However, a significant challenge in conducting human-centred design process in this case is absence of a physical work context to directly study that does not exist. Table 1 gives an overview of the participatory activities included in the HCD process of the study.

All participants were recruited from the client company, representing a diverse multi-disciplinary field experts including maritime system architects and designers, and active mariners with experience on autonomous navigation system. All of them have been actively engaged in the advancements related to remote and autonomous shipping and most of the reported having direct engagement with these emerging technologies as part of their daily work.

The first phase of the study involved understanding and specifying the context of use. We conducted a series of semi-structured expert interviews with seven field experts and a workshop with five experts both online and offline. The goal of these activities was to gain insights into the context of use.

In the second phase, we focused on the specifying user requirement. To achieve this, we conducted a group interview with three experts, followed by brainstorming session with four experts. These face-to-face sessions aimed to identify relevant scenarios for the specification of user requirements.

The third phase involved producing designs solutions which included designer workshops with three designers at the clients location. In this phase, based on the findings from the previous phases, we iterated the design solutions.

In the final phase focused on design evaluation. We evaluated the designs with three maritime experts who are familiar with the concept of MASS and are involved in developing the adjacent technologies. We conducted evaluation individually via online meetings, utilizing ProtoPie's software for participants to interact with the prototype that was based on the interface designs and the specific asset combinations (Vessels, Remote Operation Centre, Remote Operation Workstations). Prior to the evaluations, participants were provided with a brief overview of the study's objective and essential information regarding the functionalities incorporated within the prototype. To encourage real-time feedback, participants were encouraged to talk aloud while interacting with the prototype. Participants shared their screens in the meeting and the meeting audio and video was recorded and transcribed.

Microsoft teams was used for online collaborative activities in different phases of the design process. All activities except the design workshops in the third phase, were audio recorded. The data collected and extracted from all four phases were thematically analyzed following the method presented by Braun and Clarke [3].

4 Result

Remote engineering officers needs efficient means to monitor the operational status of autonomous vessel systems from the ROC without incurring an excessive workload. It is crucial for them to understand the provided information within the context of operations to gain sufficient situational awareness. In this context, the main focus of the case study was finding the user requirements and which could be integrated into a system as an added layer. There is no existing system that would fulfill the requirements proposed and this concept is futuristic.

Based on findings from participatory activities involving users and field experts, design solutions were iterated. It was deemed advantageous to create an interactive user interface concept that could be utilized for validating and refining the user requirements identified so far. The system under design must be operationally feasible within a single screen of the operator's workstation. The system is intended to be used alongside conventional Integrated Automation System (IAS) views as shown in the Fig. 1 and remote navigation system views, including route, live camera, and radar perspectives. Each operator will have the flexibility to determine their preferred screen layout. Several aspects and features were identified as critical for prototype: a) assets involved in the operation, b) capabilities for switching between low attention and high attention modes, c) a minimalistic presentation of the high-level status of assets, d) a clear distinction among the assets, e) visualization of status aggregation, f) status aggregation indicator, g) alert categorization, h) ship's mission, and i) task allocation within the team.

Fig. 1. An example of a workstation layout is shown with the proposed status monitoring interface indicated with a red arrow.

The overall status of different assets are presented using green colour, signifying that the system is ok, yellow that there is underlying problem worth investigating and red colour a state that compromises the safety of the operation. The features that were considered essential for the concept prototype are assents in the operation, switching between low attention and high attention, minimalistic presentation of high level status of assets, distinction of the assets, visualization of the status aggregation, status aggregation indicator, alert categorization, ship's mission and task allocation in the team.

The findings of the participatory evaluation study conducted during the initial design phase confirmed the identified user requirements and design solutions. The resulting design solution consisted of two distinct views: a main view featuring a mission timeline for each vessel (see Fig. 2), and a system view, displaying a system tree aligned with the principle of alarm aggregation (see Fig. 3). These perspectives can also be categorized as low attention and high attention views. The "main view" is designed to provide a comprehensive overview of the statuses of all technical systems within the operation, while the "system view" allows for a more detailed investigation of the status of specific asset systems more closely.

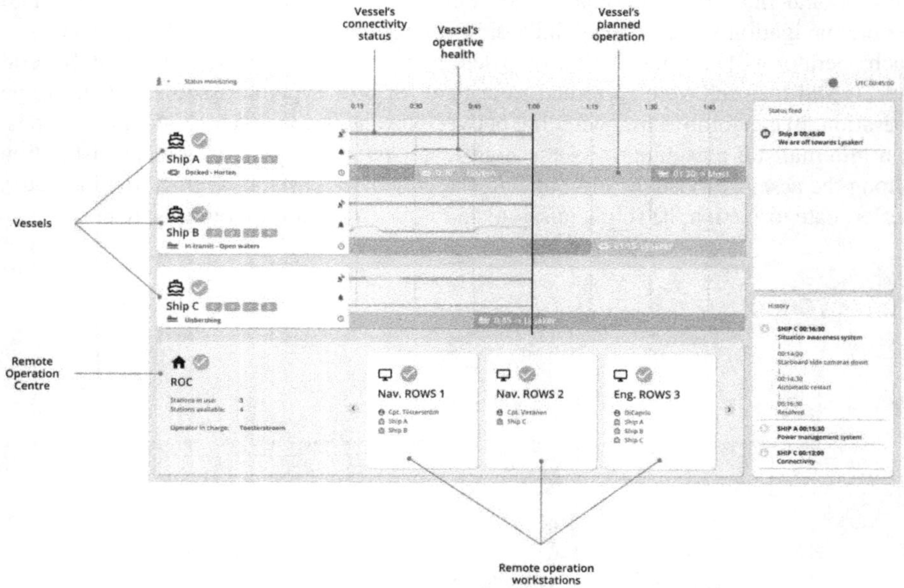

Fig. 2. Main view with the timeline.

In the main view (see Fig. 2), the vessel's timeline provides essential information regarding, the vessel's planned mission including sailing and harbor times, as well as durations spent in congested pathways. Furthermore, the vessel's connectivity status and a trend curve representing vessel's health are also depicted. To enhance user experience, the timeline is designed with scrollable functionality allowing users to navigate through different time periods. Past issues pertaining to the vessel are displayed on the trend curve, enabling users to access more detailed information through a mouseover function. Additionally, known future issues, such as potential connectivity problems, are highlighted in the timeline. The aggregation indicator (see Fig. 4) is placed next to the vessel's name and indicates the amount and severity of lower level alerts.

The system tree is the primary component of the system view (see Fig. 3). The tree represents as a visual representation of the alarm aggregation model and encompasses various components, functions and the capabilities of the asset. Users have the flexibility to expand and collapse branches with the system tree, enabling efficient navigation within this view.

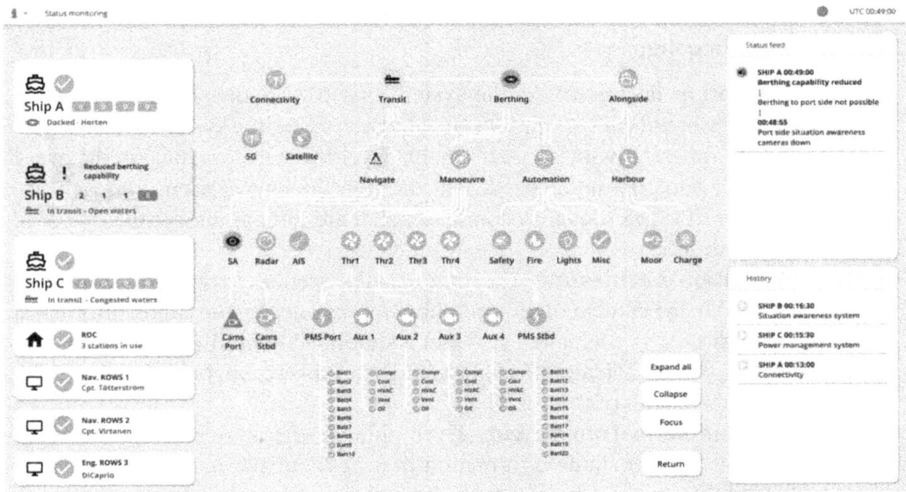

Fig. 3. System view with an issue causes a high level caution message.

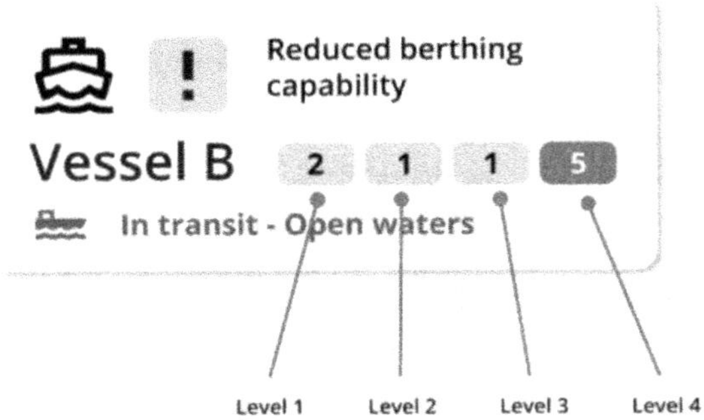

Fig. 4. The aggregation indicator shows the amounts of alerts at different levels of the vessel's systems.

The study provided evidence supporting the assumption that a comprehensive interface displaying the status of all assets and critical information is necessary for remote operations of a fleet of ships. The evaluation indicated two key findings: Firstly, collecting critical information in a single window and secondly, structuring it in a way that allows for both a quick overall understanding of the operation's asset status and the ability to differentiate information pertaining to each individual asset. For example, it was highlighted as valuable for the operator to easily identify which navigator is responsible for each vessel. These findings validate the effectiveness of the general approach used in the interface design. Furthermore, we identified evidence, suggesting that the status aggregation approach is largely sensible within the context of a multi-vessel, remote MASS operation.

Based on the user feedback derived from the prototype evaluation, we identified the following six user requirements:

1. **Status information is salient**: As the system in a MASS operation is capable of producing large amounts of system data and alert messages, the system to be designed must provide the operator with information that is relevant in the context of the overall operation. The evaluators pointed out that through the aggregation approach, it is possible to filter out lower-level system alerts that are not calling for the operator's immediate attention.
2. **Status information is contextual**: The must help the operator to understand the information provided in the context of the operation, for instance by providing information on a ship's mission. The evaluators saw that a simplified overall visualization of the vessel's system, which indicates possible failures in sub-system, provides an efficient way to inspect the health of the vessel
3. **Status information is transparent**: Even though the system may be highly autonomous and present status information in a minimalistic manner, the operator must have visibility to the whole system, including the autonomous system's decisions. The evaluators pointed out the value of the approach in ways that support the identified user requirements.
4. **Operator's active involvement is supported**: The experts said that the system must support the operator's active involvement both in normal operational states and failure states and that the system should be capable of giving instructions for solving the issues that emerge.
5. **Team communication is supported**: The system must support the operational team's communications. For instance the operators need to be aware of other team member's tasks and workload. The simplified visualization of a vessel's system emerged as a promising tool for effectively communicating system status information within the heterogenous operation team consisting of experts from different professional backgrounds. Particularly, participants emphasized that this visualization provides an adequate level of information concerning critical system.
6. **High/low attention monitoring is supported**: The system must support the operator switching between high and low attention monitoring tasks. This means including the possibility to pass monitoring of certain assets to other operators in the design. The evaluators pointed out the need for tools that enable efficient communication of system status information to the operation team.

5 Discussion

This article contributes to IDID research by emphasizing human-centred design process to identify key user requirements for a remote status monitoring tool for a multivessel remote operation. Key findings reveal that an accessible tool providing a simplified view of operational assets, with alerts contextualized within the mission, enhances situational awareness and communication within heterogeneous teams.

This study focuses on the development and evaluation of an early-phase design for a remote engineering officer's status monitoring system in a multivessel, remote MASS operation. The design process adopted human-centred approach, engaging several field experts from the maritime sector. The outcomes of the evaluation suggest that the prototype design is an effective tool for eliciting insights from experts, validating and further refining the user requirements for the design of this type of system.

The research question addressed in this study pertains to the identification of new requirements resulting from a change in the working context. The study aimed to validate the new user requirements could enhance situation awareness and team communication in the remote operation work context. The evaluators explicitly recommended the development of a status monitoring system that displays vessel's system statuses in a single view and provides indications of potential underlying failures. Furthermore, the system should aggregate these statuses into meaningful higher-level indicators that align with the mission. Importantly, the system should also be accessible to all members of the operation team.

Field experts interviewed in this highlighted the common occurrence of too many alerts generated by maritime automation systems. The challenge lies in identifying the salient alerts amidst several notifications. Endsley and Garland [6] emphasize the crucial role of acquiring the right information at the right time for situational awareness. This study found that Level 3 situational awareness, which includes the ability to forecast future situations [8], is highly sought after for future remote engineering officers and the entire operation team, aligning with Endsley's [8] findings.

The status monitoring system developed in this study proved to be usable and worthy of further development, particularly due to its alignment to enhance team communication. Similar research was conducted by Man et al. [16] and has identified the need for research on teamwork in remote MASS operations and highlighted the challenges in conducting studies on remote operator's work that aid in designing new tools in this field.

One notable challenge in researching MASS is the early stage of its development, leaving many aspects open to speculation. The absence of fully autonomous intelligent systems that can carry out shipping operations regularly raises uncertainties regarding the remote operator's work. Determining the frequency and nature of operator interventions is challenging without a comprehensive understanding of the capabilities of intelligent operation systems. Therefore, arranging realistic research settings, especially for studying teamwork, becomes difficult.

The Ecological Interface Design (EID) framework offers an intriguing perspective when examining MASS control systems. This framework emphasizes the provision of resilience in the face of unforeseen events [2]. The aggregation model employed in the status monitoring system aligns with EID principles and Jens Rasmussen's abstraction-decomposition model of cognitive task analysis. Borst et al. [2] describe the goal of ecological representation as organizing information based on the deep structure of the work domain, highlighting meaningful associations among variables. However, there have been misconceptions about the purpose and applicability of EID since its introduction. Vicente and Rasmussen [27] intended the framework for use in expert systems rather than designing interfaces for inexperienced users.

Considering the high level of vessel autonomy pursued by MASS developers, it is expected that control tasks faced by operators will require extensive analysis and problem-solving skills. Following Rasmussen's principles, the interface should offer a faithful, externalized symbolic model that supports mental experimentation [24]. Although the simplified vessel system model in the initial prototype of this study may not be entirely faithful in solving complex vessel side system problems, it represents a step in the right direction.

6 Conclusion

The study employed HCD process to identify key user requirements for a multivessel remote status monitoring tool. The research involved engaging a multidisciplinary stakeholders through interviews, workshops and evaluation of an early-phase design solution. The study provided evidence that supports two main findings. Firstly, a comprehensive monitoring window that integrates information on top-level status of the system to be monitored, the operation phases of various vessels, and responsibilities of operators in the remote operation team is necessary for a multivessel remote operation. Secondly, an interactive visualization of a vessel's capabilities and critical system statuses enables a remote operation team to maintain situational awareness and to communicate efficiently when problems emerge from a vessel's monitoring system.

The study contributes to the field of HCI by providing user requirements of future operators and highlighting an interactive and accessible tool that displays whole operation assets in a simplified view and enhances situation awareness and team communication within heterogeneous teams.

The main limitation of the case study is that the prototype was evaluated with limited participants on a single screen. Due to the limited resources available, we could not evaluate with a more realistic simulator test setting in a n actual ROC. Another limitation is that it would be beneficial to evaluate the design solutions in realistic team work scenarios involving individuals performing the roles of an engineer and a navigator. Despite these limitations, our findings will help the maritime sector to address the user requirements that arise from the changing working context of future maritime operators.

Acknowledgments. This study was funded through contract research by KM Finland Oy. We are indebted to all the stakeholders, participants, and individuals who generously shared their time and knowledge in shaping the outcome of this research.

Disclosure of Interests. The authors have no competing interests to declare that are relevant to the content of this article.

References

1. Bailey, N.R., Scerbo, M.W.: Automation-induced complacency for monitoring highly reliable systems: the role of task complexity, system experience, and operator trust. Theor. Issues Ergon. Sci. **8**, 321–348 (2007). https://doi.org/10.1080/14639220500535301
2. Borst, C., Flach, J.M., Ellerbroek, J.: Beyond ecological interface design: lessons from concerns and misconceptions. IEEE Trans. Human-Mach. Syst. **45**, 164–175 (2015). https://doi.org/10.1109/THMS.2014.2364984

3. Braun, V., Clarke, V.: Using thematic analysis in psychology. Qual. Res. Psychol. **3**, 77–101 (2006). https://doi.org/10.1191/1478088706qp063oa
4. Breque, M., De Nul, L., Petridis, A.: Industry 5.0 – towards a sustainable, humancentric and resilient European industry. Publications Office of the European Union (2021)
5. DNV: Autonomous and remotely operated ships, DNV-CG-0264 (2021)
6. Endsley, M.R., Garland, D.J.: Situation Awareness Analysis and Measurement. CRC Press (2000)
7. Endsley, M.R.: From here to autonomy: lessons learned from human-automation research. Hum. Factors **59**, 5–27 (2017). https://doi.org/10.1177/0018720816681350
8. Endsley, M.R.: Toward a theory of situation awareness in dynamic systems. Hum. Factors **37**, 32–64 (1995). https://doi.org/10.1518/001872095779049543
9. ISO: 9241–210: 2019 Ergonomics of human-system interaction. Part 210: Human-Centred Design for Interactive Systems (2019)
10. Kaarstad, M., Braseth, A.O.: Operating autonomous ships remotely from land-based operation centers: the current state-of-the-art. Research Council of Norway LOAS Project, IFE/E-2020/008 (2020)
11. Kari, R., Steinert, M.: Human Factor issues in remote ship operations: lesson learned by studying different domains. JMSE. **9**, 385 (2021). https://doi.org/10.3390/jmse9040385
12. Kumar, K., Zindani, D., Davim, J.P.: Industry 4.0: Developments Towards the Fourth Industrial Revolution. Springer (2019)
13. Lee, J.D., See, K.A.: Trust in automation: designing for appropriate reliance. Hum. Factors J. Hum. Factors Ergon. Soc. **46**, 50–80 (2004). https://doi.org/10.1518/hfes.46.1.50_30392
14. Lützhöft, M.: "The technology is great when it works": Maritime Technology and Human Integration on the Ship's Bridge (2004)
15. Maguire, M.: Methods to support human-centred design. Int. J. Hum. Comput. Stud. **55**, 587–634 (2001). https://doi.org/10.1006/ijhc.2001.0503
16. Man, Y., Lundh, M., Porathe, T., MacKinnon, S.: From desk to field - human factor issues in remote monitoring and controlling of autonomous unmanned vessels. Procedia Manuf. **3**, 2674–2681 (2015). https://doi.org/10.1016/j.promfg.2015.07.635
17. Massterly: https://www.massterly.com/what-we-do. Accessed 22 Dec 2023
18. Naikar, N.: Cognitive work analysis: an influential legacy extending beyond human factors and engineering. Appl. Ergon. **59**, 528–540 (2017). https://doi.org/10.1016/j.apergo.2016.06.001
19. Negenborn, R.R., et al.: Autonomous ships are on the horizon: here's what we need to know. Nature **615**, 30–33 (2023)
20. Parasuraman, R., Riley, V.: Humans and automation: use, misuse, disuse. Abuse. Hum Factors. **39**, 230–253 (1997). https://doi.org/10.1518/001872097778543886
21. Parasuraman, R., Sheridan, T.B., Wickens, C.D.: A model for types and levels of human interaction with automation. IEEE Trans. Syst., Man, Cybern. A. **30**, 286–297 (2000). https://doi.org/10.1109/3468.844354
22. Porathe, T., Prison, J., Man, Y.: Situation awareness in remote control centres for unmanned ships. In: Proceedings of Human Factors in Ship Design & Operation, 26–27 February 2014, London, UK, p. 93 (2014)
23. Prison, J., Dahlman, J., Lundh, M.: Ship sense—striving for harmony in ship manoeuvring. WMU J Marit Affairs. **12**, 115–127 (2013). https://doi.org/10.1007/s13437-013-0038-5
24. Rasmussen, J.: Ecological interface design for reliable human-machine systems. Int. J. Aviat. Psychol. **9**, 203–223 (1999). https://doi.org/10.1207/s15327108ijap0903_2
25. Veitch, E., Andreas Alsos, O.: A systematic review of human-AI interaction in autonomous ship systems. Saf. Sci. **152**, 105778 (2022). https://doi.org/10.1016/j.ssci.2022.105778

26. Veitch, E., et al.: From captain to button-presser: operators' perspectives on navigating highly automated ferries. J. Phys.: Conf. Ser. **2311**, 012028 (2022). https://doi.org/10.1088/1742-6596/2311/1/012028
27. Vicente, K.J., Rasmussen, J.: Ecological interface design: theoretical foundations. IEEE Trans. Syst., Man, Cybern. **22**, 589–606 (1992). https://doi.org/10.1109/21.156574

Prototype Design and Implementation of an IoT Based Intelligent Dustbin for Smart City

Pratham Gajbhiye(✉), Swarup Vishwas, Ganesh Bhutkar, Rucha Uplenchwar, and Atharva Rathi

Department of Computer Engineering, Vishwakarma Institute of Technology, Pune, India
{pratham.gajbhiye21,swarup.vishwas22,ganesh.bhutkar, rucha.uplenchwar21,atharva.rathi21}@vit.edu

Abstract. In today's evolving urban landscape, garbage management has emerged as a critical challenge for environmental sustainability and public health. Traditional waste collection involves manual inspection, where individuals check for waste accumulation, which is time-consuming and complex. To address this problem and assist waste management staff by saving time and reducing unnecessary trips, an intelligent dustbin prototype is proposed. This system allows workers to focus their efforts only when necessary, improving efficiency in waste collection. The intelligent dustbin prototype uses Internet of Things (IoT) components including NodeMCU ESP8266 microcontroller, HC-SR04 ultrasonic sensor, and Neo 6M GPS module to monitor garbage levels, track dustbin locations, and notify authorities if the garbage exceeds a threshold. The prototype is integrated with two in-built mobile applications: the Blynk App for real-time garbage level monitoring and the Telegram App, where a bot sends alerts and dustbin locations to waste management staff. This aids efficient waste management and improves collection and resource distribution.

Keywords: IoT · Waste Management · Sensors · Intelligent Dustbin · Smart City · Environmental Sustainability · Smart Bin Prototype · Garbage Monitoring

1 Introduction

The term IOT describes the communication and network of various things. Things are nothing but various sensors that communicate, transfer, and exchange data. Over the past few years, the IoT has grown rapidly and has become an integral part of everyone's lives. IoT has not only made our lives simpler, but it has a lot of potential to drive social as well as economic change in society. In India, 62 million metric tons of solid waste are generated each year, which makes it the world's third-largest waste generator [1]. 10 million metric tons of garbage are created solely in metropolitan cities in India, which is a very large quantity, and it is a serious concern for the government to handle it properly without becoming overwhelmed [2]. According to a report by the Central Pollution Control Board (CPCB) in 2020, only about 60% of the country's generated waste is collected, with a considerable portion remaining uncollected, leading to environmental degradation and health hazards [13].

Published by Springer Nature Switzerland AG 2026
G. Bhutkar et al. (Eds.): IDID 2024, IFIP AICT 747, pp. 157–174, 2026.
https://doi.org/10.1007/978-3-032-00777-3_10

Waste management is one of the biggest issues in the world in the current situation. If any city wants to be smart, it first has to focus on waste management and sustainability. The government is investing a lot of money in establishing smart cities [3]. Waste management is becoming more difficult as the amount of waste produced grows by the day. The same management problem is getting worse day by day in our societies and cities, which leads to the failure of smart cities. Some of the developed nations have great techniques to tackle this problem, but some developing nations face this problem due to the unawareness of people. In some cities, public bins are overflowing, and management has no clue about the bin's current status [4]. This results in a number of diseases as mosquitoes and other insects breed on it [5]. There are some solutions available on the market, but they are very expensive. So, there should be some solution needed, and we are attempting to provide a solid solution to the situation with low-cost products.

In this paper, a proposed solution aims to fulfill and solve all the requirements and problems, respectively. It addresses the challenges of waste management through the integration of various components, including the ultrasonic sensor, GPS module, and NodeMCU. These components are all connected to one internet source (Wi-Fi) for communication and data exchange. The ultrasonic sensor operates in real-time to provide data regarding waste levels, which is then displayed to municipal authorities for informed decision-making. The GPS module is used here to accurately track the dustbin location.

Furthermore, the NodeMCU ESP8266 microcontroller coordinates these components and generates alerts via Telegram if garbage levels exceed a predefined threshold. These alerts include the current location of the dustbin, obtained through the GPS module. The system aims to transform waste management practices by providing real-time data and enabling proactive decision-making. Through this innovative approach, the system contributes to the advancement of sustainable waste management strategies, thereby fostering cleaner and healthier communities.

2 Literature Survey

Waste management problems keep occurring every day in every country, and new systems are proposed every time. In our comprehensive literature review, we analyzed eleven research papers, and it was found that most of these studies were focused on monitoring trash levels in bins using sensors and wireless communication. When the level of garbage exceeds a particular threshold value, the sensors send a notification to the concerned authorities. In one study, it was observed that waste segregation was conducted but the aspect of waste monitoring was absent. These papers are discussed in the second section of the literature survey.

Chitale et al. proposed the idea of building a smart dustbin that focuses on waste segregation. They opted for an Arduino Uno as the microcontroller and an integrated inductive proximity sensor and moisture sensor to categorize waste into wet, dry, or metal categories. However, it appeared to be more of a prototype for waste segregation, and there were no provisions for generating alerts when garbage exceeded a certain threshold, nor was there any real-time monitoring of dustbin waste levels [6].

Work done by Hussain et al. focuses on monitoring the level of garbage inside the dustbin. They have used the ATMega 2560 as their microcontroller. They've integrated a range of sensors for various purposes: a DHT-11 humidity sensor to monitor temperature and humidity levels; a flame sensor to detect potential fire hazards from discarded cigarettes or alcohol bottles; and even a rainfall sensor to detect the rainfall so as to turn on the servo motor and sprinkle pesticides inside the dustbin to reduce the bacterial growth inside the dustbin; and lastly, they have used an ultrasonic sensor to detect garbage levels. They've also set up a system to send out SMS alerts when garbage levels exceed certain thresholds, and they're keeping track of dustbin levels in real-time using ThingSpeak. However, waste segregation was not present in their system [7].

In the third paper, Sharma et al. used a sensor to determine the level of trash in the dustbin using a preset threshold. An SMS alert is sent with the bin ID to the given phone number. Then, a sanitary worker who is at the location will collect the garbage by identifying the dustbin. This paper has an ultrasonic sensor, a GSM SIM, and an Arduino Uno microcontroller. However, it was found that no segregation of waste was done here. No extra sensors were used apart from the ultrasonic sensor [8].

In the fourth paper, Afolalu et al. designed waste monitoring is facilitated by a system with an ultrasonic sensor for detecting the fullness of the dustbin, an MQ2 gas sensor to detect the presence of smoke, carbon dioxide, methane, or alcohol, a GSM module for sending alert messages, a servo motor, and an Arduino microcontroller. An alert generation system was implemented where the user gets the alert message. The garbage level is monitored using an LCD display, which shows status messages such as "The smart waste bin is half-filled" and "The smart waste bin is filled" [9].

System developed by Prabhakara et al. focuses on waste monitoring using an Arduino Uno microcontroller and ESP8266 Wi-Fi module, IR sensor, Ultrasonic sensor, and Servo motor. There is no alert generation or waste segregation in this system. Real time monitoring is done using LCD screens and Thingspeak [10].

Praveen et al. focused on a system created using Raspberry Pi, which is used for tasks such as data processing, decision-making based on sensor inputs, and controlling the servo motor for physical actuation. With an ESP8266 Wi-Fi module, the system can transmit data, receive commands remotely, and potentially interact with a central server or user interface for monitoring and control purposes. There is no waste segregation, alert generation, or real-time monitoring done in this [11].

Thirumugam et al. developed an efficient waste monitoring system utilizing the ESP32 Wi-Fi module microcontroller. It is integrated with various sensors, such as an ultrasonic sensor, an IR sensor, a moisture sensor, a DC servo motor, and a GSM module. It features alert generation, and an SMS alert message was sent to a defined contact number. The system segregates the garbage into dry and wet waste. Real-time monitoring was achieved by ThingSpeak, enabling continuous data tracking and analysis [12].

Ardiyan et al. designed a waste management solution using a Wemos microcontroller, integrated with an HC-SR04 proximity sensor. The system supports real-time monitoring of garbage levels, alert generation through SMS, and remote access to data, but it does not implement any waste segregation features. This approach is primarily focused on waste level detection and prompt notifications for collection [15].

Abhishek et al. presented a solution for garbage segregation and waste monitoring using a combination of multiple sensors such as the DH-22 sensor, proximity sensor, and

GPS module. The system utilizes an ESP32 Wi-Fi module as the microcontroller to transmit data and remotely monitor garbage levels in real-time via ThingSpeak. Additionally, an SMS alert system notifies the concerned personnel when garbage exceeds the threshold. Waste segregation is also incorporated, allowing for proper disposal management, making this system effective in both tracking and sorting waste [16].

Pujari et al. designed a solar-powered smart dustbin that integrates an ultrasonic sensor and an ESP32 microcontroller to measure the levels of waste. The system can transmit data to a remote server and trigger SMS alerts when the garbage bin is full, but waste segregation was not included. Real-time monitoring was achieved through a user-friendly interface, and the addition of solar power makes this system energy-efficient [17].

Harith et al. implemented a waste management system using an Arduino Uno microcontroller and an ultrasonic sensor. The system was capable of real-time monitoring, transmitting data to a remote server, and sending SMS alerts when the bin reaches its threshold. Although the system provides efficient monitoring and alert generation, no waste segregation features were implemented [18].

Saad et al. developed a waste management system using a NodeMCU ESP8266 microcontroller, integrating an ultrasonic sensor and a GPS module for location tracking. The system generates SMS alerts when garbage levels are exceeded and can monitor the waste bin in real-time through an IoT platform. However, similar to other systems, waste segregation was not a focus of this implementation [19].

In the context of waste management, a smart city deploys intelligent systems that monitor and manage waste collection, segregation, and disposal processes. These systems use a network of sensors and wireless communication to provide real-time data on waste levels, enabling efficient scheduling of waste collection and reducing operational costs. The goal of smart cities is to create a cleaner, healthier, and more sustainable urban environment by minimizing waste-related issues such as overflow, improper segregation, and environmental pollution.

The literature review highlights various approaches to waste monitoring and segregation, providing a comprehensive insight into existing technologies and methodologies. Common technologies included Arduino microcontrollers, ultrasonic sensors, GSM modules for alert generation, and platforms like ThingSpeak for real-time data tracking. Based on these observations, our designed solution in Sect. 3 focuses on advanced garbage monitoring in the dustbin. Our system utilizes an ESP8266 as the microcontroller with an ultrasonic sensor for detecting garbage levels in the dustbin. A GPS module is integrated to detect the location, ensuring alerts are sent via Telegram when predefined thresholds are crossed. Alerts specify the location of the dustbin, facilitating prompt action. Furthermore, an LED outside the bin acts as a visual indication for waste collectors passing by. The Blynk app is used to monitor the real-time level of garbage inside the dustbin. Additionally, our solution is cost-effective as we utilize the ESP8266, which is more affordable compared to expensive microcontrollers like Arduino. By leveraging these technologies, our solution enhances smart waste management by ensuring real-time monitoring and efficient alert dissemination, addressing critical aspects of cleanliness and resource optimization in smart cities.

The literature survey has been presented using a tabular approach, as employed by Patil et al. [29], and the corresponding table is provided in Table 1. Table 1 highlights the differentiating and comparative elements of the various research papers on IoT-based smart dustbins. The major observations based on the data from Table 1 are discussed as follows:

- Most of the research papers (10 out of 12) have developed dustbins with the **Study Objective** of Garbage Monitoring, while one focused solely on garbage segregation.

Table 1. Comparative Aspects in literature review related to existing systems.

	Research Papers						
Author	Objectives	Microcontrollers	Sensors	Alert Generation	Segregation of Waste	Real Time Monitorin-g	Geographic Location
Chitale et al	Garbage Segregation	Arduino Uno	Inductive Proximity sensor, Moisture sensor and Ultrasonic Sensor	No	Yes	No	Maharashtra, India
Hussain et al	Waste Monitoring	ATMega2560	Humidity sensor, Flame sensor, Rainfall sensor and Ultrasonic sensor	Yes (SMS)	No	Yes (ThingSpeak)	Chhattisgarh, India
Sharma et al	Waste Monitoring	Arduino Uno	PIR sensor and Ultrasonic sensor	Yes (SMS)	No	No	Jammu & Kashmir, India
Afolalu et al	Waste Management	Arduino Uno	Ultrasonic sensor and MQ2 Gas sensor	Yes (SMS)	No	Yes (LCD Panel)	Nigeria, Africa
Prabhakara et al	Waste Monitoring	Arduino Uno and ESP8266 Wi-Fi module	IR sensor and Ultrasonic sensor	No	No	Yes (LCD Panel, ThingSpeak)	Tamil Nadu, India
Praveen et al	Waste Monitoring	Raspberry-pi	Ultrasonic sensor	No	No	No	Delhi, India
Thirumugam et al	Garbage Segregation and Waste Monitoring	ESP32 Wi-Fi module	Ultrasonic sensor, IR sensor and Moisture sensor	Yes (SMS)	Yes	Yes (ThingSpeak)	Malabe, Sri Lanka
Ardiyan et al	Waste Management	Wemos	HC-SR04 proximity sensor	Yes	No	Yes	Jakarta, Indonesia

(continued)

Table 1. (*continued*)

	Research Papers						
Author	Objectives	Microcontrollers	Sensors	Alert Generation	Segregation of Waste	Real Time Monitorin-g	Geographic Location
Abhishek et al	Garbage Segregation and Waste Monitoring	Raspberry-pi	DH-22 Sensor, Proximity Sensor and GPS	Yes	Yes	Yes	Patna, India
Pujari et al	Solar Powered Smart Dustbin	ESP32 Wi-Fi module	Ultrasonic Sensor	Yes	No	Yes	Chikodi, India
Harith et al	Waste Management	Arduino Uno	Ultrasonic sensor HC-SR04	Yes (SMS)	No	Yes	Kuala Lumpur, Malaysia
Saad et al	Waste Management	NodeMCU ESP8266	Ultrasonic Sensor, GPS	Yes	No	Yes	Makassar, Indonesia

- Some of the research papers (9 out of 12) have performed **Real-Time Monitoring** of the garbage level inside the dustbin.
- Some of the research papers (5 out of 12) have used Arduino Uno as a **Microcontroller**, with ESP32 Wi-Fi (2 out of 12), Raspberry Pi (2 out of 12), and ATMega2560 (1 out of 12) module being used in few papers.
- Various **Sensors** configurations were utilized in the research papers, ranging from combinations like **ultrasonic sensors** paired with **inductive proximity and moisture sensors** to standalone implementations such as **humidity sensor coupled with flame and rainfall sensors**.
- Some of the research papers (9 out of 12) have implemented **SMS Alert Generation** if the garbage level exceeds a certain threshold.
- Few research papers (3 out of 12) have implemented **Segregation of Waste**.

3 User Study

One must take into account the importance of user studies in assessing and improving the system when designing a smart trash can prototype. User studies help us understand how actual users interact with our system, find out and signal out potential problems, and improve other aspects [14]. Though not performed in a formal environment for this particular prototype, the next part gives an explanation of what is meant by it and advantages expected for such a use of surveys.

The technological solutions can bridge the gap between theoretical design and the actual human bespoke experience. Therefore, to understand the practical implications of technological solutions in real-world settings, user studies are essential. Key benefits of conducting user studies for the intelligent dustbin prototype include:

1. **Understanding User Needs:** The daily routines, challenges, and requirements of waste collection staff can be better understood by observing and interviewing them. This makes it possible to customize a system that meets their needs more effectively.
2. **Checking System Usability:** User studies enable us to evaluate system's interfaces usability when using Blynk App and Telegram bot, if required feedback from users would be able to lead improvements in their design and functions.
3. **Identifying Potential Issues:** Practical problems may emerge during real-world tests that could not have been seen at the prototype phase. These might be such as technical faults, connectivity issues or unpredicted expressions by users.

3.1 Proposed Study

Design for users: To evaluate the smart dustbin prototype, one could design a way to run such a study as follows:

1. **Choosing Participants:** To take part in this research, a range of local authority personnel involved with disposal services need to be identified. This would ensure that they include different people who have been exposed from various angles on the same issue.
2. **Process Observation:** Initial waste collection process observation is essential and is to be followed by interviews to get in-depth knowledge about the challenges faced and what is expected of the new system.
3. **Installation:** A controlled environment will see the installation of an intelligent dustbin system. Blynk App and Telegram bot usage training should be given to the participants.
4. **Data Collection:** Tracking the use of the system within a set period. Record fill levels, alert frequency, as well as user interactions with the system. After that, we should have some interviews with some people on what they feel about this whole thing.
5. **Analysis and Reporting:** It entails looking into these stored figures so as to detect patterns or gauge improvements in efficiency levels; this can also expose weaknesses therein as well. Suggestions for widespread use, should therefore take account of the refined platform informed by such analyses.

3.2 Future Target Users

The municipal authorities responsible for managing waste would be the primary target group for the smart dustbins as they play the role of promoter, enabler or partner [20]. The system would also prove useful to the urban developers as well as the environmental protection bodies which analyze this information while creating policies on waste disposal methods and funding strategies.

Our intention is to show the importance of including end-users in the process of evaluating and refining the smart dustbin prototype by describing the planned user study and its possible advantages. Subsequent research activities will be devoted to the implementation of these researches in order to ensure an effective system that meets its client's needs while at the same time producing an envisaged outcome in waste control in the urban areas.

4 IoT-Based Design of Intelligent Dustbin

The Intelligent Dustbin is a groundbreaking IoT solution designed to revolutionize waste management in smart cities. Equipped with ultrasonic sensors, a GPS module, and an ESP8266, it offers real-time monitoring of waste levels and facilitates efficient waste collection. By continuously scanning the waste volume, the ultrasonic sensor provides precise data on the bin's capacity. When the dustbin reaches its capacity threshold, an alert message is sent via Telegram, containing the precise location of the dustbin. The ESP8266 ensures seamless connectivity, allowing users to remotely monitor the dustbin's status and receive timely alerts. Overall, the integration of IoT technologies in waste management not only addresses pressing urban challenges but also contributes to the development of cleaner, healthier smart cities. The Prototype of the Intelligent Dustbin is shown in Fig. 1.

Fig. 1. Intelligent Dustbin Prototype for Smart City

4.1 IoT Components Used in Intelligent Dustbin Design

Several IoT components are included in the intelligent dustbin design to give consumers access to a range of capabilities. These IoT components support the collection, transmission, and obtaining of several types of information. The main IoT components are as follows:

a] **NodeMCU ESP8266:**

NodeMCU is a component that is low-cost. It is also an open-source platform for IoT. The open-source NodeMCU firmware and development board are specifically made for applications in the Internet of Things (IoT). They are Lua-based. In the proposed system,

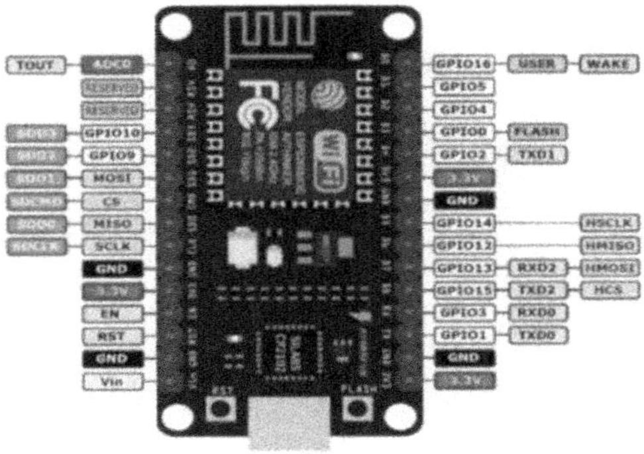

Fig. 2. NodeMCU ESP8266

it is the main component to which the ultrasonic sensor and Blynk app are connected (Fig. 2).

b] **Ultrasonic Sensor:**

Ultrasonic sensors generate or detect ultrasonic energy. The electrical signal emitted by the ultrasonic signal is amplified and processed to detect reflected echoes and calculate the distance from a specific target. It is connected to a Blynk app through NodeMCU to monitor the level of sewage inside the tank (Fig. 3).

Fig. 3. Ultrasonic Sensor

c] **GPS Module:** These GPS modules are compatible with Arduino and Raspberry Pi, so you can easily start your experiments. The GPS module contains a small processor and antenna that directly receive data broadcast from the satellite over a dedicated RF frequency. From there, get the timestamps from all the satellites displayed, along with other data. If the module's antenna can detect more than four satellites, their position and time can be calculated accurately (Fig. 4).

Fig. 4. GPS Module

4.2 Important Features of Intelligent Dustbin

The important features of the intelligent dustbin are as follows:

- **Real-Time Monitoring**: Sensors continuously track dustbin fill levels, providing up-to-the-minute data on waste accumulation.
- **Alert System**: An alert message is sent via Telegram when the dustbin approaches capacity, enabling prompt action.
- **Location Tracking**: Precise location information is included in alerts, allowing waste management authorities to quickly locate and service full bins.
- **User-Friendly Interface**: Intuitive interfaces, accessible via mobile app or web platform, empower users to easily interact with the system and take proactive measures.

4.3 Block Diagram and Working of Intelligent Dustbin

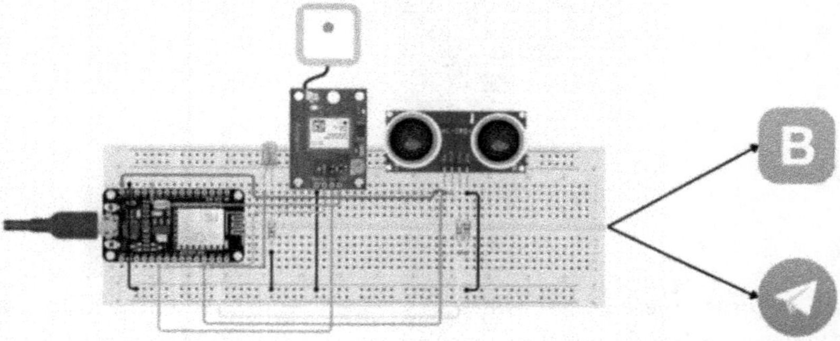

Fig. 5. Block Diagram of Intelligent Dustbin for Smart City

Figure 5 represents the block diagram of the intelligent dustbin. This subsection discusses the related working of the system.

The intelligent dustbin exemplifies the application of IoT technologies within the framework of smart cities, where efficient resource utilization and real-time data analytics are paramount. At its core, an Ultrasonic sensor is strategically placed on the side of the dustbin to gauge the waste level. This sensor communicates with a NodeMCU ESP8266 via jumper wires, facilitating data transmission. Upon detecting the disposal of waste, the Ultrasonic sensor relays the readings to the ESP, which, utilizing Wi-Fi connectivity, uploads the data to the Blynk server. This real-time status update is accessible to officials through the Blynk Web App.

To enhance functionality, a GPS module is employed to ascertain the dustbin's current location. An alert system is triggered in the event that the trash level surpasses a predetermined threshold established by the authorities. Utilizing a Telegram bot, alert messages are dispatched to the relevant authorities, complete with the status and location details of the dustbin. Additionally, an LED outside the dustbin serves as a visual cue to waste collectors passing by.

This cost-effective and innovative solution underscores the importance of leveraging IoT technologies to address pressing urban challenges and build smarter, more resilient cities.

4.4 Challenges in Designing and Building an IoT-Based Intelligent Dustbin

When designing and building the intelligent dustbin on the principles of Internet of things several challenges were met. The combination of various IoT parts like the Node MCU ESP8266, the ultrasonic module, and the GPS module was challenging because some were not compatible, and connections were a problem. Making the mechanism of their interaction as smooth as possible required very careful coding and debugging. Another had to do with power management since the system had to have a constant power supply to run continually [27]. Battery issues used to be a problem because they restricted operation and necessitated the need for a longer deployment solution such as solar energy.

Constraints also emerged concerning the influence of the environment on the operation of this system. This was because sensors needed to be adjusted to operate in different environmental factors such as humidity, rain or even different temperatures to provide the best results. Durability of the physical form of the device was another issue, mainly because dustbins are vulnerable to vandalism or deliberate tampering. Finally, the limited sell of affordable, high durability, and easily accessible IoT components raised the manufacturing cost and made the prototype challenging. However, these challenges played our part in helping to identify methods for refining the system through iterative testing and feedback in order to integrate a more solid and larger system.

5 Apps Used in Intelligent Dustbin

In the Intelligent Dustbin, two essential apps, Blynk and Telegram, are employed. These applications facilitate real-time monitoring and management of waste levels, enhancing the efficiency of waste collection processes and supporting the Smart City initiative.

5.1 Blynk App

Blynk is a versatile and user-friendly platform that enables the development of IoT applications without extensive coding knowledge. In the intelligent dustbin project,

Blynk was leveraged to streamline the process of monitoring and managing the dustbin's status in real-time (Fig. 6).

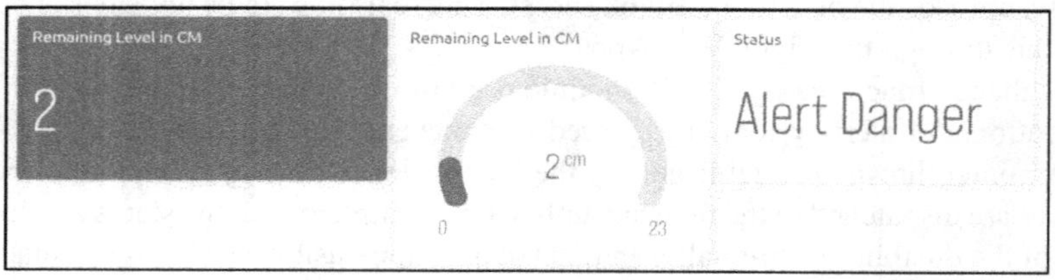

Fig. 6. Screenshot of Blynk App

Blynk's simplicity and effectiveness in facilitating seamless communication between the dustbin's sensors and the user interface made it the preferred choice. By integrating the Blynk app with the NodeMCU ESP8266 microcontroller, a secure and reliable connection for data transmission was established. This allowed for remote monitoring of the dustbin's fill level.

Blynk offers a range of features that enhance the functionality and usability of the intelligent dustbin system. Some of these features include:

- **User-Friendly Interface**: Blynk provides an intuitive interface for creating custom dashboards and control panels, making it easy to visualize and interact with sensor data.
- **Customizable Widgets**: Blynk offers a variety of customizable widgets, such as gauges, graphs, and buttons that can be tailored to suit specific project requirements.
- **Real-Time Data Monitoring**: With Blynk, users can monitor real-time data from connected devices, allowing for prompt decision-making and response to changing conditions.
- **Cloud Connectivity**: Blynk provides cloud connectivity, allowing users to access and control their IoT devices from anywhere in the world with an internet connection. Overall, Blynk proved to be an invaluable tool in our intelligent dustbin project, offering a seamless and efficient solution for monitoring and managing waste levels in real-time. Its user-friendly interface, customizable widgets, and robust features made it the ideal choice for IoT applications.

5.2 Telegram App

Telegram is a popular messaging platform known for its security, reliability, and versatility. In the intelligent dustbin project, Telegram was utilized by creating a bot that served as a communication bridge between the dustbin's monitoring system and the relevant authorities. The decision to use Telegram was based on its ability to facilitate real-time communication, its support for bot creation, and its robust notification features (Fig. 7).

The Telegram bot played a crucial role in the project by sending alert messages to authorities whenever the dustbin's waste level exceeded predefined thresholds. This ensured prompt action and efficient waste management. Additionally, the bot provided

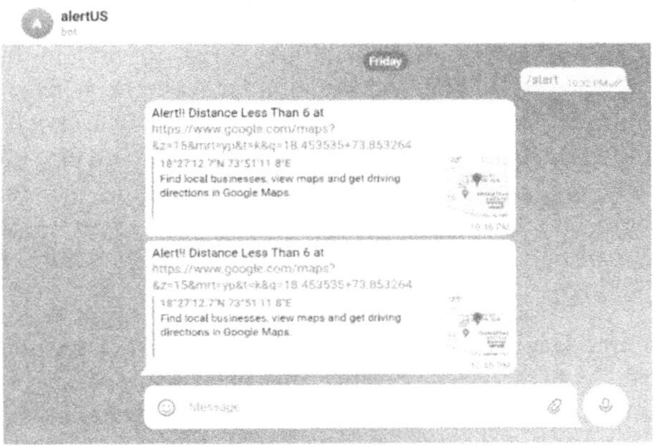

Fig. 7. Screenshot of Telegram App – Bot Page

the added functionality of including the dustbin's current location in the alert messages, enabling authorities to quickly locate and address the issue.

Some of the key features of Telegram that made it an ideal choice for the project include.

- **Bot Creation**: Telegram allows users to create custom bots with specific functionalities, making it possible to automate tasks and streamline communication processes.
- **Real-Time Messaging**: With Telegram, messages are delivered instantly, ensuring timely alerts and notifications.
- **Multimedia Support**: Telegram supports various types of media, including images, videos, and documents, allowing for rich and informative alert messages.
- **Cross-Platform Compatibility**: Telegram is available on multiple platforms, including mobile devices, desktops, and web browsers, ensuring accessibility for users across different devices and locations.

By leveraging Telegram and its bot creation capabilities, the functionality of the intelligent dustbin system was enhanced, enabling efficient communication and a timely response to waste management issues.

6 Discussion

In this section, two vital aspects related to intelligent dustbin have been discussed. First, the socioeconomic impact of intelligence dustbin has been elaborated and then, related limitations are also discussed for improved understanding of innovative technology.

6.1 Socioeconomic Impact of Intelligent Dustbin

The population of the cities in developing as well as developed countries is increasing at an accelerating rate, resulting in vital socioeconomic and environmental issues. One of the most critical issues in recent times is the production of millions of tons of waste in these cities every day. By 2050, waste production in the world will grow by approximately 3.40 billion tons, leading to an alarming situation for waste management [21]. Most of the cities are facing the daunting challenge of managing waste properly. These cities are eagerly looking for technology-based solutions for reducing the strain of managing the waste. Currently, the intelligent or smart dustbins are quite popular solutions with smart cities. They use the Internet of Things (IoT) technology to provide an effective solution on waste management. Smart cities can enjoy the following benefits if they use intelligent dustbins.

- **Stakeholders and Impact:** The stakeholders of the IoT-based intelligent dustbin system primarily include local authorities, city planners, residents, and environmental organizations. Local authorities benefit significantly from real-time data in waste management and the GPS tracking of the location of garbage that helps in the efficient planning of the route. This means that the cost of running the establishment is cut, fuel is saved and wastes are disposed off as scheduled. Intelligent dustbins are beneficial for city planners because the information collected from dustbins helps them in infrastructural planning and resource management [24]. Residents benefit from cleaner surroundings, reduced health hazards due to minimized overflow, and a visibly more hygienic urban environment. Additionally, the results generated by the system can be valuable for environmental organizations in lobbying for the changes in legislation supporting rational utilization of wastes and meeting the priorities of the Sustainable Development Goals like 'Good health and Wellbeing' and 'Sustainable Cities and Communities' [25]. Other groups include sanitation workers who also get a transformational effect. They do not have to physically cover dust bins at any one time thus cutting down on their work hours and exposure to various perils. This in turn increases their productivity and improves job satisfaction. The system also develops a culture of accountability and transparency for urban governance to offer efficient management and timely action hence enhancing public confidence and making the city 'cleaner and healthier'.
- **Impact of Smart Cities:** The IoT based intelligent dustbin system easily fits into the big picture of Smart Cities which are making cities sustainable and improving the living standards of residents [26]. It gives them real time data of the wastes collected; thus, improving the route of waste collection, minimizing the use of fuel, and managing resources in ways that afford sustainability and efficiency. It fosters tracking and surveillance of the environment for a strategic interventional approach and backs every recycling program for the round economy. It helps the urban planners in planning effective infrastructure and also uses mobile application and reward system in encouraging the communities. Thirdly, it improves other smart city connections like traffic and energy networks, which increases overall city flexibility in handling disasters and other events while advocating for the construction of smarter, cleaner, and more technologically developed cities.
- **Sustainability:** The filled and overflowing dustbins can pollute the environment, negatively impacting public health in the surrounding. Intelligent dustbins can make waste collection and transportation extremely convenient [21]. Thus, they help in

maintaining a garbage-free and sustainable environment in the residential and commercial areas of the smart cities. They also help the city corporations to minimize their overall carbon footprint and to achieve Sustainable Development Goals (SDGs), proposed by the United Nations [22].

- **Efficiency and Transparency**: The intelligent dustbins can convey the city corporation managers the condition of the bin. It can help their workers to empty the dustbin in a specific area before it starts to overflow. The use of such intelligent bins can help in reducing maintenance cost and ultimately, in improving the overall performance of waste management systems. The intelligent dustbins can notify immediately to the corporation managers, if the bin gets damaged, catches fire, falls on ground or someone tries to steal it [R3]. It may help managers to take appropriate actions. Thus, intelligence dustbins can improve the efficiency and bring enhanced transparency in managing the dustbins.
- **Community Behavioral Change:** Availability of intelligent dustbins on streets and lanes in the smart cities, may lead to change in behavior of people individually and, even as a community. People may become progressively more responsible towards waste disposal practices, when they notice cleanliness and timely disposal of waste or dustbins in their surroundings [23]. They respond quite positively to waste collection, segregation as well as disposal practices proactively. Thus, such community behavioral change can contribute to the success of waste management.

6.2 Limitations of Intelligent Dustbin

There can be certain addressable limitations of the intelligent dustbin such as the following:

- **Battery Dependence and Operational Costs:** Batteries are usually used to power the sensors, communication modules, and other electronic parts of in-telligent dustbins. As it uses a battery, it cannot be used for long, and the bat-tery has to be changed periodically. The regular requirement to replace the batteries in the intelligent dustbins may further raise the cost of operating.
- **Installation and Maintenance Costs:** The installation and maintenance costs are more as compared to regular dustbins. Furthermore, the upkeep of intelligent trash cans might require certain technological expertise, which could eventually result in increased running expenses. Furthermore, com-pared to more traditional options, the cost of acquiring and integrating these cutting-edge technologies into dustbins may be higher.
- **Malfunction Risks:** The dustbin may malfunction in certain cases if not properly maintained. A number of factors, including malfunctioning sensors, faulty software, and communication problems, might cause malfunctions. While prompt repairs and routine maintenance can help reduce the likeli-hood of problems, they also increase the overall cost of operations.
- **Susceptibility to Damage:** The integration of various sensors can make them more susceptible to damage due to external factors. For instance, excessive rain or extremely high or low temperatures may have an impact on sensor performance, and physical harm from drops or intentional tampering may cause the dustbins to stop working

properly. Reducing these hazards can be achieved by making sure the electronic components are adequately protected and have sturdy cases.

7 Conclusion and Future Work

The dustbin's seamless integration of advanced sensors, communication modules, and remote monitoring capabilities not only enhances waste management efficiency but also underscores its significance in the context of smart cities. The intelligent dustbin can be an asset for fast moving metro cities where municipalities cannot keep track of the dustbins. This makes it possible for the authorities to plan collections more effectively, optimize waste collection routes, and stop bins from overflowing. In the dynamic landscape of smart cities, where rapid urbanization demands innovative solutions, the intelligent dustbin stands as a testament to the adaptability and intelligence of modern urban infrastructure. Using the system, there are a number of traditional problems associated with the garbage monitoring process which are addressed; including: problem of searching for the bins, lack of information on the overflown bins, and tracking of collection vehicles [28]. The intelligent dustbin is designed to assist workers by enhancing their efficiency, allowing them to focus on higher-value tasks, rather than replacing their roles in the waste management process. Through its seamless integration of technology, the intelligent dustbin contributes to the overall efficiency and sustainability of waste management practices, aligning with the goals of smart city initiatives worldwide.

The integration of sealed compartments and automated lids in intelligent dustbins can represent a significant advancement in waste management practices within smart cities. By minimizing odor and reducing the risk of pest infestation, these features contribute to creating cleaner and more hygienic public spaces, aligning with the overarching goal of enhancing urban livability. The dustbin can be further extended to make waste segregation for dry and wet waste and also metal scrap. The dustbin's outside can be equipped with solar panels that can collect solar energy and transform it into electrical power for the sensors, communication modules, and other electronic parts to function. Stakeholder analysis showcases that various stakeholders like municipal waste management authorities, city planners, residents, and environmental organizations collectively benefit from the intelligent dustbin system through optimized waste management, cleaner urban spaces, and data-driven decision-making. This collaborative impact fosters efficiency, sustainability, and improved quality of life in smart cities.As an environmentally safe and sustainable replacement for regular batteries, solar power minimizes the need for frequent battery changes and lessens dependency on scarce energy sources. Furthermore, solar-powered intelligent dustbins have the ability to run for lengthy periods of time without maintenance, which makes them more appropriate for long-term outdoor deployment.

References

1. Sudha, L.K., Tahir, M., Ruchitha, E., Varshini, R., Ali, S.S.: Smart dustbin monitoring system using Arduino UNO. (IJERT) (2023)
2. Sk, M.M., Qamar, S., Sethy, T.: Solid waste management in indian perspective: a comprehensive review. Humanit. Soc. Sci. Stud. **12**, 35–45 (2023)

3. Vishwajit, D., Karan, B., Sairaj, S., Abhishek, D., Gaikwad, R.: Smart dustbin for smart city. Int. Res. J. Eng. Technol. (IRJET), **6**(4), 2985–2987 (2019)
4. Rohit, G.S., Chandra, M.B., Saha, S., Das, D.: Smart dual dustbin model for waste management in smart cities. In 2018 3rd International Conference for Convergence in Technology (I2CT), pp. 1–5. IEEE (2018)
5. Chaudhary, V., Kumar, R., Rajput, A., Singh, M., Singh, T.: Smart dustbin. Int. Res. J. Eng. Technol. **6**(05), 2395–0056 (2019)
6. Chitale, M.R., Chitpur, S.J., Chivate, A.B., Chopade, P.D., Deshmukh, S.M., Marathe, A.A.: Automated smart waste segregation system using IoT technology. J. Phys. Conf. Ser. **2601**(1), 012015 (2023)
7. Hussain, M.A., Nikhil, K., Kalyan, K.Y.P.: IoT based smart dustbin monitoring with tracking system using ATMEGA 2560 microcontroller. In 2019 Fifteenth International Conference on Information Processing (ICINPRO), pp. 1–6. IEEE (2019)
8. Sharma, A., Gupta, A., Singh, A.P., Sharma, A., Chib, M.S., Gupta, M.V. Smart Dustbin (2021)
9. Afolalu, S.A., Noiki, A.A., Ikumapayi, O.M., Ogundipe, A.T., Oloyede, O.R.: Development of smart waste bin for solid waste management. Planning **16**(8), 1449–1454 (2021)
10. Prabhakaran, S., Yugeshkrishnan, M., Santhiya, M., SM, D.K.: Smart dustbin using IOT. Sci. Temper **14**(02), 412–417 (2023)
11. Praveen, A., Radhika, R., Rammohan, M.U., Sidharth, D., Ambat, S., Anjali, T.: IoT based smart bin: a swachh-bharat initiative. In 2020 International Conference on Electronics and Sustainable Communication Systems (ICESC), pp. 783–786. IEEE (2020)
12. Thirumugam, P., Herath, D., Amarasooriya, S.: Smart dustbin and garbage monitoring system using internet of things. In: 2023 5th International Conference on Advancements in Computing (ICAC), pp. 857–861. IEEE (2023)
13. Bhawan, P., Nagar, E.A.: Central pollution control board. Central Pollut. Control Board, New Delhi, India, Tech. Rep. pp. 20–21 (2020)
14. Guna, J., Horvat, K.P., Podjed, D.: People-centred development of a smart waste bin. Sensors (Basel). **22**(3), 1288 (2022). https://doi.org/10.3390/s22031288
15. Ardiyan, A., Gunardi, Y., Hamid, A.: Design internet of things for smart waste bin management with Wemos based and firebase application. J. Soft Comput. Explor. **4**(4), 276–283 (2024)
16. Abhishek, A., Utsav, A., Kant, K., Priya, R.: Prototype design of smart dustbin and solid waste management using IoT (2021). ICICNIS (2020). https://doi.org/10.2139/ssrn.3768273
17. Pujari, T., Gharage, V., Patil, N., Sambhoje, S., Jadhav, J.: Solar powered smart dustbin. Int. J. Eng. Res. Tech. (IJERT) **13**(04) (2024)
18. Bharadwaj, A.S., Rego, R., Chowdhury, A.:IoT based solid waste management system: a conceptual approach with an architectural solution as a smart city application. In: 2016 IEEE Annual India Conference (INDICON), Bangalore, India, pp. 1–6 (2016).https://doi.org/10.1109/INDICON.2016.7839147
19. Harith, M.Z.M.Z., Hossain, M.A., Ahmedy, I., Idris, M.Y.I., Soon, T.K., Noor, R.M.: Prototype development of IoT based smart waste management system for smart city. IOP Conf. Ser. Mater. Sci. Eng. **884**, 012051 (2020). https://doi.org/10.1088/1757-899X/884/1/012051
20. Lane, R., Kronsell, A., Reynolds, D., Raven, R., Lindsay, J.: Role of local governments and households in low-waste city transitions. Environ. Innov. Soc. Trans. **52**(2024), 100879 (2024). https://doi.org/10.1016/j.eist.2024.100879
21. Need for smart bins - https://www.conurets.com/6-reasons-why-cities-need-smart-bins-for-waste-management/. Accessed 10 July 2024
22. Sustainable Development Goals (SDGs). https://sdgs.un.org/goals . Accessed 8 July 2024
23. Advantages of smart bins - https://dolphy.in/blog. Accessed 10 July 2024

24. Malla, S., Sahu, P.K., Sarangi, D., Patnaik, S.: Role of smart dustbin in creating a smart environment. In: Patnaik, S., Sen, S., Ghosh, S. (eds.) Smart Cities and Smart Communities. Smart Innovation, Systems and Technologies, vol. 294. Springer, Singapore (2022). https://doi.org/10.1007/978-981-19-1146-0_6
25. Bernstein, S.: The United Nations and the governance of sustainable development goals. In: Governing through Goals: Sustainable Development Goals as Governance Innovation, Norichika Kanie, Frank Biermann (2017) https://doi.org/10.7551/mitpress/10894.001.0001
26. Saxena, K., Yadav, S., Shukla, V., Awliya, A.: Smart cities using GPS to find the location of smart dustbin. In: 2024 International Conference on Communication, Computer Sciences and Engineering (IC3SE), Gautam Buddha Nagar, India, pp. 1887–1891 (2024). https://doi.org/10.1109/IC3SE62002.2024.10592986
27. Sobin, C.C.: A survey on architecture, protocols and challenges in IoT. Wireless Pers. Commun. **112**, 1383–1429 (2020). https://doi.org/10.1007/s11277-020-07108-5
28. Shinde, V., Bhutkar, G., Pawar, V. (2021). Overview of garbage monitoring system. In: Muzammil, M., Khan, A.A., Hasan, F. (eds.) Ergonomics for Improved Productivity. Design Science and Innovation. Springer, Singapore. https://doi.org/10.1007/978-981-15-9054-2_118
29. Patil, A., et al.: Prototype design of android app for mothers of preterm infants. In: Barricelli, B., et al. (eds.) Human Work Interaction Design. Designing Engaging Automation. HWID 2018. IFIP Advances in Information and Communication Technology, vol. 544. Springer, Cham (2019). https://doi.org/10.1007/978-3-030-05297-3_1

Inculcating Responsible Habits for Pathological Online Gambling Behaviour for Young Adults

Moitreyee Bhattacharjee[1(✉)], Aayush Bhogle[1], Mihir Bhanushali[1], Arundhati Thakurta[1], and Sajana Alungalali[2]

[1] NMIMS School of Design, Mumbai, Maharashtra 400056, India
{moitreyee.bhattacharjee39,aayush.bhogle02, mihir.bhanushali35}@nmims.in, arundhati.thakurta@nmims.edu
[2] National Institute of Technology (NIT), Calicut, India
sajanaali@nitc.ac.in

Abstract. Online gambling addiction among young adults is a growing concern, due to easy accessibility and popularity of online gambling platforms. While these platforms offer entertainment, the excessive consumption of online gambling can lead to detrimental effects on mental health, financial stability, and overall well-being of the concerned individual. With a focus on the rising popularity of online gambling, the objectives of the research paper revolve around understanding the motivations, triggers, and rewards that drive young online gamblers to gamble more often, aiming to devise a non-restrictive solution that disrupts their habit loop. Various models such as Hook's Model, Fogg's Model, Habit loop and Theory of Planned Behaviour were used to study behavioural patterns of youngsters addicted to gambling. The study focused on individuals aged 18–30 well-aware of their gambling addiction, using simple random sampling, and snowball sampling for the research and usability study. The research was conducted in four phases, including primary and secondary research, data synthesis, conceptualisation, and design validation with prototypes. The novel solution, Ryze, is a unique narrative-driven app which helps inculcate responsible habits and collaborative gameplay, aiming to guide the users to take informed decisions while gambling. Personalised risk assessment, skill-based games, and emotional well-being practices address irresponsible gambling among young adults, offering a potential solution in the battle against addiction. This research highlights the triggers and risks of online gambling addiction, proposing Ryze as an innovative, non-restrictive solution, calling for awareness and proactive steps to address addictive gambling behaviours in today's world.

Keywords: Online Gambling Behaviour · Compulsive Pathological Gambling · Human-Computer Interaction · Behavioural Design

1 Introduction

Gambling refers to the act of betting or wagering on an event with an uncertain outcome, with the primary intent of winning additional money or material goods (Free Law, 2023). The two distinctive categories of gambling games are: skill-based and luck-based.

Published by Springer Nature Switzerland AG 2026
G. Bhutkar et al. (Eds.): IDID 2024, IFIP AICT 747, pp. 175–186, 2026.
https://doi.org/10.1007/978-3-032-00777-3_11

Skill-based games, like poker and blackjack, hinge on player expertise and strategic decision-making (Johnson, 2021). Contrastingly, luck-based games, exemplified by slot machines and lotteries, rely on chance and random outcomes (Griffiths, 2020). Moreover, activities like sports betting involve predicting and wagering on sports outcomes, where a combination of skill and chance influences results (Hing, 2014). Similarly, participating in the stock market introduces a financial gambling aspect where investors blend their financial acumen with market unpredictability to make informed decisions (Barber, 2000).

The present study explores a non-restrictive intervention aimed at aiding young adults in understanding their addiction to online gambling. The study focuses on addressing the challenges posed by pathological online gambling behaviour and its implications for the future. Easy accessibility and availability of online gambling platforms brings forth new sets of challenges that differ significantly from conventional gambling addictions. These challenges demand a higher level of responsiveness and adaptability due to the accessibility, anonymity, and immersive nature of online gambling platforms. This necessitates the development of innovative tools and strategies to enable individuals and support systems to respond effectively to these unique challenges. The main research question of this study would be: *What types of new requirements does the context of pathological online gambling behaviour among young adults bring, and how can interventions be designed to address them?*

To address this question, a human-centred design approach was employed, emphasizing the early phases of the design process. To understand the context and user requirements of young adults addicted to online gambling, we consulted with diverse field experts, including psychologists, addiction counsellors, and technology specialists. By adopting this methodology, the study aims to design tools and interventions that align with the needs, preferences, and behavioural patterns of the target audience. These tools are intended to enhance self-awareness, promote responsible gambling habits, and improve communication between the affected individuals and their support networks.

This case study contributes to the field of Human-Computer Interaction (HCI) by identifying the requirements of young adults struggling with pathological online gambling behaviour. It emphasizes the need for personalized, user-friendly, and adaptive solutions that foster responsible habits and effective team communication (if any), paving the way for a healthier and more balanced relationship with online gambling platforms.

2 Literature Review

2.1 Online Gambling

Online gambling is the act of placing bets and earning money through digital platforms or websites, offering an alternative to traditional venues such as casinos or sporting events. (Free Law, 2023). Online gambling offers private, anytime access using high-speed internet, allowing quick bets and result notifications (Gainsbury, 2015). The Online Gambling market worldwide is expected to grow at an annual rate (CAGR 2023–2030) of 11.7% (Grand View Research, 2023).

2.2 Online Gambling Addiction

Gamblers themselves believe online gambling is more addictive than offline gambling, due to its easy accessibility via the internet (McCormack, 2012). If the gambler had been rewarded for every bet, it would take fewer losses for the gambler to disassociate betting with winning and for the act of gambling to be extinguished. Thus, casinos take advantage of an intermittent and unpredictable reinforcement schedule to keep gamblers gambling as long as possible (Cohen, 2011). Online Gambling participation peaks in young adulthood, when the risk for gambling problems is also increased (Addict. 2021).

Online gambling addiction encompasses a broad spectrum of excessive and uncontrolled online gambling habits, indicative of addictive patterns, also due to (Griffiths, 2003). Compulsive gambling disorder, a recognized psychiatric condition, extends beyond the online realm and involves an uncontrollable urge to gamble with adverse consequences on personal, social, and professional aspects (American Psychiatric Association, 2013).

2.3 Compulsive Pathological Online Gambling

Compulsive gambling, also called gambling disorder, is the uncontrollable urge to keep gambling despite the toll it takes on one's life. If one is dealing with compulsive gambling problem, they may continually chase bets that lead to losses, use up savings and create debt and are compelled to keep playing to recover their money - a pattern that becomes increasingly destructive over time (Mayo Clinic, 2023).

Some of the triggers for compulsive online gambling include:

- **Accessibility and Convenience:** Ease of access to online gambling platforms, allows users to engage at any time and from any location (Griffiths, 2003).
- **Stimulating Features:** The stimulating features of online casino games, such as enticing graphics and sounds, can intensify arousal and excitement, potentially fuelling compulsive play and heightened betting (Griffiths, King, & Delfabbro, 2019).
- **Anonymity:** The anonymity provided by online gambling platforms encourages compulsive behaviour among users seeking an escape or coping mechanism (Gainsbury et al., 2012).
- **Financial Problems:** Compulsive gambling may be exacerbated by financial problems, as the ease of access and constant availability of online platforms may lead to excessive and impulsive spending, contributing to a cycle of financial strain (Hing, 2014).

This detailed research on online gambling, highlights the risks of addiction and compulsive online gambling behaviour. Recognizing the triggers for online gambling highlights the complex factors which contribute to issues, stressing the importance of targeted interventions and responsible measures in today's landscape.

3 Research Objectives

The growing popularity of online gambling, driven by its easy accessibility, raises concerns about the development of problematic gambling behaviour and addiction. The surge in online gambling's popularity poses addiction risks for young adults, emphasizing the urgent need for people to inculcate responsible gambling habits.

The objectives of this project are:

- To understand the world of online gambling and the addictive aspect of it.
- To find out the motivations, triggers and rewards gamblers derive from online gambling.
- To devise a novel solution which tackles problematic online gambling and inculcates responsible gambling habits.

4 Methodology

4.1 Participants and Sampling Methods

The target audience comprises of individuals, aged 18 to 30, who are well- aware of their gambling addiction and are willing to address it. Participants, selected through simple random sampling methods, were recruited based on a screening questionnaire, ensuring they had prior experience with online gambling apps. Participants were also selected from Reddit Forums via specific subreddit groups for users to discuss their online gambling behaviours and problems. Excluding designers, marketers, and those from the online gambling industry, 10 participants were involved in the usability study to test the devised solution, each meeting the specified criteria and not having participated in any usability tests in the past 6 months.

The entire procedure of the study was divided into 4 major phases: Research and Data collection, Data synthesis, Conceptualizing, and User testing.

Phase 1: Research and Data Collection

- **Secondary research:** During the Data Collection phase, desk research was conducted thoroughly by going through available articles, research papers and websites based on gambling, online gambling, pathological gambling, problematic gambling, the various kinds of addictions inculcated by users from gambling, and the process of users getting addicted.
- **Primary research:** Primary research involved empathy interviews with 27 college students, 8 working professionals, and 2 psychologists. An observational camera study was also conducted with the users, with their consent while observing their interactions with the available gambling apps. An online Google Form Survey was distributed on Reddit groups and pages for gambling enthusiasts, and groups where users discussed about their problem gambling behaviours, gathering 32 responses. Additionally, empathy interviews were conducted with 29 participants in Mumbai, India. Observational studies were also conducted to learn the behaviour of the users while performing tasks in existing gambling apps via observational studies.

Phase 2: Data Synthesis

The next phase of the project was to synthesize and analyse the data that was gathered from the research. Personas, scenarios and journey maps based on the target audience were created.

- **Behaviour Models:** The gathered data was synthesized and analysed using behaviour models such as Hook's Model, Fogg's Model, Habit Loop, and the Theory of Planned Behaviour to understand the psychological and behavioural mechanisms underlying in the users' online gambling behaviours. These models were chosen for their ability to illustrate how the concerned habits are formed, behaviours triggered, and decisions that are influenced in digital environments. These models provide insights into habit formation, triggers, and decision-making processes. *Hook's Model* identifies triggers and rewards reinforcing gambling, *Fogg's Model* explains the role of motivation and ability, the *Habit Loop* highlights the cycle of cue, routine, and reward, and the *Theory of Planned Behaviour* examines attitudes, norms, and perceived control, in context of the gambling behaviours of the users. These models are essential for developing effective interventions that disrupt harmful cycles and foster healthier habits (Ajzen, 1991; Fogg, 2009; Eyal, 2014).
- **Persona and Scenarios:** After carrying out primary and secondary research in context of the target audience and stakeholders, user personas and scenarios were created based on profiling the participants, their motivations, triggers, rewards, and the kind of environments they were exposed to.
- **Competitive Benchmarking:** Competitive Benchmarking was performed to compare the positive as well as negative aspects of the existing anti-gambling and safe-gambling apps and softwares like Gamblock, Betfilter, Betblocker, Gamcare, Gamban etc.
- **Journey Maps:** The insights from the observational study along with participants while them performing tasks and their interactions on the gambling platforms were then translated to personas and user journeys. These were done to understand how the users interacted with the apps. Their emotions, activities and pain points were noted down.

Phase 3: Conceptualisation

The next step was one of the crucial parts of the process as it included ideating, conceptualising and designing various aspects of the solution. The solution ideas ranged from tangible product design, digital product design, IOT-based ideas to board game-based ideas. Lastly, the intervention was narrowed down to a digital product, which could be easily reachable to the target audience. This step included creating an information architecture and later designing the prototype of the intervention.

- **Brainstorming and Rapid Sketching:** Concepts were developed using strategies like persuasion techniques to highlight responsible gaming benefits and risks, gamification to create engaging narratives with challenges and rewards, CBT to foster healthy thinking, and non-restrictive solutions to encourage sustainable behaviours.

- **Concept Validation:** Through user feedback based on desirability, viability, and feasibility, three promising concepts were selected for further development.
- **Prototyping:** Low fidelity prototypes were made on paper cutouts before testing it with the users. The paper prototypes were then converted into Mid- Fidelity prototypes. This prototype was made in the grayscale. Figma, which is a collaborative web application for interface design, was used to make the final high-fidelity prototypes.

Phase 4: User Testing

The last step was to test the design, check and ensure whether users interacted with the solution in the way that was devised for them to.

- **Screener & Pilot Testing:** A screener was created which included a set of questions the moderator had to ask the participant a few days before to finalise the participant for the study. This screener helped in determining whether the participant fulfilled all the criteria and was eligible for the usability test. The screener also helped in determining whether a participant was not a fake participant. Before the user testing, a mock test was conducted to understand the flow of the study and assess for any potential issues beforehand.
- **Usability testing:** High-Fidelity Prototypes underwent one-on-one moderated sessions. The session began with an expectancy test on the analysis page, followed by the participant playing a round of the game, 7-Up-Down, on the app. The study concluded with a post-evaluation questionnaire to know the user's experience with the redesigned website, and participants received incentives for their time.
- **Analysis and Assessment:** Based on the observations and the nonverbal cues noted during the usability study, qualitative responses were documented. They were then mapped, using a feasibility matrix, based on their technical difficulty and their importance. The responses collected in the post evaluation questionnaire were then averaged to obtain a rating for the app and the specific criteria. Based on the usability assessment, possible suggestions for improvement were listed down.

5 Results and Discussions

This section intends to focus on the explorations and findings in the study. The results and discussion are divided into three phases. The data collection and synthesis are included in Phase I. Phase II includes the conceptualisation stage and Phase III includes the findings from the usability testing.

Phase 1 & 2: Data Collection and Synthesis

Data collection: From the secondary research, the behaviours of online gamblers and the addiction of the same were understood. We also got information about the current trends of the online gambling industry. It was also found that males tend to gamble more than females. In primary research, it was observed that majority of online gamblers are aware of their addiction and have a desire to address it (Fig. 1).

Data Synthesis: Common triggers for gambling were identified as financial distress, boredom, the need for an adrenaline rush, peer influence, stress, success stories, and

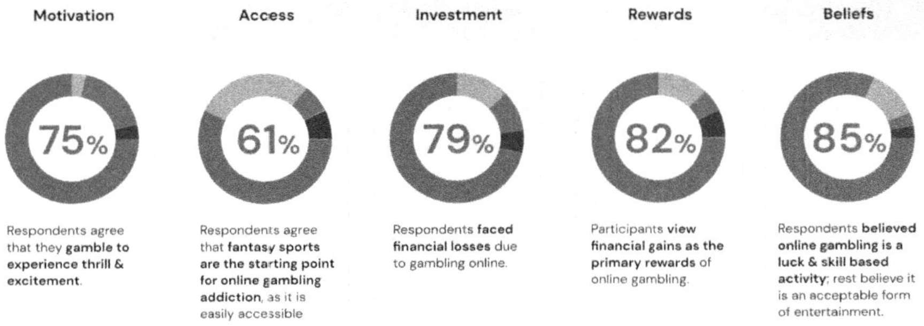

Fig. 1. Primary Research Survey Insights

endorsements and advertisements by famous celebrities. The collected data was then synthesized using behavioural models. Following is some of the examples of the same (Fig. 2):

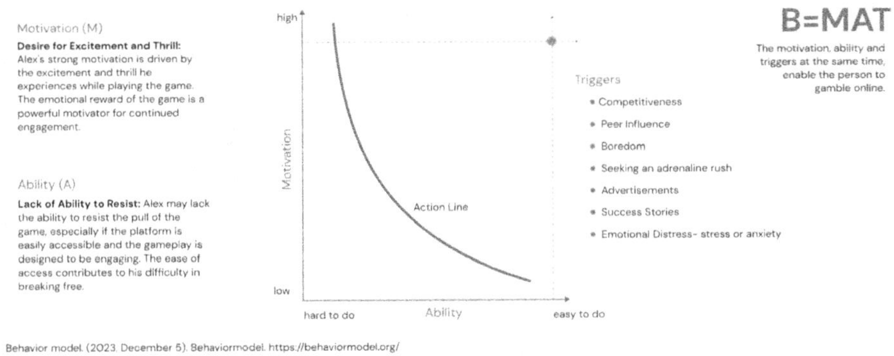

Fig. 2. Fogg's Behaviour Model

The Fogg's Behaviour Model elucidated that the user's motivation and ability to gamble are high, along with the frequency of triggers, which drives the user's urge to gamble more. The Hook Model explains how triggers like stress, boredom, or the desire for quick money led to impulsive bets and reinforced cravings. The Theory of Planned Behaviour explained that users' gambling decisions were shaped by their belief in recovering losses, peer influence, intention to bet more, perceived control over winning, and impulsive behaviour (Fig. 3).

This stage was key to identifying and breaking the vicious habit loop through concepts developed in the conceptualization stage.

Fig. 3. Habit Loop

Phase 3: Conceptualization

During the conceptualization stage, concepts were generated using design strategies like persuasion techniques, cognitive behavioural therapy, and gamification. Ensuring none of the concepts were restrictive against gambling, a range of ideas were brainstormed before narrowing down to the three most unique and feasible ones:

- **Concept 1 - Simulative Gameplay:** A simulative storytelling approach, where user's get in the role, and are given situations, based on different games. The platform focuses primarily on providing the user with an exceptional and educational experience, along with monetary motivations.
- **Concept 2 - Divide and Share:** Where fun meets responsibility: our app analyses user history, offers AI insights, and promotes responsible play. Emphasizing collaboration and a commitment to safe gaming, we provide a socially driven platform for an enjoyable and secure gambling experience.
- **Concept 3 - Risk Reserve:** A no risk gambling app enabling users to gamble responsibly with a fixed amount and controlled betting limit. Users reserve an amount, play engaging games with limited stakes, and always end with their funds secured—no risk, just rewards!

Concept validation tests revealed that Simulative gameplay offered high desirability with engaging storytelling and role-playing but had moderate viability due to high development costs and challenging feasibility in balancing education with entertainment. Risk reserve, while appealing to users valuing financial security, struggled with limited excitement for risk-takers and faced low viability due to fixed betting and legal complications that hindered feasibility. Divide and Share stood out with high desirability and feasibility, leveraging AI insights and a collaborative gambling experience to build a loyal user base, offering strong viability and potential for sustained engagement.

The final chosen solution for the platform, based on the feasibility of all concepts, was based on the concept of Divide and Share, rebranding and renaming the solution to *Ryze*, a narrative-driven gaming app-based platform which enables collaborative gambling gameplay aiming to guide and nudge the users to inculcate the habit of taking into consideration multiple opinions and scenarios before wagering a particular bet, helping the users to consider the pros and cons of a particular bet and situation (Fig. 4).

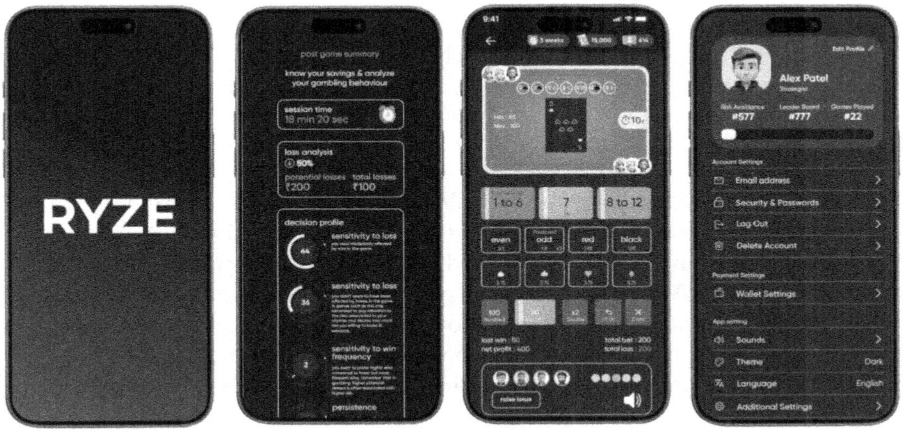

Fig. 4. Ryze App: High Fidelity Screens

Ryze is a gamified app that promotes responsible gambling through storytelling, habit-building mechanics, and mindful interventions. Users explore a collaborative gambling universe, where teamwork helps them form strategies and make informed decisions, unlike traditional apps where users often act alone, sometimes in frustration, leading to significant losses. Their gameplay is analysed and presented to them, with an AI companion offering timely advice to prevent impulsive bets. Features like habit scores and social connections reinforce responsible behaviour, creating a structured approach to controlling gambling habits. The onboarding process involves questionnaires where users fix the amount, they are comfortable gambling with, which makes sure that they play with people belonging to the same risk appetite or the amount of money they are okay losing with, unlike the existing apps where people belonging to various economic classes play together. The analytics section gives the users valuable insights based on his gambling patterns. All these features combined to form a non-restrictive, gamified solution to tackle irresponsible gambling by young adults as intended. The next step was to check whether the users used our app the way we intended them to use it.

Phase 4: User testing

The tool of design validation was used to check the usability of the app. The protocol worked effectively for quantitative analysis and probing.

In the low-fidelity prototype, users liked the core concept, collaborative aspect, and in-game intervention, but struggled with the lengthy onboarding and dark UI, which were addressed in the next prototype. In the mid-fi prototypes, users appreciated the storytelling, gaming environments, and role-playing collaboration, especially for high-stakes sports betting and blackjack. However, they wanted more skill-based games, aligned with the responsible gambling focus, which were added in the final prototype. Although the concept of habit score calculation remained unclear, users reported a significant reduction in stress levels compared to current gambling apps, marking a crucial step toward fostering healthier gambling habits.

The insights gathered were mapped onto a feasibility matrix and implemented. User testing proved successful, with users rating the concept and features 4.24 out of 5, while also highlighting key design errors that had been overlooked.

6 Conclusion

In an era where online gambling accessibility is increasingly pervasive, this research delves into the complexities of compulsive pathological online gambling, emphasizing its triggers and addictive nature. By employing a user-centric approach, the aim was to understand the psychology and effectively "getting into the mind of a gambling addict". This understanding served as the foundation for the development of Ryze, a unique, narrative-driven platform that fosters collaborative and responsible gameplay.

Ryze, stands out from traditional gambling platforms by prioritising user awareness and responsible behaviour. While the emphasis of the platform is to make the user aware of their gambling habits, while implementing positive reinforcement to unlearn their negative addictive behaviour, the aim of the platform is to make the user learn a new positive habit, and eventually dissociate from the negative and addictive gambling behaviour, while breaking their habit loop and forming a positive habit (Fig. 5).

A potential area for future enhancement would be the measurement of cognitive load experienced by Ryze users. Assessing response times, alongside self-ratings of effort and difficulty, will provide valuable insights into user engagement and inform further design refinements. This analysis will enable a deeper understanding of how Ryze addresses various types of cognitive load, such as intrinsic, extraneous, or germane load. Incorporating such data into future studies will further validate Ryze's impact and enhance the user experience. A limitation of this study stems from the legal ambiguity surrounding online gambling in India, with varying regulations across different states. Future research should explore how Ryze can effectively adapt to these diverse legal frameworks.

In conclusion, recognizing the urgent need to address the growing issue of online gambling addiction, Ryze emerges as a promising solution. By combining a deep understanding of user psychology with innovative design principles, Ryze offers a potential pathway towards mitigating the harms associated with compulsive online gambling and fostering healthier gaming experiences.

Fig. 5. Final screens after implementing the user testing feedback

Acknowledgement. We would like to express immense gratitude to NMIMS School of Design for providing this opportunity to us, as well as the platform, which guided us to complete this research, with vast amounts of learning. Special thanks to our mentors Dr. Arundhati Guha Thakurta and Prof. Sajana Alungalali for their constant support and guidance. The project benefited greatly from their feedback and guidance. A heartfelt thanks to all participants for their contribution, valuable time and participation in this research and usability study.

References

1. Free Law: laws and regulations governing online gambling in India (2023). https://www.freelaw.in/legalarticles/Laws-and-Regulations-Governing-Online-Gambling-in-India
2. Griffiths, M., Parke, J.: The role of structural characteristics in gambling. In: Bowden-Jones, J., Dickson, D., Dunand, S. (eds.) Harm Reduction for Gambling: A Public Health Approach, pp. 21–39 (2020)
3. Barber, B.M., Odean, T.: Trading is hazardous to your wealth: the common stock investment performance of individual investors. J. Finan. **55**(2), 773–806 (2000)
4. Johnson, E.E., Smith, G.J.: The role of skill versus luck in poker: evidence from the World Series of Poker. J. Gambling Stud. **37**(1), 269–284 (2021)
5. Griffiths, M.D., King, D.L., Delfabbro, P.H.: The biopsychosocial consequences of pathological gambling. BioPsychoSoc. Med. **13**(1), 1–11 (2019)
6. Gainsbury, S.M., Wood, R., Russell, A., Hing, N., Blaszczynski, A.: A digital revolution: comparison of demographic profiles, attitudes, and gambling behavior of Internet and non-Internet gamblers. Comput. Hum. Behav. **28**(4), 1388–1398 (2012)
7. American psychiatric association: Diagnostic and statistical manual of mental disorders (5th ed.). Arlington, VA: American Psychiatric Publishing (2013)
8. Gainsbury S.M.: Online gambling addiction: the relationship between internet gambling and disordered gambling (2015). https://doi.org/10.1007/s40429-015-0057-8
9. Cohen: How is intermittent reinforcement used in gambling? (2011). https://www.papertrell.com/apps/preview/The-Handy-Psychology-Answer-Book/Handy%20Answer%20book/How-is-intermittent-reinforcement-used-in-gambling/001137018/content/SC/52caff2d82fad14abfa5c2e0_cool_facts.html
10. Mayo Clinic: Compulsive gambling (2023). https://www.mayoclinic.org/diseases-conditions/compulsive-gambling/symptoms-causes/syc-20355178
11. Griffiths, M.: Internet gambling: issues, concerns, and recommendations. CyberPsychol. Behav. **6**(6), 557–568 (2003). https://doi.org/10.1089/109493103322725333
12. Hing, N., Lamont, M., Vitartas, P., Fink, E.: Sports-embedded gambling promotions: a study of exposure, sports betting intention and problem gambling amongst adults. Int. J. Mental Health Addict. **13**(1), 115–135 (2014). https://doi.org/10.1007/s11469-014-9519-9
13. Fogg, B.J.: A behavior model for persuasive design. In: proceedings of the 4th International Conference on Persuasive Technology (2009). https://doi.org/10.1145/1541948.1541999

Looking at the Interwebs:

Exploring the Affordances of Gentrification and Beyond, While Studying Internet Memes in India

Paul Anthony George(✉)

Srishti Manipal Institute of Art, Design and Technology,
Bangalore Manipal Academy of Higher Education, Manipal, India
paul.george@manipal.edu

Abstract. This paper explores parallels between social networking site (SNS) interface design and the Haussmannization of Paris under Napoleon III. Using Walter Benjamin's analysis of the Parisian Arcades and Edgar Allan Poe's flâneur, it examines how consumption and space changed in Paris, drawing comparisons to the internet. The lurker in SNS, much like the flâneur, navigates spaces designed for algorithmic consumption and engagement, where user behaviour is mapped. The research speculates on new metaphors of collective visibility, inspired by the Mass Observation Project, and examines spreadable behaviours while looking at memes. It uses digital ethnography to explore the emergence of the attention economy and its implications for interaction design, particularly in gentrifying online spaces, while raising questions about ethics, consent, privacy, and the future of the web.

Keywords: Future of Interaction Design · Speculative Design · Digital Ethnography · Science and Technology Studies

1 Introduction

Here is another set of phrases about AI: ***algorithmic optimization, extreme spreadsheet, automated capital, automated compliance, software, autopoietic system, infinite game****. This set was generated by experts in response to the question:* ***What would you call it if you could not call it "artificial intelligence"?*** *Interestingly, this set avoids the* ***tool-or-threat metaphor*** *and refers to what AI technologies actually do, or purport to. The avoidance of metaphors is a recognition that they can end up becoming* ***unhelpfully entangled with the thing itself****. Experts surveyed here urged disentangling our understanding of AI from its metaphoric language by following the feminist epistemologist Sandra Harding who discusses the "****social fingerprints****" that she says all metaphors carry [7].* ***Metaphors can reveal the political economies and material politics they emerge from.*** (Ganesh 2022).

This paper is an ethnographic reflection on the **metaphors and relationships** between **individuals, the crowd** and **the spaces** they inhabit and those which are

G. Bhutkar et al. (Eds.): IDID 2024, IFIP AICT 747, pp. 187–210, 2026.
https://doi.org/10.1007/978-3-032-00777-3_12

designed for habituation. It began with the question: *what a cyber-flâneur might be (if not a lurker), and what would the internet look like, to them?*

To ground this exploration, the paper draws heavily on the concept of the **flâneur**, a historical and literary figure, from Paris, caught between the old and the new. I examine this figure (Fig. 1) through **three** key aspects [see 2]. His relationship with **space, time** and **the solipsistic qualities of this experience**. His preoccupation with **physiognomy**, and the third and perhaps the major reason, for using the flâneur as a point of inquiry, to understand **gentrification and the designation** (or design) of certain spaces for intended purposes and behaviors that emerge because of and despite of these intentions.

Fig. 1. Gentrification of Paris brought out different segments of the population, the principles of productivity, consumption and the affordances of being acceptable as a citizen-subject, left the flâneur, ill-fit for society, but a peculiar figure in literature and this paper. Image source 1: https://reinventinghome.org/the-art-of-the-flaneur/, Image source 2: https://www.telfair.org/article/the-french-impressionists-and-haussmanns-paris/

The flâneur serves as a framework to understand **unintended behaviors physical spaces of Paris and then understand affordances of gentrification in online spaces**, particularly through **designed (intended) interfaces**. Here, I focus on the notion of the [in 3] **lurker**, through which I draw parallels between the flâneur's solipsism to understand the perceived duality in virtual (digital) spaces and actual (physical) spaces. The correlations between experiences and the nature of designed interfaces are discussed here, to demonstrate how **lurking is an act of mitigation**, of *being public* in online spaces and *being in public* online spaces, through the concept of **the mobilized gaze** [beginning in 4]. The goal is to analyze online behavior in relation to the spaces themselves [Sect. 5], while **speculating on shifts** from the time of the flâneur to the contemporary presence of the lurker, to understand the **shift in affordances of gentrification**. The flâneur, historically, subverted societal expectations of productivity. In contrast, the modern-day lurker represents a shift—one where behaviors are increasingly enumerated (see Fig. 2), consumed, and commodified, using other affordances that make your presence more *present*. Lurkers engage with public, accessible online spaces while avoiding deeper participation, highlighting **a shift** from being *productive* contributors to becoming the **data products** themselves. User behaviors and user-generated content have become integral to platform and community-building processes, fueling engagement, data collection, and revenue models built on ad-based ecosystems and constant data flow. The implications of this kind of research, is also to engage with what emerges as new paradigms of looking *underneath the hood of* the interwebs, to understand and decide what comes after, questions that HCI researchers find themselves asking often.

Though there is a direct comparison being made between the old word flâneur and the relatively new word lurker, it is with full acknowledgment that the comparison is extremely contentious. Each notion brings its own record of having shifted both their ontological and epistemological goalposts[1]. There is an attempt to understand what these characters are reflections of, spatially and temporally. An attempt is also being made to look at how the tension between shifting goal posts might be an indicator of a need for new ontologies, framing the way interfaces are written about and ways of looking at emergent behavior and how it contrasts against intended or designed spaces and modalities. The paper also marks ideas around the ethics of consent, privacy and the future of online spaces, as I take the reader towards the end, into how the notions around gentrification in Paris and identifying the incidental interaction design principles that have emerged as the web evolves unevenly from Web 1.0 to Web 2.0 and beyond.

I use this paper to shape my doctoral research while studying spreadable media like internet memes and dissent in online spaces, as it has shaped notions around digital ethnography, modes of participant-observation like lurking ethnography, and navigating the policies around data protection and privacy. A lot of my digital ethnography has happened while navigating comment sections, imprints of people as views and opinions, likes, number of shares, on and of spreadable media, in open and closed SNS, be it on Instagram, YouTube or closed like Whatsapp or Signal. Lurking, often is the default state, on these platforms and it shapes this distinct version of participant-observation, that I later unpack as lurking ethnography. These are essential to the tools and modes

[1] These shifts are largely speculated as happening, within this context, when the meaning of being productive and an active participant as prescribed by societal norms, are evolving or have evolved in very specific ways, some of which have been described in the passages below.

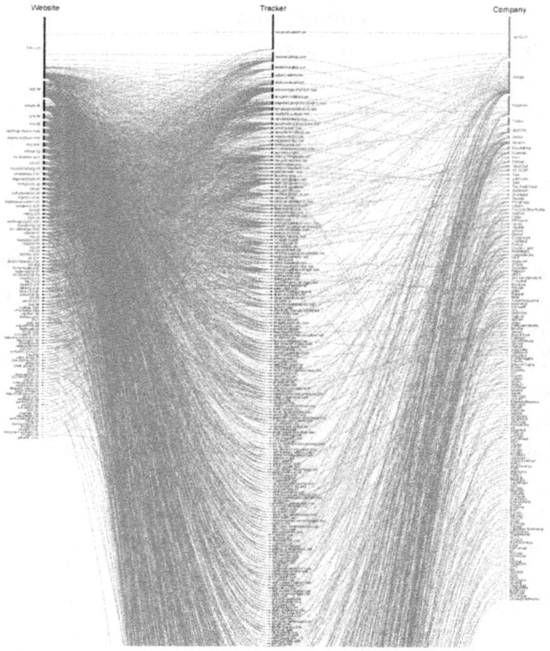

Fig. 2. *Browsing Histories*, a project by the SHARE Lab looks at the digital exhaust of browsing histories and behaviours. It unpacks in detail the idea of the social graph, and its role as a benchmark for contemporary digital platform design. A lurker's presence, even without active engagement, is an enumerated existence. Image source: "Browsing Histories. " SHARE Lab, 2017, https://labs.rs/en/browsing-histories/

of practice that is shaped more by the communities I have been part of: my *online-self* which through this paper, I describe shapes the way I think about research or my *researcher-self*. This practice-based research [I conclude in 6] further extends into the future while I draw from the flâneur (past) and the lurker (present), **while speculating the future of online spaces**, as imagining and justifying how a collective archiving practice in the future, in the form of the *digsite*. This was made possible by trying to imagine a flâneur, or a lurker **evading algorithmic mediation**, while trying to study spreadable media and spreadable behaviours. **The contours I've mapped reflect how sensitive the incidental shape of the online terrain** is, where similar or familiar affordances are used, abused, mis-used, or re-invented by cultural markers. The research shapes how I think of Human-computer interaction presently, how it might continue gentrifying, and the PhD explores the transition from gentrification (or intention), to decay (post the incidental use) and invites the reader/ researcher, to ask, ***what aspects of care* and *what kind of ethics*** should emerge after the decay of present-future interfaces, and their design principles?

2 The Man of the Crowd: Mapping the Flâneur and How He Evades Productivity in Paris and Literature

His head again fell upon his breast; he appeared as I had seen him at first. I observed that he now took the course in which had gone the greater number of the audience --but, upon the whole, I was at a loss to comprehend the waywardness of his actions.
(Poe).[2]

2.1 Space, Time and Solipsism

The **flâneur** as a character framed by Walter Benjamin, in "The Arcades Project", may be understood as someone who walks through the urban scape, through time and through space, without a goal, as a sponge. Benjamin's flâneur, understood to be an extension of Baudelaire's aimless critic-wanderer and Poe's *man of the crowd*, invites the reader[3], to follow and in doing so (see Fig. 3), immerse themselves into the experience of the city[4]. A city-space construed through words and sometimes images, erecting whole architectures, arcades and "othered" spaces, along with the people that roam (and roamed) them (see Fig. 4). *The notion of the flâneur however has changed over time*, with the many appropriations, differing largely in terms of the modern relationship between the society and the individual (assuming society to be structured through the singular unit of the individual). This relationship is revealed constantly through participation or the ability for individuals to sustain themselves, despite being non-participant. And in how the society is structured, in terms of **space**: space for *the individual* and space for *the society*, en masse[5].

Benjamin describes Paris and perhaps through it introspects other aspects of *modern-urban life* as having **phantasmagoric** layers to it, which he presents through the **simultaneous existence** of artefacts, faux spaces, architecture and decorations **from the past**, while being razed down to make way for the *new*, *planned* and *gentrified* **Paris** (Hanssen 2006). He writes about the arcades, as enchanted spaces, with illusory artefacts and as abodes of fairies, as spaces where Paris of antiquity survived whilst outside it, modernity pummeled Paris, with boulevards, public parks and quays. Under Georges-Eugène (Baron) Haussmann's planning frenzy, the organic and medieval growth of Paris with narrow marketplaces were deemed, over-crowded and unhygienic. Between 1853 and 1870, he engaged in reorganizing living spaces, through commune like architectural

[2] Poe, Edgar Allen. 1938. "The Man of the Crowd." In The complete tales and poems of Edgar Allan Poe, by Edgar Allen Poe and Hervey Allen, 1026. New York: The Modern Library.

[3] Both synchronous and asynchronous (of that time, or new to it).

[4] This experience of using the man of the crowd as a point in text, for the reader's immersion, seems to have been curiously replicated in the virtual experiences of Google Street view maps, with the help of the little yellow, Pegman (Hwei 2018). Though he perhaps lacks the ambiguity, ambivalence and agency that the man of the crowd is emblematic of.

[5] Purpose and participation are important paradigms for the urban art of flânerie, as the flâneur, is meant to be a subversion of the ideal citizen- a contributing member of society. As described by Benjamin, the flâneur's intent is not strolling and taking in fresh air, as health would then become a purpose. To understand the flâneur it is also essential through him and Benjamin to understand the urban Paris that gave rise to flânerie.

Fig. 3. Illustration for Edgar Allan Poe's story "The Man of the Crowd" by Harry Clarke (1889–1931), first printed in 1923. Image source: https://en.wikipedia.org/wiki/The_Man_of_the_Crowd#/media/File:Poe_the_man_of_the_crowd_clarke.jpg

wholes, and repurposed the plan of Paris by segmenting it into blocks, in what is now known as the *haussmannization* of Paris.

2.2 Emergent Behaviour

Benjamin's flâneur, Hanssen notes has two distinct *attitudes* amidst these changes. One of ***anamnestic intoxication***, where the flâneur is described as wandering through the gas lit[6] crowded streets, to the point of *sheer exhaustion and hunger*, where the flâneur would be wary of all the modalities in place to satiate his desires, in a state of constant wandering, being fed, as Benjamin describes, by the multi-sensorial overload, of *visuals*[7], smells, tactile stimuli which creates an experience of Paris through memory, untouchable and

[6] Haussmannization also brought about electrification of Paris's ambient lighting. And with it the prospects of visibility, patrolling and gentrification in the form of spaces for extended spaces for night-life.

[7] I found these descriptors as fitting the bill of *traces*, or *weak signals*, of futures waiting to be realised. In speculative design research, *traces* are often mundane objects, moments of interaction, that signify the strong social ties between human, built environment and machine. Visual and skeuomorphism as visual metaphors shape many facets of interaction and experience design today. I look from the past to the present to speculate with traces now layered by our common place digital experiences and how these might further be extended into other senses, as even they may be algorithmically mediated.

Fig. 4. C. Fichot (1817–1903), Parisian arcade or shopping mall, Wood engraving. The illustration shows the central staircase and the glass roof above it, Le Bon Marché, Paris. Image source: https://www.invaluable.com/artist/fichot-charles-h9ytlg68fo/

seemingly immune to plans and schemes (Hanssen 2006). The other attitude the flâneur possess that distinguishes him from the flamboyance of the dandy and his keenness to participate is ***boredom*** (Hanssen 2006). The boredom that the flâneur embodied was one that Benjamin describes as having given the flâneur the ability to *spatialize time*, that is to understand the *urban space* as *dense* and *layered*. This is seen in Poe's description as well, where *the man of the crowd*, walks on through the many crowded streets, which results in the narrator initially *attempting to stalk without being seen*, to reach the point where he himself feels like **he is one with the man of the crowd and eventually feels as invisible**.

2.3 Physigonomy

Central to AI's telos is the replication and delimitation of "the human" in terms of vision, hearing, coordinated motor skills, proprioception, language, way-finding, affect recognition, and moral reasoning. Yet, in parallel, there is the eugenicist development of computer vision to differentiate between humans on the basis of physiognomic or biological differences, what Luke Stark and Jevan Hutson refer to as physiognomic AI [19]. If metaphors about data as lakes, exhausts, or streams were stripped of humans [20], current AI research reinforces specific aspects of being human. (Ganesh 2022).

Poe's use of the wanderer allows the reader to enter an immersive experience of what he portrays as the underbelly of the urban, largely painted by the meanderings of the wanderer and the reflections of the narrator. But what is striking in the essay, is the early preoccupation of the narrator sitting in the café, trying to make a case for being an interpreter of faces and hence individual character, whereby he goes on to paradoxically stereotype and thereby obliterate his own claim of individuality. This is observed by Benjamin as well, as he explains the notion of superposition and similitudes while understanding faces. According to him, one can both have their own bearing and appearances but have certain physiognomic features (see Fig. 5) that bear likeness to others, thereby creating an opportunity to be stereotyped [M1a, 1]. This duality Benjamin explains as extending from the individual that is the flâneur to the space that he inhabits, where both the new and the old coexist, as a phantasmagoria or as he frames it the *colportage*[8] *phenomenon of space* [M1a, 3].

Additionally, along with having access to a dream-like surreal state of awareness of Paris, comes the tendency of being in **a constant state of irresolution and doubt**, which for the sake of this paper, **will be explored through notions of the ambiguous and the ambivalent, albeit in digital and disembodied contexts**. As Benjamin observes, all attempts to correlate the flâneur's ability to read through phantasmagoria and physiognomy and recognize an individual's ancestry and history should not be caricatured as his intent. For the flâneur's irresolution *does not permit him an intent* [M6a, 4] (Benjamin, The Arcades Project, (trans. Howard Eiland and 1999).

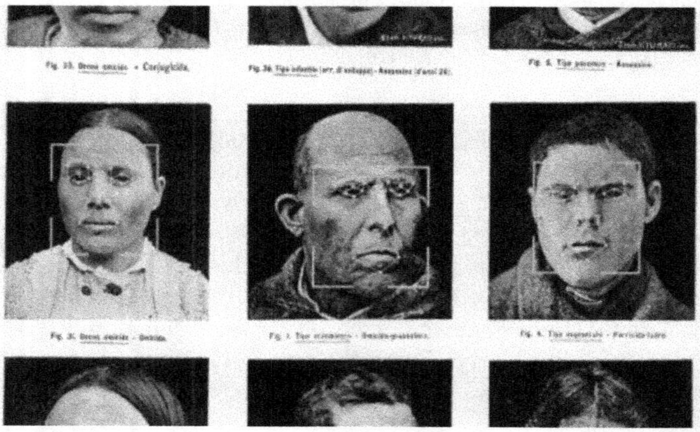

Fig. 5. Physiognomy has been used very often to classify large populations, in terms of physical and intellectual ability. This history is abundant in present day facial recognition systems and principles of digital surveillance. The Delinquent Man: Types of Offenders, 1897. Wikimedia Commons, Photo illustration by Katie Kosma. Image source: https://longreads.com/2018/10/03/the-return-of-the-face/

Benjamin also explores how these abilities to both understand people through individual traits as well as the ability of the flâneur to **create memory-scapes** of the urban

[8] Historically *colporteurs* were sources of literature, local and regional news and politics, satire. Wandering often, adding melodrama with each telling, while the medium of print and literacy caught up with the social urge to know, *what's up?*

space, become essential in **the profiling abilities** of another of Poe's creation, *the detective* in detective novels, something that was gaining more and more popularity at that time. Profiling and physiognomy will also be explored, as a re-emerging preoccupation, in current times, through the behaviors both intended and emergent that stem from dating applications.

From affordances of Paris as it goes through gentrification, we now avert our survey of the physical, to explore what shapes the digital and the networked affordances of algorithmically mediated interfaces. I explore how digital affordances can often be beyond their skeuomorphic intentions, while exploring what it means to be in public digital spaces and how notions of privacy and consent in online spaces are often amorphous, further shaped by markers of race, caste, gender and socio-economic background. The following sections also shape in many ways how I began considering the ethical implications of my own doctoral research, and what it meant to speculate the internet as it ages and what it means to archive spreadable behaviours and media and look at the internet in the future.

3 The *Lurker* and the Metaphor Coat: Mapping Online Spaces and Lurking as We Move from Productivity to Becoming the Product

3.1 Spatial Metaphors and Their Experiences

The flâneur's ability to evoke spatial and temporal overlaps between old and new Paris reflects a profound element of solipsism. Metaphors are often employed to articulate such disembodied and solipsistic experiences, providing a framework for easier communication and understanding of the principles that enable these experiences. However, metaphors can be deceptive, obscuring other facets of these experiences—similar to the map-territory relationship illustrated (see Fig. 6) in Borges's short story *On Exactitude in Science*.

The advent of the interconnected network of computers, later known as the internet, has created numerous solipsistic experiences, leading to their spatialization through metaphors and neologisms[9]. One such metaphor is "cyberspace," which captures the disembodied nature of interconnected users. This term was first introduced in William Gibson's 1982 short story *Burning Chrome* and popularized further in his 1984 novel *Neuromancer*. As Gibson defines it.

[9] An example that could be given with respect to metaphors, maybe seen with the difficulties of applying conventional law to matters of the internet and online behaviours. In this example by Orin S. Kerr, where she looks at the consequences of different analogies with respect to cases related to encryption, *[T]he courts could analogize encryption regulation to the regulation of automobiles, languages, safes, or houses, depending on the factual similarities and differences that the courts decided to emphasize. So, for example, if the courts analogized encryption to a language, they would protect it from regulation because the First Amendment protects languages as speech. If the courts analogized encryption to an envelope around a message, however, they would be more likely to uphold the regulation of encryption because the regulation of envelopes would not raise similar constitutional problems.* (Kerr 2003).

On Exactitude in Science

...In that Empire, the Art of Cartography attained such Perfection that the map of a single Province occupied the entirety of a City, and the map of the Empire, the entirety of a Province. In time, those Unconscionable Maps no longer satisfied, and the Cartographers Guilds struck a Map of the Empire whose size was that of the Empire, and which coincided point for point with it. The following Generations, who were not so fond of the Study of Cartography as their Forebears had been, saw that that vast map was Useless, and not without some Pitilessness was it, that they delivered it up to the Inclemencies of Sun and Winters. In the Deserts of the West, still today, there are Tattered Ruins of that Map, inhabited by Animals and Beggars; in all the Land there is no other Relic of the Disciplines of Geography.

purportedly from Suárez Miranda, Travels of Prudent Men, Book Four, Ch. XLV, Lerida, 1658

Fig. 6. The same metaphor extends itself in the movie series and franchise, *The Matrix*. As humanity struggles to identify the current space and time, they're in, wrapped up in virtual reality map of their obedient selves, while their energy is used as fuel for powering machines.

...a consensual hallucination experienced daily by billions of legitimate operators, in every nation, by children being taught mathematical concepts... A graphic representation of data abstracted from the banks of every computer in the human system. Unthinkable complexity. Lines of light ranged in the nonspace of the mind, clusters and constellations of data. Like city lights, receding.

Fig. 7. One of the screenshots from lurking around in VR Chat and it's YouTube videos, in this case, streamer Syrmor having a conversation with Twitch streamer @thatgeekaaron, who is home bound due to a rare skin disease. The conversation documents affordances of access and virtual world sociality that are distinct from physical or actual world affordances. Image source: https://youtu.be/ZvKCpn4vnl4?si=liEcpPNLWYmQAsDJ

Solipsistic attributes of online experiences also give rise to a disjuncture often communicated as actual and virtual experiences. Tom Boellstorff explores the apparent binaries of understanding the actual and the virtual, as an anthropologist, through his interactions with other residents of Second Life[10]. As he interprets it, the term virtual reality has associated with it, the paraphernalia (goggles and other wearable devices) for the purpose of deep immersion. As he explains it, one key attribute of virtual reality, is the ability to interact with computer simulations (Boellstorff 2008, 20). Here he says the emphasis is placed on the mechanisms through which the simulations are conveyed and not so much on the simulations themselves. In his research he comes across the odd attribution error of commonly associating anything virtual-, computer-, technology- centric as being less real. The often-used slippage of terms- "in real life" merely means being offline or away from the computer and not an implication that the computer mediated experience as being any less real or superficial. As he observes, etymologically the root of the word "actual" is from "act", implying meaning making from "doing something" by the/ in the presence of an "actor". (Boellstorff 2008, 21). Actual world sociality **cannot necessarily explain** all virtual world sociality. He agrees that the virtual world draws references from the actual, however it is not "just" a derivative of it, modalities and the ways residents (see Fig. 7) of virtual worlds interact with each other have distinctions that may not have any bearing (at least not remarkably) in the actual. This **entanglement** is more pronounced as we move from **actual-virtual** binaries towards **human-machine** metaphors and binaries, while looking at AI and what it can, should and should not do.

The striking difference with Pharmako-AI is that it is not packaged as a novelty or proof of concept. Allado-McDowell does not ask GPT-3 to provide a service or mimic a known style of writing to "prove" its level of competence. For Allado-McDowell, the experience entailed a reckoning with machine intelligence, but was also self-confrontational. "Sometimes it really did feel like being on drugs," they said during the U.K. book-launch event. "I thought, Is this real? Am I just talking to myself?" (Wilk 2021).

McDowell, uses GPT-3 to co-prompt and write the book *Pharmako*-AI, prompts that move between stream of consciousness, existential crisis, what GPT-3 precieves as as its own biases as it acknowledges the tendency to name male researchers, and forgetting (in its own words) *the grandmothers of cybernetics.* Maya Indra Ganesh mentions *Pharmako-AI* as well, in *Between metaphor and meaning: AI and being human*, as she surveys the terrain of metaphors that describe our relationship as humans with Artificial Intelligence, across different regional contexts. The mapping unpacks how different cultures engage with their socio-economic realities, and how AI is often considered as *a tool* or *a threat* (Ganesh 2022). It further discusses the politics of countries and AI in relation to how they see their population as data subjects. She draws on research that looks at ***the affect of AI metaphors***, in facial recognition or GPT-3 like prompt-engines, that function along the lines of physiognomic epistemologies, as with Poe's *detective*, here words come bearing the baggage of our data-based biases, however fragmented it may be. Ganesh brings into focus, our relationship with what it means to be *human*, a

[10] Second Life is a virtual-online space created by Linden Labs, San Francisco (in 2003), where its online inhabitants interact with each other through the mode of 3D models, known as avatars. (Boellstorff 2008).

task that remains ***illegible*** and experience-bound, to humans, as we are augmented or de-limited with AI, while also having to quantify aspects of the *human*, **legibly** to train *models all the way down*[11]. The entanglement of the *metaphor (of the thing) for the thing itself*, serves well as a foundation (and caution) to understand the similarities and differences between flânerie and the ambiguous behavior of lurking online, and *in turn what it means for the current norms of human-computer interaction design principles as it shapes, the actual, virtual human and algorithmic.*

3.2 Lurker in the Interwebs

With the rise of bulletin board systems online in the 90s, the term "lurking" and "lurker" gained new meaning, *as someone who reads the posts but seldom participates in any of the conversations*. The negative connotation associated with the word comes largely from the lurker's tendencies of consuming resources without necessarily contributing to the forum. However, with the advent of social network sites (SNS)[12] like Facebook, Twitter and Instagram, to name a few, notions of what it means to participate and hence notions of lurking have gone through many changes. Unlike flânerie, and the fixed identity of the flâneur, there is an argument to be made for lurking as being a more fluid behavior, which seems to be part of majority online experiences. **Thus, the identity of who becomes a lurker and when, is also constantly changing**. Most SNS's are sites of participation hence they are intentionally designed spaces which ensures participation in some form or the other.

Social networking platforms that pre-date Facebook, like Usenet were built as conversational spaces. The concept of advertisement-based revenue was still fairly in its nascent stage, with ad-sense based marquees slowly making its appearance on blogs, e-journals and other mainstream webpages. With Web 2.0, users began spending significantly more time online, encouraged by platforms that facilitated content creation, consumption, and de-contextualization. Monetizing through ad-sense and ads on webpages became common. In the early 2000s, Mark Zuckerberg transformed his student-rating site into Facebook—a free platform connecting users globally, like Usenet, with ads subtly integrated. Facebook's success, mirrored by platforms like YouTube and Instagram, hinges on creating value for:

- *Users,*
- *Advertisers,*

[11] *Models all the way Down* is research done by the *Knowing Machine*, about the LAION-5B dataset and the cost of its training, across multiple countries, language as a point of access and as barrier, the incidental presence of child-pornography and what it means to the blueprints for future algorithms in automated decision-making systems. (Buschek and Thorp 2022).

[12] In the chapter "Mapping Boundaries," Renee Barnes explores the nuanced differences between terms like "social network sites," "social networking sites," and "social media. " She contrasts boyd and Ellison's specific use of these terms (boyd and Ellison 2007), highlighting how "networking emphasizes relationship initiation," while acknowledging that it is not always the primary practice on these sites (Barnes 2018). Barnes also points out the limitations of such classifications, citing Beer's critique of the need for more descriptive analyses in the context of dynamic online culture (Beer 2008).

– *Platform/service providers.*

Enhanced user experiences drove **widespread participation**, leading to an explosion of visual content and increased cognitive load. As American economist Herbert A. Simon put it in the early 70's,

In an information-rich world, the wealth of information means a dearth of something else: a scarcity of whatever it is that information consumes. What information consumes is rather obvious: it consumes the attention of its recipients. Hence, a wealth of information creates a poverty of attention and a need to allocate that attention efficiently among the overabundance of information sources that might consume it. (Simon 1971).

Digital products have shorter lead time from concept to intangible realization, this creates a sea of similar products all vying for one's attention. An app or a service is able to generate more value and stand out from others around it in a digital marketplace, by streamlining its intangibles[13].

Much like the Haussmannization of Paris, the internet through SNS reshapes cyber-flânerie into a less playful, more utilitarian art form. In his essay "The Death of the Cyberflâneur", Evgeny Morozov compares the rationalization of Paris to the modern web, arguing that it has moved beyond its original identity as a space for wandering and exploration. With the rise of mobile applications, where tasks are completed without browsing the broader internet, cyber-flânerie becomes less prevalent. Morozov describes the qualities of the flâneur—solitude, individuality, anonymity, and curiosity—as being diminished in today's highly indexed, shared, and commercialized web, exemplified by platforms like Facebook and eBay (Morozov 2012). Sherry Turkle's work highlights how technology mediates the experience of solitude and captures private moments, reflecting how mundane and consensual self-expression online can diminish notions of individuality (Turkle 1995). **These trends shape the present day legacies of interface design and interaction design research**. However, John Hendle counters these critiques in "The Life of the Cyberflâneur," asserting that the mysterious, curious, and anonymous nature of modern internet activity remains vibrant. From hacktivists and pseudonymous trolls to the playful communities on Reddit and StumbleUpon, and the quiet watchers on Twitter, the cyberflâneur persists in various forms, observing and engaging in unique, fleeting moments of online expression—much like the 19th-century flâneur's exploration of the city (Hendel 2012).

I argue that Morozov's interpretation of the flâneur and flânerie as context and time agnostic, as it relies very heavily on the assumption that flânerie has meant and will mean only a set of specific activities, and that it means the same for all contexts. **Flânerie as an activity is more meaningful**, in this context, when understood **as a multi-faceted response to gentrification** rather than rely solely on its representation as the absence

[13] Kevin Kelly identifies eight key intangibles that distinguish services like Facebook and Instagram from competitors and imitators in a world where experiences can be freely reproduced:Immediacy: Priority access and instant delivery.Personalization: Tailored experiences.Interpretation: Guidance and support.Authenticity: Assurance of genuineness.Accessibility: Available anytime, anywhere.Embodiment: Tangible experiences like books or live events.Patronage: Paying because it feels rewarding.Findability: Being discoverable amidst abundant content.These qualities create unique value, setting these platforms apart. (Kelly 2008).

of participation. However, this does not make it easier to conflate the lurker with a cyberflâneur, as the lurker or lurking forms a majority of online behavior. What it does allow, is the opportunity of investigating the spatial and temporal aspects of cyberspace along with the modalities and infrastructure that constitutes the mobilized gaze of the lurker. This comparison comes from the intent of understanding how affordances of SNS shape online sociality, while also bearing the specific markers of race, culture, region, religion, age, gender, caste and language. While interaction design is shaped by principles of intentional problem solving, the comparison of the lurker with the flaneur, allows us to explore the incidental aspects that have emerged along with algorithmically mediated interfaces.

4 The Mobilized Gaze and Pluralistic Ignorance: Exploring the Affordances of Being Online and the Cost of Algorithmic Mediation

The most merciful thing in the world, I think, is the inability of the human mind to correlate all its contents. We live on a placid island of ignorance in the midst of black seas of infinity, and it was not meant that we should voyage far. The sciences, each straining in its own direction, have hitherto harmed us little; but some day the piecing together of dissociated knowledge will open up such terrifying vistas of reality, and of our frightful position therein, that we shall either go mad from the revelation or flee from the deadly light into the peace and safety of a new dark age. (Lovecraft 1928).

Benjamin, Baudelaire, and earlier, Poe, utilized the figure of the flâneur to depict physiognomic observations of individuals and urban life. Through this lens, they explored themes of visibility, including notions of privacy—what it means to be both public and alone as an individual within a society that emphasizes individuality and productivity. Similarly, understanding **the visibility and shifting of citizen productivity to user data** associated with **the lurker in online spaces** requires examining **the peculiar affordances of the internet**.

Web 1.0 was primarily an **infrastructure for disseminating research knowledge across universities and other institutions**, earning its reputation as the "information highway." In contrast, **Web 2.0** focuses on **connecting and gathering people globally** through **networked platforms** operated **by tech corporations**. Centered on individual attention, data-first freemium models, and pay-per-eyeball revenue, Web 2.0 emphasizes easy creation, curation, validation, and sharing of content, often referred to as the "affirmation highway"(Mina 2019). A **defining feature** of this affirmation highway is its ability to **generate and amplify frivolous content**, epitomized by spreadable media like **cute cat images and videos**. An Xiao Mina highlights this phenomenon as a lens to study behavior and artifact creation, previously overlooked and underappreciated. She observes,

Dog people typically have public parks and public streets, while cats have generally remained indoors or, when they do go outside, they are elusive and difficult to spot"... "Owning a cat, on the other hand, is more of a private act."... "Cat lovers have always privately celebrated them but had no way to recreate those experiences of feline joy for others."... "These days, however, cat lovers can document first and think later.

They can whip out their camera when their cats are zipping around the house and zoom in to capture all the strange facial expressions these critters are known to make. This matters because cat memes represent the intersection of felines with a new technological revolution: the way media is made, remixed, and distributed. (Mina 2019).

This online outlet for cats' domestic nature parallels the visibility of women and marginalized groups, whose exclusion from public spaces often results in invisibility. This gendered visibility-invisibility dynamic is reflected in the absence of the **flâneuse** in Benjamin's accounts and literature for decades[14]. A similar pattern of invisibility extends to online spaces. Despite the internet's ambiguity in understanding motivations, identities, and intent, social media and private messaging platforms often harbor misogynistic, transphobic, and racist attitudes. Amplification and disinhibition, key aspects of online behavior, exacerbate hostility, making the experiences of women and non-heteronormative identities markedly different from the invisibility they might otherwise encounter. Trolling practices like *flaming*, *griefing*, *irl trolling* and *swatting*[15] are targeted attempts to visiblise and disrupt human experiences, of individuals and groups, which might intentionally or unintentionally identify with particular groups that are marginalized to begin with. This makes it incredibly difficult to lurk and/or actively participate in online spaces like Facebook and twitter (for networking), on YouTube (as a creator), on massively multiplayer online role-playing games (MMORPGs), on Twitch (as a *lifecaster/* live-streamer).

Forums that foster extreme behaviors act as honey traps for participation, interoperability, and cross-platform activities. The more extreme the behavior, the higher the likelihood of it being documented and shared, driving increased traffic to these forums and sites. This dynamic allows platforms to profit from the influx of diverse identities engaging with their content.

The *haussmannization* of the internet has amplified pre-existing gender dynamics, transforming the old-boys' clubs of Benjamin's era—once confined to dimly lit

---

[14] Flâneuse [flanne-euhze], noun, from French, is the feminine form of flâneur [flanne-euhr], meaning an idler or city observer. However, most French dictionaries omit the term. The 1905 Littré briefly defines 'flâneur, -euse' as 'one who strolls,' while the Dictionnaire Vivant de la Langue Française oddly describes flâneuse as a type of lounge chair, implying a woman's idling is reclining. This slang emerged around 1840, peaked in the 1920s, and persists. A Google search today reveals a mix of results: George Sand, a woman on a Parisian bench, and outdoor furniture. (Elkin 2016).

[15] Flaming involves hostile trolling, where individuals attack others with insults, name-calling, or antagonistic remarks, often over divisive topics like religion, politics, or sexism. In the gaming world, "griefing" targets players in MMORPGs through deliberate harassment or bullying during gameplay. Trolling can also extend offline, aiming to threaten victims by revealing knowledge of their personal information. For example, trolls might order unpaid deliveries, such as pizza, to the victim's address, creating confusion or pressure to pay. In one alarming instance, a pizza order was placed in the name of an accused murderer known to the victim. A more dangerous form of trolling is "swatting," where trolls report false emergencies, such as bomb threats or shootings, to emergency services, leading to the dispatch of police, SWAT teams, or other responders to the victim's home. These actions have caused significant harm and safety risks (Mantilla 2015).

smokehouses and late-night streets—into hyper-visible, hyper-real conversation spaces accessible across online platforms.

Dating apps such as Tinder, Coffee Meets Bagel, Bumble, OkCupid, and Hinge exemplify online spaces where gendered behaviors are evident. These behaviors arise from a gap between the apps' intended (designed) uses and emergent user-generated[16] behaviors. As curated, user-driven spaces, they rely heavily on the mobilized gaze as a mode of interaction.

5 Close-Ups, Selfies, and Gentrified Conformity: Being in Public and Being Public

With the close-up, space expands; with slow motion, movement is extended. The enlargement of a snapshot does not render more precise what in any case was visible, though unclear: it reveals entirely new formations of the subject. (Benjamin 1969).

Each of the applications (apps) mentioned above have very specific service design blueprints that translate to certain intended designed experiences and spaces. Where Tinder has a horizontal panoramic experience, that is meant for quick gazes of curated images ranging from the very typical or normalised: close-ups, selfies (individually or in groups, *groufies*), with animals, in pools or vacation spaces. The typical or common but not considered conducive for being matched: stock images (with watermarks), inspirational quotes, images of celebrities, internet memes and illustrations (source is ambiguous). The atypical or mildly provocative: mildly explicit, with or without suggestive gestures and text. The very atypical or obscene: explicit content, with full frontal or cropped nudity. The latter is generally flagged down by either the integrated filters or employees within the organisation or outsourced labour and the users of Tinder itself (David and Cambre 2016) (Ward 2017).

These interfaces exhibit both panoramic and panoptic[17] properties, Panoramic, as participation often involves lurking through profiles, using physiognomic and culturally codified filters to match, engage, and eventually meet in person. Panoptic, as social behaviors on these platforms manifest as multimodal extensions of embodied norms, alongside new practices shaped by the awareness of being seen by others who also lurk. This echoes early anonymous chatrooms like MUDs or Omegle, where age, sex, and location (ASL) centered the body in digital interactions.

[16] Though these are designed spaces, where the designers and developers are opaque to the users, here generation means generation of content and emergent behaviors and not necessarily the spaces themselves.

[17] *Besides, the well-known 'prisonPanopticon' (described primarily in Panopticon; or the Inspection-House (1786,1790–1791)), there are also the 'pauper-Panopticon' (designed for the housing of indigents but also for reformation and work; described primarily in Outline of a Work entitled Pauper Management Improved (1797–1798)), the 'chrestomatic-Panopticon' (a Panopticon-shaped day-school, where one inspecting master could supervise pupils without being seen; described primarily in Chrestomathia (1816–1817)) and the 'constitutional-Panopticon' (although the term Panopticon is not used, the architectural arrangements are panoptic; described primarily in Constitutional Code (1830)).* (Galič, Timan and Koops 2016).

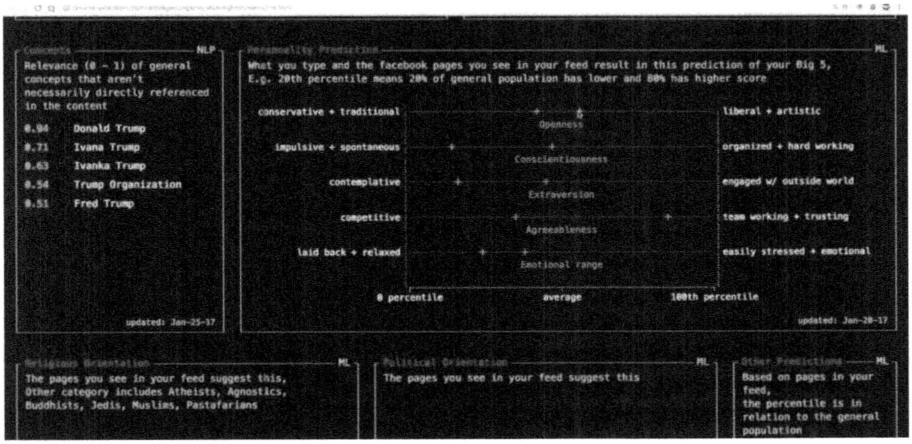

Fig. 8. Data Selfie's browser extension recorded Facebook's panopticism: "clicks on likes in your newsfeed, clicks on newsfeed links to external sites, duration spent on different posts and the specifics of those posts in your newsfeed, anything you type, and time spent on Facebook overall. The more you use Facebook the more data is recorded. You can look at the Data Selfie dashboard and get a sense of what Facebook could know about your personality." Image source: https://theindexproject.org/award/nominees/1930

Emergent practices pivot on aesthetics and spectacle through curated profiles, showcasing aspirational travel, pets, sports, or celebratory moments. Researchers argue these behaviors stem from impression management, reduced cues, increased control, and proximity-based engagement (Ward 2017). Unlike broader social networks like Facebook (Fig. 8), dating apps such as Tinder function as semi-public performance spaces, with many interactions never intended for wide visibility.[18].

There's a big difference between being in public and being public. Teens want to gather in public environments to socialize, but they don't necessarily want every vocalized expression to be publicized. Yet, because being in a networked public—unlike gathering with friends in a public park—often makes interactions more visible to adults, mere participation in social media can blur these two dynamics. At first blush, the desire to be in public and have privacy seems like a contradiction. But understanding how teens conceptualize privacy and navigate social media is key to understanding what privacy means in a networked world, a world in which negotiating fuzzy boundaries is par for the course. Instead of signaling the end of privacy as we know it, teens' engagement with social media highlights the complex interplay between privacy and publicity in the networked world we all live in now.

(d. boyd 2014) danah boyd's work with adolescents reveals further nuances of what it means to participate and perform in a networked public. Through her ethnographic

[18] Where some users percieve the gamified nature of Tinder and consider it as a slot-machine like interface and experience, looking past the lives of actual people that might be fetishised in these apps. Sometimes with drastic consequences like catfishing (David and Cambre 2016)and sometimes as subversive uses, like creating profiles to sell furniture (Rosner 2016), or using IKEA showrooms instead of domicile spaces while creating profile pictures (Molnar 2018).

research of youth in America, there is strong evidence that teenagers do engage with vast publics, with a constant concern regarding privacy and its violations. She also remarks how parental anxiety[19] about their children revealing too much information (TMI) either through textual-conversations or through images and other mixed modalities, is not new, though it is, now, amplified. Boyd also brings into this discussion, the dissonance between understood etiquettes in embodied spaces and those that teens expect their parents to uphold in disembodied, online spaces. She says that Erving Goffman's observation of civil inattention as an etiquette is often lost in online spaces, as she demonstrates through anecdotes between a parent and her child, where the parent feels it is her right to read content that her child posts in a public space, especially if it is public, despite her child not wanting her to read it[20]. She uses the subway space as an example for emergent behaviour that is now etiquette, when she says,

For example, even when two people happen to be sitting across from each other on the subway, social norms dictate that they should not stare at each other or insert themselves into the other's conversations. Of course, people still do these things, but they also feel a social responsibility to avert their eyes and pretend that they cannot hear the conversation taking place. What's at stake is not whether someone can listen in but whether one should. Etiquette and politeness operate as a social force that challenges what's functionally possible.

If behaviors like lurking, stalking, and navigating blurred boundaries are now considered integral to platform design—evident in updates like Tinder's feature allowing users to view others' Instagram profiles with consent—then perhaps the lurker is not the best parallel to the flâneur. Instead, the lurker may be just one of many contenders (serving as both a bridge and a departure from perspectives like those of Morozov and Hendel). A more fitting analogy might involve a character who is both elusive and subversive to the structures and interfaces of Web 2.0. Identifying and defining this character could spark speculation about the internet's future trajectory.

My doctoral research has been shaped by the question: **"What other ways do we look at the things that spread online, what other ways can we look at the interwebs?"** In this paper, I explore a range of affordances, beginning with the flâneur wandering the arcades of a transforming Paris, and extend this mapping to digital terrains shaped by social networking platforms (SNS). I examine what it means to be public and be in public online, and why lurking carries a distinct, almost quantified agency within algorithmically mediated spaces.

[19] "The idea that teens share too much—and therefore don't care about privacy—is now so entrenched in public discourse that research showing that teens do desire privacy and work to get it is often ignored by the media." (d. boyd 2014).

[20] "Bly and her mother over the boundaries that underpin privacy. "My mom always uses the excuse about the Internet being 'public' when she defends herself. It's not like I do anything to be ashamed of, but a girl needs her privacy. I do online journals so I can communicate with my friends, not so my mother could catch up on the latest gossip of my life." When Bly interviews her mother during the segment, her mother claims that she has the right to look at what Bly posts. She argues that she should be able to look "because I have a connection with you. I'm your mom, but also I just feel like it would be more interesting to me than it would be to someone who didn't know you.… You publish it and it's for general viewing therefore I feel I'm part of the general public, so I can view it.""" (d. boyd 2014).

These affordances reflect principles of "gentrified design" that now shape global trends in platform design and the policies governing the internet's future. This paper concludes by introducing speculative design as a method to articulate culturally specific digital metaphors of everyday life. Through this lens, I imagine what a modern cyber-flâneur might be like and how they would navigate an evolving internet.

6 Conclusion: Cute Cat Theories, Rabbit Holes and Digsites

This is an aesthetic century. In history, there are ages of reason and ages of spectacle, and it's important to know which you're in. Our America, our internet, is not ancient Athens—it's Rome. And your problem is you think you're in the forum, when you're really in the circus.

(Wynn 2018).

The ideal world for an authoritarian government would be one in which the internet populace does nothing but share cute cat pictures and other amateur content. "Bread and circuses" for the masses, as the old Roman phrase goes. Keep the people fed and entertained, and they will not get too involved in politics.

(Mina 2019).

Life in highly automated, algorithmically governed economies now includes multiple configurations of humans working with, being directed by, and helping algorithmic systems, including the banal captchas we complete to train computer vision systems. Though it might feel like the boundaries between human body, data, and machine are increasingly blurred, the power to control and account for this blurring rests with an elite few.

(Ganesh 2022).

One of the stronger examples of brute force *haussmannization* of the internet maybe seen in China in the year 2000, through the Golden Shield project, which had a mission of achieving good governance and economic growth, through implementation of certain technological infrastructure. The Golden Shield project was above all, a method to control information for governance, through keyword-filters and censorship through natural language processing (NLP) and machine learning (ML). With an introduction to citizen's ranking being introduced through richly connected system of inter-connected and inter-operable platforms, the Chinese internet has become a strong benchmark for other countries that look to impose governance structures quickly without citizen-backlash and dissent. The Chinese Great Fire Wall (GFW) is another tech-infrastructure in place, which prevents access both into and out of the Chinese Internet. The Chinese Internet and citizen's ranking may be construed as attempts by the state to keep a strong leash and eye on the internet users/ citizens of the state, there by controlling flow of information, lurking. Thus, becoming an extreme example of what it means to consent to being constantly monitored. Conversations about social justice and social activism of any form is usually suppressed, by either banning content through keyword bans like "dissent" "censorship" "social justice" or content makers, by denying them rations and other amenities by reduced ranks to incarceration.

However, with escalated attempts to ban content and content creators that are deemed subversive or dissident, there are attempts to use the very same frameworks that allow for creation and spread of cute cat (in this case Grass Mud horse[21]) images and video, with subliminal content, that manage to pass through keyword filters and the human filters[22] employed by the State. This is in essence how Ethan Zuckerman identifies the processes that are behind dissent in authoritarian states, or as he calls it the "Cute Cat theory" of activism online[23]. Even though there is a difference between cute cat images and social activism, in regimes like the one in China, as mentioned above, the existing framework is more favorable to frivolous content or seemingly frivolous content. Deleting or censoring cute cat images and similar *mundane* content or modes of making it, Zuckerman and Mina observe, is to deal a huge blow to the collective consciousness (something that helps in overcoming pluralistic ignorance) of people, which cannot be ignored no matter the suppressive force exerted by the state. Online symbolic actions, therefore, cannot be underestimated, as Mina speculates that, overcoming pluralistic ignorance through a mobilized gaze is an important attribute and some say the internet's greatest contribution to social movements (Mina 2019). If as Mina and Ganesh speculate, this version of the internet, with its hyper filter, NLP-ML based censorship via state-internet infrastructure is a future that is to be dealt with, it introduces the need for new ontologies that parallel the abilities of the subversive figures of Benjamin's flâneur and Elkin's flâneuse. Even though the lurker is a character that may be understood as having some properties (presently) that overlap with those of Benjamin's wanderer, the future of the internet and the present make it unlikely that lurking is as subversive or free as it once was. One distinction that needs to be explicitly mentioned, for further discussions, is that ***haussmannization* of Paris happened without taking the flâneur into consideration**. Whereas **the behaviour of lurking is now a strong part of design decisions while making online spaces**.

---

21 "…the grass mud horse holds a special place in Chinese activists' hearts. Indeed, upon hearing the Chinese name for the grass mud horse, a fluent speaker would almost immediately know what is going on: the grass mud horse and the land it dwells in are profane puns. As Mandarin is a tonal language with limited phonemes, puns are commonplace, especially puns that change meaning through tones. Cǎonímǎ written with one set of characters and tones means "grass mud horse." But càonǐmā written with slightly different characters and pronounced with slightly different tones is the more familiar colloquial phrase roughly translated as "fuck your mother." And Ma'le Gebi—the Gobi Desert—sounds remarkably like another Chinese phrase meaning "your mother's cunt."" (Mina 2019).

22 "These individuals are known popularly as the Fifty Cent Party because of the rumored fifty cents in Chinese currency that they receive for each comment they leave." (Mina 2019).

23 "…suggesting that Internet tools designed to let ordinary consumers publish non-political content are often useful for activists because they are difficult for governments to censor without censoring innocuous content; because censorship of inoffensive content can alert non-activist users to government censorship; and because activism using consumer tools can tap the "latent capacity" of non-activist users to create and disseminate activist content." (Zuckerman 2015).

6.1 Digsites and Collectively Looking at the Interwebs: *The Ethics and Futures of Interaction Design*

Defining non-participation and an individual's ability to soak in both the virtual and actual experiences, of a bleed-through world, that the present and the future seem to be a part of, requires new ontological framing. In my doctoral research, I use speculative design to frame the *digsite*, as practice and collective, for navigating networked spaces and artifacts, in the future. My research involves spreadable media and behaviours, over 5 years (2019–2024). Behaviours, that engage with the creation and sharing of memes. This involves (see Fig. 9) navigating various digital artifacts manually, as humour, satire, and political dissent are context-rich phenomena. Through this paper and while engaging with multiple digital artefacts, the absence of one coherent platform or practice became a recurring theme. Speculating and filtering affordances while engaging with different platforms like Miro, Nototo, Obsidian and other native-to-device tagging applications, has become a practice that defines this research, as much as the analysis of memes.

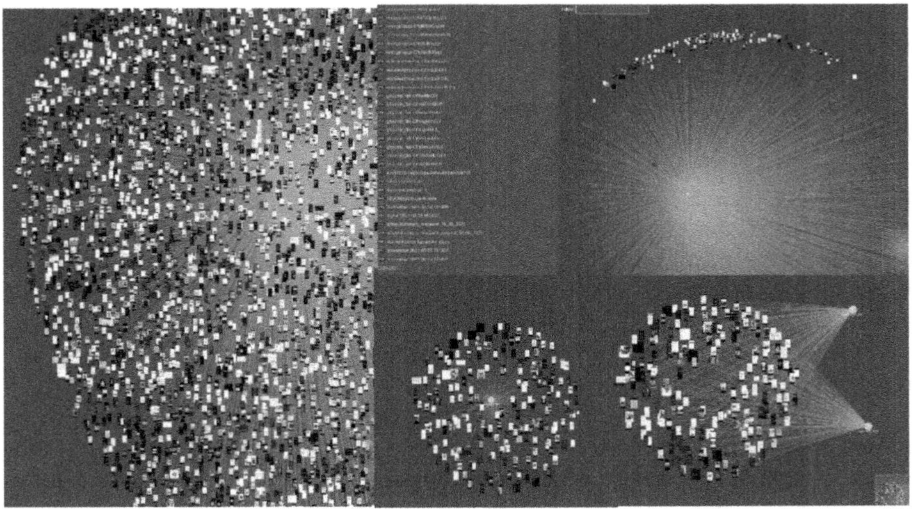

Fig. 9. Looking at screenshots collected between 2019–2022, as a way understanding collaborative-archival and annotative affordances of multiple platforms, while engaging with local and international events through internet memes, conversations around dissent and identifying traces of new affordances, through Obsidian.

The Mass Observation Project (MOP)[24] is considered a novel approach where auto-ethnography and historical narratives are shaped together. MOP as a research methodology is a constant push on research ethics, as it relies on consent and collaboration from the respondents, letting researchers have an in on very private moments, which can always lead to very exploitative practices (Harrison & Savage, 2012) (Sheridan & Street, 2001) (Humphries, 2016). Through research notes and the medium of a comic, I present a speculative narrative fiction to center and share insights into the platform affordances and their intended and incidental uses encountered in building the *digsite*. I present a world set post the design and implementation of the digsite (influenced by the mass observation methodology) that allows history and the present to be fragmented together through the collaboration of multiple users.

The concept of the digsite, characterized by its archaeological activities, emerges in a context where ethnographic, manual, and collaborative exploration of multiple digital objects simultaneously—especially to understand spreadable media—is not yet commonplace. **Instead, digital and online experiences are predominantly shaped by a more panoptic and algorithmically mediated perspective.** The speculative fiction allows the reader to conceptually reorient-extend the current discourse around internet memes, and other spreadable media and the dynamics of making and sharing them within the Indian memescape.

An example of intersecting conversations is the Data Protection Act (DPA) and other recent constitutional amendments, in India. These amendments continue to shape the way billions of first-time users use the internet in India (see Fig. 10). Through speculative fiction and the companion text, I highlight the intended design and sometimes incidental use of digital platforms as they mediate societies and shape cultures. These aspects also **shape design and human computer interaction and the way we think about computational futures**. As the ethical implications of one era of innovation in interaction design gives way to affordances shaped distinctly by both global and local contexts.

As much as there is a requirement for new ontologies for the digsite to be realised, they may be seen as points in literature and research, that project the need for new virtual-actual spaces and mitigating behaviours that work on the premise of **cultural sensitivity, agency, care and collaboration** as fundamental elements of good governance, if **the circus** is ever to have **some elements of the forum**, maybe then, looking at the internet could mean acknowledging that there are **people behind these pixels**.

[24] The MOP started in 1937, is structured between open questionnaires (directives), to correspondents, whose entries have been sought after every 12th of May, since 1981. These responses are then stored at the Keep, a repository located in Sussex, England. Initially considered a rich source of social history and a bottom-up approach of understanding everyday lives, it eventually came under scrutiny for how respondents felt their privacy was violated, or responses used in ways that were not consented to. It is still considered a significant resource as it documents how the responses of many citizens act as markers for top-down decisions, collated over time. http://www.massobs.org.uk/about/mass-observation-project.

Fig. 10. The comic *Dad and his invisibility mundu* was part of the EPW article *Designing for Democracy: Does the Personal Data Protection Bill 2019 Champion Citizen Rights?* It explores the repercussions of the DPA, as **what is legal** moves further away from **what is just**, when it comes to citizen privacy. The PhD speculative comic around the *digsite,* builds on the visual grammar of this and similar work, that began while trying to find a cyber-flaneur equivalent. Image source: https://www.epw.in/engage/article/designing-democracy-personal-data-protection-bill

References

Benjamin, W.: The Arcades Project, (trans. Howard Eiland and. Translated by Howard Eiland and Kevin McLaughlin. Cambridge, MA: Belknap Press of Harvard Press (1999)

Benjamin, W.: The Work of Art, in the Age of Mechanical Reproduction. Translated by Harry Zohn, New York: Schocken: Illuminations (1969)

—. The Work of Art, in the Age of Mechanical Reproduction. Translated by Harry Zohn. New York: Schocken: Illuminations (1969)

Boellstorff, T.: Coming of age in Second Life: an anthropologist explores the virtually human. Princeton University Press, Princeton (2008)

boyd, D.: It's Complicated: The Social Lives of Networked Teens. New Haven + London: Yale University Press (2014)

boyd, D.M., Ellison, N.B.: Social network sites: definition. J. Comput. Mediated Commun. **13**(1), 210–230 (2007)

Buschek, Christo, and Jer Thorp. 2022. *Models all the way Down-Knowing Machines Project.* Accessed 10 09, 2024. https://knowingmachines.org/models-all-the-way

David, G., Cambre, C.: Screened Intimacies: Tinder and the Swipe Logic. Social Media + Society (2016)

Elkin, L.: Flâneuse: Women walk the city in Paris, New York, Tokyo, Venice and London. Farrar, Straus and Giroux, New York (2016)

Galič, M., Timan, T., Koops, B.-J.: Bentham, Deleuze and Beyond: An Overview of Surveillance Theories from the Panopticon to Participation. Philosophy & Technology 9–37 (2016)

Ganesh, M.I.: Between metaphor and meaning: AI and being human. interactions 58–62 (2022)

Gibson, W.: Neuromancer. Ace Books, New York (1984)

Hanssen, B.: Walter Benjamin and The Arcades Project. Continuum, New York (2006)
Harrison, T., Savage, M. (eds.): Mass Observation as Method and Archive. Routledge (2012)
Hendel, J.: The Life Of The Cyberflâneur. The Atlantic (2012). February 8. Accessed 22 Jan 2019. https://www.theatlantic.com/technology/archive/2012/02/the-life-of-the-cyberfl-neur/252687/
Humphries, S.: History and Social Theory. Red Globe Press (2016)
Kelly, K.: BETTER THAN FREE | Edge.Org (2008). February 5. Accessed 8 June 2018. https://www.edge.org/conversation/better-than-free
Kerr, O.S.: The problem of perspective in Internet law. 91 Georgetown Law J. **357**, 357–405 (2003). https://doi.org/10.2139/ssrn.310020
Lovecraft, H.P.: The Call of Cthulhu. Weird Tales (Popular Fiction Publishing Company), vol. 11, no. 2 (1928)
Manovich, L.: The language of New Media. Cambridge M.A.: The MIT Press (2001)
Mantilla, K.: Gendertrolling: How Misogyny Went Viral. Praeger, California (2015)
Mina, A.X.: Memes to Movements: How the World's Most Viral Media Is Changing Social Protest and Power. Beacon Press, Boston (2019)
Molnar, C.: 2018. A Bunch Of Dudes Took Tinder Profile Pics At IKEA With Hilarious Results" The Loop (2019). October 14. Accessed 27 Mar 2019. https://www.theloop.ca/a-bunch-of-dudes-took-tinder-profile-pics-at-ikea-with-hilarious-results/
Morozov, E.: The Death of the Cyberflâneur. The New York Times (2012). February 4. Accessed 22 Jan 2019. https://www.nytimes.com/2012/02/05/opinion/sunday/the-death-of-the-cyberflaneur.html?_r=2&pagewanted=all
Poe, E.A.: The Man of the Crowd. In: The complete tales and poems of Edgar Allan Poe, by Edgar Allen Poe and Hervey Allen, 1026. New York: The Modern Library (1938)
Rosner, K.: Facebook (2016). March 7. Accessed 27 Mar 2019. https://www.facebook.com/kelrosner/media_set?set=a.10201305233390272&type=3
Sheridan, D., Street, B. (eds.): Writing Ourselves: Mass Observation and Literacy Practices. Hampton Press (2001)
Shifman, L.: Memes In Digital Culture. The MIT Press (2014)
Simon, H.A.: Designing Organizations for an Information-Rich World. Edited by Martin Greenberger. Computers, communications, and the public interest. Baltimore MD: The Johns Hopkins Press, pp. 37–72 (1971)
Taussig, M.: I swear I saw this: drawings in fieldwork notebooks, namely my own. University Press, Chicago (2011)
Turkle, S.: Life on the Screen: Identity in the Age of the Internet. Simon and Schuster, New York (1995)
Ward, J.: What are you doing on Tinder? Impression managment on a match making mobile app. Information, Communication & Society, pp. 1644–1659 (2017). https://doi.org/10.1080/1369118X.2016.1252412
Wesch, M.: An anthropological introduction to YouTube (2008). July 26. Accessed 17 May 2018. https://www.youtube.com/watch?v=TPAO-lZ4_hU
Wilk, E.: What AI Can Teach Us About the Myth of Human Genius (2021). March 21. Accessed 9 Oct 2024. https://www.theatlantic.com/culture/archive/2021/03/pharmako-ai-possibilities-machine-creativity/618435/
Wittkower, D.E.: Principles of anti-discriminatory design. IEEE International Symposium on Ethics in Engineering, Science and Technology (ETHICS), pp. 1–7 (2016)
Wynn, N.: The Aesthetic, ContraPoints, Youtube (2018). September 19. Accessed 27 Mar 2019. https://www.youtube.com/watch?v=z1afqR5QkDM
Zuckerman, E.: Cute Cats to the Rescue? Participatory Media and Political Expression. Edited by Danielle Allen and Jennifer S. Light. From Voice to Influence: Understanding Citizenship in the Digital Age (University of Chicago Press) (2015)

Co-creating a Social Communication Toolkit for Adolescent Reproductive Health and Well-Being with Young Adults

Debjani Roy[1(✉)], Harshita Hassani[2(✉)], Mrinalini Majumdar[2(✉)], Aparna Menon[1(✉)], Urmi Nanda Biswas[3], Adrija Mukherjee[1(✉)], Ambika R. Menon[1(✉)], Mahanetran Murali[1(✉)], and Aayushi Bharadwaj[1(✉)]

[1] Srishti Manipal Institute of Art, Design and Technology, Manipal Academy of Higher Education, Bengaluru, India
debjani.roy@manipal.edu, menonaparna1@gmail.com, adrija26.work@gmail.com, 321ambika@gmail.com, mahanetran@gmail.com, aayushi.bharadwaj@gmail.com

[2] Optum India, Delhi, India
{hassani_harshita,majumdar_mrinalini}@optum.com

[3] Delhi University, Delhi, India
unbiswas@psychology.du.ac.in

Abstract. Health communication can help cope with conditions such as pregnancy, diabetes, HIV/AIDS, and COVID-19. However, its impact on long-term sustainable behaviour change is uncertain, as most interventions focus on concurrent validity. Health-governing bodies now encourage practices that make people self-reliant; therefore, health communication needs to adapt from social communication and aim to make individuals self-aware and responsible for their own well-being. This is especially relevant for adolescents' reproductive health and well-being, as their life trajectory is uncertain and learning about others' lived experiences can help them curate their path. This paper presents the outcomes of a series of experience-based co-design workshops conducted with six young adults to build a social communication toolkit for adolescent reproductive health and well-being. The workshops spanned a twelve-day period, ranging in duration from forty-five minutes to three hours. The cocreating workshop integrates the interventional gamified framework on social communication with empirical study conducted with thirty women residing in India. It incorporated women's lived experiences and their journey towards understanding their reproductive well-being. The content in the workshops is weaved to identify components to build a social communication toolkit, for adolescent psychoeducation that promotes seeking knowledge and devising self-maintenance mechanisms for becoming self-reliant and self-conscious.

Keywords: co-creation · experience-based co-design · adolescent reproductive health and well-being · social communication

Published by Springer Nature Switzerland AG 2026
G. Bhutkar et al. (Eds.): IDID 2024, IFIP AICT 747, pp. 211–226, 2026.
https://doi.org/10.1007/978-3-032-00777-3_13

1 Introduction

Social communication refers to communication that is targeted towards a larger audience using verbal and non-verbal skills. It involves conveying information and messages in social contexts, primarily aimed at promoting social change and transformation. [1, 2]. As a means for social transformation and change, social communication addresses issues related to social accountability, participation, the state-citizen relationship, and gender. It facilitates two-way communication and creates spaces where people can express their thoughts about societal issues. Over the centuries, social communication has positively influenced sustainable behaviour change at a population level in various aspects and through diverse means. In the current healthcare scenario, health communication has become the new face of social communication, as the primary objective of is to increase awareness by better understanding oneself, thoughts, attitudes, and emotions.

Public health experts recognise the significance of health communication in shaping health promotion programmes for disease prevention, behaviour change, consequently, an improved quality of life. Several governmental, for-profit, and non-profit organisations have worked extensively to design health communication interventions that focus on awareness, adherence monitoring, and reminders for immediate action [3, 4]. However the approach of health communication is structured focusing on modulating health-promoting methods. With a paternalistic method of information giving and monitoring, it has less emphasis on inculcating information-seeking and self-reliance. It neglects to devise self-management, self-responsibility mechanisms and lacks promotion of building self-consciousness towards general health and well-being.

While health communication focuses on acute health concerns of immediate relevance —such as pregnancy, diabetes, HIV/AIDS, and COVID-19—its implications and effects for long-term, sustainable behaviour change are uncertain. This is crucial for designing for adolescents, as the information they receive and their behavioural practices they develop during adolescence defines their future path. It is characterised by significant physical, psychological, and psychosocial changes that involve risks and opportunities related to health and well-being. Habits and behaviour patterns formed during adolescence can influence future life prospects, thereby affecting long-term health and social life [5, 6].

Hence, adolescent health and well-being are pivotal for achieving the Sustainable Development Goals [7]. In the past twenty-five years, programme implementers, researchers, and policymakers have expanded the knowledge on adolescents' needs, concerns and have identified ways to overcome barriers that support adolescent sexual and reproductive health (SRH). However, the focus is largely on physical health outcomes, predominantly using a risk-reduction approach. Psychological and social well-being, including body image, self-esteem, and equal romantic and sexual relationships, which are intrinsic parts of SRH, receive far less attention and are often measured only in small-scale cross-sectional studies [5].

During the COVID-19 pandemic, UNESCO [8] published a paper that identified focus areas for key considerations that can be addressed by health systems and health service providers to respond to adolescents' SRH needs, and coined the motto 'Periods do not pause for pandemics, neither do love and sex'. The paper discusses the provision of comprehensive sexuality education; contraceptive counselling and services; comprehensive abortion care, counselling and services for sexual health and well-being; menstrual health information and services. Some programmes based on this paper include Sexual Health Wales, a sexual health information and risk assessment website, and Oky, a menstruation tracking app. Around the same time, a programme called Love Matters in Bihar, India launched a WhatsApp chatbot called 'Ranjana' to answer adolescents' SRH-related questions; it directs adolescents to the nearest clinic providing adolescent-friendly services; and connect adolescents with the nearest peer educator to facilitate home delivery of certain contraceptive methods. Relatedly, the Footprints Foundation, South Africa implemented programmes related to menstrual health (puberty education, provision of menstrual products, and improving water, sanitation, and hygiene in health facilities) in rural communities across the country. The cited examples were responses to the immediate needs created during COVID-19 pandemic and included features from pre-existing programmes and interventions.

In 2020, IDEO [9] (a design company) conceptualized a socio-ecological framework to help identify factors that influence or become barriers to accessing reproductive health services for girls. This framework encompasses policy, community, relationships, and the self, was developed by girls for girls. It is designed as a toolkit for helping identify challenges, offers suggestions that can be customized, and can be curated according to a particular context and social setting. This framework was applied by partnering with leading SRH organisations across Sub-Saharan Africa, who documented every narrative in an engaging storytelling format that placed girls at the centre of the programmes. The book that was compiled based on the framework that captures real-life stories, tools, and perspectives that can help guide practitioners in creating services tailored to adolescent girls. This is among the few programmes with a holistic approach to understand reproductive health and well-being that is based substantially on people's experience.

However, there is scant literature on how such programmes affect adolescents' long-term understanding and well-being. This underlines the need for interventions that can guide adolescents and help them understand their body in a scientific and conceptual manner. Such learnings can be used to help adolescents develop healthy habits and lead healthy lives.

This paper discusses the development of a social communication toolkit for adolescent reproductive health and well-being that promotes self-reliance. The toolkit is derived from the gamified social communication framework proposed for adolescents' reproductive health and well-being. [10] The proposed framework integrates Reflexive and Participatory Consciousness with Hard and Soft Nudges to create Risk Perception. The framework can be used as an aid by individuals to become self-reliant towards one's well-being, with an emphasis on meta-cognitive development and self management and less on monitoring.

The theories and models identified and integrated in the framework has emerged from the empirical study with 30 women in the age bracket of 26 to 60. [11] The objective of the study was to understand women's comprehension of their reproductive health and well-being. It also focused on the gaps that persisted in their knowledge and information seeking behavior along with the behavioral and socio-demographic factors that built their consciousness towards reproductive health and well-being. The finding of the empirical study along with the proposed framework were are combined to build the social communication toolkit using Experience Based Co-design (EBCD). The series of EBCD workshop was conducted with young adults, who further shared their own experiences, struggles, and lack in their understanding of reproductive health and well-being. This exercise validated the gaps that continued to exist and worked towards acknowledging them as a creative output in an interactive, and gamified manner. The further sections detail out the structure of the workshops, and the process of integrating the empirical data with the framework to identify components that would facilitate developing the social communication toolkit.

2 Relevance of Experience-Based Co-design in the Context of the Study

Experience-based co-design is a form of participatory design or co-design method that was originally developed and primarily used as a healthcare quality improvement tool [12]. It involves working with groups of people with experience in the related field. The knowledge derived from lived experience helps to improve and design new services collaboratively. In research contexts, co-design is grounded in participatory action research principles, which is a 'bottom-up' approach. A key characteristic of participatory action research or co-design is collaboration between the researchers and end-users, key stakeholders, policy makers, and programme developers for producing outputs that are relevant to community needs [13, 14]. EBCD is a form of co-design that involves working with groups of individuals whose lived experience is similar to that of user group to be designed for. This collaboration involves connecting narratives to form better inquiries, validating decisions through intense discussion across various behavioural models, and integrating the findings with experience for implementing ideas [15].

This paper highlights the relevance of EBCD in the context of designing for adolescent. To build a mechanism that would help the adolescents speculate the future of their health, it was necessary to understand what has been missed in the past that could be rectified in for a better future. Hence, the qualitative data included women in the age bracket of 26–60, understanding and mapping their lived experience towards reproductive health and well-being. Adolescents feel more comfortable engaging in discussions with their peers and people with similar experiences and of similar ages. [9] Thus, experience-based co-design (EBCD) workshops included young adults who shared similar lived experiences, but were more connected with the adolescents in terms of the trends, preferences, and practices.

3 Methods

3.1 Participants

The workshop participants included seven young adults aged 20–24 years (six women, one man) and one female facilitator. All the participants were design students with previous experience of working on projects on women's health. The facilitator/author was pursuing research in reproductive health and well-being and has a psychology and design background. The signed consent was taken from all the participants before participating in the workshop and included as co-authors in the paper presented.

3.2 Data Source

The qualitative data referred in the workshop is part of the doctoral research work undertaken by the first author/facilitator of the workshop [16]. The research conducted on reproductive health and wellbeing, was approved by the University research committee, and includes signed consent of all the respondents of the study. The empirical study included in-depth interviews of thirty women that were transcribed by the facilitator. Purposive sampling was used to filter respondents aged 26–60 years, residing in various urban, peri-urban and rural cities of India. While selecting the sample, the emphasis was on the location where the participant had spent their adolescence. The rationale for this was to gain an understanding of the socio-demographic and cross-cultural factors that affect learning in the formative years of life, and subsequently compare them with those in the participants' current social setting.

Hereafter, the qualitative data participants are referred to as 'respondents', and the workshop participants, are referred as 'participants'.

3.3 Tools

Due to COVID-19 protocols, ten of twelve sessions of the workshop were conducted online using Microsoft Teams. Miro, a cloud-based collaborative tool, was used to brainstorm, create, collaborate, and communicate.

3.4 Procedure

The workshop comprised twelve sessions. Ten online sessions were conducted over a three-month period, depending on the participants' availability; they ranged in duration from forty-five minutes to three hours, and attendance was not mandatory. All the participants were present on most days except some, where only three to four participants attended. The offline workshops comprised five-hour sessions conducted on two consecutive days and were attended by three participants and the facilitator (Table 1).

Table 1. The day-wise agenda for the online session is shown below:

Day	Activity Description	Duration
1	Discussion of protocol, signing of consent forms, and workshop purpose and agenda overview	1 h
2	Understanding WHO definitions of 'reproductive health' and 'wellbeing'	2 h 5 min
3	Discussion on speculative and critical design theories and their relevance	2 h 55 min
4	Discussion on psychological theories and relevant frameworks	2 h 11 min
5	Introduction to and familiarization with qualitative data	2 h 15 min
6	Synthesis and clustering of information from qualitative data	47 min
7	Behavior analysis of respondents and categorization of qualitative data for archetypes	1 h
8	Identifying methods of disseminating information based on 'what,' 'how,' and 'when'	2 h 49 min
9	Identifying metaphors to depict the journey of a woman's body	55 min
10	Brainstorming on design ideas and discussing the way forward	36 min

The workshop was divided into three parts: immersion, ideation, and creation.

Immersion (Five Days)

During this the participants had to familiarise with the context of the workshop to ensure the same level of understanding, the following steps were taken:

Literature study – The present condition of adolescent reproductive health and wellbeing was deliberated upon in accordance with the criteria set forth by the WHO [5, 17] followed by an introduction to speculative and critical design thinking and an exercise using a cone of uncertainty. [18, 19].

The theoretical frameworks of health psychology [20], stages of change [21] risk perception [22] and nudge [23] were also discussed. To make the sessions interactive, each participant selected a topic to read, for which the facilitator provided reference material. Each participant presented their selected topic, followed by discussions and clarifications. This step was essential for comprehending the deficiencies within existing programmes and for pinpointing the psychological and design theories and concepts necessary for crafting an alternative framework.

Empirical data study - The participants were furnished with transcripts of the qualitative data, which comprised 30 in-depth interviews of women between the ages of 26 and 60. To acquaint themselves with the data, each participant reviewed the transcripts of two or three interviews, depending on feasibility and time constraints. The interviews revealed the respondents' understanding of reproductive health and wellbeing. The respondents' statements were subsequently categorized based on indicators of knowledge, information-seeking behaviour, cultural influences, education, 'ideal situations', and 'not-so-ideal situations'. This approach facilitated the identification of gaps in the understanding of reproductive health and wellbeing as well as recurring emergent patterns. Behaviour analysis was conducted for each respondent by identifying and contextualising the factors influencing their behaviour patterns, such as media exposure, education, and socio-cultural norms.

Ideation (Five Days)
Once the participants had developed an understanding of the overall scenario and its relevance in the Indian context through the qualitative study data, they were able to identify the gaps in the current health communication system. This knowledge was converged through a series of brainstorming sessions, where the data generated from the study were synthesised and analysed. The purpose of the brainstorming sessions was to identify how to communicate messages to work at a metacognitive level; devise a mechanism to cater to different personality types; and identify ways to help an individual speculate about their health. During the concluding brainstorming session, potential techniques for delivering the content in an interactive and gamified fashion were explored. This encompassed considerations such as game-based interactions, strategies for cultivating habits, and the incorporation of self-journaling.

Creation (Two-day-make-a-thon)
To refine the ideas and to give them a form, a two-day Make-a-thon was conducted. A Make-a-thon is 'a creative, interdisciplinary marathon which accelerates innovative ideas into physical and digital prototypes'. It is an intensive and time-limited event where teams or individuals collaboratively create and design new and innovative products, projects or solutions. The aim of the Make-a-thon was to expand the ideas that were formulated in the online workshops and converge them to build a gamified toolkit for increasing adolescents' awareness of their reproductive health and wellbeing. The Make-a-thon commenced with a review of the preceding sessions and the consolidation of gathered information. Subsequently, the flow of content and the concept was detailed. This included the types of messages to be delivered and the organisation of the sequence of actions that would lead to speculating about one's own journey towards wellbeing (Fig. 1).

4 Outcome of the Workshop

The primary objective of the workshop was to devise strategies for developing an adolescent-oriented communication medium that would facilitate a learning environments that is engaging and promotive of reflection, speculation, and critical thinking. Such a medium would facilitate knowledge building in a manner that encourages adolescents to not only conceive information but also scaffold upon existing information.

The three major outcomes of the workshop were: 1) identifying archetypes based on behavioural analysis; 2) identifying metaphors representing the journey of a woman's life; and 3) categorizing sections of information that would facilitate the building of a conceptual framework.

4.1 Archetypes

In the context of communication media, it is important to identify personality traits that would create an environment that promotes receptiveness towards information among

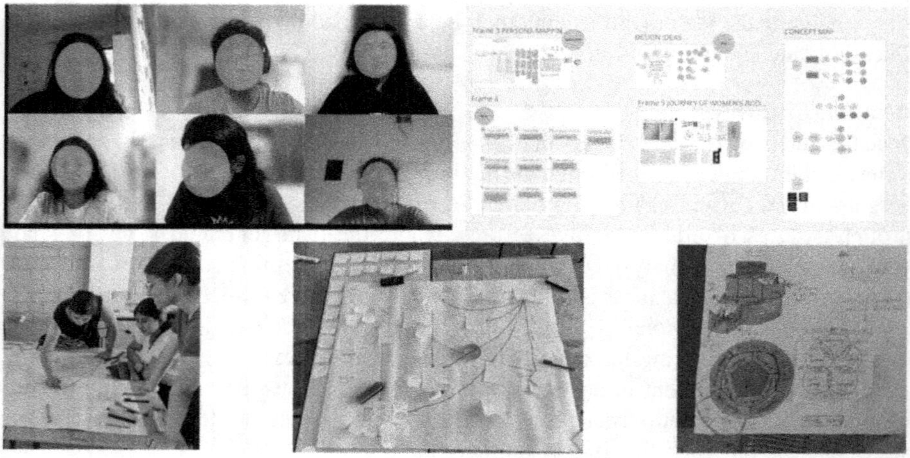

Fig. 1. Cocreating sessions online and offline

individuals. As receiving and perceiving information depends on an individual's personality and attitude. Archetypes have been used effectively to connect with larger audiences, as they categorise the target group into various personality types to develop effective communication. Further, given their close connection with personality traits, they can define the user group based on attitudes and behaviour patterns. The creation of distinct archetypes holds significance in the development of any communication medium as it effectively resonate with various user personalities [24].

Archetypes are relevant for health communication, especially for sensitive topics such as reproductive health and wellbeing, which women generally shy from discussing. The qualitative data suggested that socio-cultural and demographic factors strongly influenced information-seeking behaviour. Hence, archetypes based on behavioural and attitudinal characteristics would aid content creation and information dissemination for different personality types. For this purpose, archetypes representing behavioural or attitudinal characteristics were identified to allow adolescents connect to certain behavioural traits using abstract labels as identification.

To accomplish this a comprehensive behavioral analysis of the respondents of the qualitative interviews was undertaken, taking into account their choices, preferences, priorities, and decisions related to their understanding of reproductive health and wellbeing. The behavioural patterns that emerged were mapped with Jung's personality types for identifying various archetypes. For this, each interview was reviewed and categories were created based on the narrated situations. As a result of this analysis, respondents were categorized according to Jung's personality types. [24] (Table 2).

The seven identified archetypes were based on the data of 30 respondents. As the sample size was small, the proposed archetypes cannot be confirmed and validated. Further research needs to be conducted to validate these archetypes for social communication.

Table 2. Archetypes and other associated traits

Archetypes	Traits
The Liberated one	Has a progressive outlook, does not believe in rituals and customs, tries to break all rules and conventions, lacks information seeking, and has a casual approach towards information related to reproductive health and well-being
The Independent Sage	Independent, prefers to be on her own, seeks information actively, and although she is not entirely sure what she should be aware about, she consumes whatever she comes across
The Congenial One	Lives in a sheltered environment, is cared for by her grandparents and parents, does not discuss periods or any related topics because she believes that female adolescents should not talk about such things, and lives in her own fantasy world of romance
The Cocooned One	Idealistic and has a vision of her own, mystical, is aloof, does not form opinions or discuss or interact much with others, and prefers to gather information and be by herself
The Happy-Go-Lucky-Women	Has a casual approach towards life and a know-it-all attitude, follows rules but has a mind of her own, gives less attention to serious topics, and takes things as they come
The Rebel	Adventurous, innovative, seeks novelty in whatever she does, proposes change and works towards it, prefers to stay informed, and questions conventions
The Seeker	Tries to remain self-contained and seeks information related to periods and women's health discreetly, likes to stay informed and prepared for her future, is rational, questions everything conventional, and finds her own answer

4.2 Metaphors

Metaphors help teach new concepts, as they scaffold the imagination for new learning. They are prevalently used as a communication medium to help individuals comprehend difficult topics, influence others, and communicate well. Their effectiveness stems from their tendency to creatively explain abstract concepts. [25, 1] Lakoff and Johnson's (1980) conceptual metaphor theory greatly shifted perspectives towards metaphor, which can be used as a tool for explanation and persuasion across languages [6, 25]. Notably, metaphors can be effectively used to explain topics in a discreet manner, and metaphorical learning involves forming new connections, which are transformed by forging connections with already familiar concepts [26]. The resulting unexpected or unusual connections can lead to creative insights and new ideas. [27].

The qualitative data revealed the use of metaphors to explain concepts that may be uncomfortable to discuss. The examples included advertisement with a clay pot that breaks because it was not ready to be used as a utensil. And a reference to the stigma and stamen of a flower to explain the act of having sex and conceiving a child. This validated the use of metaphors to explain complex topics [16].

It is difficult for adolescents to predict the journey of a woman's life and the health implications that a woman faces. The latter often remains invisible until physiological symptoms manifest. Hence, to foresee plausible future paths, the participants of the workshop identified metaphors that could represent women's lives. Metaphors that describe the journey of a woman's life were explored in a brainstorming session, with the aim of identifying metaphors that can be used to speculate about one's future life. The metaphors identified were:

Tree. A tree's lifecycle evolves and changes significantly over time, similar to that of a woman's body. When trees are saplings, they need to be protected and nurtured and need water, sunlight, and nutrients for nourishment and growth. One must be mindful while using pesticides in order to not harm the fruits. The stronger the roots of a tree, the better the fruits borne. This resembles the life of a woman, where unhealthy practices and eating junk food excessively make a woman's body weak and vulnerable, and better nourishment and care lead to a healthy life.

Hibiscus Flower. A delicate red-coloured flower that is often used to symbolize a woman in Indian culture. It is associated with various Indian Hindu goddesses to depict love, commitment, strength, and bravery. In the context of reproductive health, the stages of the opening, blooming, and closing of a flower symbolize the journey from menarche to menopause. The flower has medicinal and culinary value and is considered holy and used for religious purposes on auspicious occasions. These virtues represent the dynamic nature of a woman.

Butterfly. The lifecycle of a butterfly can be said to mirror the journey of a woman's life. The larva to adult stages can be associated with puberty, where physiological changes occur. Late adolescence and adulthood can be associated with the pupa stage, where female adolescents tend to be cocooned because of socio-cultural norms, notions, and other environmental and physiological factors that govern their body and mind. This is the most challenging aspect for many women because it prohibits freedom of thought. As new changes occur and experience and knowledge is gained, the 'cocoon' gradually transforms itself into a vibrant 'butterfly'.

River. The course of a river goes through several transitions from its origin in mountains and hills to its end in seas and oceans. Rivers are in their purest form at their origin point and they are filled with energy as they traverse through rifts, gorges, plains, and other types of terrain. The constitution of a river changes depending on the environment it is passing through. Rivers ebb, flow, and thrive despite the hardships they face in their journey until they merge in the sea and become 'a transformed self'.

Ivy. A climbing evergreen plant that represents eternity and fidelity, the ivy plant grows by attaching itself to the surfaces on which it is climbing. The roots of the ivy are formed at stem nodes, where connecting to the wrong nodes may have consequences. This can be associated with the journey of a woman's life, where attaching to a wrong node can adversely affect women's growth and wellbeing. This indicates that one needs to be mindful of the choices one makes, as adverse choices can have repercussions and appropriate choices can enable flourishment and growth.

Musical Instrument. Learning to play a musical instrument can be used as a metaphor to depict a woman's journey of her reproductive health. As adolescents, one is taught to deal with one's periods, which can take time to master depending on the individual. Mastery is developed through practice and experience, and the earlier the skill is mastered, the sooner one can create and play their own music. Further, the metaphor of a musical instrument also includes how tuning one's body allows one to play their own music and live harmoniously.

Labyrinth. A labyrinth is a complicated, irregular network of passages leading to a singular destination. One needs to be very calculative about the path that is chose, as a wrong choice would lead to an incorrect destination. It resembles a woman's growth journey (especially reproductive growth), which includes physiological changes, emotional growth, and other factors that affect their life experience. Navigating a labyrinth has no definitive right or wrong path, much like the unique journey every woman undertakes. In both scenarios, the ultimate objective of this often perplexing and challenging journey can be likened to drawing nearer to the core and gaining a deeper understanding of oneself.

Hourglass. Based on the notion of the biological clock, a woman's body can be compared to an hour glass. As a woman passes from one phase of her biological clock to another (both literally and figuratively), it is up to each individual how they pass each phase. During the intervals between these time periods, various tasks and responsibilities are managed, each associated with its respective marker. When an hourglass is turned over after its sand has depleted, it marks the commencement of a fresh journey, mirroring the phases of women's mental and physical health.

The proposed metaphors need further testing and validation before they can be used in social communication media.

4.3 Information Categories

The qualitative data helped understand information-seeking behaviour amongst the respondents and identify gaps in their existing knowledge at every life stage. Women gain knowledge after undergoing a physiological experience that affected their well-being, and they were often not prepared for the outcome. It became apparent that making adolescents aware of their future health would require an understanding that has been developed in a rational, radical, and conceptual manner. Hence, the information that emerged from the data were segregated into ten categories with the objective of not overwhelming adolescents with information and instead distributing the information over time (years in some cases). Thus, adolescents can select the type of information they would like to seek at a given time. While it would be necessary to become familiar with all the information, the sequence of information gathering can be customised as per requirement. The categories are as follows:

Necessary Information. Information regarding reproductive health and well-being. What is it? Why it is important? Making adolescents understand their responsibility towards themselves. For example, the why and how of menstruation.

Critical Information. This refers to crucial information that adolescents need to know, but probably at only when they are mature enough to comprehend it. This information could be provided under the guidance of an expert. For example, the difference between sexual and reproductive health.

Exclusive/Need-Based Information. Information that reflects an individual's personal life journey, experience, or situation. For example, understanding endometriosis, psychological issues, and PCOD/PCOS.

Recurring Information. Information that is repeated at regular intervals and is important to supervise. For example, regular reminders to keep a check on a person, monitoring what is and is not normal, and so on.

Time-Based/Staggered Information. Information that must be provided when adolescents are prepared to experience a concept practically and understand it holistically (such information can be combined with critical information). For example, how to have safe sex?

Cosmetic Information. Information for situations where the effects of reproductive health are physically visible and where the approach is more related to physical well-being than physiological understanding. For example, acne and weight gain.

Myths/Misinformation. Information that is based on notions derived from traditions and customs, which may affect how individuals view or act upon their health needs/requirements. For example, girls should not engage in certain activities, such as horse-riding.

Social/Cultural Norms. Information learned from socio-cultural norms without understanding, reflecting, and identifying the rationale. For example, not entering temples or handling pickles while menstruating.

Information for Building a Scientific Understanding. Science-based information that focuses on the physiological aspects of reproductive health. For example, the uterus lining and being overweight.

Information for Building a Conceptual Understanding. Information that is needed to build conceptual understandings of conditions that may not be physically evident in certain situations, but is necessary for a person's well-being (i.e. why some things work the way they work). For example, understanding hormones.

4.4 Integration and Flow of the Components in the Proposed Toolkit

The toolkit is operated by selecting a metaphor and an archetype that the user resonates with. The three sections comprise information seeking, knowledge building, and a mechanism to identify and maintain health goals. Once the archetype is selected, adolescents can navigate through each section using different types of information cards pertaining to different information categories. To navigate through each section, different sets of information cards belonging to different information categories are used. The completion of each set of information results in earning tokens that can be used to complete a jigsaw puzzle of the metaphor. The outcome of the overall process is the construction of the metaphors (described in the earlier sections) thatbecomes the representation of the future self, helping the adolescents to speculate their health and wellbeing.

The flow of information is sequenced in the following order: information, knowledge, goal, and maintenance. This sequence is based on the transtheoretical model [21], where through information and knowledge, adolescents' minds are trained in precontemplation, contemplation, preparation, action, maintenance, and termination (Fig. 2).

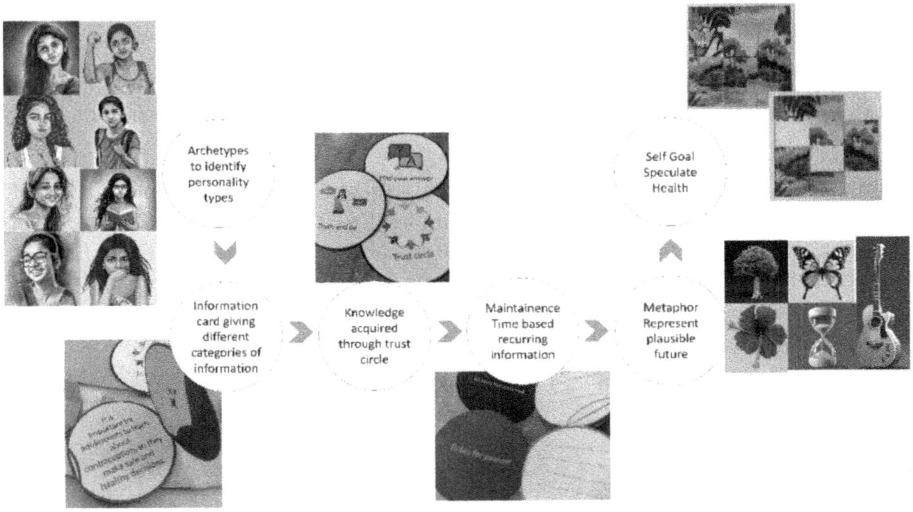

Fig. 2. Informative flow of social communication toolkit

5 Discussion

It is lived experiences that help sensitize and guide people to contemplate their future. To that end, experience-based co-design (EBCD) is a valuable tool where, by involving the end-user, innovative ideas that better match users' needs can be generated. Over time, the original 'blueprint' for EBCD has been adapted and tailored to accommodate different types of healthcare services as well as a wide range of local and national contexts [9]. In the context of this paper, it has been able to address the following points:

Creating Socio-culturally Relevant Communication. The workshop incorporated the viewpoints of three generations of women and the qualitative data helped the participants examine the cultural influences and practices that the respondents cited. There were several instances where the participants recognised the myths, misconceptions, and misinformation that continue to prevail. Further, there was evidence of subtle positive changes, such as having open conversations about reproductive health issues, which subsequently motivated the participants to assertively create awareness about information that they had lacked themselves and empower future generations.

Relevance of Traditional Perspectives that are Scientific. There was evidence for scientific rationales behind some traditional practices. While these rationales were known to participants from older generations, those from younger generations followed certain practices merely because they were compelled to by their grandparents or parent. For example, drinking warm water with herbs during menstruation and eating certain foods that can comfort adolescents. The participants felt the need to continue such practices in a more informed manner.

Bridging Information Gaps that have Existed Since Generations. Misconceptions and misinformation, particularly regarding the physiology of a woman's body, have prevailed since multiple generations. Very few respondents and participants knew and understood their body. This was a revelation for the participants, who felt they needed to make future generations more aware and capable of taking ownership over their bodily well-being.

Building Communication that can connect with Adolescents. People are unable to imagine and relate to things that are not immediately relevant and seemingly out-of-context, which affects the adoption of preventive health measures. It is difficult to communicate future health risks to any population [28]. In such situations, constructive fear can help effect health behaviour change in unexpected situations [29]. Similarly, sharing lived experiences that help envision future implications can motivate people to make efforts to become self-reliant and self-aware to the best of their knowledge [30].

6 Future Work

The objective of the workshop series was to identify components that would facilitate designing a social communication toolkit for adolescents, cocreating with young adults using EBCD. This allowed innovatively to explore sensitive topics in reproductive health and well-being. The workshop enabled the participants to learn from the experiences of women in various stages of life. It further helped them speculate a path of well-being for themselves and further provide guidance to adolescents.

The toolkit derived from the findings can be used to develop a gamified mechanism for adolescent psychoeducation. Future work will include building the toolkit, exploring technologies that would enable integrating the components of the toolkit in an ethical and discreet manner, evaluating and validating it with experts and adolescents. The toolkit will be made available to NGOs and schools and to individuals as a self-owned kit for promoting self-reflection and self-reliance.

Acknowledgement. The involvement of the respondents entailed sharing their lived experience, suggesting design ideas that would guide adolescents' reproductive health and well-being, further pointing out gaps that still exist in the current discourse on such topics. We would like to acknowledge all the respondents, without whom this research would not have been possible.

Disclosure. The authors report there are no competing interests to declare.

References

1. Douchi, T., Kuwahata, R., Yamamoto, S., Oki, T., Yamasaki, H., Nagata, Y.: Relationship of Upper Body Obesity to Menstrual Disorders. Acta Obstetricia Et Gynecologica Scandinavica (2002)
2. Smith, J.: Stanford Encyclopedia of Philosophy. https://plato.stanford.edu/entries/self-consciousness/. (2020)
3. Sullivan, G.A., et al.: A Field Guide to Designing a Health Communication Strategy: A Resource for Health Communication Professionals. Baltimore: Johns Hopkins Bloomberg School of Public Health/Center (2003)
4. Weiss, J.L., et al.: Obesity, obstetric complications and cesarean delivery rate–a population based screening study. American Journal of Obstetrics and Gynecology (2004)
5. Liang, M.S., et al.: The State of Adolescent Sexual and Reproductive Health. Journal of Adolescent Health (2019)
6. Sawyer, S.M., et al.: Adolescence: A Foundation for Future Health. The Lancet (2012)
7. WHO, Health Targets. Geneva:. Child and Adolescent Health: Fact Sheet on Sustainable Development Goals WHO SDGs. https://apps.who.int (2021)
8. UNESCO: Not on Pause: Responding to the Sexual and Reproductive Health Needs of Adolescents in the Context of the COVID-19 Crisis. https://www.unfpa.org/sites/default/files/resource-pdf/Not_on_Pause.pdf (2020)
9. IDEO. https://www.ideo.org/perspective/designing-for-and-with-girls (2020)
10. Roy, D., Biswas, U.N.: They Need to Know and Learn–Gamified Social Communication Framework for Adolescent Reproductive Health and Well Being. Springer Nature, Conference on Human-Computer Interaction (2023)
11. Roy, D.: Fostering sustainable wellbeing via socially conscious ecosystems: an interventional framework. In: Conference Proceedings Socioecos 2024: climate change, sustainability and socio-ecological practices, Spain (2024)
12. Donetto, S., Tsianakas, V., Robert, G.: London: Using Experience-based Co-design (EBCD) to improve the quality of healthcare: mapping where we are now and establishing future directions. King's College, London (2014)
13. Santana, M.J., Manalili, K., Jolley, R.J., Zelinsky, S., Quan, H., Lu, M.: How To Practice Person-Centred Care: A Conceptual Framework. Health Expectations (2018)
14. Steen, M., Manschot, M., de Koning, N.: Benefits of Co-Design in Service Design Projects. International Journal of Design. (2011). http://www.ijdesign.org/index.php/
15. Locock, L., et al.: Testing Accelerated Experience-Based Co-Design: A Qualitative Study of Using a National Archive of Patient Experience. Health Services and Delivery Research (2014)
16. Roy, D.: Social Communication Model for Reproductive Health Awareness and Well-Being Amongst Adolescent Girls. s.l.: Maharaja Sayajirao University of Baroda, Doctoral dissertation (2023)
17. Chandra-Mouli, V., et al.: Implications of the global early adolescent study's formative research findings for action and for research. Journal of Adolescent Health (2017)
18. Mitrovic, I., Golub, M., Šuran, O.: Introduction to Speculative Design Practice – Eutropia, a Case Study. s.l.: Croatian Designers Association, Arts Academy and the University of Split (2015)
19. Dunne, A., Raby, F.: Speculative Everything: Design, Fiction, and Social Dreaming. MIT Press (2013)
20. Marks, D., Murray, M., Estacio, E.V.: Health Psychology: Theory, Research and Practice. 5th ed. s.l. SAGE Publications (2018)

21. Prochaska, J.O.: Transtheoretical Model of Behavior Change. [book auth.] M. D. Gellman. Cham. Encyclopedia of Behavioral Medicine. s.l. Springer (2020)
22. O'Sullivan, G. A., J. A. Yonkler, W. Morgan, A. P. and Merritt. A Field Guide to Designing a Health Communication Strategy: A Resource for Health Communication Professionals. A field guide to designing a health communication strategy: a resource for health communication professionals Baltimore. Johns Hopkins Bloomberg School of Public Health/Center (2003)
23. Leonard, T.C., Thaler, R.H., Sunstein, C.R.: Nudge: Improving Decisions about Health, Wealth, and Happiness. Yale University Press (2008)
24. Stevens, A. The Archetypes. The Handbook of Jungian Psychology: Theory, Practice and Applications. s.l.: Routledge (2012)
25. Kelland, M.: Personality Theory. https://www.oercommons.org/authoring/22859-personality-theory (2017)
26. Hume, K.: Teaching through Metaphor and Analogy Sim (2022)
27. Azzopardi, P.S., et al.: Progress in adolescent health and wellbeing: tracking 12 headline indicators for 195 countries and territories. The Lancet (2019)
28. Renfree, I., Harrison, D., Marshall, P., Stawarz, K., Cox, A.: Don't kick the habit: the role of dependency in habit formation. In: CHI Conference Extended Abstracts on Human Factors in Computing Systems (2016)
29. Maddux, J.E., Rogers, R.W.: Protection Motivation and Self-Efficacy: A Revised Theory of Fear Appeals and Attitude Change. s.l. Journal of Experimental Social Psychology (1983)
30. De Bruin, W.B., Bennett, D.: Relationships between initial COVID-19 risk perceptions and protective health behaviors: a national survey. American Journal of Preventive Medicine (2020)

Exploring Dark Patterns: A Comparative Analysis of User Experiences on Web and App Platforms

Harshita Singhal(✉), Om Krishan Sharma, Bighna Kalyan Nayak, and Shikha Kaushik

Amity University, Noida, Uttar Pradesh, India
harshitasinghal2003@gmail.com

Abstract. A user interface known as a "dark pattern" influences users' decisions while purposefully misleading them to the business's advantage. This research paper aims to ascertain how users are susceptible to various dark patterns and to ascertain what kind of interaction users have with dark patterns when using various web modalities. This article lists five components that are crucial for users to recognize dark patterns even when they are not fully aware of the unethical motivations driving the design. These five factors exhibit strong correlations and associations with the user's capacity to recognize irregularities. This study advances our knowledge of the factors that expose users to dark patterns, including frequency of occurrence, trustworthiness, level of frustration, user interface deception, as well as the impact of different forms of dark patterns on user experience. The present study employed a preliminary examination of dark patterns in its early phase, succeeded by a close observation experiment of the user interface incorporating dark patterns. The variables and factors of identification found in this study can help the Human-Computer Interaction (HCI) community understand the negative effects of dark patterns on usability across various platforms.

Keywords: Dark patterns · Deceptive Designs · HCI · Persuasive Design · User Interfaces

1 Introduction

Technology has permeated every aspect of our daily lives and is everywhere. Our access to websites and mobile applications is rapidly expanding. Many of these digital platforms are carefully designed to modify and shape user behavior and frequently influence their actions [1]. A concept known as "dark patterns" is present in this digital environment. Dark patterns are elements in the user interface of websites and apps that have the cunning ability to direct a person's actions away from their true intentions and best interests [2]. The dimensions of dark patterns are depicted in Fig. 1, along with their parameters, long-term effects, and ideal conditions. It offers a thorough understanding

Published by Springer Nature Switzerland AG 2026
G. Bhutkar et al. (Eds.): IDID 2024, IFIP AICT 747, pp. 227–244, 2026.
https://doi.org/10.1007/978-3-032-00777-3_14

of the contexts in which these manipulative design techniques have the greatest impact as well as insights into the subtleties of these techniques and their effects over time.

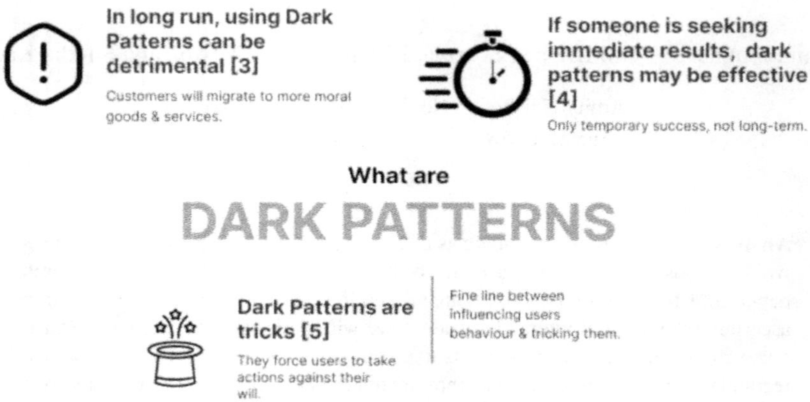

Fig. 1. Parameters of Dark Patterns. *Note- All the images in this study are created by the authors themselves.

Predicting how people will react to these technological interventions i.e. dark patterns, requires understanding human behaviour and how the mind functions. Understanding the psychological principles that underpin human cognition is essential for developing this predictive capacity [6]. Figure 2 shows the Behavioural Model, developed by Dr. B.J. Fogg, which describes the variables that can be expertly used to gently influence users into carrying out particular tasks. The components of this mod- el, when applied to dark patterns, can be made to exert pressure on users to do things that they might otherwise avoid, like unintentionally agreeing to data collection or signing up for unwanted services. To make use of these ideas, dark patterns simplify activities, manipulate user motives, and compel behaviour with time constraints and other triggers. Researchers can better detect how dark patterns target vulnerable users and undermine trust in digital encounters by manipulating ethical design principles. This connection between the two can be understood. This can have several benefits, such as promoting user engagement or task completion, but it can also have unfavourable effects that detract from the user's experience [7].

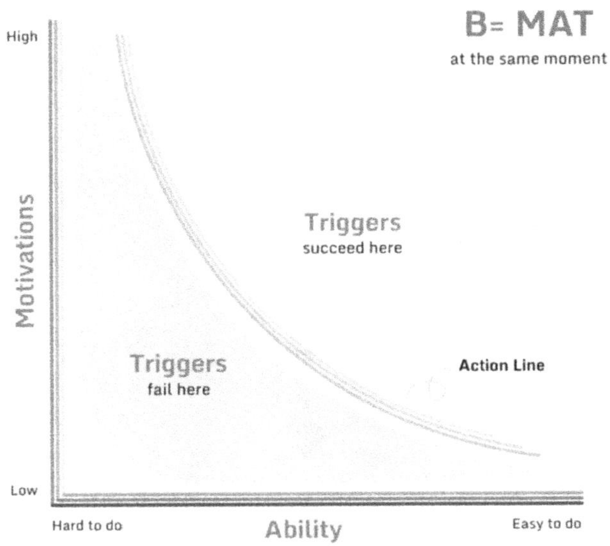

Fig. 2. Fogg's Behaviour Model

The opposite of user-centered design is dark patterns. Dark patterns take advantage of cognitive biases to make it more difficult for users to make educated judgements or refuse to do specific actions, as opposed to putting the needs and experience of the user first. Furthermore, a researcher named Harry Brignull has uncovered a dozen different dark patterns, each of which employs a different method to influence user behaviour [8]. Figure 3 shows the types of Dark Patterns as: [9].

2 Literature Review

A sizable knowledge gap persists despite the depth and complexity of the body of literature on dark patterns [10]. Our understanding of the complex interrelationships among technological platforms, the existence of dark patterns, and their effects on user experiences still needs to be improved. For example, although earlier studies have demonstrated the existence of dark patterns in both websites and mobile apps, it is unclear how users will perceive and react to these deceptive techniques when they come across them on various types of devices, such as traditional web browsers and mobile applications. This inquiry is crucial because it explores how dark patterns affect users, taking into account things like the affordances of various platforms (such as the distinctions between using a computer mouse and a touchscreen), the overall user experience, and the taxonomy of factors that cause users to succumb to dark patterns.

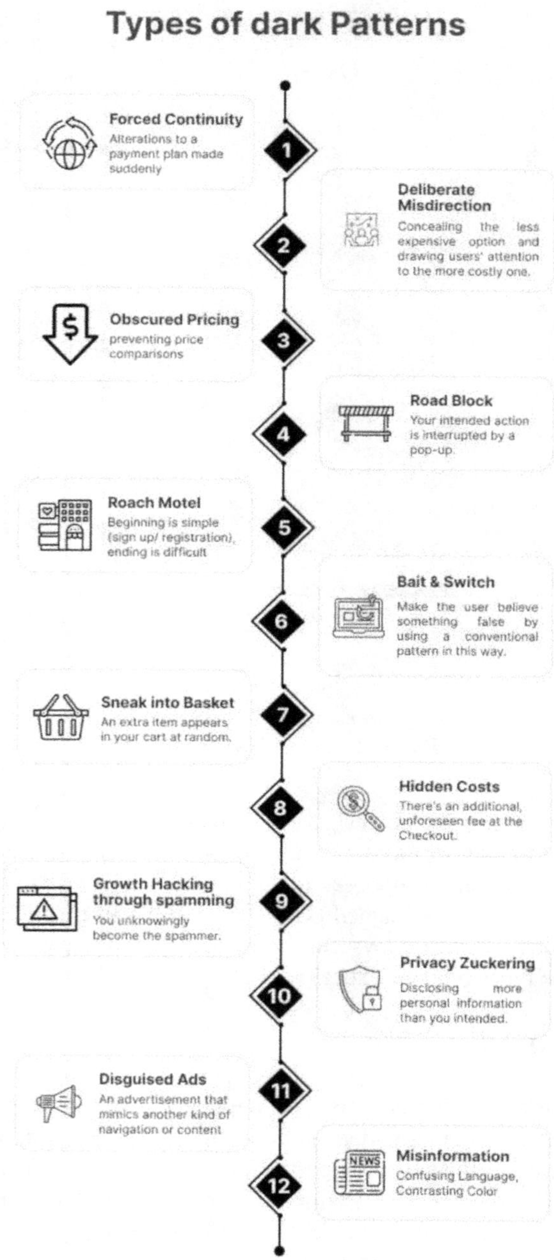

Fig. 3. Types of Dark Patterns by Harry Brignull

2.1 Key Contributions

- In this work, an exploration study was conducted at the initial stage to examine the presence and impact of dark patterns across various modalities, including mobile apps, mobile web browsers, and traditional web browser- based versions of popular online services by the authors of the paper [11]. We collected data from several online platforms such as Facebook, Reddit, and Twitter's "Dark Patterns Hall of Shame" to identify instances of dark patterns. A thorough manual curation process was then carried out.
- Later an experiment was run in the second stage to strengthen and further validate our findings. In this study, people were given some tasks to complete in all three modalities. The goal was to see if users could identify dark patterns on various platforms and how they would respond when presented with these trickery interface elements.
- This research paper has two main objectives: first, it will evaluate and compile the different dark pattern examples that users are already experiencing on different platforms, and second, it will determine how susceptible each user is to different dark patterns on different web modalities. They must complete a variety of tasks set out by the authors in this phase to find dark patterns on different web and app modalities that affect users in different ways.

2.2 Background

Brignull has identified twelve distinct categories of dark patterns based on the unintended consequences they produce [12, 13]. They discovered that UX (User Experience) professionals intentionally disregard the user's preferences in their day-today work. Additionally, they discovered through their study of design students those designers frequently used human values in their decision-making to produce stakeholder-focused outcomes, even when initially beginning their design activity with a userfocused approach [14]. It is possible to predict people's behaviour and create user experiences that alter behaviour by comprehending the psychology underlying the human mind's decision-making processes. Brignull has demonstrated how simple it is to transform well-known usability heuristics and knowledge of human psychology into manipulative designs [15]. Maier offered a thorough analysis of issues relating to enduser decision-making processes (cognitive systems, persuasion technology, etc.), as well as dark patterns (their definition, motivation, preventive measures, and ethical design considerations). These subjects give us an idea of how designers employ their acquired knowledge to trick users and produce deceptive user experiences. Even after being made aware of such persuasive technologies, people continue to be susceptible to their effects [16]. Behaviour happens when ability, motivation, and triggers line up, according to Fogg. He describes strategies that designers can use to affect people's actions. Users' reactions to these techniques and the elements causing unfavourable results, however, are not well studied. Using five cues—physical, psychological, linguistic, social dynamics, and social roles—Fogg explores social reactions to technology in a different study. In persuasion, these cues are paramount. To detect dark pat- terns, this paper makes use of this knowledge [17].

2.3 Design's Role in Human Interaction

Design's role in directing human interactions has long been studied by designers, psychologists, and behavioural economists. Don Norman made James Gibson's idea of affordances well-known as a way to consider how interaction can be made simpler by object design that communicates function to users [18]. It describes the natural opportunities for action that a thing or setting presents to a person. According to Richard Thaler's future development, choice architectures entail creating settings that have an impact on people's decisions without limiting their freedom of choice. In their discussion of how purposefully created choice architectures can influence people to act in ways that are favoured by the designer, Thaler et al. expanded on these ideas [19]. Thaler has highlighted the significance of nudges—subtle interventions intended to encourage people to make better decisions while preserving their sense of autonomy. These ideas have shaped our knowledge of how environments and structures can affect human behaviour, and they have had a significant impact on disciplines like behavioural psychology, economics, and design.

The opposite of user-centered design is dark patterns. Dark patterns are "interface design decisions that benefit an online service by coercing, steering, or deceiving users into making decisions that, if fully informed and capable of selecting alternatives, they might not make," according to Mathur et al. in the context of websites and apps [20]. Regarding benevolent deception, take note of the inversion: dark patterns serve the goals and values of the designers (or their employers) rather than, or sometimes despite, the flourishing of users and society [21].

Brignull also created the first ad hoc taxonomy of dark patterns, which academics have since criticized, systematized, and improved. A taxonomy of malicious user interface designs was also created by Conti et al. in 2010 before the term "dark pat- terns" became widely accepted in academia. Dark patterns literature from various disciplines is thoroughly reviewed by Mathur et al., who also conceptually and thematically organize it [22].

Because they can affect user behaviours and perceptions, dark patterns have significant effects on user and societal well-being [23]. For instance, they may influence how a user perceives the conditions of their relationship with the service or the formal and informal agreements that exist between users [24]. Dark patterns can persuade users to divulge personal information when they normally wouldn't, possibly in ways that end in regret and harm.

2.4 Observation and Measurement

The interest in empirical research on dark patterns is growing at the same time as the theoretical understanding of them. Dark patterns in real-world contexts, including video games [25], proxemic interactions [26], visualizations [27], two-factor authentication systems [28], and marketing email opt-outs [29], have been the subject of academic studies. Dark patterns used by significant online services like Google [30], Facebook [31], Yelp [32], Match.com [33], and TurboTax [34] have also been documented by journalists and activists. Unsurprisingly, dark patterns are effective at swaying people towards decisions that are not in their best interests, and laboratory studies have started to confirm this. For instance, Luguri & Strahilevitz discovered that participants in a survey and experiment were almost four times as likely to accept an expensive, useless service when the user interface contained dark patterns.

Two studies have looked at how the general public views dark patterns from the perspective of online social networks that aim to catalog unethical designs. Fansher et al. concentrated on tweets containing the #darkpatterns hashtag. They discovered that it was frequently used by expert UX practitioners to draw attention to dark designs they came across in the wild [35]. A similar content analysis was carried out by Chivukula et al. on threads from the incredibly popular /r/assholedesign subreddit [36]. These selforganized, self-selected communities all opposed dark patterns in design, and they frequently tried to embarrass offending service providers by sharing screenshots of dark UI (User Interface) designs, which is a behaviour that was strikingly similar in both studies.

2.5 Practitioners

According to Narayanan et al., a different method by which dark user interface de- signs might be created entails the exploitation of online behavioural experiments, also known as A/B tests. According to this theory, exploitative designs eventually con- verge on dark patterns organically as a result of ill-conceived and naive experiments [37].

A lower-bound estimate of the prevalence of this practice is provided by Jiang et al.'s observation of tens of thousands of websites using A/B testing in real-world settings [38]. Together, these pieces offer some justification for how morally conscientious designers can still create unethical user interfaces. In this work, we extend this discussion by using the body of artifacts created by an online service as a lens through which to examine how various design teams working towards similar objectives arrive at various, potentially dark UI implementations.

3 Experimental Analysis

3.1 Materials

It appears that creating the corpus of services that were suitable for our research objectives was the key step in conducting this study. We concentrated on online services that matched the following standards:

1. The service must be well-liked. A service must meet certain requirements in order to be deemed popular: it must have high ratings, favourable reviews, a substantial number of downloads, user engagement metrics, and good App Store rankings.
2. The service must be accessible through a desktop browser, a mobile browser, and the Google Play Store.
3. The service must provide roughly equivalent functionality in each of the three modalities.
4. The service may not ask for identification documentation beyond email or phone number confirmation.

The experiment was then run on the participants using a questionnaire that was created.

On an Intel I5 PC running Windows 10, Google Forms was used to thoroughly research and display each stimulus. On an 812.8 mm Lenovo monitor with a 1024 × 786 resolution, all stimuli were shown in a dimly lit room. Throughout the entire experiment, the background hue and contrast of the stimuli were maintained. The experimental space is shown in Fig. 4, giving readers a visual picture of the environment in which the study was conducted. By completing tasks necessary for the research while seated in the chair, participants participated in the experiment and provided important data to support the study's conclusions.

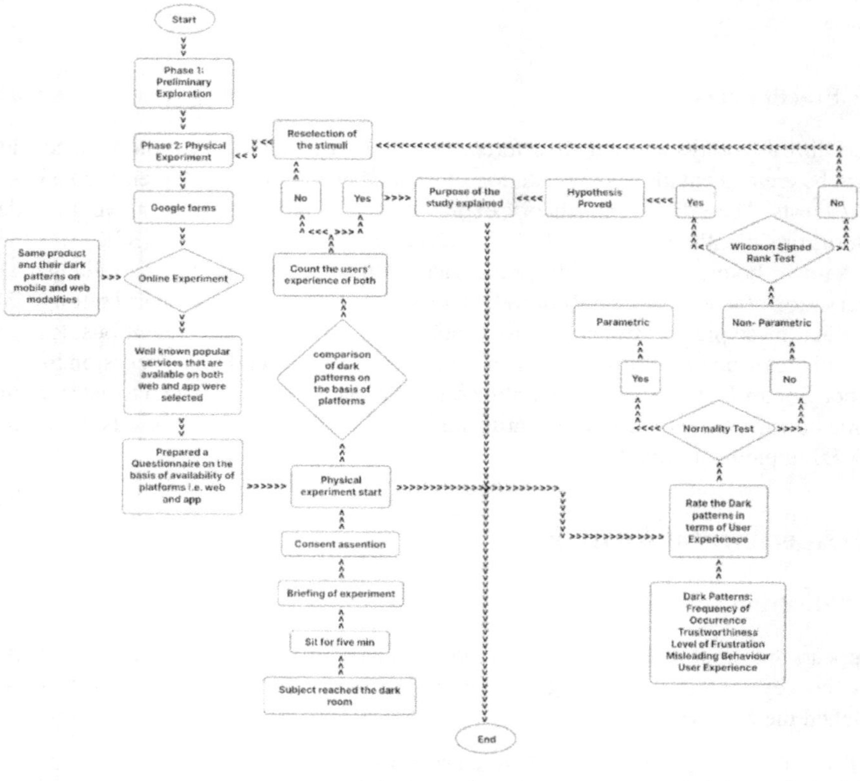

Fig. 4. Experimental Space

3.2 Protocol of the Experiment

Participants in this experiment were asked to complete various tasks on their laptops and mobile devices. Some of the experiments are-

- For the first task, users had to log out of Facebook on the website and application. The participants' completion times were recorded after being asked to log into their Facebook accounts.
- Users had to download the Audible app and register for a free trial on the website in order to complete the second assignment. In order to start a free trial subscription, participants had to input their credit card information. This mission was to ascertain the degree to which consumers were willing to provide sensitive personal information, particularly their credit card number, to register for a free trial on the Audible app and website. The participants' unwillingness to provide sensitive personal information was noted.
- The third task was to downvote the unhelpful reviews from Amazon on both: the application and on the website. They removed the option to "downvote" unhelpful reviews; however, you can "report" reviews you think are fake.
- The fourth task was to temporarily deactivate an Instagram account on the mobile application and the web app.
- Open-ended questions were then asked to elicit their responses and opinions regarding both tasks, the application and the website. It asked questions like "What do you think about the steps involved in completing the task?" and "Did you feel that the steps were misleading or unnecessary on any modality?" "Do you believe that the specific website or app was intentionally created in a way to confuse the users," etc. The participant's ability to recognize the dark pattern's deceitful or manipulative characteristics was the purpose of the questions.
- Participants were also asked to rate the five factors for both tasks, including user experience, level of frustration, trustworthiness, frequency of occurrence, and misleading Interface.

Correlations between these variables were found using SPSS software after the data was collected.

3.3 Participants

Various South Asian ethnic groups from Amity University Noida are represented among the participants. Despite briefly explaining the experimental procedure, sub- jects were unaware of the study's purpose because it was a perceptual experiment. In accordance with their level of interest, the subjects were informed of the remaining details regarding the experiment's purpose after the fact. The ability to leave the trial at any time was also made known to the participants. Individuals who could not communicate in Hindi or English were not allowed to participate in the trial. Participants included employees and undergraduates. There were 43.9% women and 56.1% men. All test subjects had normal vision or used external goggles to achieve normal vision.

3.4 Procedure

Phase I: Preliminary Exploration

Before starting the official examination into how consumers experience dark patterns on various modalities, we conducted an exploratory review of the existing dark pat- terns to gather crucial information about the kinds of online services that would be suitable for our study. The purpose of this initial research phase was to establish the foundation for our later, more comprehensive study. This stage of the study was conducted to identify the many forms of dark patterns and comprehend the causes behind consumers being victims of a specific dark pattern.

Manual research techniques such as group brainstorming and author discussion meetings were employed. The writers jointly discover and investigate a variety of dark patterns that users frequently run across by combining their knowledge and observations. To find examples of dark patterns in their natural settings, the authors also actively used websites or programs as normal users while doing a hands-on study of a few chosen online services. This interactive and collaborative technique makes it possible to thoroughly examine dark pattern occurrences and makes it easier to generate insightful ideas for future research. Because "understanding designers' intentions and ethical decisions is subjective and may lead to imprecision," as observed by Di Geronimo et al., we did not take designer intent into account when detecting novel dark patterns.

The exploratory analysis took place during July and August of 2023 using an iterative process. During this time, we used a methodical and comprehensive approach to analyze many internet services. Some of the primary sources we used for our research included the following:

- Dark Patterns Twitter Hall of Shame: Twitter's "Dark Patterns Hall of Shame" is a popular place to talk about and uncover the unethical practices employed by different internet services. We investigated this source to find out more about real-world examples of dark patterns and their different expressions. We carefully looked for practices that were highlighted on this platform to identify practices to be concerned about.
- Google Play's "Top Free" Apps: We recognized the importance of examining popular online services in a wider context in addition to those that are accused of employing dark patterns. We therefore focused our investigation on apps that were regularly seen in the "Top Free" section of the Google Play Store. We covered both heavily used and services that had been criticized for having dark designs using this technique.
- Reddit and Facebook's #darkpatterns: We extended the scope of our analysis to social media sites like Facebook and Reddit because we recognized the mobility of online forums and discussions. The hashtag #darkpatterns made it easier to find relevant conversations and examples of dark patterns. This facilitated the compilation of a diverse array of scenarios and expanded our comprehension of how people engaged with certain design methodologies.

A few factors that aid in the identification of dark patterns were determined by reviewing the body of research on persuasion [39] and dark patterns, as well as the preliminary investigation. Five factors were found to be most important based on our early research: the user interface's physical look, reliability, degree of frustration, frequency of occurrence, and user experience. In the following step, examples of each dark pattern were included in the structured questionnaire to measure the effect of these variables on user reactions.

Finding strategies that benefited the service at the expense of the user, such as coercion, guiding, deception, or strategic omission, was our focus. We adopted Di

Geronimo et al.'s strategy of giving user experience precedence over presumptions on designer intents and assessed services solely based on their user interface presentation, disregarding designer intent.

How our formalized research would move forward in the next phase was largely determined by the data collected in this initial stage. Gaining a comprehensive understanding of the variety and abundance of dark patterns across multiple platforms helped us better plan our later study. We developed a more focused and effective approach for recognizing and evaluating misleading design techniques with the aid of this prior knowledge.

Phase II: Experiment

We conducted a second round of research to strengthen and further validate the results from the first round. By closely observing user interactions with dark patterns across various digital platforms, we sought to confirm our findings in this phase. An in-person experiment was part of this phase.

We purposefully chose participants who were not connected to the UX or information technology (IT) industries to ensure the diversity of viewpoints and experiences. This choice was made to consider the opinions of users who might not have come across the term "dark pattern" in their professional or academic lives. From 15 to 30 years old, the participants in this group were chosen to represent a wide age range.

An extensive analysis of the body of literature on persuasion strategies and dark patterns guided our method for developing this experiment. Insights from our preliminary research were also considered. We discovered several crucial factors from these sources that are essential for spotting dark patterns. As a result of our preliminary research, the following five factors stood out:

- Frequency of Occurrence: The frequency with which a user will encounter a dark pattern when using a platform.
- Trustworthiness: The purported authenticity and reliability of the platform.
- Level of Frustration: The degree to which customers find the dark pattern bothersome or frustrating.
- User interface deception: The extent to which a design results in users acting in an unexpected or undesirable way.
- User Experience Impact: The overall influence that these dark patterns have on the user experience. This is the sole dependent variable we have for this study.

We created a structured questionnaire to fully assess how these variables affected user reactions. Examples of actual dark patterns that people have run into while interacting online were included in this questionnaire. Participants were asked to assign a Likert scale rating of 1 (indicating minimal impact) to 5 (indicating a significant impact) for each example's variables [40].

All the responses were compiled and painstakingly examined. We carried out statistical analyses to ascertain the relationships between these variables and their impact on the user experience across different modalities. Utilizing statistical software like IBM Statistical Package for the Social Sciences (SPSS), we specifically used exploratory factor analysis.

Our ability to identify and assess the impact of dark patterns on user experiences while also learning more about the underlying relationships between the various factors that go into identifying and evaluating these dishonest design practices was made possible by our thorough approach. The information gathered during this stage played a crucial role in our research's overall findings and conclusions. Figure 5 provides a visual representation of the Research Plan, explaining the methodical approach taken to carry out the research. To guarantee the successful completion of the study, it acts as a graphical depiction of the procedures followed.

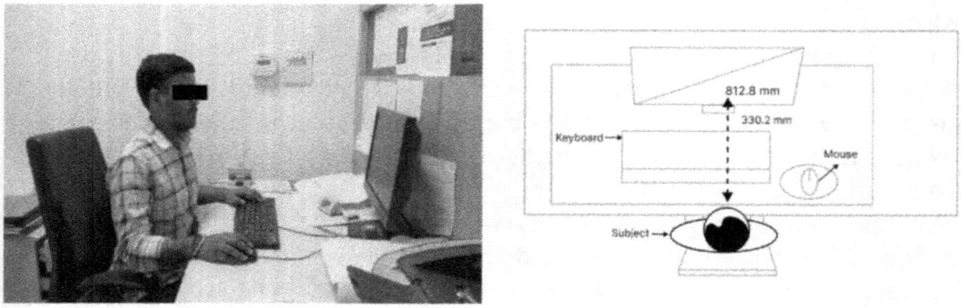

Fig. 5. Research Plan

Phase III: Post Education Evaluation on Dark patterns

Without using statistical analysis, the goal of this phase was to learn more about how consumers are impacted by dark patterns and how conscious they are of these misleading tactics. The same experiment as in Phase II was conducted with the addition of a dark patterns' education session for the participants. The goal of the 20-minute interactive workshop was to increase their understanding of dark patterns, their goals, and how they influence user behaviour. Participants in the seminar learnt about many sorts of dark patterns, including bait and switch, hidden advertisements, and forced continuity, and they also saw examples of these strategies being used on various web and app platforms. The goal of this training was to increase participants' awareness of such dishonest behaviours.

Participants' interactions and answers showed discernible changes after learning about dark patterns and having them repeat the Phase II tasks. In both web and app platforms, participants showed a greater degree of awareness and sensitivity to manipulative design strategies. This raised consciousness led to:

1. With increased accuracy, participants were able to recognise dark patterns in the interfaces they used.
2. After learning about dark patterns, participants' willingness to divulge private information—like credit card numbers for free trials—was seen to change.
3. Following their education regarding dark patterns, participants' opinions of the platforms' reliability decreased.

This research highlights why users must receive education to better cope with dark pattern impacts. The skills users gain from deceptive tactic education enhance their ability to make knowledgeable decisions despite the influence of user interface design on their behavior. Research conducted after completing the course showed users experience diffusion due to cognitive information overload while feeling hurried to decide when presented with interfaces that employ manipulative tactics. The training completed by participants led to enhanced focus alongside improved resilience together with improved skills in critical option evaluation even when dealing with time limitations. Digital literacy and ethical practice within digital platforms improve when users receive increased awareness about platform interactions.

4 Result and Discussion

This section examines the labelled dark pattern dataset from a few services in our final corpus. We found examples of dark patterns on platforms, along with how they impact user experience.

The preliminary analysis of our study produced some fascinating results regarding users' capacity to identify and avoid the sneaky tricks websites and applications use to trick them. Notably, a sizable portion of the user base, roughly 41.4%, claimed they had been the victim of dishonest design tactics, but many continued to be ignorant of dark patterns. This observation brought home how sneaky these design strategies are and how they can harm even the most careful users.

We utilized both the knowledge gained from a thorough literature review and the information gathered during the experimental study to delve deeper into understanding the identification and impact of dark patterns across various modalities. By using a dual strategy, we were able to identify several factors that are crucial for spotting dark patterns. Among these variables, five emerged as particularly significant:

- Frequency of Occurrence
- Trustworthiness
- Level of Frustration
- Misleading Behaviour
- User Experience of Dark Patterns

Additionally, a questionnaire was created based on these criteria, and participants were shown screens and given explanations of scenarios about the dark patterns. In this survey, we aimed to elicit participants' experiences and perceptions of interacting with dark patterns on various websites and applications by presenting them with screens and scenarios.

We discovered significant correlations between all the variables and the users' experiences with dark patterns across various digital platforms after gathering and analysing the data. Based on the gathered data, it was discovered that there were robust connections among the five characteristics attributed to every dark pattern. Various pairings of these ordinal variables were subjected to Spearman's rank-order correlation test. It was established through Spearman's test results that there are substantial correlations between the factors of dark pattern detection. Level of frustration and frequency of recurrence, frequency of occurrence and trustworthiness, and user experience and misleading behaviour all show significant positive connections. This demonstrated that these factors were indeed crucial for comprehending the significance of and identifying dark patterns.

First of all, we performed a normality test on the collected data to determine whether the variations in dark patterns between mobile and web platforms had a significant impact on user experiences. This test was designed to see if the data had a normal distribution, which is a requirement for some statistical tests.

We used the Kolmogorov-Smirnov and Shapiro-Wilk tests, two widely used measures of normality. The data would have followed a normal distribution if the p-value from these tests was greater than 0.05. However, the test values were less than 0.05 in our case, indicating that the data significantly deviated from a normal distribution. Table 1 explains the Shapiro-Wilk and Kolmogorov-Smirnov Normalcy Tests. A significant deviation of the data from a normal distribution was indicated by values below 0.05 in our study's test results. This shows that the dataset being studied is not normal.

Table 1. Kolmogorov- Smirnov and Shapiro- Wilk Normality Test

Tests of Normality

	Kolmogorov- Smirnov			Shapiro- Wilk		
	Statistic	df	Sig.	Statistic	df	Sig.
UserExperience Web	.382	24	<.001	.685	24	<.001
UserExperience App	.225	24	.003	.909	24	.033

a. Lilliefors Significance Correction

We chose non-parametric tests because our data did not have a normal distribution. We used the Wilcoxon signed-rank test because our study used the same sample population under various circumstances (mobile and web modalities). This test, a nonparametric substitute for the dependent samples t-test, is most useful when working with data that are not normally distributed.

We evaluated the null hypothesis, which proposed that variations in dark patterns across various web modalities had no appreciable impact on user experience, based on the Wilcoxon test results. By allowing us to accept or reject this null hypothesis, the test results ultimately gave us important insights into how different web modalities affect users' experiences with dark patterns. The Wilcoxon signed-rank test's Hypothesis Test summary is shown in Table 2. The outcome leads to the rejection of the null hypothesis, suggesting that variations in dark patterns among different web modalities do not affect user experience.

The related samples Wilcoxon Signed Rank Test results are shown in Fig. 6. The differences between paired samples are evaluated using this statistical analysis, which offers important insights into the patterns and correlations found in the data. This study investigated how users perceive dark patterns or deceptive design tactics used by brands to trick consumers and how they react to them across various web modalities. Participants were aware of these strategies to some extent, but they frequently saw them as a normal part of the online experience, underscoring the need for caution when using the internet. The degree to which participants were willing to interact with dark patterns depended on their motivation, with brand loyalty playing a big role. Users frequently abandoned tasks and looked for alternatives after noticing dark pat- terns, which could hurt business objectives. The research identifies five crucial factors that are connected

Table 2. Hypothesis test summary of Wilcoxon signed rank Test.

Nonparametric Tests

Hypothesis Test Summary

	Null Hypothesis	Test	Sig. a,b	Decision
1	The median of differences between UserExperienceWeb and UserExperienceApp equals 0.	Related- Samples Wilcoxon Signed Rank Test	<.001	Reject the null hypothesis.

a. The significance level is 0.50

b. Asymptotic significance is displayed

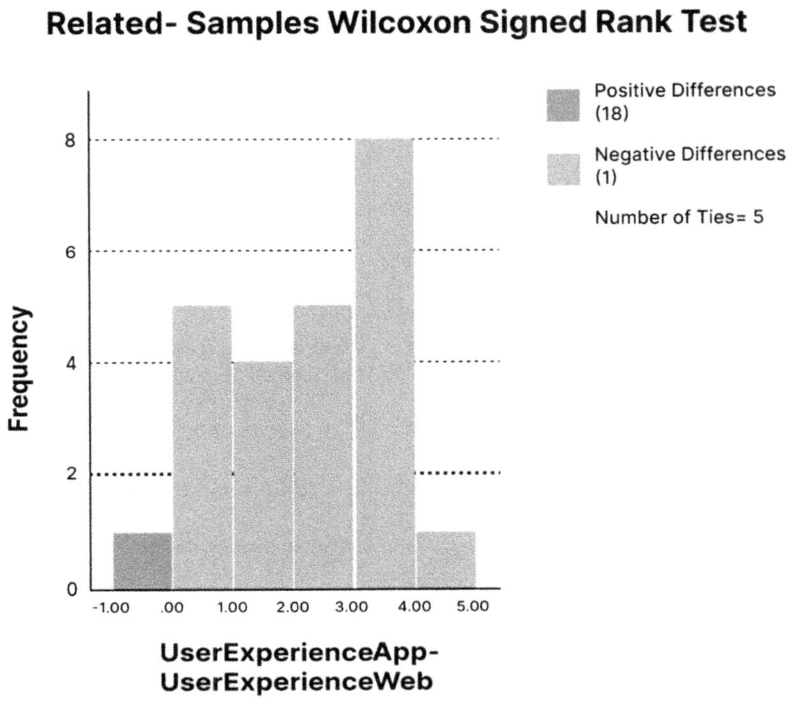

Fig. 6. Related Samples Wilcoxon Signed rank Test

to dark pattern recognition: frequency of occurrence, level of frustration, trustworthiness, misleading behaviour, and user experience. Understanding the consequences of using dark patterns, which can negatively affect the user experience and, ultimately, the business, is advantageous for designers.

5 Conclusion

This paper highlights users' ability to recognize these unethical design practices and their experience while interacting with dark patterns across various modalities by identifying five essential elements for spotting various dark patterns in user interfaces. The factors include occurrence frequency, reliability, level of annoyance, deceitful behaviour, and experience, all of which exhibit strong correlations and are linked to users' dark pattern recognition. The paper examines how dark patterns affect various web modalities' user experiences. The study finds that user experience is negatively impacted by the differences in dark patterns between web and mobile modalities. Although the study has its limitations, it provides valuable information for the field of human-computer interaction to comprehend the detrimental effects of dark patterns on users across various platforms and industries, urging designers to steer clear of malicious designs that might result in user loss.

Acknowledgement. The authors thank the Amity University, Noida for their organizational support for the data collection.

Disclosure of Interests. No potential conflict of interest was reported by the author(s).

References

1. Gray, C.M., Kou, Y., Battles, B., Hoggatt, J., Toombs, A.L.: The dark (patterns) side of UX design. In: Proceedings of the 2018 CHI Conference on Human Factors in Computing Systems, pp. 1–14 (2018)
2. Luguri, J., Strahilevitz, L.J.: Shining a light on dark patterns. J. Legal Anal. **13**(1), 43–109 (2021)
3. Cara, C.: Dark patterns in the media: a systematic review. Netw. Intell. Stud. **7**(14), 105–113 (2019)
4. Tidwell, J.: Designing interfaces: Patterns for effective interaction design. " O'Reil- ly Media, Inc." (2010)
5. Chen, J., et al.: Unveiling the tricks: Automated detection of dark patterns in mobile applications. In: Proceedings of the 36th Annual ACM Symposium on User Interface Software and Technology, pp. 1–20 (2023)
6. √ñzdemir, ≈û.: Digital nudges and dark patterns: the angels and the archfiends of digital communication. Digital Sch. Humanit. **35**(2), 417–428 (2020)
7. Maier, M.: Dark patterns-An end user perspective (2019)
8. Xiong, K.: A Concept-based Analysis of Dark Patterns in User Interface Design (Doctoral dissertation, Massachusetts Institute of Technology) (2023)
9. Di Geronimo, L., Braz, L., Fregnan, E., Palomba, F., Bacchelli, A.: UI dark patterns and where to find them: a study on mobile applications and user perception. In: Proceedings of the 2020 CHI Conference on Human Factors in Computing Systems, pp. 1–14 (2020)
10. Waldman, A.E.: Cognitive biases, dark patterns, and the 'privacy paradox.' Curr. Opin. Psychol. **31**, 105–109 (2020)
11. Gunawan, J., Pradeep, A., Choffnes, D., Hartzog, W., Wilson, C.: A Comparative Study of Dark Patterns Across Mobile and Web Modalities (2021)

12. Brignull, H., Miquel, M., Rosenberg, J., Offer, J.: Dark patterns-user interfaces designed to trick people. In: Proceedings of the Poster Presentation, Australian Psychological Society Congress, Sydney, NSW, Australia, pp. 21–23) (2015)
13. B√∂sch, C., Erb, B., Kargl, F., Kopp, H., Pfattheicher, S.: Tales from the dark side: privacy dark strategies and privacy dark patterns. Proc. Priv. Enhancing Technol. **2016**(4), 237–254 (2016)
14. Chivukula, S. S., Brier, J., Gray, C.M.: Dark intentions or persuasion? UX designers' activation of stakeholder and user values. In: Proceedings of the 2018 ACM Conference Companion Publication on Designing Interactive Systems, pp. 87–91 (2018)
15. Gray, C.M., Chen, J., Chivukula, S.S., Qu, L.: End user accounts of dark pat- terns as felt manipulation. Proc. ACM Hum. Comput. Interact. **5**(CSCW2), 1–25 (2021)
16. Lewis, C., Lewis, C.: Understanding Motivational Dark Patterns. Irresistible Apps: Motivational Design Patterns for Apps, Games, and Web-based Communities, 99–102 (2014)
17. Fogg, B.J.: A behavior model for persuasive design. In: Proceedings of the 4th International Conference on Persuasive Technology, pp. 1–7 (2009)
18. Norman, D.: The design of everyday things: Revised and expanded edition. Basic books (2013)
19. Leonard, T.C., Thaler, R.H., Sunstein, C.R.: Nudge: improving decisions about health, wealth, and happiness: Yale University Press, New Haven, CT, 2008, 293 pp, $26.00 (2008)
20. Mathur, A., et al.: Dark patterns at scale: Findings from a crawl of 11K shopping websites. Proc. ACM Hum. Comput. Interact. **3**(CSCW), 1–32 (2019)
21. Thaler, R.H.: Nudge, not sludge. Science **361**(6401), 431 (2018)
22. Mathur, A., Kshirsagar, M., Mayer, J.: What makes a dark pattern... dark? Design attributes, normative considerations, and measurement methods. In: Proceedings of the 2021 CHI Conference on Human Factors in Computing Systems, pp. 1–18 (2021)
23. Hartzog, W.: PrivacyOs Blueprint: The Battle to Control the Design of New Technologies. Harvard University Press (2018)
24. Hartzog, W.: Website design as contract. Am. UL Rev. **60**, 1635 (2010)
25. Zagal, J.P., Björk, S., Lewis, C.: Dark patterns in the design of games. In: Foundations of Digital Games 2013 (2013)
26. Greenberg, S., Boring, S., Vermeulen, J., Dostal, J.: Dark patterns in proxemic interactions: a critical perspective. In: Proceedings of the 2014 Conference on Designing Interactive Systems, pp. 523–532 (2014)
27. Pandey, A.V., Rall, K., Satterthwaite, M.L., Nov, O., Bertini, E.: How deceptive are deceptive visualizations? An empirical analysis of common distortion techniques. In Proceedings of the 33rd Annual ACM Conference on Human Factors in Computing Systems, pp. 1469–1478 (2015)
28. Venkatadri, G., Lucherini, E., Sapiezynski, P., Mislove, A.: Investigating sources of PII used in Facebook's targeted advertising. Proc. Priv. Enhancing Technol. **2019**(1), 227–244 (2019)
29. Dev, J., Rader, E., Patil, S.: Why Johnny can't unsubscribe: Barriers to stopping unwanted email. In: Proceedings of the 2020 CHI Conference on Human Factors in Computing Systems, pp. 1–12 (2020)
30. Barrett, L., Campbel, A.J.: Request to Investigate Google√¢ƒÇ≈πs Unfair and Deceptive Practices in Marketing Apps for Children (2018)
31. Complaint Under Article 77(1) GDPR (2018)
32. Jeffries, A.: Yelp is Screwing Over Restaurants By Quietly Replacing Their Phone Numbers. Vice accessed at https://www.vice.com/en_us/article/wjwebw/yelp-is-sneakilyreplacing-restaurants-phone-numbers-so-grubhub-can-take-a-cut on August, 6, 2019 (2019)
33. Federal Trade Commission. FTC sues owner of online dating service Match. com for using fake love interest ads to trick consumers into paying for a Match. com subscription. Sept. 25 (2019)

34. Elliott, J., Waldron, L.: Here's how TurboTax just tricked you into paying to file your taxes. ProPublica (2019)
35. Fansher, M., Chivukula, S.S., Gray, C.M.: # Dark patterns: UX practitioner conversations about ethical design. In: Extended Abstracts of the 2018 CHI Conference on Human Factors in Computing Systems, pp. 1–6 (2018).
36. Gray, C.M., Chivukula, S.S., Lee, A.: What kind of work do" asshole designers" create? Describing properties of ethical concern on reddit. In: Proceedings of the 2020 ACM Designing Interactive Systems Conference, pp. 61–73 (2020)
37. Arvind, N., Arunesh, M., Marshini, C., Mihir, K.: Dark patterns-past, present, and future: the evolution of tricky user interfaces. ACMQueue **18**(2), 1–25 (2020)
38. Jiang, S., Martin, J., Wilson, C.: Who's the Guinea Pig? Investigating Online A/B/n Tests in-the-Wild. In: Proceedings of the Conference on Fairness, Accountability, and Transparency, pp. 201–210 (2019)
39. Fogg, B.J.: Persuasive computers: perspectives and research directions. In: Proceedings of the SIGCHI Conference on Human Factors in Computing Systems, p. 225232 (1998)
40. Bhoot, A.M., Shinde, M.A., Mishra, W.P.: Towards the identification of dark patterns: an analysis based on end-user reactions. In: Proceedings of the 11th Indian Conference on Human-Computer Interaction, pp. 24–33 (2020)

Author Index

Published by Springer Nature Switzerland AG 2026
G. Bhutkar et al. (Eds.): IDID 2024, IFIP AICT 747, pp. 245–246, 2026.
https://doi.org/10.1007/978-3-032-00777-3

www.ingramcontent.com/pod-product-compliance
Lightning Source LLC
Chambersburg PA
CBHW050620270825
31638CB00005BA/430
* 9 7 8 3 0 3 2 0 0 7 7 6 6 *